Johann Wolfgang von Goethe, L. Dora Schmitz

Miscellaneous Travels of J.W. Goethe

Comprising letters from Switzerland; the campaign in France, 1792; the siege of Mainz; and a tour on the Rhine, Maine, and Neckar, 1814-1815

Johann Wolfgang von Goethe, L. Dora Schmitz

Miscellaneous Travels of J.W. Goethe

Comprising letters from Switzerland; the campaign in France, 1792; the siege of Mainz; and a tour on the Rhine, Maine, and Neckar, 1814-1815

ISBN/EAN: 9783337384449

Printed in Europe, USA, Canada, Australia, Japan

Cover: Foto ©Andreas Hilbeck / pixelio.de

More available books at **www.hansebooks.com**

New Edition, with a New Biographical Supplement of upwards of 9700 Names.

WEBSTER'S COMPLETE DICTIONARY
OF THE ENGLISH LANGUAGE, AND GENERAL BOOK OF LITERARY REFERENCE. With 3000 Illustrations. Thoroughly revised and improved by CHAUNCEY A. GOODRICH, D.D., LL.D., and NOAH PORTER, D.D., of Yale College.

In One Volume, Quarto, strongly bound in cloth, 1919 pages, price £1 11s. 6d.; half-calf, £2; calf or half-russia, £2 2s.; russia, £2 10s.

Besides the matter comprised in the WEBSTER'S GUINEA DICTIONARY, this volume contains the following Appendices, which will show that no pains have been spared to make it a complete Literary Reference-book:—

A Brief History of the English Language. By Professor JAMES HADLEY. This Work shows the Philological Relations of the English Language, and traces the progress and influence of the causes which have brought it to its present condition.

Principles of Pronunciation. By Professor GOODRICH and W. A. WHEELER, M.A. Including a Synopsis of Words differently pronounced by different authorities.

A Short Treatise on Orthography. By ARTHUR W. WRIGHT. Including a Complete List of Words that are spelt in two or more ways.

An Explanatory and Pronouncing Vocabulary of the Names of Noted Fictitious Persons and Places, &c. By W. A. WHEELER, M.A. This Work includes not only persons and places noted in Fiction, whether narrative, poetical, or dramatic, but Mythological and Mythical names, names referring to the Angelology and Demonology of various races, and those found in the romance writers; Pseudonyms, Nick-names of eminent persons and parties, &c., &c. In fact, it is best described as explaining every name which is not strictly *historical*. A reference is given to the originator of each name, and where the origin is unknown a quotation is given to some well-known writer in which the word occurs.

This valuable Work may also be had separately, post 8vo., 5s.

A Pronouncing Vocabulary of Scripture Proper Names. By W. A. WHEELER, M.A. Including a List of the Variations that occur in the Douay version of the Bible.

A Pronouncing Vocabulary of Greek and Latin Proper Names. By Professor THACHER, of Yale College.

An Etymological Vocabulary of Modern Geographical Names. By the Rev. C. H. WHEELER. Containing:—I. A List of Prefixes, Terminations, and Formative Syllables in various Languages, with their meaning and derivation; II. A brief List of Geographical Names (not explained by the foregoing List), with their derivation and signification, all doubtful and obscure derivations being excluded.

Pronouncing Vocabularies of Modern Geographical and Biographical Names. By J. THOMAS, M.D.

A Pronouncing Vocabulary of Common English Christian Names, with their derivations, signification, and diminutives (or nick-names), and their equivalents in several other languages.

A Dictionary of Quotations. Selected and translated by WILLIAM G. WEBSTER. Containing all Words, Phrases, Proverbs, and Colloquial Expressions from the Greek, Latin, and Modern Foreign Languages, which are frequently met with in literature and conversation.

A New Biographical Dictionary of upwards 9700 Names of Noted Persons, Ancient and Modern, including many now living—giving the Name, Pronunciation, Nationality, Profession, and Date of Birth and Death.

A List of Abbreviations, Contractions, and Arbitrary Signs used in Writing and Printing.

A Classified Selection of Pictorial Illustrations (70 pages). With references to the text.

"The cheapest Dictionary ever published, as it is confessedly one of the best. The introduction of small woodcut illustrations of technical and scientific terms adds greatly to the utility of the Dictionary."—*Churchman*.

To be obtained through all Booksellers.

STANDARD WORKS PUBLISHED BY

WEBSTER'S DICTIONARY.

From the QUARTERLY REVIEW, *Oct.* 1873.

"Seventy years passed before JOHNSON was followed by Webster, an American writer, who faced the task of the English Dictionary with a full appreciation of its requirements, leading to better practical results."
. . . .

"His laborious comparison of twenty languages, though never published, bore fruit in his own mind, and his training placed him both in knowledge and judgment far in advance of Johnson as a philologist. Webster's 'American Dictionary of the English Language' was published in 1828, and of course appeared at once in England, where successive re-editing *has as yet kept it in the highest place as a practical Dictionary.*"

"The acceptance of an American Dictionary in England has itself had immense effect in keeping up the community of speech, to break which would be a grievous harm, not to English-speaking nations alone, but to mankind. The result of this has been that the common Dictionary must suit both sides of the Atlantic." . . . .

"The good average business-like character of Webster's Dictionary, both in style and matter, made it as distinctly suited as Johnson's was distinctly unsuited to be expanded and re-edited by other hands. Professor Goodrich's edition of 1847 is not much more than enlarged and amended, but other revisions since have so much novelty of plan as to be described as distinct works." . . . .

"The American revised Webster's Dictionary of 1864, published in America and England, is of an altogether higher order than these last [The London Imperial and Student's]. It bears on its title-page the names of Drs. Goodrich and Porter, but inasmuch as its especial improvement is in the etymological department, the care of which was committed to Dr. MAHN, of Berlin, we prefer to describe it in short as the Webster-Mahn Dictionary. Many other literary men, among them Professors Whitney and Dana, aided in the task of compilation and revision. On consideration it seems that the editors and contributors have gone far toward improving Webster to the utmost that he will bear improvement. The *vocabulary has become almost complete,* as regards usual words, *while the definitions keep throughout to Webster's simple careful style,* and the derivations are assigned with the aid of good modern authorities."

"On the whole, the Webster-Mahn Dictionary as it stands, is most respectable, and CERTAINLY THE BEST PRACTICAL ENGLISH DICTIONARY EXTANT."

LONDON: GEORGE BELL & SONS, YORK STREET, COVENT GARDEN.

SPECIAL DICTIONARIES AND WORKS OF REFERENCE.

Dr. Richardson's Philological Dictionary of the ENGLISH LANGUAGE. Combining Explanation with Etymology, and copiously illustrated by Quotations from the Best Authorities. *New Edition*, with a Supplement containing additional Words and further Illustrations. In 2 vols. 4to. £4 14s. 6d. Half-bound in Russia, £5 15s. 6d. Russia, £6 12s.—The Supplement separately. 4to. 12s.
An 8vo. edition, without the Quotations, 15s. Half-russia, 20s. Russia, 24s.

A Supplementary English Glossary. Containing 12,000 Words or Meanings occurring in English Literature not found in any other Dictionary. With Illustrative Quotations. By T. LEWIS O. DAVIES, M.A. Demy 8vo. 16s.

Folk-Etymology. A Dictionary of Corrupted Words which have been Perverted in Form or Meaning by False Derivation or Mistaken Analogy. By the Rev. A. S. PALMER, Author of "A Word-Hunter's Note-book." Demy 8vo. 21s.
"Most interesting, instructive, and valuable contribution to the study of language."—*Athenæum*.

Synonyms Discriminated. A Catalogue of Synonymous Words in the English Language, with their various Shades of Meaning, &c. Illustrated by Quotations from Standard Writers. By the late Ven. C. J. SMITH, M.A. Demy 8vo. *New Edition, revised and enlarged.* 14s.

A Dictionary of Quotations. From the English Poets. By HENRY G. BOHN, F.R.A.S., F.L.S., &c. Large post 8vo. 10s. 6d.
"Mr. Bohn's volume has the rare recommendation of being entirely free from the rubbish which is commonly thrust into similar collections. His selections have been made from a long and extensive course of reading, and it everywhere bears evidence of a scholar's eye and taste. There must be, as we judge, nearly 8,000 quotations in the volume, ranging from Chaucer to Tennyson."—*Times*.

A Biographical Dictionary. By THOMPSON COOPER, F.S.A., Editor of "Men of the Time," and Joint Editor of "Athenæ Cantabrigienses." 1 vol. 8vo. With Supplement to 1883. 15s. Supplement separate, 3s. 6d.
This volume is not a mere repetition of the contents of previous works, but embodies the results of many years' laborious research in rare publications and unpublished documents. Any note of omission which may be sent to the Publishers will be duly considered.
"It is an important original contribution to the literature of its class by a painstaking scholar. . . . . It seems in every way admirable, and fully to justify the claims on its behalf put forth by its editor."—*British Quarterly Review*.

Bryan's Biographical and Critical Dictionary of Painters and Engravers. With a List of Ciphers, Monograms, and Marks. *Enlarged Edition, thoroughly revised* by R. E. GRAVES, British Museum. In monthly parts, 5s. each. Parts 1-4 ready.

The Cottage Gardener's Dictionary. With a Supplement, containing all the new plants and varieties to the year 1869. Edited by GEORGE W. JOHNSON. Post 8vo. Cloth. 6s. 6d.

LONDON: GEORGE BELL & SONS, YORK STREET, COVENT GARDEN.

STANDARD WORKS PUBLISHED BY

THE ALDINE SERIES OF THE BRITISH POETS.
CHEAP EDITION.

In Fifty-two Volumes, Bound in Cloth, at Eighteenpence each Volume.

Akenside, with Memoir by the Rev. A. Dyce, and additional Letters. 1s. 6d.

Beattie, with Memoir by the Rev. A. Dyce. 1s. 6d.

Burns, with Memoir by Sir Harris Nicolas, and additional Copyright Pieces. 3 vols. 4s. 6d.

Butler, with Memoir by the Rev. J. Mitford. 2 vols. 3s.

Chaucer, edited by R. Morris, with Memoir by Sir Harris Nicolas. 6 vols. 9s.

Churchill, Tooke's Edition, revised, with Memoir, by James Hannay. 2 vols. 3s.

Collins, edited, with Memoir, by W. Moy Thomas. 1s. 6d.

Cowper, including his Translations. Edited, with Memoir, and Additional Copyright Pieces, by John Bruce, F.S.A. 3 vols. 4s. 6d.

Dryden, with Memoir by the Rev. R. Hooper, F.S.A. Carefully revised. 5 vols. 7s. 6d.

Falconer, with Memoir by the Rev. J. Mitford. 1s. 6d.

Goldsmith, with Memoir by the Rev. J. Mitford. Revised. 1s. 6d.

Gray, with Notes and Memoir by the Rev. John Mitford. 1s. 6d.

Kirke White, with Memoir by Sir H. Nicolas, and additional Notes. Carefully revised. 1s. 6d.

Milton, with Memoir by the Rev. J. Mitford. 3 vols. 4s. 6d.

Parnell, with Memoir by the Rev. J. Mitford. 1s. 6d.

Pope, with Memoir by the Rev. A. Dyce. 3 vols. 4s. 6d.

Prior, with Memoir by the Rev. J. Mitford. 2 vols. 3s.

Shakespeare, with Memoir by the Rev. A. Dyce. 1s. 6d.

Spenser, edited, with Memoir, by J. Payne Collier. 5 vols. 7s. 6d.

Surrey, edited, with Memoir, by James Yeowell. 1s. 6d.

Swift, with Memoir by the Rev. J. Mitford. 3 vols. 4s. 6d.

Thomson, with Memoir by Sir H. Nicolas. Annotated by Peter Cunningham, F.S.A., and additional Poems, carefully revised. 2 vols. 3s.

Wyatt, edited, with Memoir, by James Yeowell. 1s. 6d.

Young, with Memoir by the Rev. J. Mitford, and additional Poems. 2 vols. 3s.

Complete sets may be obtained, bound in half-morocco. £9 9s.

N.B.—Copies of the Fine Paper Edition, with Portraits, may still be had, price 5s. per volume (except Collins, 3s. 6d.).

LONDON: GEORGE BELL & SONS, YORK STREET, COVENT GARDEN.

THE ALDINE EDITION OF THE BRITISH POETS.

SUPPLEMENTARY SERIES.

THE fifty-two volumes which have hitherto formed the well-known Aldine Series, embody the works of nearly all the more popular English poetical writers, whether lyric, epic, or satiric, up to the end of the eighteenth century. But since that time the wonderful fertility of English literature has produced many writers equal, and in some cases far superior, to the majority of their predecessors; and the widely augmented roll of acknowledged English poets now contains many names not represented in the series of "Aldine Poets."

With a view of providing for this want, and of making a series which has long held a high place in public estimation a more adequate representation of the whole body of English poetry, the Publishers have determined to issue a second series, which will contain some of the older poets, and the works of recent writers, so far as may be practicable by arrangement with the representatives of the poets whose works are still copyright.

One volume, or more, at a time will be issued at short intervals; they will be uniform in binding and style with the last fine-paper edition of the Aldine Poets, in fcap. 8vo. size, printed at the Chiswick Press. Price 5s. per volume.

Each volume will be edited with notes where necessary for elucidation of he text; a memoir will be prefixed and a portrait, where an authentic one is accessible.

The following are already published:—

THE POEMS OF WILLIAM BLAKE. With Memoir by W. M. Rossetti, and portrait by Jeens.

THE POEMS OF SAMUEL ROGERS. With Memoir by Edward Bell, and portrait by Jeens.

THE POEMS OF THOMAS CHATTERTON. 2 vols. Edited by the Rev. W. Skeat, with Memoir by Edward Bell.

THE POEMS OF SIR WALTER RALEIGH, SIR HENRY WOTTON, and Selections from other Courtly Poets. With Introduction by the Rev. Dr. Hannah, and portrait of Sir W. Raleigh.

THE POEMS OF THOMAS CAMPBELL. With Memoir by W. Allingham, and portrait by Jeens.

THE POEMS OF GEORGE HERBERT. (Complete Edition.) With Memoir by the Rev. A. B. Grosart, and portrait.

THE POEMS OF JOHN KEATS. With Memoir by Lord Houghton, and portrait by Jeens.

SACRED POEMS AND PIOUS EJACULATIONS BY HENRY VAUGHAN. With Memoir by Rev. H. F. Lyte.

COLERIDGE'S POEMS. By T. Ashe. [*In the Press.*

LONDON: GEORGE BELL & SONS, YORK STREET, COVENT GARDEN.

STANDARD WORKS PUBLISHED BY

In Ten Volumes, price 2s. 6d. each; in half-morocco, £2 10s., or, with Plates, £3 the set.

CHEAP ALDINE EDITION OF
SHAKESPEARE'S DRAMATIC WORKS.

EDITED BY S. W. SINGER.

Uniform with the Cheap Edition of the Aldine Poets.

THE formation of numerous Shakespeare Reading Societies has created a demand for a cheap portable edition, with LEGIBLE TYPE, that shall provide a sound text with such notes as may help to elucidate the meaning and assist in the better understanding of the author. The Publishers therefore determined to reprint Mr. Singer's well-known Edition, published in 10 vols., small 8vo., for some time out of print, and issue it in a cheap form, uniform with the well-known Aldine Edition of British Poets.

CONTENTS.

Vol. I. The Life of Shakespeare. The Tempest. The Two Gentlemen of Verona. The Merry Wives of Windsor. Measure for Measure.

Vol. II. Comedy of Errors. Much Ado about Nothing. Love's Labour Lost. Midsummer Night's Dream. Merchant of Venice.

Vol. III. As You Like It. Taming of the Shrew. All's Well that Ends Well. Twelfth Night, or What You Will.

Vol. IV. Winter's Tale. Pericles. King John. King Richard II.

Vol. V. King Henry IV., Parts I. and II. King Henry V.

Vol. VI. King Henry VI., Parts I. II. and III. King Richard III.

Vol. VII. King Henry VIII. Troilus and Cressida. Coriolanus.

Vol. VIII. Titus Andronicus. Romeo and Juliet. Timon of Athens. Julius Cæsar.

Vol. IX. Macbeth. Hamlet. King Lear.

Vol. X. Othello. Antony and Cleopatra. Cymbeline.

Uniform with the above, price 2s. 6d; in half-morocco, 5s.

CRITICAL ESSAYS ON THE PLAYS OF SHAKESPEARE,

BY WILLIAM WATKISS LLOYD;

Giving a succinct account of the origin and source of each play, where ascertainable and careful criticisms on the subject-matter of each.

A few copies of this Work have been printed to range with the fine-paper Edition of the Aldine Poets. The price for the Eleven Volumes (not sold separately) is £2 15s.

LONDON: GEORGE BELL & SONS, YORK STREET, COVENT GARDEN.

POCKET VOLUMES.

A SERIES of Select Works of Favourite Authors, adapted for general reading, moderate in price, compact and elegant in form, and executed in a style fitting them to be permanently preserved. Imperial 32mo., cloth,

Gatty's Parables from Nature. 2 vols. 5s.
Captain Marryat's Masterman Ready, 2s. 6d.
Lamb's Elia. Eliana and Last Essay with Memoir, by BARRY CORNWALL. 2 vols. 5s.
Bacon's Essays. 2s. 6d.
Burns's Poems. 3s.
———— Songs. 3s.
Coleridge's Poems. 3s.
C. Dibdin's Sea Songs and Ballads. And others. 3s.
Midshipman, The. Autobiographical Sketches of his own early Career, by Captain BASIL HALL, R.N., F.R.S. 3s. 6d.
Lieutenant and Commander. By Captain BASIL HALL, R.N., F.R.S. 3s. 6d.
George Herbert's Poems. 2s. 6d.
———— Remains. 2s.

George Herbert's Works. 3s. 6d.
The Sketch Book. By WASHINGTON IRVING. 3s. 6d.
Tales of a Traveller. By WASHINGTON IRVING. 3s. 6d.
Charles Lamb's Tales from Shakspeare. 2s.
Longfellow's Evangeline and Voices, Sea-side, and Poems on Slavery. 3s.
Milton's Paradise Lost. 3s.
———— Regained, & other Poems. 3s.
Robin Hood Ballads. 3s.
Southey's Life of Nelson. 3s.
Walton's Complete Angler. Portraits and Illustrations. 3s.
———— Lives of Donne, Wotton, Hooker, &c. 3s. 6d.
White's Natural History of Selborne. 3s. 6d.

Shakspeare's Plays & Poems. KEIGHTLEY's Edition. 13 Vols. in cloth case, 21s.

ELZEVIR SERIES.

Small fcap. 8vo.

THESE Volumes are issued under the general title of "ELZEVIR SERIES," to distinguish them from other collections. This general title has been adopted to indicate the spirit in which they are prepared; that is to say, with the greatest possible accuracy as regards text, and the highest degree of beauty that can be attained in the workmanship.

They are printed at the Chiswick Press, on fine paper, with wide margins, and issued in a neat cloth binding.

Longfellow's Evangeline, Voices, Sea-side and Fire-side. 4s. 6d. With Portrait.
———— Hiawatha, and The Golden Legend. 4s. 6d.
———— Wayside Inn, Miles Standish, Spanish Student. 4s. 6d.
Burns's Poetical Works. 4s. 6d. With Portrait.
———— Songs and Ballads. 4s. 6d.
These Editions contain all the copyright pieces published in the Aldine Edition.
Cowper's Poetical Works. 2 vols., each 4s. 6d. With Portrait.
Coleridge's Poems. 4s. 6d. With Portrait.

Irving's Sketch Book. 5s. With Portrait.
———— Tales of a Traveller. 5s.
Milton's Paradise Lost. 4s. 6d. With Portrait.
———— Regained. 4s. 6d.
Shakspeare's Plays and Poems. Carefully edited by THOMAS KEIGHTLEY. In seven volumes. 5s. each.
Southey's Life of Nelson. 4s. 6d. With Portrait of NELSON.
Walton's Angler. 4s. 6d. With a Frontispiece.
———— Lives of Donne, Hooker, Herbert, &c. 5s. With Portrait.

LONDON: GEORGE BELL & SONS, YORK STREET, COVENT GARDEN.

STANDARD WORKS PUBLISHED BY

HISTORY AND TRAVELS.

Rome and the Campagna. A Historical and Topographical Description of the Site, Buildings, and Neighbourhood of ancient Rome. By the Rev. ROBERT BURN, late Fellow and Tutor of Trinity College, Cambridge. With eighty engravings by JEWITT, and numerous Maps and Plans, and an Appendix, bringing the Work down to 1876. Demy 4to. £3 3s.

Old Rome. A Handbook of the Ruins of the Ancient City and the Campagna, for the use of Travellers. By R. BURN, M.A. With Illustrations, Maps, and Plans. Demy 8vo. 10s. 6d.

Ancient Athens; its History, Topography, and Remains. By THOMAS HENRY DYER, LL.D., Author of "The History of the Kings of Rome." Super-royal 8vo. Illustrated, cloth. £1 5s.

The History of the Kings of Rome. By Dr. T. H. DYER, Author of the "History of the City of Rome;" "Pompeii: its History, Antiquities," &c., with a Prefatory Dissertation on the Sources and Evidence of Early Roman History. 8vo. 16s.

Modern Europe, from the Fall of Constantinople in 1453. By THOMAS HENRY DYER, LL.D. Second Edition, Revised and Continued. In 5 vols. £2 12s. 6d.

The Decline of the Roman Republic. By the late GEORGE LONG, M.A., Editor of "Cæsar's Commentaries," "Cicero's Orations," &c. 8vo.
Vol. I. From the Destruction of Carthage to the End of the Jugurthine War. 14s.
Vol. II. To the Death of Sertorius. 14s.
Vol. III. Including the third Mithridatic War, the Catiline Conspiracy, and the Consulship of C. Julius Cæsar. 14s.
Vol. IV. History of Cæsar's Gallic Campaigns and of contemporaneous events. 14s.
Vol. V. From the Invasion of Italy by Julius Cæsar to his Death. 14s.

A History of England during the Early and Middle Ages. By C. H. PEARSON, M.A., Fellow of Oriel College, Oxford, and late Lecturer in History at Trinity College, Cambridge. Second Edition, revised and enlarged. 8vo. Vol. I. to the Death of Cœur de Lion. 16s. Vol. II. to the Death of Edward I. 14s.

Historical Maps of England. By C. H. PEARSON, M.A. Folio. Third Edition, revised. 31s. 6d.
An Atlas containing Five Maps of England at different periods during the Early and Middle Ages.

The Desert of the Exodus. Journeys on Foot in the Wilderness of the Forty Years' Wanderings, undertaken in connection with the Ordnance Survey of Sinai and the Palestine Exploration Fund. By the late E. H. PALMER, M.A., Lord Almoner's Professor of Arabic and Fellow of St. John's College, Cambridge, Member of the Asiatic Society, and of the Société de Paris. With Maps, and numerous Illustrations from Photographs and Drawings taken on the spot by the Sinai Survey Expedition and C. F. TYRWHITT DRAKE. 2 vols. 8vo. 28s.

LONDON: GEORGE BELL & SONS, YORK STREET, COVENT GARDEN.

GEORGE BELL & SONS.

STANDARD WORKS.

Corpus Poetarum Latinorum. Edited by E. WALKER.
One thick vol. 8vo. Cloth, 18s.
Containing:—Catullus, Lucretius, Virgilius, Tibullus, Propertius, Ovidius, Horatius, Phaedrus, Lucanus, Persius, Juvenalis, Martialis, Sulpicia, Statius, Silius Italicus, Valerius Flaccus, Calpurnius Siculus, Ausonius, and Claudianus.

Cruden's Concordance to the Old and New Testament,
or an Alphabetical and Classified Index to the Holy Bible, specially adapted for Sunday School Teachers, containing nearly 54,000 references. Thoroughly revised and condensed by G. H. HANNAY. Fcap. 2s.

Perowne (Canon). The Book of Psalms. A New Translation, with Introductions and Notes, Critical and Explanatory. By the Very Rev. J. J. STEWART PEROWNE, Dean of Peterborough. 8vo. Vol. I., Fifth Edition, 18s.; Vol. II., Fifth Edition, 16s.

——— ABRIDGED EDITION for Schools. Fourth Edition. Crown 8vo. 10s. 6d.

Adams (Dr. E.). The Elements of the English Language. By ERNEST ADAMS, Ph.D. Eighteenth Edition. Post 8vo. 4s. 6d.

Whewell (Dr.). Elements of Morality, including Polity.
By W. WHEWELL, D.D., formerly Master of Trinity College, Cambridge. Fourth Edition. In 1 vol. 8vo. 15s.

BIOGRAPHIES BY THE LATE SIR ARTHUR HELPS, K.C.B.

The Life of Hernando Cortes, and the Conquest of MEXICO. Dedicated to Thomas Carlyle. 2 vols. Crown 8vo. 15s.

The Life of Christopher Columbus, the Discoverer of AMERICA. Fourth Edition. Crown 8vo. 6s.

The Life of Pizarro. With Some Account of his Associates in the Conquest of Peru. Second Edition. Crown 8vo. 6s.

The Life of Las Casas, the Apostle of the Indies.
Second Edition. Crown 8vo. 6s.

The Life and Epistles of St. Paul. By THOMAS LEWIN, Esq., M.A., F.S.A., Trinity College, Oxford, Barrister-at-Law, Author of "Fasti Sacri," "Siege of Jerusalem," "Cæsar's Invasion," "Treatise on Trusts," &c. With upwards of 350 Illustrations finely engraved on Wood, Maps, Plans, &c. Fourth Edition. In 2 vols., demy 4to. £2 2s.

"This is one of those works which demand from critics and from the public, before attempting to estimate its merits in detail, an unqualified tribute of admiration. The first glance tells us that the book is one on which the leisure of a busy lifetime and the whole resources of an enthusiastic author have been lavished without stint. . . . This work is a kind of British Museum for this period and subject in small compass. It is a series of galleries of statues, gems, coins, documents, letters, books, and relics, through which the reader may wander at leisure, and which he may animate with his own musings and reflections. It must be remembered throughout that this delightful and instructive collection is the result of the devotion of a lifetime, and deserves as much honour and recognition as many a museum or picture-gallery which has preserved its donor's name for generations."
—*Times.*

LONDON: GEORGE BELL & SONS, YORK STREET, COVENT GARDEN.

STANDARD WORKS PUBLISHED BY

ILLUSTRATED OR POPULAR EDITIONS OF STANDARD WORKS.

Dante's Divine Comedy. Translated by the Rev. HENRY FRANCIS CARY. With all the Author's Copyright Emendations. Post 8vo. 3s. 6d.

Shakespeare. Shakespeare's Plays and Poems. With Notes and Life by CHARLES KNIGHT, and 40 engravings on wood by HARVEY. Royal 8vo. Cloth. 10s. 6d.

Fielding. Works of Henry Fielding, complete. With Memoir of the Author by THOMAS ROSCOE, and 20 Plates by GEORGE CRUIKSHANK. Medium 8vo. 14s.

Fielding. The Novels separately. With Memoir by THOMAS ROSCOE, and Plates by GEORGE CRUIKSHANK. Medium 8vo. 7s. 6d.

Swift. Works of Jonathan Swift, D.D. Containing interesting and valuable passages not hitherto published. With Memoir of the Author by THOMAS ROSCOE. 2 vols. Medium 8vo. 24s.

Smollett. Miscellaneous Works of Tobias Smollett. Complete in 1 vol. With Memoir of the Author by THOMAS ROSCOE. 21 Plates by GEORGE CRUIKSHANK. Medium 8vo. 14s.

Lamb. The Works of Charles Lamb. With a Memoir by Sir THOMAS NOON TALFOURD. Imp. 8vo. 10s. 6d.

Goldsmith's Poems. Illustrated. 16mo. 2s. 6d.

Wordsworth's White Doe of Rylstone; or, the Fate of THE NORTONS. Illustrated. 16mo. 3s. 6d.

Longfellow's Poetical Works. With nearly 250 Illustrations by BIRKET FOSTER, TENNIEL, GODWIN, THOMAS, &c. In 1 vol. 21s.

Longfellow's Evangeline. Illustrated. 16mo. 3s. 6d.

Longfellow's Wayside Inn. Illustrated. 16mo. 3s. 6d.

Adelaide Anne Procter's Legends and Lyrics. The Illustrated Edition. With Additional Poems, and an Introduction by CHARLES DICKENS, a Portrait by JEENS, and 20 Illustrations by Eminent Artists, and a short Memoir by Mrs. EWING. Fcap. 4to. Ornamental cloth. 21s.

Mrs. Gatty's Parables from Nature. A Handsomely Illustrated Edition; with Notes on the Natural History, and numerous Full-page Illustrations by the most eminent Artists of the present day. *New complete edition, with Short Memoir* by J. H. EWING. Fcap. 4to. 21s.

The Book of Gems. Selections from the British POETS. Illustrated with upwards of 150 Steel Engravings. Edited by S. C. HALL. 3 vols. Handsomely bound in walnut. 21s. each.

FIRST SERIES—CHAUCER TO DRYDEN.
SECOND SERIES—SWIFT TO BURNS.
THIRD SERIES—WORDSWORTH TO TENNYSON.

LONDON: GEORGE BELL & SONS, YORK STREET, COVENT GARDEN.

BOOKS FOR THE YOUNG.

CAPTAIN MARRYAT'S BOOKS FOR BOYS.

Poor Jack. With Sixteen Illustrations after Designs by CLARKSON STANFIELD, R.A. Twenty-second Edition. Post 8vo., 3s. 6d. Gilt, 4s. 6d.
——— People's Edition, Illustrated. Demy 4to., 6d.
——— Cheap Edition. Fcap. 8vo., 6d.

The Mission; or, Scenes in Africa. With Illustrations by JOHN GILBERT. Post 8vo., 3s. 6d. Gilt, 4s. 6d.

The Settlers in Canada. With Illustrations by GILBERT and DALZIEL. Post 8vo., 3s. 6d. Gilt, 4s. 6d.

The Privateers Man. Adventures by Sea and Land IN CIVIL AND SAVAGE LIFE, ONE HUNDRED YEARS AGO. Illustrated with Eight Steel Engravings. Post 8vo., 3s. 6d. Gilt, 4s. 6d.

Masterman Ready; or, the Wreck of the Pacific. Embellished with Ninety-three Engravings on Wood. Post 8vo., 3s. 6d. Gilt, 4s. 6d.
——— People's Edition, Illustrated. Demy 4to., 6d.
——— Cheap Edition. Fcap. 8vo., 6d.

The Pirate and Three Cutters. Illustrated with Eight Steel Engravings from Drawings by CLARKSON STANFIELD, R.A. With a Memoir of the Author. Post 8vo., 3s. 6d. Gilt, 4s. 6d.

A Boy's Locker. A Smaller Edition of the above Tales, in 12 volumes, enclosed in a compact cloth box. 21s.

Hans Christian Andersen's Tales for Children. With Forty-eight Full-page Illustrations by Wehnert, and Fifty-seven Small Engravings on Wood by W. THOMAS. A new Edition. Very handsomely bound. 6s.

Hans Christian Andersen's Fairy Tales and Sketches. Translated by C. C. PEACHEY, H. WARD, A. PLESNER, &c. With 104 Illustrations by OTTO SPECKTER and others. 6s.
   This volume contains several tales that are in no other Edition published in this country, and with the above volume it forms the most complete English Edition.

Mrs. Alfred Gatty's Presentation Box for Young PEOPLE. Containing "Parables from Nature," "Aunt Judy's Tales," and other Popular Books, 9 volumes in all, beautifully printed, neatly bound, and enclosed in a cloth box. 31s. 6d. Any single volume at 3s. 6d.

Anecdotes of Dogs. By EDWARD JESSE. With Illustrations. Post 8vo. Cloth. 5s. With Thirty-four Steel Engravings after COOPER, LANDSEER, &c. 7s. 6d.

The Natural History of Selborne. By GILBERT WHITE. Edited by JESSE. Illustrated with Forty Engravings. Post 8vo. 5s.; or with the Plates Coloured, 7s. 6d.

A Poetry Book for Schools. Illustrated with Thirty-seven highly-finished Engravings by C. W. COPE, R.A., HELMSLEY, PALMER, SKILL, THOMAS, and H. WEIR. Crown 8vo. 1s.

Select Parables from Nature. By Mrs. GATTY. For the Use of Schools. Fcap. 1s.
   Besides being reprinted in America, selections from Mrs. Gatty's Parables have been translated and published in the German, French, Italian, Russian, Danish, and Swedish languages.

LONDON: GEORGE BELL & SONS, YORK STREET COVENT GARDEN.

STANDARD WORKS PUBLISHED BY

SOWERBY'S ENGLISH BOTANY:

Containing a Description and Life-size coloured Drawing of every British Plant. Edited and brought up to the Present Standard of Scientific Knowledge by T. BOSWELL, LL.D., F.L.S., &c. With Popular Descriptions of the Uses, History, and Traditions of each Plant, by Mrs. LANKESTER, Author of "Wild Flowers Worth Notice," "The British Ferns," &c. The Figures by J. E. SOWERBY, JAMES SOWERBY, F.L.S., J. DE. C. SOWERBY, F.L.S., and J. W. SALTER, A.L.S. In Eleven Volumes, super-royal 8vo.; or in 83 Parts, 5s. each.

"Under the editorship of T. Boswell Syme, F.L.S., assisted by Mrs. Lankester, 'Sowerby's English Botany,' when finished, will be exhaustive of the subject, and worthy of the branch of science it illustrates. . . . In turning over the charmingly executed hand-coloured plates of British plants which encumber these volumes with riches, the reader cannot help being struck with the beauty of many of the humblest flowering weeds we tread on with careless step. We cannot dwell upon many of the individuals grouped in the splendid bouquet of flowers presented in these pages, and it will be sufficient to state that the work is pledged to contain a figure of every wild flower indigenous to these isles."—*Times.*

"Will be the most complete Flora of Great Britain ever brought out. This great work will find a place wherever botanical science is cultivated, and the study of our native plants, with all their fascinating associations, held dear."—*Athenæum.*

"A clear, bold, distinctive type enables the reader to take in at a glance the arrangement and divisions of every page. And Mrs. Lankester has added to the technical description by the editor an extremely interesting popular sketch, which follows in smaller type. The English, French, and German popular names are given, and, wherever that delicate and difficult step is at all practicable, their derivation also. Medical properties, superstitions, and fancies, and poetic tributes and illusions, follow. In short there is nothing more left to be desired."—*Guardian.*

"Without question, this is the standard work on Botany, and indispensable to every botanist. . . . The plates are most accurate and beautiful, and the entire work cannot be too strongly recommended to all who are interested in botany."—*Illustrated News.*

Sold separately, prices as follows:—

	Bound cloth.	Half morocco.	Morocco elegant.
	£ s. d.	£ s. d.	£ s. d.
Vol. I. (Seven Parts)	1 18 0	2 2 0	2 8 6
II. ditto	1 18 0	2 2 0	2 8 6
III. (Eight Parts)	2 8 0	2 7 0	2 13 6
IV. (Nine Parts)	2 8 0	2 12 0	2 18 6
V. (Eight Parts)	2 8 0	2 7 0	2 13 6
VI. (Seven Parts)	1 18 0	2 2 0	2 8 6
VII. ditto	1 18 0	2 2 0	2 8 6
VIII. (Ten Parts)	2 13 0	2 17 0	3 3 6
IX. (Seven Parts)	1 18 0	2 2 0	2 8 6
X. ditto	1 18 0	2 2 0	2 8 6
XI. (Six Parts)	1 13 0	1 17 0	2 3 6

Or, the Eleven Volumes, 22l. 8s. in cloth; 24l. 12s. in half-morocco; and 28l. 3s. 6d. whole morocco.

Volume XII., by Prof. BOSWELL, containing ferns and other cryptogamous plants, with an Index to the whole work, is now being issued. Part I. with 22 coloured plates is now ready, price 5s.

LONDON: GEORGE BELL & SONS, YORK STREET, COVENT GARDEN.

LIBRARY OF NATURAL HISTORY.

"Each volume is elegantly printed in royal 8vo., and illustrated with a very large number of well-executed engravings, printed in colours. . . . . They form a complete library of reference on the several subjects to which they are devoted, and nothing more complete in their way has lately appeared."—*The Bookseller.*

BREE'S BIRDS OF EUROPE AND THEIR EGGS, not observed in the British Isles. With 252 beautifully coloured Plates. Five vols. 5*l*. 5*s*.

COUCH'S HISTORY OF THE FISHES OF THE BRITISH ISLANDS. With 252 carefully coloured Plates. Four vols. 4*l*. 4*s*.

GATTY'S (MRS. ALFRED) BRITISH SEAWEEDS. Numerous coloured Illustrations. Two vols. 2*l*. 10*s*.

HIBBERD'S (SHIRLEY) NEW AND RARE BEAUTIFUL-LEAVED PLANTS. With 64 coloured Full-page Illustrations. Executed expressly for this work. One vol. 1*l*. 5*s*.

LOWE'S NATURAL HISTORY OF BRITISH AND EXOTIC FERNS. With 479 finely coloured Plates. Eight vols. 6*l*. 6*s*.

LOWE'S OUR NATIVE FERNS. Illustrated with 79 coloured Plates and 900 Wood Engravings. Two vols. 2*l*. 2*s*.

LOWE'S NATURAL HISTORY OF NEW AND RARE FERNS. Containing Species and Varieties not included in "Ferns, British and Exotic." 72 coloured Plates and Woodcuts. One vol. 1*l*. 1*s*.

LOWE'S NATURAL HISTORY OF BRITISH GRASSES. With 74 finely coloured Plates. One vol. 1*l*. 1*s*.

LOWE'S BEAUTIFUL-LEAVED PLANTS: being a description of the most beautiful-leaved Plants in cultivation in this country. With 60 coloured Illustrations. One vol. 1*l*. 1*s*.

MAUNDS' BOTANIC GARDEN. New Edition. Edited by J. C. NIVEN, Curator of the Botanic Gardens, Hull. With 250 coloured Plates, giving 1247 figures. Six vols. 12*l*. 12*s*.

MORRIS' HISTORY OF BRITISH BIRDS. With 360 finely coloured Engravings. Six vols. 6*l*. 6*s*.

MORRIS' NESTS AND EGGS OF BRITISH BIRDS. With 223 beautifully coloured Engravings. Three vols. 3*l*. 3*s*.

MORRIS' BRITISH BUTTERFLIES. With 71 beautifully coloured Plates. One vol. 1*l*. 1*s*.

MORRIS' BRITISH MOTHS. With coloured Illustrations of nearly 2000 specimens. Four vols. 6*l*. 6*s*.

TRIPP'S BRITISH MOSSES. With 39 coloured Plates, containing a figure of each species. Two vols. 2*l*. 10*s*.

WOOSTER'S ALPINE PLANTS First Series. With 54 coloured Plates. 25*s*.

WOOSTER'S ALPINE PLANTS. Second Series. With 54 coloured Plates. 25*s*.

LONDON: GEORGE BELL & SONS, YORK STREET, COVENT GARDEN.

STANDARD WORKS

PUBLISHED BY

GEORGE BELL & SONS.

⁎ *For List of* BOHN'S LIBRARIES *see the end of the Volume.*

MISCELLANEOUS

TRAVELS OF J. W. GOETHE:

COMPRISING

LETTERS FROM SWITZERLAND;
THE CAMPAIGN IN FRANCE, 1792; THE SIEGE OF MAINZ; AND
A TOUR ON THE RHINE, MAINE, AND NECKAR, 1814-15.

EDITED BY

L. DORA SCHMITZ,

TRANSLATOR OF 'CORRESPONDENCE BETWEEN SCHILLER AND GOETHE,'
'ULRICI'S DRAMATIC ART,' ETC., ETC.

LONDON: GEORGE BELL AND SONS, YORK STREET,
COVENT GARDEN.
1882.

"Es ist vortheilhaft den Genius
Bewirthen; gibst du ihm ein Gastgeschenk,
So läszt er dir ein schöneres zurück."

Goethe's *Tasso*.

CONTENTS.

	PAGE
LETTERS FROM SWITZERLAND	1
PART THE FIRST	3
PART THE SECOND, OCTOBER 3 TO NOVEMBER 13, 1779	15
THE CAMPAIGN IN FRANCE 1792	69
DIGRESSION	190
VISIT TO JACOBI IN PEMPELFORT	194
VISIT TO PLESSING IN DUISBURG	204
VISIT TO THE PRINCESS GALLIZIN IN MÜNSTER	220
WEIMAR IN 1792 AND 1793	230
THE SIEGE OF MAINZ	249
FROM A TOUR ON THE RHINE, MAINE, AND NECKAR, IN 1814 AND 1815	289
ST. ROCH'S FESTIVAL AT BINGEN	291
AUTUMN DAYS IN THE RHINEGAU	321
ART COLLECTIONS ON THE RHINE AND MAINE	335
Cologne	"
Bonn	349
Neuwied	353
Coblenz	"
Mainz	355
Biberich	357
Wiesbaden	"
Frankfort	359
Offenbach	382
Hanau	383

CONTENTS.

FROM A TOUR ON THE RHINE, MAINE, AND NECKAR, IN 1814 AND 1815—continued.

ART COLLECTIONS ON THE RHINE AND MAINE—*continued*.

	PAGE
Aschaffenburg	389
Darmstadt	390
Heidelberg	395
Supplementary Remarks on Art, in connection with the Boisserées' Collection of Paintings	418

MAP OF MAINZ, 1793 250

PREFACE.

THE travels of Goethe collected in this volume and arranged in their chronological order, comprise the account of his second tour in Switzerland in 1779, his account of the *Campaign in France in* 1792, the *Siege of Mainz* in 1793, and a tour on the Rhine, Maine, and Neckar, in 1814 and 1815. The Swiss tour is a mere reprint of a translation that has already appeared in the second volume of Goethe's Autobiography, for which, therefore, I cannot hold myself in any way responsible. The Campaign and Siege of Mainz, however, I have very carefully revised from a translation by Mr. Faric, published some years since, but which could scarcely be allowed to stand as it was. The Tour on the Rhine, Maine, and Neckar, appears here for the first time in English.

The First Part of the Swiss tour with its allusion to *Werther* has suggested the theory that Goethe intended to write a sort of prelude to that novel by way of giving it a more explicit *motif*.* If so, the design was abandoned, and the work has remained fragmentary. For this reason, I believe, it was not considered essential to translate it with absolute completeness, and a digression which has no bearing on the main course of the narrative has been abridged. In the Second Part, beginning with the date October 3, 1779, the letters assume a strictly

* See Dr. Strehlke's preface in Hempel's edition.

matter-of-fact tone, and the work may almost be regarded as a continuation of the Autobiography.

The account of the *Campaign in France* may likewise be regarded as mainly autobiographical, for the diaries of which it is composed were certainly never meant to form a regular history of the military events, as is proved by the title of the first edition, published in 1822, bearing the words, *Aus meinem Leben*. That the account was not meant to be an historical record is still more evident from the fact that Goethe's experiences during the campaign are immediately followed by accounts of visits to Jacobi at Pempelfort, to Plessing at Duisburg, and to the Princess Gallizin at Münster. It seems, in fact, certain that Goethe had no thought whatever at the time of writing a report of the military proceedings for publication; for on various important occasions, when disinclined for the task, or when he happened to find other occurrences more attractive, he even omitted to note down what had taken place, and, as he himself admits, made use of a journal kept by the Duke of Weimar's chamberlain, to supplement his own. His interest, throughout his stay with the army in France, was directed more to his human surroundings, to scientific observations and to nature generally, than to the actual course or consequences of the war. It was not till the year 1822 that Goethe first thought of adding his experiences during the campaign as a part of his autobiography, and some new additions were then made to the diary from other sources. The chapter headed a Digression was written wholly from memory in the winter of 1821, and Zelter in a letter to Goethe speaks of the impression made upon him by the finished work.

The *Siege of Mainz*, on the other hand, seems more strictly a regular report of the military proceedings. It is only occasionally that we find Goethe's own personal experiences brought prominently forward. Fuller details of his thoughts and work during those days will be found more especially in his letters to Herder and Jacobi. The invasion of France in 1792 was made by the allied army under the command of the King of Prussia and the Duke of Brunswick. The Duke of Weimar took his place at the head of his own regiment, and it seems that, being unwilling to be without Goethe's genial society, he sent for him to join the regiment as his guest, as Goethe had been requested to do on a previous occasion in Silesia. During the following winter he was again in Weimar, and so busily engaged with the direction of the theatre, with his *Bürger-General*, *Reinecke Fuchs*, a contemplated visit to Jena, and other matters, that when the Duke, in February, again requested him to come and watch the proceedings before Mainz, Goethe was somewhat loth to leave home; this may, at least, be inferred from the lines with which he closes his account of the campaign. However, being anxious to comply with the wishes of his friend, the Duke, Goethe did again join the army in May, and remained to see the capitulation and evacuation of the city.

The *Tour on the Rhine, Maine, and Neckar*, shows us Goethe under a completely different aspect. In the summer of 1814 he was at Wiesbaden taking the waters, and from there, in company with his friends Cramer and Zelter, made the excursion to Rüdesheim to which we owe his charming description of the festival held in celebration of the restoration of St. Roch's Chapel near Bingen. The pleasant excursions in the Rheingau were enjoyed while on a week's visit to the Brentano family, who had a country residence at Winkel. In the essays on the Art Collections we find Goethe devoting his attention chiefly to the so-called Christian art of the Middle Ages, a style of art which it would seem had lost its attraction for him for many years, after the first great impression made upon him by the Strassburg Cathedral, and which led him to publish a pamphlet full of enthusiasm on the subject—an enthusiasm which in subsequent years appeared so incomprehensible to him that he was with difficulty persuaded to include this treatise among his other works.. The essays on the Art Collections were probably written with the view of drawing the attention of the public to the Boisserées' work on Cologne Cathedral, which was to embrace drawings of all the more important monuments of early German architecture on the Lower Rhine. Goethe had become personally acquainted with Sulpiz Boisserée in 1811, after many letters had passed between them on the subject of the latter's work on the Cathedral. Boisserée, in his admiration of Goethe's genius, was anxious to have his approval of the work, and also to seek his advice on various other points. The essays were first published in an Art Magazine edited by Goethe, and originally called *Ueber Kunst und Alterthum in den Rhein- und Main- Gegenden*, but which subsequently received the more general name of *Kunst und Alterthum*, and appeared under Goethe's supervision up to the time of his death. The Boisserées' splendid collection in Heidelberg likewise reawakened Goethe's interest in the early German and Netherland schools of painting, an historical sketch of which closes his observations on the collections he had visited in the different towns.

In this volume, therefore, in spite of the warlike headings of the two main portions of the contents, we shall find Goethe the same calm, observant and peace-loving man he proved himself throughout life, delighting in all that is beautiful in nature and art, and true to his own words:

  Manches Herrliche der Welt
   Ist in Krieg und Streit zerronnen;
  Wer beschützet und erhält,
   Hat das schönste Loos gewonnen.

London, 1882.

           L. DORA SCHMITZ.

LETTERS FROM SWITZERLAND.

TRANSLATED BY

THE REV. A. J. W. MORRISON, M.A.

AUTHOR'S INTRODUCTION.

When, a few years ago, the copies of the following letters were first made known to us, it was asserted that they had been found among Werther's papers, and it was pretended that before his acquaintance with Charlotte, he had been in Switzerland. We have never seen the originals: however we would not on any account anticipate the judgment and feelings of our readers; for whatever may be their true history, it is impossible to read them without sympathy

LETTERS FROM SWITZERLAND.

PART THE FIRST.

How all my descriptions disgust me, when I read them over. Nothing but your advice, your command, your injunction could have induced me to attempt anything of the kind. How many descriptions, too, of these scenes had I not read before I saw them. Did these, then, afford me an image of them,—or at best but a mere vague notion? In vain did my imagination attempt to bring the objects before it; in vain did my mind try to think upon them. Here I now stand contemplating these wonders, and what are my feelings in the midst of them? I can think of nothing—I can feel nothing,—and how willingly would I both think and feel. The glorious scene before me excites my soul to its inmost depths, and impels me to be doing; and yet what can I do—what do I? I set myself down and scribble and describe!—Away with you, ye descriptions—delude my friend —make him believe that I am doing something—that he sees and reads something.

Free, then, are these Switzers? Free, those opulent burghers in their little pent-up towns—free, those poor devils on their rocks and crags? What is it that man cannot be made to believe, especially when he cherishes in his heart the memory of some old tale of marvel? Once, forsooth, they did break a tyrant's yoke, and might for the moment fancy themselves free; but out of the carcase of the single oppressor the good sun, by a strange new birth, has hatched a swarm of petty tyrants. And so now they are ever telling that old tale of marvel: one hears it till one is sick of it. They formerly made themselves free, and have ever since remained free! and now they sit behind their walls, hugging themselves with their customs and laws—their philandering and philistering. And there, too, on the rocks, it is surely fine to talk of liberty, when for six months of the year they, like the marmot, are bound hand and foot by the snow.

Alas! how wretched must any work of man look, in the midst of this great and glorious Nature, but especially such sorry, poverty-stricken works as these black and dirty little towns—such mean heaps of stones and rubbish! Large rubble and other stones on the roofs too, that the miserable thatch may not be carried off from the top of them, —and then the filth, the dung, and the gaping idiots! When here you meet with man and the wretched work of his hands, you are glad to fly away immediately from both.

That there are in man very many intellectual capacities which in this life he is unable to develope, which therefore point to a better future, and to a more harmonious state of existence: on this point we are both agreed. But further than this I cannot give up that other fancy of mine, even though on account of it you may again call me, as you have so often done already, a mere enthusiast. For my part, I do think that man feels conscious also of corporeal qualities, of whose mature expansion he can have no hope in this life. This most assuredly is the case with "*flying.*" How strongly at one time used the clouds, as they drove along the blue sky, to tempt me to travel with them to foreign lands! and now in what danger do I stand, lest they should carry me away with them from the mountain peak as they sweep violently by. What desire do I not feel to throw myself into the boundless regions of the air—to poise over the terrific abyss, or to alight on some otherwise inaccessible rock. With what a longing do I draw deeper and deeper breath, when, in the dark blue depth below, the eagle soars over rocks and forests, or in company, and in sweet concord with his mate, wheels in wide circles round the eyrie to which he has entrusted his young. Must I then never do more than creep up to the summits? Must I always go on clinging to the highest rocks, as well as to the lowest plain; and when I have at last, with much toil, reached the desired eminence, must I still anxiously grasp at every holding place, shudder at the thought of return, and tremble at the chance of a fall.

With what wonderful properties are we not born,—what vague aspirations rise within us! How rarely do imagination and our bodily powers work in opposition! Peculiarities of my early boyhood again recur. While I am walking, and have a long road before me, my arms go dangling by my side, I often make a grasp, as if I would seize a javelin, and hurl it I know not at whom, or what; and then I fancy an arrow is shot at me which pierces me to the heart; I strike my hand upon my breast, and feel an inexpressible sweetness; and then after this I soon revert to my natural state. Whence comes this strange phenomenon,—what is the meaning of it? and why does it invariably recur under the same figures, in the same bodily movement, and with the same sensation?

I am repeatedly told that the people who have met me on my journey are little satisfied with me. I can readily believe it, for neither has any one of them contributed to my satisfaction. I cannot tell how it comes to pass, that society oppresses me,—that the forms of politeness are disagreeable to me,—that what people talk about does not interest me,—that all that they show to me is either quite indifferent, or else produces quite an opposite impression to what they expect. When I am shown a drawing or painting of any beautiful spot, immediately a feeling of disquiet arises within me which is utterly inexpressible. My toes within my shoes begin to bend, as if they would clutch the ground—a cramp-like motion runs through my fingers. I bite my lips, and I hasten to leave the company I am in, and throw myself down in the presence of the majesty of nature on the first seat however inconvenient. I try to take in the scene before me with my eye—to seize all its beauties, and on the spot I love to cover a whole sheet with scratches, which represent nothing exactly, but which, nevertheless, possess an infinite value in my eyes, as serving to remind me of the happy moment whose bliss even this bungling exercise could not mar. What means, then, this strange effort to pass from art to nature, and then back again from nature to art? If it gives promise of an artist, why is steadiness wanting to me? If it calls me to enjoyment, wherefore, then, am I not able to seize it? I lately had a present of a basket of fruit. I was in raptures at the sight of it as of something heavenly,—such riches, such abundance, such variety and yet such affinity! I could not persuade myself to pluck off a single berry—I could not bring myself to take a single peach or a fig. Most assuredly this gratification of the eye and the inner sense is the highest and most worthy of man; in all probability it is the design of Nature, when the hungry and thirsty believe that she has exhausted herself in marvels merely for the gratification of their palate. Ferdinand came and found me in the midst of these meditations: he did me justice, and then said, smiling, but with a deep sigh, "Yes, we are not worthy to consume these glorious products of Nature; truly it were a pity. Permit me to make a present of them to my beloved?" How glad was I to see the basket carried off! How did I love Ferdinand—how did I thank him for the feeling he had excited in me—for the prospect he gave me? Aye, we ought to acquaint ourselves with the beautiful; we ought to contemplate it with rapture, and attempt to raise ourselves up to its height. And in order to gain strength for that, we must keep ourselves thoroughly unselfish—we must not make it our own, but rather seek to communicate it: indeed, to make a sacrifice of it to those who are dear and precious to us.

How sedulously are we shaped and moulded in our youth—how constantly are we then called on to lay aside now this, now that bad feeling! But what, in fact, are our so-called bad feelings but so many organs by means of which man is to help himself in life. How is not the poor child worried, in whom but a little spark of vanity is discovered! and yet what a poor miserable creature is the man who has no vanity at all. I will now tell you what has led me to make all these reflections. The day before yesterday we were joined by a young fellow, who was most disagreeable to me and to Ferdinand. His weak points were so prominent, his emptiness so manifest, and his care for his outward appearance so obvious, that we looked down upon him as far inferior to ourselves, yet everywhere he was better received than we were. Among other of his follies, he wore a waistcoat of red satin, which round the neck was so cut as to look like the ribbon of some order or other. We could not restrain our jokes at this piece of absurdity, but he let them all pass, for he drew a good profit from it, and perhaps secretly laughed at us. For host and hostess, coachman, waiter and chambermaid, and indeed not a few of our fellow-travellers, were taken in by this seeming ornament, and showed him greater politeness than ourselves. Not only was he always first waited upon, but, to our great humiliation, we saw that all the pretty girls in the inns bestowed all their stolen glances upon him; and then, when it came to the reckoning, which his eminence and distinction had enhanced, we had to pay our full shares. Who, then, was the fool in the game?—not he, assuredly.

There is something pretty and instructive about the symbols and maxims which one here sees on all the stoves. Here you have the drawing of one of these symbols which particularly caught my fancy. A horse tethered by his hind foot to a stake is grazing round it as far as his tether will permit; beneath is written, "Allow me to take my allotted portion of food." This, too, will be the case with me, when I come home, and, like the horse in the mill, shall have to work away at your pleasure, and in return, like the horse here on the stove, shall receive a nicely-measured dole for my support. Yes, I am coming back, and what awaits me was certainly well worth all the trouble of climbing up these mountain heights, of wandering through these valleys, and seeing this blue sky—of discovering that there is a nature which exists by an eternal voiceless necessity, which has no wants, no feelings, and is divine, whilst we, whether in the country or in the towns, have alike to toil hard to gain a miserable subsistence, and at the same time struggle to subject everything to our lawless caprice, and call it liberty!

Aye, I have ascended the Furca,—the summit of S. Gotthard. These sublime, incomparable scenes of nature, will ever stand before my eye. Aye, I have read the Roman history, in order to gain from the comparison a distinct and vivid feeling what a thoroughly miserable being I am.

Never has it been so clear to me as during these last few days, that I too could be happy on moderate means—could be quite as happy as any one else, if only I knew a trade—an exciting one, indeed, but yet one which had no consequences for the morrow, which required nothing but industry and attention at the time, without calling for either foresight or retrospection. Every mechanic seems to me the happiest of mortals: all that he has to do is already settled for him, what he can do is fixed and known. He has not to rack his brains over the task that is set him; he works away without thinking, without exertion or haste, but still with diligence and pleasure in his work, like a bird building its nest, or a bee constructing its cells. He is but a degree above the beasts, and yet he is a perfect man. How do I envy the potter at his wheel, or the joiner behind his bench!

Tilling the soil is not to my liking—this first and most necessary of man's occupations is disagreeable to me. In it man does but ape nature, who scatters her seeds everywhere, whereas man would choose that a particular field should produce none but one particular fruit. But things do not go on exactly so—the weeds spring up luxuriantly—the cold and wet injures the crop, or the hail cuts it off entirely. The poor husbandman anxiously waits throughout the year to see how the cards will decide the game with the clouds, and determine whether he shall win or lose his stakes. Such a doubtful ambiguous condition may be right suitable to man, in his present ignorance, while he knows not whence he came, nor whither he is going. It may then be tolerable to man to resign all his labours to chance; and thus the parson, at any rate, has an opportunity, when things look thoroughly bad, to remind him of Providence, and to connect the sins of his flock with the incidents of nature.

So then I have nothing to joke Ferdinand about! I too have met with a pleasant adventure. Adventure! why do I use the silly word? There is nothing of adventure in a gentle attraction which draws man to man. Our social life, our false relations, those are adventures, these are monstrosities and yet they come before us as well-known and as nearly akin to us, as Uncle and Aunt.

We had been introduced to Herr Tüdou, and we found ourselves very happy among this family—rich, open-hearted, good-natured, lively people, who in the society of their children, in comfort and without care, enjoy the good which each day brings with it—their property and their glorious neighbourhood. We young folks were not required, as is too often the case, in so many formal households, to sacrifice ourselves at the card-table, in order to humour the old. On the contrary, the old people, father, mother, and aunts, gathered round us, when for our own amusement, we got up some little games, in which chance, and thought, and wit, had their counteracting influence. Eleonora—for I must now at last mention her name—the second daughter—her image will for ever be present to my mind—a slim slight-frame, delicately chiselled features, a bright eye—a palish complexion, which in young girls of her age is rather pleasing than disagreeable, as being a sign of no very incurable a malady—on the whole, her appearance was extremely agreeable. She seemed cheerful and lively and every one felt at his ease with her. Soon—indeed I may venture to say at once,—at once, on the very first evening she made me her companion; she sat by my side, and if the game separated us a moment, she soon contrived to find her old place again. I was gay and cheerful—my journey, the beautiful weather, the country—all had contributed to produce in me an immoderate cheerfulness—aye, I might almost venture to say, a state of excitement. I derived it from everything and imparted it to everything; even Ferdinand seemed to forget his fair one. We had almost exhausted ourselves in varying our amusements when we at last thought of the "Game of Matrimony." The names of the ladies and of the gentlemen were thrown separately into two hats, and then the pairs were drawn out one by one. On each couple, as determined by the lot, one of the company whose turn it might happen to be, had to write a little poem. Every one of the party, father, mother, and aunts, were obliged to put their names in the hats; we cast in besides the names of our acquaintances, and to enlarge the number of candidates for matrimony, we threw in those of all the well-known characters of the literary and of the political world. We commenced playing, and the first pairs that were drawn were highly distinguished personages. It was not every one, however, who was ready at once with his verses. *She*, Ferdinand and myself, and one of the aunts who wrote very pretty verses in French—we soon divided among ourselves the office of secretary. The conceits were mostly good and the verses tolerable. Her's especially, had a touch of nature about them which distinguished them from all others; without being really clever they had a happy turn; they were playful without being bitter, and shewed good will towards every one. The father laughed heartily, and his face was lit up with joy when his daughter's verses were declared to be the best after mine. Our unqualified approbation highly delighted him,—we praised as men praise unexpected merit—as we praise an author who has bribed us. At last out came my lot, and chance had taken honourable care of me. It was no less a personage than the Empress of all the Russias, who was drawn to be my partner for life. The company laughed heartily at the match, and Eleonora maintained that the whole company must try their best to do honour to so eminent a consort. All began to try: a few pens were bitten to pieces; she was ready first, but wished to read last; the mother and the aunt could make nothing of the subject, and although the father was rather matter-of-fact, Ferdinand somewhat humorous, and the aunts rather reserved, still, through all you could see friendship and goodwill. At last it came to her turn; she drew a deep breath, her ease and cheerfulness left her; she did not read but rather lisped it out—and laid it before me to read it to the rest. I was astonished, amazed. Thus does the bud of love open in beauty and modesty! I felt as if a whole spring had showered upon me all its flowers at once! Every one was silent, Ferdinand lost not his presence of mind. "Beautiful," he exclaimed, "very beautiful! he deserves the poem as little as an Empire." "If, only we have rightly understood it," said the father; the rest requested I would read it once more. My eyes had hitherto been fixed on the precious words, a shudder ran through me from head to foot; Ferdinand who saw my perplexity, took the paper up and read it. She scarcely allowed him to finish before she drew out the lots for another pair. The play was not kept up long after this and refreshments were brought in.

Shall I or shall I not? Is it right of me to hide in silence any thing from him to whom I tell so much—nay, all? Shall I keep back from you a great matter, when I yet weary you with so many trifles which assuredly no one would ever read but you who have taken so wonderful a liking for me? or shall I keep back anything from you because it might perhaps give you a false, not to say an ill opinion of me? No—you know me better than I even know myself. If I should do anything which you do not believe possible I could do, you will amend it; if I should do anything deserving of censure, you will not spare me,—you will lead me and guide me whenever my peculiarities entice me off the right road.

My joy, my rapture at works of art when they are true, when they are immediate and speaking expressions of Nature afford the greatest delight to every collector, to every dilettante. Those indeed who call themselves connoisseurs are not always of my opinion; but I care nothing for their connoisseurship when I am happy. Does not living nature vividly impress itself on my sense of vision? Do not its images remain fixed in my brain? Do not they there grow in beauty, delighting to compare themselves in turn with the images of art which the mind of others has also embellished and beautified? I confess to you that my fondness for nature arises from the fact of my always seeing her so beautiful, so lovely, so brilliant, so ravishing, that the similation of the artist, even his imperfect imitation transports me almost as much, as if it were a perfect type. It is only such works of art, however, as bespeak genius and feeling that have any charms for me. Those cold imitations which confine themselves to the narrow circle of a certain meagre mannerism, of mere painstaking diligence, are to me utterly intolerable. You see, therefore, that my delight and taste cannot well be riveted by a work of art, unless it imitates such objects of nature as are well known to me, so that I am able to test the imitation by my own experience of the originals. Landscape, with all that lives and moves therein—flowers and fruit-trees, Gothic churches,—a portrait taken directly from Nature, all this I can recognize, feel, and if you like, judge of. Honest W—— amused himself with this trait of my character, and in such a way that I could not be offended, often made merry with it at my expense. He sees much further in this matter, than I do, and I shall always prefer that people should laugh at me while they instruct, than that they should praise me without benefitting me. He had noticed what things I was most immediately pleased with, and after a short acquaintance did not hesitate to avow that in the objects that so transported me there might be much that was truly estimable, and which time alone would enable me to distinguish.

But I turn from this subject and must now, however circuitously, come to the matter which, though reluctantly, I cannot but confide to you. I can see you in your room, in your little garden, where, over a pipe of tobacco, you will probably break the seal and read this letter. Can your thoughts follow me into this free and motley world? Will the circumstances and true state of the case become clear to your imagination? And will you be as indulgent towards your absent friend as I have often found you when present?

When my artistic friend became better acquainted with me, and judged me worthy of being gradually introduced to better pieces of art, he one day, not without a most mysterious look, took me to a case, which, being opened, displayed a Danae, of the size of life, receiving in her bosom the golden shower. I was amazed at the splendour of the limbs—the magnificence of the posture and arrangement—the intense tenderness and the intellectuality of the sensual subject; and yet I did but stand before it in silent contemplation. It did not excite in me *that* rapture, *that* delight, *that* inexpressible pleasure. My friend, who went on descanting upon the merits of the picture, was too full of his own enthusiasm to notice my coldness, and was delighted with the opportunity this painting afforded him of pointing out the distinctive excellences of the Italian School.

But the sight of this picture has not made me happy—it has made me uneasy. How! said I to myself—in what a strange case do we civilized men find ourselves with our many conventional restraints! A mossy rock, a waterfall rivets my eye so long that I can tell everything about it—its heights, its cavities, its lights and shades, its hues, its blending tints and reflections—all is distinctly present to my mind; and whenever I please, comes vividly before me, in a most happy imitation. But of that masterpeice of Nature, the human frame—of the order and symmetry of the limbs, of all this I have but a very general notion—which in fact is no notion at all. My imagination presents to me anything but a vivid image of this glorious structure, and when art presents an imitation of it, to my eye it awakens in me no sensation and I am unable to judge of the merits of the picture. No, I will remain no longer in this state of stupidity. I will stamp on my mind the shape of man, as well as that of a cluster of grapes or of a peach-tree.

I sought an occasion and got Ferdinand to take a swim in the lake. What a glorious shape has my friend; how duly proportioned are all his limbs: what fulness of form; what splendour of youth! What a gain to have enriched my imagination with this perfect model of manhood! Now I can people the woods, the meadow, and the hills, with similar fine forms! I can see him as Adonis chasing the boar, or as Narcissus contemplating himself in the mirror of the spring.

But alas! my imagination cannot furnish, as yet, a Venus, who holds him from the chace, a Venus who bewails his death, or a beautiful Echo casting one sad look more on the cold corpse of the youth before she vanishes for ever! I have therefore resolved, cost what it will, to see a female form in the state that I have seen my friend.

When, therefore, we reached Geneva, I made arrangements in the character of an artist to complete my studies of the nude figure, and to-morrow evening my wish is to be gratified.

I cannot avoid going to-day with Ferdinand to a grand party. It will form an excellent foil to the studies of this evening. Well enough do I know those formal parties where the old women require you to play at cards with them, and the young ones to ogle with them; where you must listen to the learned, pay respect to the parson, and give way to the noble, where the numerous lights show you scarcely one tolerable form, and that one hidden and buried beneath some barbarous load of frippery. I shall have to speak French, too,—a foreign tongue—the use of which always makes a man appear silly, whatever he may think of himself, since the best he can express in it is nothing but common place, and the most obvious of remarks, and that, too, only with stammering and hesitating lips. For what is it that distinguishes the blockhead from the really clever man but the peculiar quickness and vividness with which the latter discerns the nicer shades and proprieties of all that come before him, and expresses himself thereon with facility; whereas the former, (just as we all do with a foreign language,) is forced on every occasion to have recourse to some ready found and conversational phrase or other? To-day I will calmly put up with the sorry entertainment, in expectation of the rare scene of nature which awaits me in the evening.

My adventure is over. It has fully equalled my expectation —nay, surpassed it; and yet I know not whether to congratulate, or to blame myself on account of it.*

* The conclusion of this Part is somewhat abridged in the translation.—ED.

LETTERS FROM SWITZERLAND.*

PART THE SECOND.

Moutier, October 3, 1779. Sunday evening.

From Basle you will receive a packet containing an account of my travels up to that point, for we are now continuing in good earnest our tour through Switzerland. On our route to Bienne we rode up the beautiful valley of the Birs, and at last reached the pass which leads to this place.

Among the ridges of the broad and lofty range of mountains the little stream of the Birs found of old a channel for itself. Necessity soon after may have driven men to clamber wearily and painfully through its gorges. The Romans in their time enlarged the track, and now you may travel through it with perfect ease. The stream, dashing over crags and rocks, and the road run side by side, and except at a few points, these make up the whole breadth of the pass which is hemmed in by rocks, the top of which is easily reached by the eye. Behind them the mountain chain rose with a slight inclination; the summits, however, were veiled by a mist.

Here walls of rock rise precipitously one above another; there immense strata run obliquely down to the river and the road—here again broad masses lie piled one over another, while close beside stands a line of sharp-pointed crags. Wide

---

* At this point commence the genuine records of Goethe's second tour in Switzerland. Originally written as letters to the Frau von Stein, they were soon afterwards arranged for reading aloud to the Court circle at Weimar. In the year 1796 they appeared in a more abridged form in Schiller's *Horen*, and it is this version, afterwards corrected and somewhat enlarged by reference to the original MSS., that appears in the editions of Goethe's works.—ED.

clefts run yawning upwards, and blocks, of the size of a wall, have detached themselves from the rest of the stony mass. Some fragments of the rock have rolled to the bottom; others are still suspended, and by their position alarm you, as also likely at any moment to come toppling down.

Now round, now pointed, now overgrown, now bare are the tops of these rocks among and high above which some single bald summit boldly towers, while along the perpendicular cliffs and among the hollows below, the weather has worn many a deep and winding cranny.

The passage through this defile raised in me a grand but calm emotion. The sublime produces a beautiful calmness in the soul which entirely possessed by it, feels as great as it ever can feel. How glorious is such a pure feeling, when it rises to the very highest, without overflowing. My eye and my soul were both able to take in the objects before me, and as I was pre-occupied by nothing, and had no false tastes to counteract their impression, they had on me their full and natural effect. When we compare such a feeling with that we are sensible of, when we laboriously harass ourselves with some trifle, and strain every nerve to gain as much as possible for it, and as it were, to patch it out, striving to furnish joy and aliment to the mind from its own creation; we then feel sensibly what a poor expedient, after all, the latter is.

A young man, whom we have had for our companion from Basle, said his feelings were very far from what they were on his first visit, and gave all the honour to novelty. I however would say, when we see such objects as these for the first time, the unaccustomed soul has to expand itself, and this gives rise to a sort of painful joy—an overflowing of emotion which agitates the mind, and draws from us the most delicious tears. By this operation the soul, without knowing it, becomes greater in itself, and is of course not capable of ever feeling again such a sensation, and man thinks in consequence that he has lost something, whereas in fact he has gained. What he loses in delight he gains in inward riches. If only destiny had bidden me to dwell in the midst of some grand scenery, then would I every morning have imbibed greatness from its grandeur, as from a lonely valley I would extract patience and repose.

After reaching the end of the gorge I alighted, and went

back alone through a part of the valley. I thus called forth another profound feeling—one by which the attentive mind may expand its joys to a high degree. One guesses in the dark about the origin and existence of these singular forms. It may have happened, when and how it may,—these masses must, according to the laws of gravity and affinity, have been formed grandly and simply by aggregation. Whatever revolutions may subsequently have upheaved, rent and divided them, the latter were only partial convulsions, and even the idea of such mighty commotions gives one a deep feeling of the eternal stability of the masses. Time, too, bound by the everlasting law, has had here greater, here less, effect upon them.

Internally their colour appears to be yellowish. The air, however, and the weather has changed the surface into a bluish-grey, so that the original colour is only visible here and there in streaks and in the fresh cracks. The stone itself slowly crumbles beneath the influence of the weather, becoming rounded at the edges, as the softer flakes wear away. In this manner have been formed hollows and cavities gracefully shelving off, which when they have sharp slanting and pointed edges, present a singular appearance.

Vegetation maintains its rights on every ledge, on every flat surface, for in every fissure the pines strike root, and the mosses and plants spread themselves over the rocks. One feels deeply convinced that here there is nothing accidental; that here there is working an eternal law which, however slowly, yet surely governs the universe,—that there is nothing here from the hand of man but the convenient road, by means of which this singular region is traversed.

Geneva, October 27, 1779.

The great mountain-range which, running from Basle to Geneva, divides Switzerland from France, is, as you are aware, named the Jura. Its principal heights run by Lausanne, and reach as far as Rolle and Nyon. In the midst of this summit ridge Nature has cut out—I might almost say washed out—a remarkable valley, for on the tops of all these limestone rocks the operation of the primal waters is manifest. It is called La Vallée de Joux, which means the Valley of the Rock, since Joux in the local dialect signifies a rock. Before I proceed with the further description of our journey, I will give you a brief geographical account of its situation. Lengthwise it stretches like the mountain range itself almost directly from south to north, and is locked in on the one side by Sept Moncels, and on the other by Dent de Vaulion, which, after the Dôle, is the highest peak of the Jura. Its length, according to the statement of the neighbourhood, is nine short leagues, but according to our rough reckoning as we rode through it, six good leagues. The mountainous ridge which bounds it lengthwise on the north, and is also visible from the flat lands, is called the Black Mountain (Le Noir Mont). Towards the west the Risou rises gradually, and slopes away towards Franche Comté. France and Berne divide the valley pretty evenly between them; the former claiming the upper and inferior half, and the latter possessing the lower and better portion, which is properly called La Vallée du Lac de Joux. Quite at the upper part of the valley, and at the foot of Sept Moncels, lies the Lac des Rousses, which has no single visible origin, but gathers its waters from the numerous springs which here gush out of the soil, and from the little brooks which run into the lake from all sides. Out of it flows the Orbe, which after running through the whole of the French, and a great portion of the Bernese territory, forms lower down, and towards the Dent de Vaulion, the Lac de Joux, which falls on one side into a smaller lake, the waters of which have some subterraneous outlet. The breadth of the valley varies; above, near the Lac des Rousses it is nearly half a league, then it closes in to expand again presently, and to reach its greatest breath, which is nearly a league and a-half. So much to enable you better to understand what follows; while you read it, however, I would beg you now and then to cast a glance upon your map, although, so far as concerns this country, I have found them all to be incorrect.

October 24*th*. In company with a captain and an upper ranger of the forests in these parts, we rode first of all up Mont, a little scattered village, which much more correctly might be called a line of husbandmen's and vinedressers' cottages. The weather was extremely clear; when we turned to look behind us, we had a view of the Lake of Geneva, the mountains of Savoy and Valais, and could just catch

Lausanne, and also, through a light mist, the country round Geneva, Mont Blanc, which towers above all the mountains of Faucigni, stood out more and more distinctly. It was a brilliant sunset, and the view was so grand, that no human eye was equal to it. The moon rose almost at the full, as we got continually higher. Through large pine forests we continued to ascend the Jura, and saw the lake in a mist, and in it the reflection of the moon. It became lighter and lighter. The road is a well-made causeway, though it was laid down merely for the sake of facilitating the transport of the timber to the plains below. We had been ascending for full three leagues before the road began gently to descend. We thought we saw below us a vast lake, for a thick mist filled the whole valley which we overlooked. Presently we came nearer to the mist, and observed a white bow which the moon formed in it, and were soon entirely enveloped in the fog. The company of the captain procured us lodgings in a house where strangers were not usually entertained. In its internal arrangement it differed in nothing from usual buildings of the same kind, except that the great room in the centre was at once the kitchen, the ante-room, and general gathering-place of the family, and from it you entered at once into the sleeping-rooms, which were either on the same floor with it, or had to be approached by steps. On the one side was the fire, which was burning on the ground on some stone slabs, while a chimney, built durably and neatly of planks, received and carried off the smoke. In the corner were the doors of the oven; all the rest of the floor was of wood, with the exception of a small piece near the window around the sink, which was paved. Moreover, all around, and over head on the beams a multitude of domestic articles and utensils were arranged in beautiful order, and all kept nice and clean.

October 25th.—This morning the weather was cold but clear, the meadows covered with hoar frost, and here and there light clouds were floating in the air. We could pretty nearly survey the whole of the lower valley, our house being situated at the foot of the eastern side of Noir Mont. About eight we set off, and in order to enjoy the sun fully, proceeded on the western side. The part of the valley we now traversed was divided into meadows, which, towards the lake were rather swampy. The inhabitants either dwell in detached houses built by the side of their farms, or else have gathered closer together in little villages, which bear simple names derived from their several sites. The first of those that we passed through was called "Le Sentier." We saw at a distance the Dent de Vaulion peeping out over a mist which rested on the lake. The valley grew broader, but our road now lay behind a ridge of rock which shut out our view of the lake, and then through another village called " Le Lieu." The mist arose, and fell off highly variegated by the sun. Close hereto is a small lake, which apparently has neither inlet nor outlet of its waters. The weather cleared up completely as we came to the foot of Dent de Vaulion, and reached the northern extremity of the great lake, which, as it turns westward, empties itself into a smaller by a dam beneath the bridge. The village just above is called " Le Pont." The situation of the smaller lake is what you may easily conceive, as being in a peculiar little valley which may be called pretty. At the western extremity there is a singular mill, built in a ravine of the rock which the smaller lake used formerly to fill. At present it is dammed out of the mill which is erected in the hollow below. The water is conveyed by sluices to the wheel, from which it falls into crannies of the rock, and being sucked in by them, does not show itself again till it reaches Valorbe, which is a full league off, where it again bears the name of the Orbe. These outlets (*entonnoirs*) require to be kept clear, otherwise the water would rise and again fill the ravine, and overflow the mill as it has often done already. We saw the people hard at work removing the worn pieces of the limestone and replacing them by others.

We rode back again over the bridge towards " Le Pont," and took a guide for the Dent du Vaulion. In ascending it we now had the great Lake directly behind us. To the east its boundary is the Noir Mont, behind which the bald peak of the Dôle rises up; to the west it is shut in by the mountain ridge, which on the side of the lake is perfectly bare. The sun felt hot: it was between eleven and twelve o'clock. By degrees we gained a sight of the whole valley, and were able to discern in the distance the " Lac des Rousses," and then stretching to our feet the district we had just ridden through and the road which remained for our return. During the ascent my guide discoursed of the whole range of the country, and the lordships which, he said, it was possible to distinguish from the peak. In the midst of such talk we reached the summit. But a very different spectacle was prepared for us. Under a bright and clear sky nothing was visible but the high mountain chain, all the lower regions were covered with a white sea of cloudy mist, which stretched from Geneva northwards, along the horizon and glittered brilliantly in the sunshine. Out of it, rose to the east, the whole line of snow and ice-capt mountains acknowledging no distinction of names of either the Princes or Peoples, who fancied they were owners of them, and owning subjection only to one Lord, and to the glance of the Sun which was tinging them with a beautiful red. Mont Blanc, right opposite to us, seemed the highest, next to it were the ice-crowned summits of Valais and Oberland, and lastly, came the lower mountains of the Canton of Berne. Towards the west, the sea of mist which was unconfined to one spot; on the left, in the remotest distance, appeared the mountains of Solothurn; somewhat nearer those of Neufchatel, and right before us some of the lower heights of the Jura. Just below, lay some of the masses of the Vaulion, to which belongs the Dent, (tooth) which takes from it its name. To the west, Franche-Comté, with its flat, outstretched and wood-covered hills, shut in the whole horizon; in the distance, towards the north-west, one single mass stood out distinct from all the rest. Straight before us, however, was a beautiful object. This was the peak which gives this summit the name of a tooth. It descends precipitously, or rather with a slight curve, inwards, and in the bottom it is succeeded by a small valley of pine-trees, with beautiful grassy patches here and there, while right beyond it lies the valley of the Orbe (Val-orbe), where you see this stream coming out of the rock, and can trace, in thought, its route backwards to the smaller lake. The little town of Valorbe, also lies in this valley. Most reluctantly we quitted the spot. A delay of a few hours longer, (for the mist generally disperses in about that time), would have enabled us to distinguish the low lands with the lake—but in order that our enjoyment should be perfect, we must always have something behind still to be wished. As we descended we had the whole valley lying perfectly distinct before us. At Le Pont we again mounted our horses, and rode to the east side of the lake, and passed through l'Abbaye de Joux, which at present is a village, but once was a settlement of monks, to whom the whole valley belonged. Towards four, we reached our aubèrge and found our meal ready, of which we were assured by our hostess that at twelve o'clock it would have been good eating, and which, overdone as it was, tasted excellently.

Let me now add a few particulars just as they were told me. As I mentioned just now, the valley belonged formerly to the monks, who having divided it again to feudatories, were with the rest ejected at the Reformation. At present it belongs to the Canton of Berne, and the mountains around are the timber-stores of the Pays de Vaud. Most of the timber is private property, and is cut up under supervision, and then carried down into the plains. The planks are also made here into deal utensils of all kinds, and pails, tubs, and similar articles manufactured.

The people are civil and well disposed. Besides their trade in wood, they also breed cattle. Their beasts are of a small size. The cheese they make is excellent. They are very industrious, and a clod of earth is with them a great treasure. We saw one man with a horse and car, carefully collecting the earth which had been thrown up out of a ditch, and carrying it to some hollow places in the same field. They lay the stones carefully together, and make little heaps of them. There are here many stone-polishers, who work for the Genevese and other tradesmen, and this business furnishes occupation for many women and children. The houses are neat but durable, the form and internal arrangements being determined by the locality and the wants of the inmates. Before every house there is a running stream, and everywhere you see signs of industry, activity, and wealth. But above all things is the highest praise due to the excellent roads, which, in this remote region, as also in all the other cantons, are kept up by that of Berne. A causeway is carried all round the valley, not unnecessarily broad, but in excellent repair, so that the inhabitants can pursue their avocations without inconvenience, and with their small horses and light carts pass easily along. The air is very pure and salubrious.

26*th Oct.*—Over our breakfast we deliberated as to the road we should take on our return. As we heard that the Dôle, the highest summit of the Jura, lay at no great distance from the upper end of the valley, and as the weather promised to be most glorious, so that we might to-day hope to enjoy all that chance denied us yesterday, we finally determined to take this route. We loaded a guide with bread and cheese, and butter and wine, and by 8 o'clock mounted our horses. Our route now lay along the upper part of the valley, in the shade of Noir Mont. It was extremely cold, and there had been a sharp hoar-frost. We had still a good league to ride through the part belonging to Berne, before the causeway which there terminates branches off into two parts. Through a little wood of pine trees we entered the French territory. Here the scene changed greatly. What first excited our attention was the wretched roads. The soil is rather stony; everywhere you see great heaps of those which have been picked off the fields. Soon you come to a part which is very marshy and full of springs. The woods all around you are in wretched condition. In all the houses and people you recognise, I will not say want, but certainly a hard and meagre subsistence. They belong, almost as serfs, to the canons of S. Claude; they are bound to the soil (*glebæ astricti*), and are oppressed with imposts (*sujets à la main-morte et au droit de la suite*), of which we will hereafter have some talk together, as also of a late edict of the king's repealing the droit de la suite, and inviting the owners and occupiers to redeem the main-morte for a certain compensation. But still even this portion of the valley is well cultivated. The people love their country dearly, though they lead a hard life, being driven occasionally to steal the wood from the Bernese, and sell it again in the lowlands. The first division is called the Bois d'Amant; after passing through it, we entered the parish of Les Rousses, where we saw before us the little Lake des Rousses and Les Sept Moncels,— seven small hills of different shapes, but all connected together, which form the southern limit of the valley. We soon came upon the new road which runs from the Pays de Vaud to Paris. We kept to this for a mile downwards, and now left entirely the valley. The bare summit of the Dole was before us. We alighted from our horses, and sent them on by the road towards S. Cergues while we ascended the Dôle. It was near noon; the sun felt hot, but a cool south wind came now and then to refresh us. When we looked round for a halting-place, we had behind us Les Sept Moncels, we could still see a part of the Lac des Rousses, and around it the scattered houses of the parish. The rest of the valley was hidden from our eye by the Noir Mont, above which we again saw our yesterday's view of Franche-Comté, and nearer at hand southwards, the last summits and valleys of the Jura. We carefully avoided taking advantage of a little peep in the hill, which would have given us a glimpse of the country, for the sake of which in reality our ascent was undertaken. I was in some anxiety about the mist; however, from the aspect of the sky above, I drew a favourable omen. At last we stood on the highest summit, and saw with the greatest delight that to-day we were indulged with all that yesterday had been denied us. The whole of the Pays de Vaux and de Gex lay like a map before us: all the different holdings divided off with green hedges like the beds of a parterre. We were so high that the rising and sinking of the landscape before us was unnoticeable. Villages, little towns, country-houses, vine-covered hills, and higher up still, where the forests and Alps begin, the cow-sheds mostly painted white, or some other light colour, all glittered in the sunshine. The mist had already rolled off from Lake Leman. We saw the nearest part of the coast on our side, quite clear; of the so-called smaller lake, where the larger lake contracts itself, and turns towards Geneva, which was right opposite to us, we had a complete view; and on the other side the country which shuts it in was gradually clearing. But nothing could vie with the view of the mountains covered with snow and glaciers. We sat down before some rocks to shelter us from the cold wind, with the sunshine full upon us, and highly relished our little meal. We kept watching the mist, which gradually retired; each one discovered, or fancied he discovered, some object or other. One by one we distinctly saw Lausanne, surrounded with its houses, and gardens; then Vevay, and the castle of Chillon; the mountains, which shut out from our view the entrance into Valais, and extended as far as the lake; from thence the borders of Savoy, Evian, Repaille, and Tonon, with a sprinkling of villages and farm-houses between them. At last Geneva stood clear from the mist, but beyond and towards the south, in the neighbourhood of Mont Credo and Mont Vouache, it still hung immoveable. When the eye turned to the left it caught sight of the whole of the lowlands from Lausanne, as far as Solothurn, covered with a light halo. The nearer mountains and heights, and every spot that had a white house on it, could be closely distinguished. The guides pointed out a glimmering which they said was the castle of Chanvan, which lies to the left of the Neuburg-lake. We were just able to guess whereabouts it lay, but could not distinguish it through the bluish haze. There are no words to express the grandeur and beauty of this view. At the moment every one is scarcely conscious of what he sees:—one does but recall the names and sites of well-known cities and localities, to rejoice in a vague conjecture that he recognizes them in certain white spots which strike his eye in the prospect before him.

And then the line of glittering glaciers was continually drawing the eye back again to the mountains. The sun made his way towards the west, and lighted up their great flat surfaces, which were turned towards us. How beautifully before them rose from above the snow the variegated rows of black rocks:—teeth,—towers,—walls! Wild, vast, inaccessible vestibules! and seeming to stand there in the free air in the first purity and freshness of their manifold variety! Man gives up at once all pretensions to the infinite, while he here feels that neither with thought nor vision is he equal to the finite!

Before us we saw a fruitful and populous plain. The spot on which we were standing was a high, bare mountain rock, which, however, produces a sort of grass as food for the cattle, which are here a great source of gain. This the conceited lord of creation may yet make his own:—but those rocks before his eyes are like a train of holy virgins which the spirit of heaven reserves for itself alone in these inaccessible regions. We tarried awhile, tempting each other in turn to try and discover cities, mountains, and regions, now with the naked eye, now with the telescope, and did not begin to descend till the setting sun gave permission to the mist,—his own parting breath,—to spread itself over the lake.

With sunset we reached the ruins of the fort of S. Cergues. Even when we got down in the valley, our eyes were still rivetted on the mountain glaciers. The furthest of these, lying on our left in Oberland, seemed almost to be melting into a light fiery vapour; those still nearer stood with their sides towards us, still glowing and red; but by degrees they became white, green, and grayish. There was something melancholy in the sight. Like a powerful body over which death is gradually passing from the extremities to the heart, so the whole range gradually paled away as far as Mont

Blanc, whose ampler bosom was still covered all over with a deep red blush, and even appeared to us to retain a reddish tint to the very last,—just as when one is watching the death of a dear friend, life still seems to linger, and it is difficult to determine the very moment when the pulse ceases to beat.

This time also we were very loth to depart. We found our horses in S. Cergues; and that nothing might be wanting to our enjoyment, the moon rose and lighted us to Nyon. While on the way, our strained and excited feelings were gradually calmed, and assumed their wonted tone, so that we were able with keen gratification to enjoy, from our inn window, the glorious moonlight which was spread over the lake.

At different spots of our travels so much was said of the remarkable character of the glaciers of Savoy, and when we reached Geneva we were told it was becoming more and more the fashion to visit them, that the Count* was seized with a strange desire to bend our course in that direction, and from Geneva to cross Cluses and Sallanches, and enter the valley of Chamouni, and after contemplating its wonderful objects, to go on by Valorsine and Trient into Valais. This route, however, which was the one usually pursued by travellers, was thought dangerous in this season of the year. A visit was therefore paid to M. de Saussure at his country-house, and his advice requested. He assured us that we need not hesitate to take that route; there was no snow as yet on the middle-sized mountains, and if on our road we were attentive to the signs of the weather and the advice of the country-people, who were seldom wrong in their judgment, we might enter upon this journey with perfect safety. Here is the copy of the journal of a day's hard travelling.

Cluses in Savoy, Nov. 3, 1779.

To-day on departing from Geneva our party divided. The Count with me and a huntsman took the route to Savoy. Friend W. with the horses proceeded through the Pays de Vaud for Valais. In a light four-wheeled cabriolet we proceeded first of all to visit Hüber at his country-seat,—a man out of whom, mind, imagination and imitative tact, oozes at

* The Duke Charles Augustus of Weimar, who travelled under the title of Count.—Tr.

every pore.—one of the very few thorough men we have met with. He saw us well on our way, and then we set off with the lofty snow-capped mountains, which we wished to reach, before our eyes. From the Lake of Geneva the mountain-chains verge towards each other to the point where Bonneville lies, half way between the Môle, a considerable mountain, and the Arve. There we took our dinner. Behind the town the valley closes right in. Although not very broad, it has the Arve flowing gently through it, and is on the southern side well cultivated, and everywhere the soil is put to some profit. From the early morning we had been in fear of its raining some time at least before night, but the clouds gradually quitted the mountains, and dispersed into fleeces,—a sign which has more than once in our experience proved a favourable omen. The air was as warm as it usually is in the beginning of September, and the country we travelled through beautiful. Many of the trees being still green; most of them had assumed a brownish-yellow tint, but only a few were quite bare. The crops were rich and verdant; the mountains caught from the red sunset a rosy hue, blended with violet; and all these rich tints were combined with grand, beautiful, and agreeable forms of the landscape. We talked over much that was good. Towards 5 we came towards Cluses where the valley closes, and has only one outlet, through which the Arve issues from the mountains, and by which also we propose to enter them to-morrow. We ascended a lofty eminence, and saw beneath us the city, partly built on the slightly inclined side of a rock, but partly on the flat portion of the valley. Our eyes ranged with pleasure over the valley, and sitting on the granite rocks we awaited the coming of night in calm and varied discourse. Towards seven, as we descended, it was not at all colder than it is usually in summer about nine. At a miserable inn (where, however, the people were ready and willing, and by their patois afforded us much amusement) we are now going, about ten o'clock, to bed, intending to set out early to-morrow, before the morning shall dawn.

Sallanches, Nov. 4. 1779. *Noon.*

Whilst a dinner is being prepared by very willing hands, I will attempt to set down the most remarkable incidents of our yesterday's journey, which commenced with the early morning. With break of day we set out on foot from Cluses, taking the road towards Balme. In the valley the air was agreeably fresh; the moon, in her last quarter, rose bright before the sun, and charmed us with the sight, as being one which we do not often see. Single light vapours rose upwards from all the chasms in the rocks. It seemed as if the morning air were awakening the young spirits, who took pleasure in meeting the sun with expanded bosoms and gilding them in his rays. The upper heaven was perfectly clear; except where now and then a single cloudy streak, which the rising sun lit up, swept lightly across it. Balme is a miserable village, not far from the spot where a rocky gorge runs off from the road. We asked the people to guide us through the cave for which the place is famous. At this they kept looking at one another, till at last one said to a second, "Take you the ladder, I will carry the rope,—come, gentlemen." This strange invitation did not deter us from following them. Our line of descent passed first of all among fallen masses of limestone rock, which by the course of time had been piled up step by step in front of the precipitous wall of rock, and were now overgrown with bushes of hazel and beech. Over these you reach at last the strata of the rock itself, which you have to climb up slowly and painfully by means of the ladder and of the steps cut into the rock, and by help of branches of the nut-trees, which hung over head, or of pieces of rope tied to them. After this you find yourself, to your great satisfaction, in a kind of portal, which has been worn out of the rock by the weather, and overlooks the valley and the village below. We now prepared for entering the cave; lighted our candles and loaded a pistol which we proposed to let off. The cave is a long gallery, mostly level and on one strand; in parts broad enough for two men to walk abreast, in others only passable by one; now high enough to walk upright, then obliging you to stoop, and sometimes even to crawl on hands and feet. Nearly about the middle a cleft runs upwards and forms a sort of a dome. In one corner another goes downwards. We threw stones down it, and each time counted slowly seventeen to nineteen before it reached the bottom, after touching the sides many times, but always with a different echo. On the walls a stalactite forms its various devices; however it is only damp in a very few places, and forms for the most part long drops, and not those rich and rare shapes which are so remarkable in Baumann's cave. We penetrated as far as we could for the water, and as we came out let off our pistol, which shook the cave with a strong but dull echo, so that it boomed round us like a bell. It took us a good quarter of an hour to get out again, and on descending the rocks, we found our carriage and drove onwards. We saw a beautiful waterfall like the Staubbach; neither its height was very great nor its volume very large, and yet it was extremely interesting, for the rocks formed around it, as it were, a circular niche in which its waters fell, and the pieces of the limestone as they were tumbled one over another formed the most rare and unusual groups.

We arrived here at mid-day, not quite hungry enough to relish our dinner, which consisted of warmed fish, cow beef, and very stale bread. From this place there is no road leading to the mountains that is passable for so stately an equipage as we have with us; it therefore returns to Geneva, and I now must take my leave of you, in order to pursue my route a little further. A mule with my luggage will follow us as we pick our way on foot.

Chamouni, Nov. 4, 1779.
Evening, about 9 *o'clock:*

It is only because this letter will bring me for awhile nearer to yourself that I resume my pen; otherwise it would be better for me to give my mind a little rest.

We left Sallanches behind us in a lovely open valley; during our noonday's rest the sky had become overcast with white fleecy clouds, about which I have here a special remark to make. We had seen them on a bright day rise equally fine, if not still finer, from the glaciers of Berne. Here too it again seemed to us as if the sun had first of all attracted the light mists which evaporated from the tops of the glaciers, and then a gentle breeze had, as it were, combed the fine vapours, like a fleece of foam over the atmosphere. I never remember at home, even in the height of summer, (when such phenomena do also occur with us,) to have seen any so transparent, for here it was a perfect web of light. Before long the ice-covered mountains from which it rose lay before us; the valley began to close in; the Arve was gushing out of the rock; we now began to ascend a mountain, and went up higher and higher, with the snowy summits right before us. Mountains and old pine forests, either in the hollows below or on a level with our track, came out one by one before the eye as we proceeded. On our left were the mountain-peaks, bare and pointed. We felt that we were approaching a mightier and more massive chain of mountains. We passed over a dry and broad bed of stones and gravel, which the watercourses tear down from the sides of the rocks, and in turn flow among and fill up. This brought us into an agreeable valley, flat, and shut in by a circular ridge of rocks, in which lies the little village of Servoz. There the road runs round some very highly variegated rocks, and takes again the direction towards the Arve. After crossing the latter you again ascend; the masses become constantly more imposing, nature seems to have begun here with a light hand, to prepare her enormous creations. The darkness grew deeper and deeper as we approached the valley of Chamouni, and when at last we entered it, nothing but the larger masses were discernible. The stars came out one by one, and we noticed above the peaks of the summits right before us, a light which we could not account for. Clear, but without brilliancy, like the milky way, but closer, something like that of the Pleiades; it rivetted our attention until at last, as our position changed, like a pyramid illuminated by a secret light within, which could best be compared to the gleam of a glow-worm, it towered high above the peaks of all the surrounding mountains, and at last convinced us that it must be the peak of Mont Blanc. The beauty of this view was extraordinary. For while, together with the stars which clustered round it, it glimmered, not indeed with the same twinkling light, but in a broader and more continuous mass, it seemed to belong to a higher sphere, and one had difficulty in thought to fix its roots again in the earth. Before it we saw a line of snowy summits, sparkling as they rested on the ridges covered with the black pines, while between the dark forests vast glaciers sloped down to the valley below.

My descriptions begin to be irregular and forced; in fact, one wants two persons here, one to see and the other to describe.

Here we are in the middle village of the valley called "Le Prieuré," comfortably lodged in a house, which a widow caused to be built here in honour of the many strangers who visited the neighbourhood. We are sitting close to the hearth, relishing our Muscatel wine from the Vallée d'Aost, far better than the lenten dishes which were served up for our dinner.

Nov. 5, 1779. Evening.

To take up one's pen and write, almost requires as great an effort as to take a swim in the cold river. At this moment I have a great mind to put you off, by referring you to the description of the glaciers of Savoy, given by that enthusiastic climber Bourritt.

Invigorated however by a few glasses of excellent wine, and by the thought that these pages will reach you much sooner than either the travellers or Bourritt's book, I will do my best. The valley of Chamouni, in which we are at present, lies very high among the mountains, and, from six to seven leagues long, runs pretty nearly from south to north. The characteristic features which to my mind distinguish it from all others, are its having scarcely any flat portion, but the whole tract, like a trough, slopes from the Arve gradually up the sides of the mountain. Mont Blanc and the line of mountains which runs off from it, and the masses of ice which fill up the immense ravines, make up the eastern wall of the valley, on which, throughout its entire length, seven glaciers, of which one is considerably larger than the others, run down to the bottom of the valley.

The guides whom we had engaged for the Mer-de-Glace came to their time. One was a young active peasant, the other much older, who seemed to think himself a very shrewd personage, who had held intercourse with all learned foreigners, well acquainted with the nature of the ice-mountains, and a very clever fellow. He assured us that for eight and twenty years,—so long had he acted as guide over the mountains,—this was the first time that his services had been put in requisition so late in the year—after All Saints' Day, and yet that we might even now see every object quite as well as in June. Provided with wine and food we began to ascend Mont Anvert, from which we were told the view of the Ice-sea would be quite ravishing. Properly I should call it the ice-valley or the ice-stream; for looking at it from above, the huge masses of ice force themselves out of a deep valley in tolerable smoothness. Right behind it ends a sharp-pointed mountain, from both sides of which waves of ice run frozen into the principal stream. Not the slightest trace of snow was as yet to be seen on the rugged surfaces, and the blue crevices glistened beautifully. The weather by degrees became overcast, and I saw grey wavy clouds, which seemed to threaten snow, more than it had ever yet done. On the spot where we were standing is a small cabin, built of stones, loosely piled together as a shelter for travellers, which in joke has been named " The Castle of Mont Anvert." An Englishman, of the name of Blaire, who is residing at Geneva, has caused a more spacious one to be built at a more convenient spot, and a little higher up, where, sitting by a fire-side, you catch through the window a view of the whole Ice-Valley. The peaks of the rocks over against you, as also in the valley below, are very pointed and rugged. These jags are called needles, and the Aiguille du Dru is a remarkable peak of this kind, right opposite to Mont Anvert. We now wished to walk upon the Ice-sea itself, and to consider these immense masses close at hand. Accordingly we climbed down the mountain, and took nearly a hundred steps round about on the wave-like crystal cliffs. It is certainly a singular sight, when standing on the ice itself, you see before you the masses pressing upwards, and divided by strangely shaped clefts. However, we did not like standing on this slippery surface, for we had neither come prepared with ice-shoes, nor with nails in our usual ones; on the contrary, those which we ordinarily wore had become smooth and rounded with our long walk; we, therefore, made our way back to the hut, and after a short rest were ready for returning. We descended the mountain, and came to the spot where the ice-stream, step by step, forces its way to the valley below, and we entered the cavern, into which it empties its water. It is broad, deep, and of the most beautiful blue, and in the cave the supply of water is more invariable than further on at the mouth, since great pieces of ice are constantly melting and dissolving in it.

On our road to the auberge we passed the house where there were two albinos,—children between twelve and fourteen, with very white complexions, rough white hair, and with red and restless eyes like rabbits. The deep night which hangs over the valley invites me to retire early to bed, and I am hardly awake enough to tell you, that we have seen a tame young ibex, who stands out as distinctly among the goats as the natural son of a noble prince from the burgher's family, among whom he is privately brought up and educated. It does not suit with our discourses, that I should speak of anything out of its due order. Besides, you do not take much delight in specimens of granite, quartz, or in larch and pine trees, yet, very soon you must contrive to see some remarkable fruits of our botanising. I think I am stupid with sleep,— I cannot write another line.

Chamouni, Nov. 6, 1776. Early.
Content with seeing all that the early season allows us to see, we are ready to start again, intending to penetrate as far as Valais to-day. A thick mist covers the whole valley, and reaches half way up the mountains, and we must wait and see what sun and wind will yet do for us. Our guide purposes that we should take the road over the Col-de-Balme, a lofty eminence, which lies on the north side of the valley towards Valais, from the summit of which, if we are lucky, we shall be able to take another survey of the valley of Chamouni, and of all its remarkable objects.

Whilst I am writing a remarkable phenomenon is passing along the sky. The mists which are shifting about, and breaking in some places, allow you through their openings as through skylights, to catch a glance of the blue sky, while at the same time the mountain peaks, which rising above our roof of vapour, are illuminated by the sun's rays. Even without the hope it gives of a beautiful day, this sight of itself is a rich treat to the eye.

We have at last obtained a standard for judging the heights of the mountains. It is at a considerable height above the valley, that the vapour rests on the mountains. At a still greater height are clouds, which have floated off upwards from the top of the mist, and then far above these clouds you see the summits glittering in the sunshine.

It is time to go. I must bid farewell to this beautiful valley and to you.

*Martinac, in Valais,
Nov. 6, 1779. Evening.*

We have made the passage across without any mishap, and so this adventure is over. The joy of our good luck will keep my pen going merrily for a good half hour yet.

Having packed our luggage on a mule, we set out early (about 9,) from Pricuré. The clouds shifted, so that the peaks were now visible and then were lost again; at one moment the sun's rays came in streaks on the valley, at the next the whole of it was again in shade. We went up the valley, passing the outlet of the ice-stream, then the glacier d'Argentière, which is the highest of the five, the top of it however was hidden from our view by the clouds. On the plain we held a counsel, whether we should or not take the route over Col de Balme, and abandon the road over Valorsine. The prospect was not the most promising; however, as here there was nothing to lose and much perhaps to gain, we took our way boldly towards the dark region of mists and clouds. As we approached the Glacier du Tour, the clouds parted, and we saw this glacier also in full light. We sat down awhile and drank a bottle of wine, and took something to eat. We now mounted towards the sources of the Arve, passing over rugged meadows and patches scantily covered with turf, and came nearer and nearer to the region of mists, until at last we entered right into it. We went on patiently for awhile till at last as we got up higher, it began again to clear above our heads. It lasted for a short time, so we passed right out of the clouds, and saw the whole mass of them beneath us spread over the valley, and were able to see the summits of all the mountains on the right and left that enclosed it, with the exception of Mont Blanc, which was covered with clouds. We were able to point them out one by one, and to name them. In some we saw the glaciers reaching from their summits to their feet, in others we could only discern their tracks, as the ice was concealed from our view by the rocky sides of the gorges. Beyond the whole of the flat surface of the clouds, except at its southern extremity, we could distinctly see the mountains glittering in the sunshine. Why should I enumerate to you the names of summits, peaks, needles, icy and snowy masses, when their mere designations can furnish no idea to your mind, either of the whole scene or of its single objects?

It was quite singular how the spirits of the air seemed to be waging war beneath us. Scarcely had we stood a few minutes enjoying the grand view, when a hostile ferment seemed to arise within the mist, and it suddenly rose upwards and threatened once more to envelope us. We commenced stoutly ascending the height, in the hope of yet awhile escaping from it, but it outstripped us and enclosed us on all sides. However, perfectly fresh, we continued to mount, and soon there came to our aid a strong wind, blowing from the mountain. Blowing over the saddle which connected two peaks, it drove the mist back again into the valley. This strange conflict was frequently repeated, and at last, to our joy, we reached the Col de Balme. The view from it was singular, indeed unique. The sky above the peaks was overcast with clouds; below, through the many openings in the mist, we saw the whole of Chamouni, and between these two layers of cloud the mountain summits were all visible. On the east we were shut in by rugged mountains, on the west we looked down on wild valleys, where, however, on every green patch human dwellings were visible. Before us lay the valley of Valais, where at one glance the eye took in mountains piled in every variety of mass one upon another, and stretching as far as Martinac and even beyond it. Surrounded on all sides by mountains which, further on towards the horizon, seemed continually to multiply and to tower higher and higher, we stood on the confines of Valais and Savoy.

Some contrabandists, who were ascending the mountains with their mules, were alarmed at seeing us, for at this season they did not reckon on meeting with any one at this spot. They fired a shot to intimate that they were armed, and one advanced before the rest to reconnoitre. Having recognised our guide and seen what a harmless figure we made, he returned to his party, who now approached us, and we passed one another with mutual greetings.

The wind now blew sharp, and it began to snow a little as we commenced our descent, which was rough and wild enough, through an ancient forest of pines, which had taken root on the faces of the gneiss. Torn up by the winds, the trunks and roots lay rotting together, and the rocks which were loosened at the same time were lying in rough masses among them.

At last we reached the valley where the river Trient takes its rise from a glacier, and passing the village of Trient, close upon our right, we followed the windings of the valley along a rather inconvenient road, and about six reached Martinac, which lies in the flatter portion of the Valais. Here we must refresh ourselves for further expeditions.

Martinac, Nov. 6, 1779.
Evening.

Just as our travels proceed uninterruptedly, so my letters one after another keep up my conversation with you. Scarcely have I folded and put aside the conclusion of " Wanderings through Savoy," ere I take up another sheet of paper in order to acquaint you with all that we have further in contemplation.

It was night when we entered a region about which our curiosity had long been excited. As yet we have seen nothing but the peaks of the mountains, which enclose the valley on both sides, and then only in the glimmering of twilight. We crept wearily into our auberge, and saw from the window the clouds shifting. We felt as glad and comfortable to have a roof over our heads, as children do when with stools, table-leaves and carpets, they construct a roof near the stove, and therein say to one another that outside " it is raining or snowing," in order to excite a pleasant and imaginary shudder in their little souls. It is exactly so with us on this autumnal evening in this strange and unknown region.

We learn from the maps that we are sitting in the angle of an elbow, from which the smaller part of Valais, running almost directly from south to north, and with the Rhone, extends to the lake of Geneva, while the other and the larger portion stretches from west to east, and goes up the Rhone to its source, the Furca. The prospect of riding through the Valais is very agreeable, our only anxiety is how we are to cross over into it. First of all, with the view of seeing the lower portion, it is settled that we go to-morrow to S. Maurice, where we are to meet our friend, wno with the horses has gone round by the Pays de Vaud. Tomorrow evening we think of being here again, and then on the next day shall begin to go up the country. If the advice of M. de Saussure prevails, we shall perform the route to the Furca on horseback, and then back to Brieg over the Simplon, where, in any weather, the travelling is good over Domo d'Osula, Lago Maggiore, Bellinzona, and then up Mount Gotthard. The road is said to be excellent, and everywhere passable for horses. We should best prefer going over the Furca to S. Gotthard, both for the sake of the shorter route, and also because this detour through the Italian provinces was not within our original plan, but then what could we do with our horses; they could not be made to descend the Furca, for in all probability the path for pedestrians is already blocked up by the snow.

With regard to the latter contingency, however, we are quite at our ease, and hope to be able, as we have hitherto done, to take counsel, from moment to moment, with circumstances as they arise.

The most remarkable object in this inn is a servant-girl, who with the greatest stupidity gives herself all the airs of one of our would-be delicate German ladies. We had a good laugh, when after bathing our weary feet in a bath of red wine and clay, as recommended by our guide, we had in the affected hoyden to wipe them dry.

Our meal has not refreshed us much, and after supper we hope to enjoy our beds more.

S. Maurice, Nov. 7, 1779.
Nearly Noon.

On the road it is my way to enjoy the beautiful views, in order that I may call in one by one my absent friends, and converse with them on the subject of the glorious objects. If I come into an inn it is in order to rest myself, to go back in memory and to write something to you, when many a time my overstrained faculties would much rather collapse upon themselves, and recover their tone in a sort of half sleep.

This morning we set off at dawn from Martinac; a fresh

breeze was stirring with the day, and we soon passed the old castle which stands at the point where the two arms of Valais make a sort of Y. The valley is narrow, shut in on its two sides by mountains, highly diversified in their forms, and which without exception are of a peculiar and sublimely beautiful character. We came to the spot where the Trient breaks into the valley around some narrow and perpendicular rocks, so that one almost doubts whether the river does not flow out of the solid rock itself. Close by stands the old bridge, which only last year was greatly injured by the stream, while not far from it lie immense masses of rock, which have fallen very recently from the mountains and blocked up the road. The whole group together would make an extremely beautiful picture. At a short distance from the old bridge a new wooden one has been built, and a new road been laid down to it.

We were told that we were getting near the famous waterfall of Pisse Vache, and wished heartily for a peep at the sun, while the shifting clouds gave us a good hope that our wish would be gratified. On the road we examined various pieces of granite and of gneiss, which with all their differences seem, nevertheless, to have a common origin. At last we stood before the waterfall, which well deserves its fame above all others. At a considerable height a strong stream bursts from a cleft in the rock, falling downward into a basin, over which the foam and spray is carried far and wide by the wind. The sun at this moment came forth from the clouds, and made the sight doubly vivid. Below in the spray, wherever you go, you have close before you a rainbow. If you go higher up, you still witness no less singular a phenomenon. The airy foaming waves of the upper stream of water, as with their frothy vapour, they come in contact with the angle of vision at which the rainbow is formed, assume a flame-like hue, without giving rise to the pendant form of the bow, so that at this point you have before you a constantly varying play of fire.

We climbed all round, and sitting down near it, wished we were able to spend whole days and many a good hour of our life on this spot. Here too, as in so many other places during our present tour, we felt how impossible is was to enjoy and to be fully impressed with grand objects on a passing visit.

We next came to a village where there were some merry soldiers, and we drank there some new wine. Some of the same sort had been set before us yesterday. It looked like soap and water; however, we had rather drink it than their sour "this year's" and "two years' old" wine When one is thirsty nothing comes amiss.

We saw S. Maurice at a distance; it lies just at the point where the valley closes in, so much as to cease to be anything more than a mere pass. Over the city, on the left, we saw a small church with a hermitage close to it, and we hope to have an opportunity yet of visiting them both.

We found in the inn a note from our friend, who has stopped at Bex, which is about three quarters of a league from this place; we have sent a messenger to him. The Count is gone out for a walk to see the country before us. I shall take a morsel to eat, and then set out towards the famous bridge and the pass.

After 1 *o'clock.*

I have at last got back from the spot where one could be contented to spend whole days together, lounging and loitering about without once getting tired, holding converse with oneself.

If I had to advise any one as to the best route into Valais, I should recommend the one from the Lake of Geneva up the Rhone. I have been on the road to Bex over the great bridge from which you step at once into the Bernese territory. Here the Rhone flows downwards, and the valley near the lake becomes a little broader. As I turned round again I saw that the rocks near S. Maurice pressed together from both sides, and that a small light bridge, with a high arch, was thrown boldly across from them over the Rhone, which rushes beneath it with its roaring and foaming stream. The numerous angles and turrets of a fortress stands close to the bridge, and a single gateway commands the entrance into Valais. I went over the bridge back towards S. Maurice, and even beyond it, in search of a view which I had formerly seen a drawing of at Hüber's house, and by good luck found it.

The count is come back. He had gone to meet the horses and mounting his grey had outstripped the rest. He says the bridge is so light and beautiful that it looks like a horse in the act of leaping a ditch. Our friend too is coming, and is quite contented with his tour. He accomplished the distance from the Lake of Geneva to Bex in a few days, and we are all delighted to see one another again.

Martinac, towards 9.

We were out riding till late at night, and the road seemed much longer returning than going, as in the morning, our attention had been constantly attracted from one object to another. Besides I am for this day, at least, heartily tired of descriptions and reflections; however, I must try hastily to perpetuate the memory of two beautiful objects. It was deep twilight when on our return we reached the waterfall of the Pisse Vache. The mountains, the valley, and the heavens themselves were dark and dusky. By its greyish tint and unceasing murmur you could distinguish the falling stream from all other objects, though you could scarcely discern the slightest motion. Suddenly the summit of a very high peak glowed just like molten brass in a furnace, and above it rose a red smoke. This singular phenomenon was the effect of the setting sun which illuminated the snow and the mists which ascended from it.

Sion, Nov. 8, 1779.
about 3 *o'clock.*

This morning we missed our way riding, and were delayed in consequence, three hours at least. We set out from Martinac before dawn, in order to reach Sion in good time. The weather was extraordinarily beautiful, only that the sun being low in the heavens was shut out by the mountains, so that the road, as we passed along, was entirely in the shade. The view, however, of the marvellously beautiful valley of Valais brought up many a good and cheerful idea. We had ridden for full three hours along the high road with the Rhone on our left, when we saw Sion before us; and we were beginning to congratulate ourselves on the prospect of soon ordering our noon-day's meal, when we found that the bridge we ought to cross had been carried away. Nothing remained for us, we were told by the people who were busy repairing it, but either to leave our horses and go by a foot-path which ran across the rocks, or else to ride on for about three miles, and then cross the Rhone by some other bridges. We chose the latter; and we would not suffer any ill-humour to get possession of us, but determined to ascribe this mischance to the interposition of our good genius, who intended to take us a slow ride through this interesting region with the advantage of good day-light. Everywhere, indeed, in this narrow district, the Rhone makes sad havoc. In order to reach the other bridges we were obliged, for more than a league and a half, to ride over sandy patches, which in the various inundations are constantly shifting, and are useful for nothing but alder and willow beds. At last we came to the bridges, which were wretched, tottering, long, and composed of rotten timbers. We had to lead our horses over one by one, and with extreme caution. We were now on the left side of the Valais and had to turn backwards to get to Sion. The road itself was for the most part wretched and stony; every step, however, opened a fresh view, which was well worth a painting. One, however, was particularly remarkable. The road brought us up to a castle, below which there was spread out the most lovely scene that we had seen in the whole road. The mountains nearest to us run down on both sides slantingly to the level ground, and by their shape gave a kind of perspective effect to the natural landscape. Beneath us was the Valais in its entire breadth from mountain to mountain, so that the eye could easily take it in; the Rhone, with its ever-varying windings and bushy banks was flowing past villages, meadows, and richly cultivated highlands; in the distance you saw the Castle of Sion, and the various hills which begin to rise behind it; the farthest horizon was shut in, amphitheatre like, with a semicircular range of snow-capped mountains which, like all the rest of the scene, stood glittering in the sun's meridian splendour. Disagreeable and rough was the road we had to ride over; we therefore enjoyed the more, perhaps, the still tolerably green festoons of the vines which over-arched it. The inhabitants, to whom every spot of earth is precious, plant their grape-vines close against the walls which divide their little holdings from the road, where they grow to an extraordinary thickness, and by means of stakes and trellises are trained across the road so as almost to form one continuous arbour. The lower grounds were principally meadows: in the neighbourhood of Sion, however, we noticed some tillage. Towards this town the scenery is extremely diversified by a variety of hills, and we wished to be able to make a longer stay in order to enjoy it. But the hideousness of the town and of the people fearfully disturb the pleasant impression which the scenery leaves. The most frightful goitres put me altogether out of humour. We cannot well put our horses any further to-day, and therefore we think if going on foot to Sierre. Here in Sion the inn is disgusting, and the whole town has a dirty and revolting appearance.

Sierre, Nov. 8, 1779.
Night.

As evening had begun to fall before we set out from Sion, we reached here at night, with the sky above us clear and starry. We have consequently lost many a good view—that I know well. Particularly we should have liked to have ascended to the Castle of Tourbillon, which is at no great distance from Sion; the view from it must be uncommonly beautiful. A guide whom we took with us skilfully guided us through some wretched low lands, where the water was out. We soon reached the heights, and had the Rhone below us on our right. By talking over some astronomical matters we shortened our road, and have taken up our abode here with some very worthy people, who are doing their best to entertain us. When we think over what we have gone through, so busy a day, with its many incidents and sights, seems almost equal to a whole week. I begin to be quite sorry that I have neither time nor talent to sketch at least the outlines of the most remarkable objects; for that would be much better for the absent than all descriptions.

Sierre, Nov. 9, 1779.

Before we set out I can just bid you good morning. The Count is going with me to the mountains on the left, towards

Leukerbad; our friend will, in the meantime, stay here with the horses, and join us to-morrow at Leuk.

Leukerbad, Nov. 9, 1779.
At the Foot of Mount Gemmi.

In a little wooden house where we have been friendlily received by some very worthy people, we are sitting in a small, low room, and trying how much of to-day's highly interesting tour can be communicated in words. Starting from Sierre very early we proceeded for three leagues up the mountains, after having passed large districts laid waste by the mountain torrents. One of these streams will suddenly rise and desolate an extent of many miles, covering with fragments of rock and gravel the fields, meadows, and gardens, which (at least wherever possible) the people laboriously set to work to clear, in order within two generations, perhaps, to be again laid waste. We have had a grey day, with every now and then a glimpse of sunshine. It is impossible to describe how infinitely variegated the Valais here again becomes; the landscape bends and changes every moment. Looking around you all the objects seem to lie close together, and yet they are separated by great ravines and hills. Generally we had had the open part of the valley below us, on the right, when suddenly we came upon a spot which commanded a most beautiful view over the mountains.

In order to render more clear what it is I am attempting to describe, I must say a few words on the geographical position of the district in which we are at present. We had now for three hours been ascending the mountainous region which separates Valais from Berne. This is, in fact, the great track of mountains which runs in one continuous chain from the Lake of Geneva to Mount S. Gotthard, and on which, as it passes through Berne, rest the great masses of ice and snow. Here *above* and *below* are but the relative terms of the moment. I say, for instance, beneath me lies a village—and in all probability the level on which it is built is on a precipitous summit, which is far higher above the valley below, than I am above it.

As we turned an angle of the road and rested awhile at a hermitage, we saw beneath us, at the end of a lovely green meadowland, which stretched along the brink of an enormous chasm, the village of Inden, with its white church exactly in the middle of the landscape, and built altogether on the slope of the hill-side. Beyond the chasm another line of meadow lands and pine forests went upwards, while right behind the village a vast cleft in the rocks ran up the summit. On the left hand the mountains came right down to us, while those on our right stretched far away into the distance, so that the little hamlet, with its white church, formed as it were the focus towards which the many rocks, ravines, and mountains all converged. The road to Inden is cut out of the precipitous side of the rock, which, on your left going to the village, lines the amphitheatre. It is not dangerous although it looks frightful enough. It goes down on the slope of a rugged mass of rocks, separated from the yawning abyss on the right, by nothing but a few poor planks. A peasant with a mule, who was descending at the same time as ourselves, whenever he came to any dangerous points caught his beast by the tail, lest the steep descent should cause him to slip, and roll into the rocks below. At last we reached Inden. As our guide was well known there, he easily managed to obtain for us, from a good-natured dame, some bread and a glass of red wine, for in these parts there are no regular inns.

We now ascended the high ravine behind Inden, where we soon saw before us the Gemmiberg (of which we had heard such frightful descriptions), with Leukerbad at its foot, lying between two lofty, inaccessible, snow-covered mountains, as if it were in the hollow of a hand. It was three o'clock, nearly, when we arrived there, and our guide soon procured us lodgings. There is properly no inn even here, but in consequence of the many visitors to the baths at this place, all people have good accommodation. Our hostess had been put to bed the day before, but her husband with an old mother and a servant girl, did very creditably the honours of the house. We ordered something to eat, and went to see the warm springs, which in several places burst out of the earth with great force, and are received in very clean reservoirs. Out of the village, and more towards the mountains, there are said to be still stronger ones. The water has not the slightest smell of sulphur, and neither at its source nor in its channel does it make the least deposit of ochre or of any other earth or mineral, but like any other clear spring water it leaves not the slightest trace behind it. As it comes out of the earth it is extremely hot, and is famous for its good qualities. We had still time for a walk to the foot of the Gemmi, which appeared to us to be at no great distance. I must here repeat a remark that has been made so often already; that when one is surrounded with mountain scenery all objects appear to be extremely near. We had a good league to go, amongst fragments of rock which had fallen from the heights, and over gravel brought down by the torrents, before we reached the foot of the Gemmi, where the road ascends along the precipitous crags. This is the only pass into the canton of Berne, and the sick have to be transported along it in sedan chairs.

If the season did not bid us hasten onwards, in all probability we might make an attempt to-morrow to ascend this remarkable mountain; as it is, however, we must content ourselves with the simple view of it. On our return we saw the clouds brewing, which in these parts is a highly interesting sight. The fine weather we have hitherto enjoyed has made us forget almost entirely that it is in November that we are; besides too, as they foretold us in Berne, the autumn here is very delightful. The short days, however, and the clouds which threaten snow, warn us how late it is in the year. The strange drift which has been agitating them this evening was singularly beautiful. As we came back from the foot of the Gemmi, we saw light mists come up the ravine from Inden, and move with great rapidity. They continually changed their direction, going now forwards, now backwards, and at last, as they ascended, they came so near to Leukerbad that we saw clearly that we must double our steps if we would not before nightfall be enveloped in the clouds. We reached our quarters, however, without accident, and whilst I write this it is snowing in earnest. This is the first fall of snow that we have yet had, and when we call to mind our warm ride yesterday, from Martinac to Sion, beneath the vine-arbours, which were still pretty thick with leaves, the change does appear sudden indeed. I have been standing some time at the door, observing the character and look of the clouds, which are beautiful beyond description. It is not yet night, but at intervals the clouds veil the whole sky and make it quite dark. They rise out of the deep ravines until they reach the highest summits of the mountains; attracted by these they appear to thicken, and being condensed by the cold they fall down in the shape of snow. It gives you an inexpressible feeling of loneliness to find yourself here at this height, as it were, in a sort of well, from which you scarcely can suppose that there is even a footpath to get out by, except down the precipice before you. The clouds which gather here in this valley, at one time completely hiding the immense rocks, and absorbing them in a waste impenetrable gloom, or at another letting a part of them be seen like huge spectres, give to the people a cast of melancholy. In the midst of such natural phenomena the people are full of presentiments and forebodings. Clouds—a phenomenon remarkable to every man from his youth up—are, in the plain countries, generally looked upon at most as something foreign—something superterrestrial. People regard them as strangers, as birds of passage, which, hatched under a different climate, visit this or that country for a moment or two in passing—as splendid pieces of tapestry wherewith the gods part off their pomp and splendour from human eyes. But here, where they are hatched, man is inclosed in them from the very first, and the eternal and intrinsic energy of his nature feels itself at every nerve moved to forebode and to indulge in presentiments.

To the clouds, which, with us even produce these effects, we pay little attention; moreover as they are not pushed so thickly and directly before our eyes, their economy is the more difficult to observe. With regard to all such phenomena one's only wish is to dwell on them for a while, and to be able to tarry several days in the spots where they are observable. If one is fond of such observations the desire becomes the more vivid the more one reflects that every season of the year, every hour of the day, and every change of weather produces new phenomena which we little looked for. And as no man, not even the most ordinary character, was ever a witness, even for once, of great and unusual events, without their leaving behind in his soul some traces or other, and making him feel himself also to be greater for this one little shred of grandeur, so that he is never weary of telling the whole tale of it over again, and has gained at any rate a little treasure for his whole life; just so is it with the man who has seen and become familiar with the grand phenomena of nature. He who manages to preserve these impressions, and to combine them with other thoughts and emotions, has assuredly a treasury of sweets wherewith to season the most tasteless parts of life, and to give a pervading relish to the whole of existence.

I observe that in my notes I make very little mention of human beings. Amid these grand objects of nature, they are but little worthy of notice, especially where they do but come and go. I doubt not but that on a longer stay we should meet with many worthy and interesting people. One fact I think I have everywhere observed; the farther one moves from the highroad and the busy marts of men, the more people are shnt in by the mountains, isolated and confined to the simplest wants of life, the more they draw their maintenance from simple, humble, and unchangeable pursuits: so much the better, the more obliging, the more friendly, unselfish, and hospitable are they.

Leukerbad, Nov. 10, 1779.

We are getting ready by candle-light, in order to descend the mountain again as soon as day breaks. I have had rather a restless night. Scarcely had I got into bed before I felt as if I was attacked all over with the nettle rash. I soon found, however, that it was a swarm of crawling insects, who, ravenous of blood, had fallen upon the new comer. These insects breed in great numbers in these wooden houses. The night appeared to me extremely long, and I was heartily glad when in the morning a light was brought in.

Leuk., about 10 o'clock.

We have not much time to spare; however, before we set out, I will give you an account of the remarkable breaking up of our company, which has here taken place, and also of the cause of it. We set out from Leukerbad with daybreak this morning, and had to make our way over the meadows through the fresh and slippery snow. We soon came to Inden, where, leaving above us on our right the precipitous road which we came down yesterday, we descended to the meadow lands along the ravine which now lay on our left. It is extremely wild and overgrown with trees, but a very tolerable road runs down into it. Through the clefts in the rock the water which comes down from Leukerbad has its outlets into the Valais. High up on the side of the hill, which yesterday we descended, we saw an aqueduct skilfully cut out of the rock, by which a little stream is conducted from the mountain, then through a hollow into a neighbouring village.

Next we had to ascend a steep height, from which we soon saw the open country of Valais, with the dirty town of Leuk. lying beneath us. These little towns are mostly stuck on the hill sides; the roofs inelegantly covered with coarsely split planks, which within a year become black and overgrown with moss; and when you enter them, you are at once disgusted, for everything is dirty; want and hardship are everywhere apparent among these highly privileged and free burghers.

We found here our friend, who brought the unfavourable report that it was beginning to be injudicious to proceed further with the horses. The stables were everywhere small and narrow, being built only for mules or sumpter horses; oats too were rarely to be procured; indeed he was told that higher up among the mountains there were none to be had. Accordingly a council was held. Our friend with the horses was to descend the Valais and go by Bex, Vevay, Lausanne, Freiburg, and Berne, to Lucerne, while the Count and I pursued our course up the Valais, and endeavoured to penetrate to Mount Gotthard, and then through the Canton of Uri, and by the Lake of the Forest Towns,* likewise make for Lucerne. In these parts you may anywhere procure mules, which are better suited to these roads than horses, and to go on foot invariably proves the most agreeable in the end. Our friend is gone, and our portmanteaus packed on the back of a mule, and so we are now ready to set off and make our way on foot to Brieg. The sky has a motley appearance, still I hope that the good luck which has hitherto attended us, and attracted us to this distant spot, will not abandon us at the very point where we have the most need of it.

* *i.e.*, the Lake of Lucerne.—TR.

Brieg, Nov. 10, 1779.
Evening.

Of to-day's expedition I have little to tell you, unless you would like to be entertained with a long circumstantial account of the weather. About 11 o'clock we set off from Leuk., in company with a Suabian butcher's boy, who had run away hither, and had found a place where he served somewhat in the capacity of Hanswurst (Jack-Pudding), and with our luggage packed on the back of a mule, which its master was driving before him. Behind us, as far as the eye could reach, thick snow clouds, which came driving up the lowlands, covered everything. It had really a threatening aspect. Without expressing my fears I felt anxious lest, even though right before us it looked as clear as it could do in the land of Goshen, the clouds might nevertheless overtake us, and here, perhaps in the territory of the Valais, shut in on both sides by mountains, we might be covered with the clouds, and in one night snowed up. Thus whispered alarm which got possession almost entirely of one ear; at the other good courage was speaking in a confident tone, and reproving me for want of faith, kept reminding me of the past, and called my attention to the phenomena of the atmosphere before us. Our road went continually on towards the fine weather. Up the Rhone all was clear, and strongly as the evening breeze drove up the clouds behind us, it was little likely that they would reach us.

The following was the cause of this. Into the valley of Valais there are, as I have so often remarked already, many ravines running down from the neighbouring mountain-chains, which fall into it like little brooks into a great stream, as indeed all their waters flow off into the Rhone. Out of each of these openings rushes a current of wind, which has been forming in the inner valleys and nooks of the rocks. When now the principal drift of the clouds up the valley reaches one of these ravines, the current of the wind does not allow the clouds to pass, but contends with them, and with the wind which is driving them, and thus detains them, and disputes with them for whole hours the passage up the valley. This conflict we often witnessed, and when we believed we should surely be overtaken by the clouds, an obstacle of this kind would again arise, and after we had gone a good league, we found they had scarcely stirred from the spot.

Towards evening the sky was uncommonly beautiful. As we arrived at Brieg, the clouds got there almost as soon as we did; however, as the sun had set, and a driving east wind blew against them, they were obliged to come to a halt, and formed a huge crescent from mountain to mountain across the valley. The cold air had greatly condensed them, and where their edge stood out against the blue sky, it presented to the eye many beautiful, light, and elegant forms. It was quite clear that they were heavy with snow; however, the fresh air seemed to us to promise that much would not fall during the night.

Here we are in a very comfortable inn, and what greatly tends to make us contented, we have found a roomy chamber with a stove in it, so that we can sit by the fire-side and take counsel together as to our future travels. Through Brieg runs the usual road to Italy over the Simplon; should we, therefore, give up our plan of going over the Furca to Mont S. Gotthard, we shall go with hired horses and mules to Domo d'Ossola, Margozzo, pass up Lago Maggiore, and then to Bellinzona, and then on to S. Gotthard, and over Airolo to the monastery of the Capuchins. This road is passable all the winter through, and is good travelling for horses; however, to our minds it is not very inviting, especially as it was not in our original plan, and will not bring us to Lucerne till five days after our friend. We wish rather to see the whole of the Valais up to its extreme limit, whither we hope to come by to-morrow evening, and, if fortune favours, we shall be sitting by about the same time next day in Realp, in the canton of Uri, which is on Mont Gotthard, and very near to its highest summit. Should we find it impossible to cross the Furca, the road back to this spot will still be open to us, and then we can take of necessity the route which of free choice we are disinclined to.

You can well believe that I have here closely examined the people, whether they believe that the passage over the Furca is open, for that is the one idea with which I rise up, and lie down to sleep, and occupy myself all day long. Hitherto our route may be compared to a march to meet an enemy, and now it is as if we were approaching to the spot where he has entrenched himself, and we must give him battle. Besides our mule two horses are ordered to be ready by the evening.

Münster, Nov. 11, 1779.
Evening, 6 o'clock.

Again we have had a pleasant and prosperous day. This morning as we set out early and in good time from Brieg, our host, when we were already on the road said, " If the mountain (so they call the Furca here,) should prove too fearful, you can easily come back and take another route." With our two horses and mule we soon came upon some pleasant meadows, where the valley becomes so narrow that it is scarcely some gun-shots wide. Here are some beautiful pasture lands, on which stand large trees, while pieces of rock lie scattered about which have rolled down from the neighbouring mountains. The valley gradually grows narrower, and the traveller is forced to ascend along the side of the mountain, having the while the Rhone below him in a rugged ravine on his left. Above him, however, the land is beautifully spread out; on the variously undulating hills are verdant and rich meadows and pretty hamlets, which, with their dark-brown wooden houses, peep out prettily from among the snow. We travelled a good deal on foot, and we did so in turns to accommodate one another. For although riding is safe enough, still it excites one's alarm to see another riding before you along so narrow a track, and on so weak an animal, and just on the brink of so rugged a precipice; and as too there are no cattle to be seen on the meadows, (for the people here shut them all up in sheds at this season,) such a region looks lonely, and the thought that one is continually being hemmed in closer and closer by the vast mountains, fills the imagination with sombre and disagreeable fancies, enough to make you fall from your seat, if you are not very firm in the saddle. Man is never perfectly master of himself. As he lives in utter ignorance of the future, as indeed what the next moment may bring forth is hidden from him, consequently, when anything unusual falls beneath his notice, he has often to contend with involuntary sensations, forebodings, and dream-like fancies, at which shortly afterwards he may laugh outright, but which at the decisive moment are often extremely oppressive.

In our noonday quarters we met with some amusement. We had taken up our lodgings with a woman in whose house everything looked neat and orderly. Her room, after the fashion of the country, was wainscotted, the beds ornamented with carving; the cupboards, tables, and all the other little repositories which were fastened against the walls or to the corners, had pretty ornaments of turner's work or carving. From the portraits which hung around the room, it was easy to see that several members of the family had devoted themselves to the clerical profession. We also observed a collection of bound books over the door, which we took to be the endowment of one of these reverend personages. We took down the Legends of the Saints, and read it while our meal was preparing. On one occasion of our hostess entering the room, she asked us if we had ever read the history of S. Alexis? We said no, and took no further notice of her question, but went on reading the chapter we each had begun. When, however, we had sat down to table, she placed herself by our sides, and began again to talk of S. Alexis. We asked her whether he was the patron saint of herself, or of her family; which she denied, affirming at the same time, however, that this saintly person had undergone so much for the love of God, that his history always affected her more than any other's. When she saw that we knew nothing about him, she began to narrate to us his history. "S. Alexis," she said, "was the son of noble, rich, and God-fearing parents in Rome, and in the practice of good works he delighted to follow their example, for they did extraordinary good to the poor. All this, however, did not appear enough to Alexis; but secretly in his own heart he devoted himself entirely to God's service, and took a vow to Christ of perpetual virginity. When, then, in the course of time, his parents wished to marry him to a lovely and amiable maiden, he did not oppose their will. When, however, the marriage ceremony was concluded, instead of retiring to his bed in the nuptial chamber, he went on board a vessel which he found ready to sail, and with it passed over to Asia. Here he assumed the garb of a wretched mendicant, and became thereby so thoroughly disguised that the servants of his father who had been sent after him failed to recognise him. Here he posted himself near the door of the principal church, invariably attending the divine services, and supporting himself on the alms of the faithful. After two or three years various miracles took place, betokening the special favour of the Almighty. The bishop heard a voice in the church, bidding him to summon into the sacred temple that man whose prayer was most acceptable to God, and to keep him by his side while he celebrated divine worship. As the bishop did not at once know who could be meant, the voice went on to point out to him the beggar, whom, to the great astonishment of the people, he immediately fetched into the church. The saintly Alexis, embarrassed by having the attention of the people directed towards himself, quietly and silently departed thence, also on ship-board, intending to proceed still further in foreign lands. But by a tempest and other circumstances he was compelled to land in Italy. The saint seeing in all this the finger of God, was rejoiced to meet with an opportunity of exercising self-denial in the highest degree. He therefore set off direct for his native town, and placed himself as a beggar at the door of his parents' house. With their usual pious benevolence did they receive him, and commanded one of their servants to furnish him with lodging in the castle and with all necessary sustenance. This servant, annoyed at the trouble he was put to, and displeased with his master's benevolence, assigned to this seeming beggar a miserable hole under some stone steps, where he threw to him, as to a dog, a sorry pittance of food. The saint instead of suffering himself to be vexed thereat, first of all thanked God sincerely for it in his heart, and not only bore with patient meekness all this which he might easily have altered, but with incredible and superhuman fortitude, endured to witness the lasting grief of his parents and his wife for his absence. For he heard his much-loved parents and his beautiful spouse invoke his name a hundred times a day, and pray for his return, and he saw them wasting their days in sorrow for his supposed absence." At this passage of her narrative our good hostess could not refrain her tears, while her two daughters, who during the story had crept close to her side, kept steadily looking up in their mother's face. "But," she continued, "great was the reward which the Almighty bestowed on his constancy, giving him, at his death, the greatest possible proofs of his favour in the eyes of the faithful. For after living several years in this state, daily frequenting the service of God with the most fervent zeal, he at last fell sick, without any particular heed being given to his condition by any one. One morning shortly after this, while the pope was himself celebrating high mass, in presence of the emperor and all the nobles, suddenly all the bells in the whole city of Rome began to toll as if for the passing knell of some distinguished personage. Whilst every one was full of amazement, it was revealed to the pope that this marvel was in honour of the death of the holiest person in the whole city, who had but just died in the house of the noble Patrician.—The father of Alexis being interrogated, thought at once of the beggar. He went home and found him beneath the stairs quite dead. In his folded hands the saintly man clutched a paper, which his old father sought in vain to take from him. He returned to the church and told all this to the emperor and the pope, who thereupon, with their courtiers and clergy, set off to visit the corpse of the saint. When they reached the spot, the holy father took it without difficulty out of the hands of the dead man, and handed it to the emperor, who thereupon caused it to be read aloud by his chancellor. The paper contained the history of the saint. Then you should have seen the grief of his parents and wife, which now became excessive, to think that they had had near to them a son and husband so dear; for whom there was nothing too good that they would not have done; and then too to know how ill he had been treated! They fell upon his corpse and wept so bitterly that there was not one of the bystanders who could refrain from tears. Moreover, among the multitude of the people who gradually flocked to the spot, there were many sick, who were brought to the body and by its touch were made whole."

Our fair story-teller affirmed over and over again, as she dried her eyes, that she had never heard a more touching history, and I too was seized with so great a desire to weep that I had the greatest difficulty to hide and to suppress it. After dinner I looked out the legend itself in Father Cochem, and found that the good dame had dropped none of the purely human traits of the story, while she had clean forgotten all the tasteless remarks of this writer.

We keep going continually to the window watching the weather; and are at present very near offering a prayer to the winds and clouds. Long evenings and universal stillness are the elements in which writing thrives right merrily, and I am convinced that if, for a few months only, I could contrive, or were obliged, to stay at a spot like this, all my unfinished dramas would of necessity be completed one after another.

We have already had several people before us, and questioned them with regard to the pass over the Furca; but even here we have been unable to gain any precise information, although the mountain is only two or three leagues distant. We must, however, rest contented, and we shall set out ourselves at break of day to reconnoitre, and see how destiny will decide for us. However, in general, I may be disposed to take things as they go, it would, I must confess, be highly annoying to me if we should be forced to retrace our steps again. If we are fortunate we shall be by to-morrow evening at Realp or S. Gotthard, and by noon the next day among the Capuchins at the summit of the mountain. If things go unfortunately we have two roads open for a retreat. Back through the whole of Valais, and by the well-known road over Berne to Lucerne; or back to Brieg, and then by a wide detour to S. Gotthard. I think in this short letter I have told you that three times. But in fact it is a matter of great importance to us. The issue will decide which was in the right, our courage, which gave us a confidence that we must succeed, or the prudence of certain persons who were very earnest in trying to dissuade us from attempting this route. This much, at any rate, is certain, that both prudence and courage must own chance to be over them both. And now that we have once more examined the weather, and found the air to be cold, the sky bright, and without any signs of a tendency to snow, we shall go calmly to bed.

Münster, Nov. 12, 1776.
Early. 6 o'clock.

We are quite ready, and all is packed up in order to set out from hence with the break of day. We have before us two leagues to Oberwald, and from there the usual reckoning makes six leagues to Realp. Our mule is to follow us with the baggage as far as it is possible to take him.

Realp, Nov. 12, 1779.
Evening.

We reached this place just at nightfall. We have surmounted all difficulties, and the knots which entangled our path have been cut in two. Before I tell you where we are lodged, and before I describe to you the character of our hosts, allow me the gratification of going over in thought the road that we did not see before us without anxiety, and which, however, we have left behind us without accident, though not without difficulty. About seven we started from Münster, and saw before us the snow-covered amphitheatre of mountain summits, and took to be the Furca, the mountain which in the background stood obliquely before it. But as we afterwards learned, we made a mistake; it was concealed from our view by the mountains on our left and by high clouds. The east wind blew strong and fought with some snow-clouds, chasing the drifts, now over the mountains, now up the valley. But this only made the snow drifts deeper on the ground, and caused us several times to miss our way; although shut in as we were on both sides, we could not fail of reaching Oberwald eventually. About nine we actually got there, and dropping in at an auberge, its inmates were not a little surprised to see such characters appearing there this time of the year. We asked whether the pass over the Furca were still practicable, and they answered that their folk crossed it for the greater part of the winter, but whether we should be able to get across they could not tell. We immediately sent to seek for one of these persons as a guide. There soon appeared a strong thick-set peasant, whose very look and shape inspired confidence. With him we immediately began to treat: if he thought the pass was practicable for us, let him say so; and then take one or more comrades and come with us. After a short pause he agreed, and went away to get ready himself and to fetch the others. In the meantime we paid our muleteer the hire of his beast, since we could no longer make any use of his mule; and having eaten some bread and cheese and drank a glass of red wine, felt full of strength and spirits, as our guide came back, followed by another man who looked still bigger and stronger than himself, and seeming to have all the strength and courage of a horse, he quickly shouldered our portmanteau. And now we set out, a party of five, through the village, and soon reached the foot of the mountain, which lay on our left, and began gradually to ascend it. At first we had a beaten track to follow which came down from a neighbouring Alp; soon, however, this came to an end, and we had to go up the mountain side through the snow. Our guides, with great skill, tracked their way among the rocks, around which the usual path winds, although the deep and smooth snow had covered all alike. Next our road lay through a forest of pines, while the Rhone flowed beneath us in a narrow unfruitful valley. Into it we also, after a little while, had to descend, and by crossing a little foot-bridge we came in sight of the glacier of the Rhone. It is the hugest we have as yet had so full a view of. Of very great breadth, it occupies the whole saddle of the mountain, and descends uninterruptedly down to the point where, in the valley, the Rhone flows out of it. At this source the people tell us it has for several years been decreasing; but that is as nothing compared with all the rest of the huge mass. Although everything was full of snow, still the rough crags of ice, on which the wind did not allow the snow to lie, were visible with their glass blue fissures, and you could see clearly where the glacier ended and the snow-covered rock began. To this point, which lay on our left, we came very close. Presently we again reached a light foot-bridge over a little mountain stream, which flowed through a barren trough-shaped valley to join the Rhone. After passing the glacier, neither on the right, nor on the left, nor before you, was there a tree to be seen, all was one desolate waste; no rugged and prominent rocks—nothing but long smooth valleys, slightly inclining eminences, which now, in the snow which levelled all inequalities, presented to us their simple unbroken surfaces. Turning now to the left we ascended a mountain, sinking at every step deep in the snow. One of our guides had to go first, and boldly treading down the snow break the way by which we were to follow.

It was a strange sight, when turning for a moment your

attention from the road, you directed it to yourself and your fellow travellers. In the most desolate region of the world, in a boundless, monotonous wilderness of mountains enveloped in snow, where for three leagues before and behind, you would not expect to meet a living soul, while on both sides you had the deep hollows of a web of mountains, you might see a line of men wending their way, treading each in the deep footsteps of the one before him, and where, in the whole of the wide expanse thus smoothed over, the eye could discern nothing but the track they left behind them. The hollows as we left them lay behind us gray and boundless in the mist. The changing clouds continually passed over the pale disc of the sun, and spread over the whole scene a perpetually moving veil. I am convinced that any one who, while pursuing this route, allowed his imagination to gain the mastery, would even, in the absence of all immediate danger, fall a victim to his own apprehensions and fears. In reality, there is little or no risk of a fall here; the great danger is from the avalanches, when the snow has become deeper than it is at present, and begins to roll. However our guide told us that they cross the mountains throughout the winter, carrying from Valais to S. Gotthard skins of the chamois, in which a considerable trade is here carried on. But then to avoid the avalanches, they do not take the route that we did, but remain for some time longer in the broad valley, and then go straight up the mountain. This road is safer, but much more inconvenient. After a march of about three hours and a-half, we reached the saddle of the Furca, near the cross which marks the boundary of Valais and Uri. Even here we could not distinguish the double peak from which the Furca derives its name. We now hoped for an easier descent, but our guides soon announced to us still deeper snow, as we immediately found it to be. Our march continued in single file as before, and the foremost man who broke the path often sank up to his waist in the snow. The readiness of the people, and their light way of speaking of matters, served to keep up our courage; and I will say, for myself, that I have accomplished the journey without fatigue, although I cannot say that it was a mere walk. The huntsman Hermann asserted that he had often before met with equally deep snow in the forests of Thuringia, but at last he could not help bursting out with a loud exclamation, "The Furca is a ————."

A vulture or lammergeier swept over our heads with incredible rapidity: it was the only living thing that we had met with in this waste. In the distance we saw the mountains of Urserenthal lit up with the bright sunshine. Our guides wished to enter a shepherd's hut which had been abandoned and snowed up, and to take something to eat, but we urged them to go onwards, to avoid standing still in the cold. Here again is another group of valleys; and at last we gained an open view into the valley of Uri.

We now proceeded at a shorter pace, and after travelling about three leagues and a half from the cross, we saw the scattered roofs of Realp. We had several times questioned our guides as to what sort of an inn, and what kind of wine we were likely to find in Realp. The hopes they gave us were anything but good, but they assured us that the Capuchins there, although they had not, like those on the summit of S. Gotthard, an hospice, were in the habit of entertaining strangers. With them we should get some good red wine, and better food than at an inn. We therefore sent one of our party forwards to inform the Capuchins of our arrival, and to procure a lodging for us. We did not loiter long behind, and arrived very soon after him, when we were received at the door by one of the fathers—a portly, good-looking man. With much friendliness of manner he invited us to enter, and at the threshold begged that we would put up with such entertainment they could alone offer, as at no time and least of all at this season of the year, were they prepared to receive such guests. He therefore led us into a warm room, and was very diligent in waiting upon us, while we took off our boots, and changed our linen. He begged us once for all to make ourselves perfectly at home. As to our meat, we must, he said, be indulgent, for they were in the middle of their long fast, which would last till Christmas-day. We assured him that a warm room, a bit of bread, and a glass of red wine would, in our present circumstances, fully satisfy all our wishes. He procured us what we asked for, and we had scarcely refreshed ourselves a little, ere he began to recount to us all that concerned the establishment, and the settlement of himself and fellows on this waste spot. "We have not," he said, "an hospice like the fathers on Mont S. Gotthard.—we are here in the capacity of parish priests, and there are three of us. The duty of preaching falls to my lot; the second father has to look after the school, and the brother to look after the household." He went on to describe their hardships and toils; here, at the furthest end of a lonely valley, separated from all the world, and working hard to very little profit. This spot, like all others, was formerly provided with a secular priest, but an avalanche having buried half of the village, the last one had run away, and taken the pix with him, whereupon he was suspended, and they, of whom more resignation was expected, were sent there in his place.

In order to write all this I had retired to an upper room, which is warmed from below by a hole in the floor; and I have just received an intimation that dinner is ready, which, notwithstanding our luncheon, is right welcome news.

About 9.

The fathers, priests, servants, guides and all, took their dinner together at a common table; the brother, however, who superintended the cooking, did not make his appearance till dinner was nearly over. Out of milk, eggs, and flour he had compounded a variety of dishes, which we tasted one after another, and found them all very good. Our guides, who took a great pleasure in speaking of the successful issue of our expedition, praised us for our uncommon dexterity in travelling, and assured us that it was not every one that they would have undertaken the task of being guides to. They even confessed also that this morning, when their services were required, one had gone first to reconnoitre, and to see if we looked like people who would really go through all difficulties with them; for they were particularly cautious how they accompanied old or weak people at this time of the year, since it was their duty to take over in safety every one they had once engaged to guide, being bound in case of his falling sick, to carry him, even though it should be at the imminent risk of their own lives, and if he were to die on the passage, not to leave his body behind. This confession at once opened the flood-gates to a host of anecdotes, and each in turn had his story to tell of the difficulties and dangers of wandering over the mountains amidst which the people had here to live as in their proper element, so that with the greatest indifference they speak of mischances and accidents to which they themselves are daily liable. One of them told a story of how, on the Candersteg, on his way to Mount Gemmi, he and a comrade with him (he is mentioned on every occasion with both Christian and sur-name) found a poor family in the deep snow, the mother dying, her boy half dead, and the father in that state of indifference which verges on a total prostration of intellect. He took the woman on his back, and his comrade her son, and thus laden, they had driven before them the father, who was unwilling to move from the spot.

During the descent of Gemmi the woman died on his back, but he brought her dead as she was to Leukerbad. When we asked what sort of people they were, and what could have brought them at such a season into the mountains, he said they were poor people of the canton of Berne, who, driven by want, had taken to the road at an unseasonable period of the year, in the hope of finding some relations either in Valais or the Italian canton, and had been overtaken by a snow-storm. Moreover, they told many anecdotes of what had happened to themselves during the winter journeys over the Furca with the chamois-skins, on which expeditions, however, they always travelled in companies. Every now and then our reverend host would make excuses for the dinner, and we redoubled our assurances that we wished for nothing better. We also found that he contrived to bring back the conversation to himself and his own matters, observing that he had not been long in this place. He began to talk of the office of preaching, and of the dexterity that a preacher ought to have. He compared the good preacher to a chapman who cleverly puffs his wares, and by his pleasant words makes himself agreeable to his customers. After dinner he kept up the conversation, and, as he stood with his left hand leaning on the table, he accompanied his remarks with his right, and while he discoursed most eloquently on eloquence, appeared at the moment as if he wished to convince us that he himself was the dexterous chapman. We assented to his observations, and he came from the lecture to the thing itself. He panegyrized the Roman Catholic religion. "We must," he said, "have a rule of faith; and the great value of it consists in its being fixed, and as little liable as possible to change, We," he said, "had made Scripture the foundation of our faith, but it was insufficient. We ourselves would not venture to put it into the hands of common men; for holy as it is, and full as every leaf is of the Spirit of God, still the worldly-minded man is insensible of all this, and finds rather perplexities and stumbling-blocks throughout. What good can a mere layman extract from the histories of sinful men, which are contained therein, and which the Holy Ghost has there recorded for the strengthening of the faith of the tried and experienced children of God? What benefit can a common man draw from all this, when he is unable to consider the whole context and connection? How is such a person to see his way clear out of the seeming contradictions which occasionally occur?—out of the difficulties which arise from the ill arrangement of the books, and the differences of style, when the learned themselves find it so hard, and while so many passages make them hold their reason in abeyance? What ought we therefore to teach? A rule of faith founded on Scripture, and proved by the best of commentaries? But who then is to comment upon the Scripture? Who is to set up this rule? I, perhaps, or some other man? By no means. Every man has his own way of taking and seeing things, and represents them after his own ideas. That would be to give to the people as many systems of doctrines as there are are heads in the world, and to produce inexplicable confusion as indeed had already been done. No, it remains for the Holy Church alone to interpret Scripture to determine the rule of faith by which the souls of men are to be guided and governed. And what is the church? It is not any single supreme head, or any particular member alone. No! it is all the holiest, most learned, and most experienced men of all times, who, with the co-operation of the Holy Spirit, have successively combined together in building up that great, universal, and agreeing body, which has its great councils for its members to communicate their thoughts to one another, and for mutual edification; which banishes error, and thereby imparts to our holy religion a certainty and a stability such as no other profession can pretend to, and gives it a foundation and strengthens it with bulwarks which even hell itself cannot overthrow. And just so is it also with the text of the sacred scriptures. We have," he said, "the Vulgate, moreover an approved version of the Vulgate, and of every sentence a commentary which the church itself has accredited. Hence arises that uniformity of our teaching which surprises every one. Whether," he continued, "you hear me preaching in this most remote corner of the world, or in the great capital of a distant country are listening to the dullest or cleverest of preachers, all will hold one and the same language; a Catholic Christian will always hear the same doctrine; everywhere will he be instructed and edified in the same manner. And this it is which constitutes the certainty of our faith; which gives us the peace and confidence by which each one in life holds sure communion with his brother Catholics, and at death can calmly part in the sure hope of meeting one another again."

In his speech, as in a sermon, he let the subjects follow in due order, and spoke more from an inward feeling of satisfaction that he was exhibiting himself under a favourable aspect than from any bigotted anxiety for conversion. During the delivery he would occasionally change the arm he rested upon, or draw them both into the arms of his gown, or let them rest on his portly stomach; now and then he would, with much grace, draw his snuff-box out of his capote, and after using it replace it with a careless ease. We listened to him attentively, and he seemed to be quite content with our way of receiving his instructions. How greatly amazed would he have been if an angel had revealed to him, at the moment, that he was addressing his peroration to a descendant of Frederick the Wise.

November 13, 1779.
Among the Capuchins, on the summit of Mont S. Gotthard.
Morning, about 10 *o'clock.*

At last we have fortunately reached the utmost limits of our journey. Here it is determined we shall rest awhile, and then turn our steps towards our dear fatherland. Very strange are my feelings here, on this summit, where four years ago I passed a few days with very different anxieties, sentiments, plans, and hopes, and at a very different season of the year, when, without any foreboding of my future fortunes, but moved by

I know not what, I turned my back upon Italy, and ignorantly went to meet my present destiny. I did not even recognise the house again. Some time ago it was greatly injured by an avalanche, and the good fathers took advantage of this opportunity, and made a collection throughout the canton for enlarging and improving their residence. Both of the two fathers who reside here at present are absent, but, as I hear, they are still the same that I met four years ago. Father Seraphin, who has now passed fourteen years in this post is at present at Milan, and the other is expected to-day from Airolo. In this clear atmosphere the cold is awful. As soon as dinner is over I will continue my letter; for, I see clearly we shall not go far outside the door.

After dinner.

It becomes colder and colder; one does not like to stir from the stove. Indeed it is most delightful to sit upon it, which in this country, where the stoves are made of stone-tiles, it is very easy to do. First of all, therefore, we will tell you of our departure from Realp, and then of our journey hither.

Yesterday evening before we retired to our beds, the good father would shew us his sleeping cell, where everything was in nice order, in a very small space. His bed, which consisted of a bag of straw, with a woollen coverlid, did not appear to us to be anything very meritorious, as we ourselves had often put up with no better. With great pleasure and internal satisfaction he showed us everything—his bookcase and all other things. We praised all that we saw, and parting on the best terms with each other, we retired for the night. In furnishing our room, in order that two beds might stand against one wall, both had been made unusually small. This inconvenience kept me long awake, until I thought of remedying it by placing four chairs together. It was quite broad daylight before we awoke this morning. When we went down we found nothing but happy and friendly faces. Our guides, on the point of entering upon their return over yesterday's beautiful route, seemed to look upon it as an epoch, and as a history with which hereafter they would be able to entertain other strangers, and as they were well paid the idea of an adventure became complete in their minds. After this we made a capital breakfast and departed.

Our road now lay through the Urserenthal, which is remarkable as having, at so great an elevation, such beautiful meadows and pasturage for cattle. They make here a cheese which I prefer to all others. No trees, however, grow here. Sally bushes line all the brooks, and on the mountains little shrubs grow thickly together. Of all the countries that I know, this is to me the loveliest and most interesting,—whether it is that old recollections make it precious to me, or that the perception of such a long chain of nature's wonders excites within me a secret and inexpressible feeling of enjoyment. I take it for granted that you bear in mind that the whole country through which I am leading you is covered with snow, and that rock and meadow alike are snowed over. The sky has been quite clear, without a single cloud; the hue far deeper than one is accustomed to see in low and flat countries, and the white mountain ridges, which stood out in strong contrast to it, were either glittering in the sunshine, or else took a greyish tint in the shade.

In an hour and a half we reached Hospenthal, a little village within the canton of Uri, which lies on the road to S. Gotthard. Here at last I regained the track of my former tour. We entered an inn, and though it was as yet morning, ordered a dinner, and soon afterward began to ascend the summit. A long train of mules with their bells enlivened the whole region. It is a sound which awakens all one's recollections of mountain scenery. The greater part of the train was in advance of us, and with their sharp iron shoes had pretty well cut up the smooth icy road. We also saw some labourers who were employed in covering the slippery ice with fresh earth, in order to render it passable. The wish which I formerly gave utterance to, that I might one day be permitted to see this part of the world under snow, is now at last gratified. The road goes up the Reuss as it dashes down over rocks all the way, and forms everywhere the most beautiful waterfalls. We stood a long while attracted by the singular beauty of one which in considerable volume was dashing over a succession of dark black rocks. Here and there in the cracks, and on the flat ledges pieces of ice had formed, and the water seemed to be running over a variegated black and white

F

marble. The masses of ice glistened like veins of crystal in the sun, and the water flowed pure and fresh between them.

On the mountains there is no more tiresome a fellow-traveller than a train of mules; they have so unequal a pace. With a strange instinct they always stop a while at the bottom of a steep ascent, and then dash off at a quick pace up it, to rest again at the top. Very often too they will stop at the level spots which do occur now and then, until they are forced on by the drivers or by other beasts coming up. And so the foot passenger, by keeping a steady pace, soon gains upon them, and in the narrow road has to push by them. If you stand still a little while to observe any object, they in their turn will pass by you, and you are pestered with the deafening sound of their bells, and hard brushed with their loads, which project to a good distance on each side of them. In this way we at last reached the summit of the mountain, which you can form some idea of by fancying a bald skull surrounded with a crown. Here one finds oneself on a perfect flat surrounded with peaks. Far and near the eye falls on nothing but bare and mostly snow-covered peaks and crags.

It is scarcely possible to keep oneself warm, especially as they have here no fuel but brushwood, and of that too they are obliged to be very sparing, as they have to fetch it up the mountains, from a distance of at least three leagues, for at the summit, they tell us, scarcely any kind of wood grows. The reverend father is returned from Airolo, so frozen that on his arrival he could scarcely utter a word. Although here the Capuchins are allowed to clothe themselves a little more comfortably than the rest of their order, still their style of dress is by no means suited for such a climate as this. All the way up from Airolo the road was frozen perfectly smooth, and he had the wind in his face; his beard was quite frozen, and it was a long while before he recovered himself. We had some conversation together on the hardships of their residence here; he told us how they managed to get through the year, their various occupations, and their domestic circumstances. He could speak nothing but Italian, and so we had an opportunity of putting to use the exercises in this language which we had taken during the spring. Towards evening we went for a moment outside the house-door that the good father might point out to us the peak which is considered to be the highest summit of Mont Gotthard; but we could scarcely endure to stay out a very few minutes, so searching and pinching was the cold. This time, therefore, we shall remain close shut up within doors, and shall have time enough before we start to-morrow, to travel again in thought over all the most remarkable parts of this region.

A brief geographical description will enable you to understand how remarkable the point is at which we are now sitting. S. Gotthard is not indeed the highest mountain of Switzerland; in Savoy, Mont Blanc has a far higher elevation and yet it maintains above all others the rank of a king of mountains, because all the great chains converge together around him, and all rest upon him as their base. Indeed, if I do not make a great mistake, I think I was told at Berne, by Herr Wyttenbach, who, from its highest summit, had seen the peaks of all the others, that the latter all leaned towards it. The mountains of Schweitz and Unterwalden, joined by those of Uri range from the north, from the east those of the Grisons, from the south those of the Italian cantons, while from the west, by means of the Furca, the double line of mountains which enclose Valais, presses upon it. Not far from this house, there are two small lakes, one of which sends forth the Ticino through gorges and valleys into Italy, while from the other, in like manner, the Reuss proceeds till it empties itself in the Lake of the Forest towns.* Not far from this spot are the sources of the Rhine, which pursue an easterly course, and if then we take in the Rhone which rises at the foot of the Furca and runs westward through Valais, we shall find ourselves at the point of a cross, from which mountain ranges and rivers proceed towards the four cardinal points of heaven.

* Lake Lucerne.

CAMPAIGN IN FRANCE, 1792.

TRANSLATED BY

ROBERT FARIE,
BARRISTER-AT-LAW.

(*REVISED.*)

CAMPAIGN IN FRANCE.

23rd August, 1792.

IMMEDIATELY after my arrival in Mainz, I visited Herr von Stein,* Chamberlain and Chief Forest-Ranger to the King of Prussia, who filled in some sort the office of Resident Minister there, and was distinguished by his violent hatred of everything revolutionary. He gave me a rapid sketch of the progress of the allied army up to that time, and furnished me with an abstract of the topographical atlas of Germany, arranged by Jäger at Frankfort, and entitled " Theatre of the War."

At dinner in his house I found several Frenchwomen, whom I had reason to observe with some attention; one of them (the mistress, it was said, of the Duke of Orleans†), a stately woman, already of a certain age, with proud manners, and raven-black eyes, eyebrows, and hair; her conversation, moreover, was clever and agreeable. Her daughter, who was a youthful picture of herself, did not speak a word. The livelier, therefore, and more fascinating appeared the Princess Monaco, the intimate friend of the Prince of Condé, and the ornament of Chantilly in better days. Nothing could be more charming than this slender, fair woman; young, sparkling, and humorous, no man whose attention she wished to attract could resist her. I watched her unmoved, and was surprised at thus meeting Philina‡ again, whom I did not expect to find here, flutter-

* The elder brother of Carl von Stein, who subsequently became the Prussian Minister; Goethe's acquaintance with the latter belongs to a later period.

† Louis Philippe (Egalité), who was guillotined in November, 1793.

‡ Evidently an allusion to the character in *Wilhelm Meister;* yet the Second Book in which Philina first appears Goethe did not finish till June, 1794; hence, almost two years after the incident here mentioned.

ing about so bright and gay. She did not appear as uneasy or excited as the rest of the party, who were living in an agitation of hope, fear and anxiety. The Allies had lately entered France. Would Longwy immediately surrender or stand an assault? Would the French republican troops unite with the Allies, and every one, as had been promised, declare for the good cause, and further its progress? All this was at the moment suspended in doubt. Couriers were expected; the last had only announced the slow progress of the army, and the impediments arising from the bad state of the roads. The suppressed wish of these people became the more irksome to them, seeing that they could not conceal their desire of returning as soon as possible to their own country, that they might take advantage of the assignats, the invention of their enemies, and thus be able to live more cheaply and comfortably than they did before.

Afterwards I passed two pleasant evenings with the Sömmerings, Huber, Forsters, and other friends. Here I at once felt myself in my native air again. Almost all of them were former acquaintances and fellow-students in connection with Frankfort (Sömmering's wife was from Frankfort); all of them intimate with my mother, whose genial qualities they valued, repeating many of her happiest sayings, and asserting more than once my great resemblance to her in cheerfulness of manners and liveliness of conversation; what recollections and sympathies were excited in us by our unaffected, innate, and habitual confidence in each other! Some good-natured jokes about scientific and learned matters, which we could indulge in without restraint, put us in the best humour. About political matters we were silent, as we felt the necessity of mutual forbearance; for whilst they did not altogether repudiate republican opinions, I, on the other hand, was hastening undisguisedly to join an army which had taken the field to crush these opinions and destroy their influence.

Between Mainz and Bingen, I witnessed a scene which gave me immediately an insight into the character of the time. Our light carriage overtook another with four horses, and covered with luggage. The hollow road we were in, being up-hill and full of ruts, compelled us to get out; and the postilions having dismounted, we asked them who was in the carriage before us. The postilion of the other carriage replied, with oaths and curses, that they were Frenchwomen, who expected to make their way with paper money, but that he intended to upset them as soon as a good opportunity presented itself. We reprimanded him for his abominable ill-humour, without its having any effect upon him. As we went very slowly, I walked up to the window of the carriage before us, and addressed a few friendly words to the lady; her young pretty face, which had been somewhat overclouded by anxiety, brightened up a little.

She confided to me at once, that she was following her husband to Trèves, and wished, as soon as possible, to get from thence into France. When I represented to her the imprudence of such a step, she confessed that, besides the hope of finding her husband once more, the *necessity of living again upon paper* had induced her to take it. Moreover, she showed such confidence in the allied forces of the Prussians, Austrians, and emigrants, that, even though time and circumstances had not been against it, it would have been difficult to prevent her carrying out her plan.

In the midst of this conversation a singular occurrence took place; over the hollow road which we had entered, a wooden gutter had been thrown, to carry the water to a mill, which stood at the other side of the road. One would have thought that the height of the framework would have been calculated to allow at least a hay-waggon to pass. However that may have been, the carriage was so excessively loaded on the top—trunks and boxes heaped like a pyramid above one another—that the gutter presented an insuperable obstacle to its further progress.

Now commenced in good earnest the cursing and swearing of the postilions, as they foresaw great loss of time; however, we offered our services, and assisted in unpacking the carriage and repacking it on the other side of the dripping barrier. The young woman, who had gradually become less timid, was at a loss how to express her thanks to us; her confidence in us at the same time increased by degrees. She wrote down the name of her husband, and earnestly requested us, as we should arrive in Trèves before her, to leave his address in writing at the gate-way of the town. With every desire to comply with her request, we despaired of being able to do so, on account of the size of the place. She, however, did not give up hope.

When we arrived in Trèves we found it full of troops, vehicles of all kinds driving about, and nowhere a lodging to be found; conveyances were drawn up in the squares; the people hurrying about the streets; and the officers charged with the providing of quarters, besieged on all hands, scarcely knew what to do. A confusion of this kind is like a lottery, in which those who are fortunate obtain the prizes; and such was the case with me, for I encountered Lieutenant von Fritsch, of the Duke's regiment, who, after the kindest of greetings, conducted me to a Canon, in whose large house and extensive premises both myself and my compendious equipage were satisfactorily established, and abundant refreshment was immediately supplied to me. This young military friend whom I had known from his childhood, and who was besides a kind of *protégé* of mine, had been ordered to remain in Trèves, and was commissioned to provide for the sick and stragglers, and to receive and forward the baggage-waggons, and such other things as were delayed upon the road; his presence was of great advantage to me, although he did not relish being left in the rear of the army, where, as a young and ambitious soldier, there was not much prospect of advancement for him.

My servant had scarcely unpacked such things as I stood most in need of, when he begged permission to go and take a walk about the town; he did not return till late at night, and next morning early the same restlessness drove him out of the house. This singular behaviour was at first unintelligible to me, but at length the riddle was solved; the pretty Frenchwomen had made some impression upon him; and having searched carefully, he was lucky enough to find them in the large square amongst a crowd of carriages, having recognised them by the pyramid of trunks, but the lady had not found her husband.

On the road from Trèves to Luxembourg I was soon gratified with a view of the monument in the neighbourhood of Ygel. As I knew that the ancients always chose a favourable position for their buildings and monuments, I put aside, in imagination, all the humble buildings that surrounded it, and then its position appeared in the highest degree appropriate. The Moselle flows close by, and is joined on the opposite side by a considerable stream, called the Saar; the winding of the rivers, the undulation of the ground, and the luxuriant vegetation, giving loveliness and dignity to the spot.

The monument itself might be called an obelisk, architecto-plastically ornamented. It rises up in several stories erected artistically one above another, and ends in a pinnacle, which is decorated with scales in the manner of tiles, and is surmounted by a ball, a serpent, and an eagle. It is to be hoped that some engineer whom the present warlike events may lead to this part of the country, and perhaps keep him here for some time, will not consider it too much trouble to measure the monument, and that, if a draughtsman, he will provide us with a drawing of it, and preserve for us the figures on the four sides, as far as they are still recognisable.

What number of miserable, unornamental obelisks I have seen erected in my time, without anybody having ever thought of this one! It belongs indeed to a later period; but we still see the pleasure and desire they had of handing down to posterity sensible representations of the personalities,. together with the surrounding objects and evidences of industry. Here parents and children are seen beside each other, and feasting is going on in the family circle; but that the spectator may learn whence the abundance is derived, beasts of burden are to be seen going about, and trade and commerce are represented in various ways; for it was, in fact, war commissaries who raised this monument to themselves and their countrymen, by way of evidence that, in those days as well as at present, an abundance of all things was to be obtained in that place by industry.

The whole of this pointed structure had been built of massive unhewn blocks of sandstone, piled one upon the other, and then the architecto-plastic figures were engraved upon them as out of a rock. The preservation of this monument for so many centuries may be attributed to its having so solid a foundation.

I was unable to indulge long in this agreeable and

fruitful train of thought, for close at hand, in Grevenmachern, a spectacle of the most modern description awaited me. I found here the corps of Emigrants, consisting entirely of noblemen, mostly knights of St. Louis. They had neither servants nor grooms, but acted as their own servants, and groomed their own horses. Many a one I have seen leading the horses to drink, and holding them while they were being shod. But the most singular contrast to this humble kind of occupation was presented by the crowd of vehicles and travelling carriages of all kinds collected on a meadow. For they had come with their wives and sweethearts, children and relations, as if they wanted to make a display of the utter incongruity of their present condition.

As I was obliged to wait here several hours for post-horses in the open air, I was enabled to make further observations. I sat down in front of the window of the post-house, near the place where the box was into the opening of which unfranked letters were to be thrown. Such a crush I never saw; letters were dropped into it by the hundred. The eagerness with which every one would have liked to rush with body, soul, and spirit, back to the land of his birth through the breach thus effected, could not have been more vividly or impressively depicted.

From ennui and a wish to unravel secrets or to weave them for myself, I set about guessing what might be the contents of some of this multitude of letters. I thought I could discover there a girl who had been separated from her lover, passionately expressing the pain and misery of her privation in such a separation; one friend begging another for money to supply his urgent necessities; women, driven from their homes with children and domestics, whose funds had dwindled down to a few pieces of money; vehement adherents of the Princes, hoping that all would yet go well, exhorting each other to take courage; others who already saw mischief looming in the distance, and mournfully deploring the impending loss of their estates—pretty near the truth my guesses were, I suspect.

A variety of information was given me by the postmaster, who, in order to overcome my impatience about the horses, purposely sought to amuse me. He showed me several letters with stamps upon them from distant quarters, which were to be sent after those who had already gone forward and those who were still advancing. France, he said, was beleaguered on all its frontiers by unfortunate people of this kind, from Antwerp to Nice; on the other hand, the French armies were everywhere prepared, either for defence or attack. He related many circumstances of ominous import; and the state of things appeared to him very doubtful, to say the least of it.

As I did not seem so frantic as the others who were rushing towards France, he took me for a republican, and showed more confidence in me; he called my attention to the miseries endured by the Prussians, from the state of the weather and the roads, on their march through Coblentz and Trèves; and gave me a fearful description of the condition in which I should find the camp in the neighbourhood of Longwy. He was well informed about everything, and seemed not unwilling to impart his information to others; he begged me finally, to mark how the Prussians, either the troops themselves or the baggage-servants and stragglers, had plundered quiet and unoffending villages; the culprits apparently were punished, but the people exasperated against them to the utmost degree.

I thought then of the general in the Thirty Years' War, who, when complaint was made to him of the hostile behaviour of his troops in the territory of an ally, replied: "I cannot carry my army about in my pocket." On the whole, however, I could perceive that our rear was but ill protected.

Longwy, whose capture had already been triumphantly announced to me on the way, I left at some distance to the right, and arrived on the afternoon of the 27th August near the camp of Brocourt. It could be seen stretched out over a plain; but to reach it was an affair of some difficulty. The ground, which was wet and cut up, impeded the horses and waggons; it was strange, too, that one met neither sentinels nor outposts, nor anybody else to examine the passports, and to whom one could have applied for the requisite information. We drove through a wilderness of tents, as everybody had crept under them to get some indifferent shelter from the dreadful weather. Only after considerable difficulty we succeeded in obtaining intelligence of where the Weimar regiment was to be found, but arrived at the place at last, where we found familiar faces, and were cordially received by our fellow-sufferers. Wagner,* the chamberlain, and his black poodle were the first to greet us; both of them recognised in me an old comrade of many years' standing, who was destined again to struggle through a time of difficulty and danger with them. I heard, at the same time, of an unfortunate occurrence. The Prince's favourite horse, Amarant, after giving a frightful scream, had yesterday suddenly fallen down dead.

I found and heard of a much worse state of things in the camp than the postmaster had predicted. It stood upon a plain at the foot of a gently-inclined hill, in which of old a ditch had been dug to drain the water from the fields and meadows. This became immediately a receptacle for all kinds of filth and offal; the outlet was stopped up, heavy showers of rain during the night had broken down the dam, and brought disgusting havoc among the tents. Bones and garbage of all sorts, which the butchers had thrown aside, were borne into the sleeping-places, which had been wet and uncomfortable enough before.

I was to have had a tent provided for me, but I preferred remaining with my friends and acquaintances during the daytime, and at night went to rest in the large sleeping-waggon, the comfort of which I had known in former times. It appeared strange, however, that, although only thirty paces from the tents, it remained so difficult of access as to make it necessary for me to be carried into it in the evening, and out of it again in the morning.

28th and 29th August.

Strangely this year did my birth-day dawn upon me. We mounted our horses and rode into the captured

* Johann Conrad Wagner, Chamberlain to the Duke of Weimar, whose diary Goethe subsequently made use of to complete his own. See p. 198.

fortress. The little town, which is well built and strongly fortified, stands upon an eminence. My object was to buy some large woollen blankets. And we went at once to a shop, where we found a mother and her daughter, both of them pretty, and willing to serve us. We did not bargain with them much, but paid them handsomely, and were as polite as Germans without *tournure* could be.

The house had been the scene of some most strange occurrences during the bombardment. Several grenades in succession had fallen into the parlour, putting the inmates to flight; the mother had snatched a child from the cradle and fled, and at that very moment another grenade dashed through the cushion on which the boy had been lying. Luckily none of the grenades had burst. The furniture was broken, and the wainscot burnt, but no further damage was done, the balls not having entered the shop.

It was evident that the patriotism of the people of Longwy was not very great, for the citizens had very soon compelled the commandant to surrender the fortress, and we had scarcely moved a step from the shop, before the internal dissensions of the townspeople became manifest to us. Some adherents of royalty, and consequently friendly to our cause, and who had effected the speedy surrender of the place, expressed to us their regret that accident had brought us to that particular shop, to one of the worst of the Jacobins, who, with his whole family, was good for nothing, and that we had given him an opportunity of getting so much money from us. We were at the same time warned not to go to a showy hotel, which they named, and were given to understand that it might be dangerous to trust too much to the dishes; they pointed out a smaller one that might be depended upon, where, in fact, we were well received and tolerably well served.

And now we all sat down cheerily together again, all of us old comrades and friends; the officers of the regiment joined the official and private attendants of the Duke, and related the latest occurrences—what a commotion there had been in Aschersleben in the beginning of May, and what an imposing sight it had been to see the regiments when they received orders to hold themselves ready to march, for the Duke of Brunswick and several distinguished persons were there on a visit; the Marquis of Bouillé was also mentioned as a foreigner of importance, who had a powerful influence in the operations. As soon as the landlord, who was listening, heard this name, he demanded eagerly if we knew the gentleman. Most of the party were able to answer in the affirmative, on which he became very respectful, and expressed great hope from the co-operation of this excellent and energetic man; it appeared, in fact, as if we were better served from that time forward.

All those here assembled then professed allegiance, with soul and body, to the Prince who, during a reign of several years, had developed many great qualities, and was now about to prove his ability in the business of war, to which from youth upwards he had been devoted, and had studied for a considerable time; his health, and that of his family, was drunk in good old German fashion; but particularly the health of Prince Bernhard,* to whom, just before the marching of the troops, Sèrgeant-major von Weyrach, as delegate of the regiment, had stood godfather.

Everybody had some anecdote to tell of the march itself, how they had passed Goslar on towards Nordheim and Göttingen, leaving the Harz to the left; we heard of their good and bad quarters, of the boorishly uncivil, politely illnatured, and hypochondriacally obliging landlords that had been encountered, of nunneries, and all manner of adventures, and variations of the weather and the roads. Their route then lay along the eastern border of Westphalia to Coblentz, and many a pretty woman they had met now had her praises sung; a checkered account was further given of singular-looking priests, unexpected meetings with friends, of broken wheels, and carriages overturned.

Great complaints were made of the hilly country that had to be traversed after leaving Coblentz, of the bad roads, and want of all conveniences; and scarcely had the existing state of things been forgotten in the description of past

* Second son of the Duke of Weimar, born in May 1792, a few months before the opening of the campaign.

occurrences, when it again presented itself in its disagreeable reality. The march into France in the midst of frightful weather was described as most dismal, and as a worthy prelude to the present condition of the camp, which, on our return, could be seen stretched out before us. However, in such companionship, each man is encouraged by his neighbour; and, for my part, I took comfort in thinking of the delicious woollen blankets which my groom had tied up in a bundle behind him.

In the camp in the evening I found very good company in the large tent, where all had remained together, not being able to venture outside; all in high spirits and confident of success. The speedy surrender of Longwy seemed to confirm the predictions of the Emigrants, that we should be received everywhere with open arms, and there appeared no obstacle but the weather to our great undertaking. The same hatred and contempt for the French Revolutionists which had been proclaimed in the manifesto* of the Duke of Brunswick was displayed, without exception, by Prussians, Austrians, and Emigrants.

Indeed, it was only necessary to state the information authentically received, to show that a nation so utterly disunited, not split into contending factions, but broken up into isolated units, and paralysed to the core, could never withstand the lofty sense of unity of the gallant Confederates.

Some military achievements also were already related. Immediately after the entry into France, five squadrons of the Wolfrat hussars fell in with a thousand *chasseurs*,† who

---

* Of this manifesto Lamartine, in his "Histoire des Girondins," says: "Cet impérieux défi des rois à la liberté menaçait de mort tous les gardes nationaux qui serait pris les armes à la main défendant leur indépendance et leur patrie; et dans le cas où le moindre outrage serait commis par les factieux contre la majesté royale, il annonçait qu'on raserait Paris à la surface du sol."

† At the beginning of the Revolution Dumourier took the popular side and became connected with the Girondists, by whose interest he was appointed Minister of Foreign Affairs. Subsequently he withdrew from internal politics. After the 10th of August he was appointed to replace La Fayette in the command of the army which was to oppose the Duke of Brunswick. It is generally allowed that Dumourier's stand at Argonne was the means of saving France from a successful invasion.

had come from Sedan to watch our advance. Our troops, ably commanded, commenced the attack, and as their antagonists made a gallant defence and would accept no quarter, there was a fearful struggle, in which we conquered after dreadful slaughter, and took many prisoners, horses, carbines, and sabres; by which prelude a warlike spirit was raised, and hope and confidence were more firmly established.

On the 29th of August we left the coagulated waves of earth and water, slowly and not without difficulty; for how could the tents, baggage, uniforms, and other things, be kept even tolerably clean, as there was not a dry spot where anything could be properly laid by or spread out!

The attention, however, which was bestowed by the military commanders upon this march gave us fresh confidence. All vehicles, without exception, were most rigorously ordered to keep behind the column, only the commander of each regiment was entitled to have a light carriage in front of his men; and thus I, in my open, light little carriage, had the good luck this time to lead the main body of the army. Both commanders, the King as well as the Duke of Brunswick, had stationed themselves with their staff where everything had to pass them. I saw them from a distance; and as we came close to them, his Majesty rode up to my little vehicle, and asked in his laconic way to whom the carriage belonged. I answered, in a loud voice: "The Duke of Weimar!" and we moved forwards. One could not readily have been interrogated by a more distinguished official.

Further on we found the road here and there somewhat better. In a singular tract of country, where hill and valley alternated, there was sufficient dry space, particularly for those who were on horseback, to enable us to move forwards comfortably. I mounted my horse, and in this way got along more freely and pleasantly: our regiment had precedence in the army, we could always be in front, and escape the annoying movement of the whole body.

The line of march left the main road. We passed Arrancy, and then on our flank Chatillon l'Abbaye, as first token of the Revolution—a church property which had been sold, its walls half broken down and in ruins.

But now we saw, across hill and valley, his Majesty the King moving rapidly forwards on horseback ; he, as it were, the nucleus of a comet, followed by an attendant train. Scarcely, however, had this vision past us, with lightning speed, when a second one from another quarter crowned the hill or filled the valley. It was the Duke of Brunswick, followed and surrounded by elements of a similar description. We, although more inclined to observe than to criticise, could not avoid the consideration as to which of these two powers was in reality the highest? Which would have to decide in doubtful cases? Unanswerable questions, which left only doubt and suspicion behind them.

But what gave even more serious matter for reflection was, that we saw both commanders openly and unguardedly entering a country, where, not improbably, in every bush an exasperated mortal enemy might be lurking. However, we were obliged to confess, that a bold personal disregard of danger had in all times led to and secured victory.

In spite of a somewhat clouded sky, the sun shone very hot. The vehicles made slow progress in the splashy ground. Broken wheels of gun-carriages occasioned many a halt, while here and there worn-out fusiliers could scarcely drag themselves along. We heard the cannonading at Thionville, and wished success to our friends in that quarter.

In the evening we rested from our fatigues in the camp near Pillon. We halted in a delicious wooded meadow, and the shade had a refreshing effect upon us. Plenty of branches were ready for our kitchen fire ; a brook flowed close at hand, forming two clear basins, which were both of them in immediate danger of being polluted by men and beasts. The one I allowed them to treat as they pleased, but defended the other vehemently, and got it immediately enclosed with sticks and cords; this was not effected without some disturbance from those who were pressing round it. Here two of our troopers were very quietly cleaning their accoutrements, and one of them asked the other, "Who is that, that gives himself such airs?" "I do not know," answered the other, "but he is right."

Thus did the Prussians, Austrians, and a portion of the French, come to carry on their warlike operations on French soil. By whose power and authority did they do it? They might have done it in their own name; war had been partly declared against them, and their league was no secret—but another pretext was invented. They took the field in the name of Louis XVI.; they exacted nothing, but they borrowed by force. *Bons* had been printed, which the commander signed; but whoever had them in his possession filled them up at his pleasure, according to circumstances, and Louis XVI. was called upon to pay. Perhaps, with the exception of the manifesto, nothing had so exasperated the people against the monarchy as this treatment. I myself witnessed a scene which I remember as a most tragic one. Several shepherds, who had succeeded in uniting their flocks, in order to conceal them for safety in the forests or other secluded places, were seized by some active patrols and brought to the army, and were at first well received and kindly treated. They were asked who their different proprietors were: the flocks were separated and counted. Anxiety and fear, but still not without hope, fluctuated in the countenances of the worthy people. But when this proceeding ended in the division of the flocks among the regiments and companies, whilst the pieces of paper drawn on Louis XVI. were handed to them, and their woolly favourites slaughtered at their feet by the impatient and hungry soldiers, I confess that my eyes and spirit have seldom witnessed a more cruel spectacle, or more profound manly grief in all its gradations. The Greek tragedies alone have anything so purely, deeply pathetic.

30th August.

This day, which was to bring us towards Verdun, we had been looking forward to, and promised ourselves adventures from it; and these did not fail. The road, which ascended and descended alternately, was drier now; the waggons moved less heavily, the horsemen rode more easily and pleasantly.

A lively party of us met, and being well mounted, we rode forward so far that we came up to a troop of hussars who were properly the advanced guard of the main army. The captain, a grave man, already past middle age, did not appear to like our arrival. The strictest orders had been given him; everything was to be done with the greatest circumspection, every unpleasant coincidence to be handled with caution. He had skilfully distributed his men: they advanced singly at certain distances, and everything was being done with the greatest order and quiet. The country was void of inhabitants, the utter loneliness seemed ominous. In thus ascending and descending hill after hill, we passed Mangiennes, Damvillers, Wavrille, and Ormont, and had reached a height which afforded a beautiful view, when a shot was fired in the vineyards to the right of the road, whereupon the hussars rushed forward to search the immediate neighbourhood. They succeeded in capturing a black-haired, bearded man, who looked rather wild, and on whose person they found a bad pocket-pistol. He said, sulkily, that he was frightening the birds out of his vineyard, and intended no harm to anybody. The captain quietly considered the case, and finally released the menaced captive with a few blows, which the fellow took with him so hastily in his flight, that when his hat, amid loud shouts of laughter, was thrown after him, he seemed to feel no inclination to pick it up.

We moved forwards, diverted by what had already occurred and the thought of other adventures that might still come. It may be mentioned, that our little party, which had obtruded itself upon the hussars, and had met accidentally, consisted of the most heterogeneous elements; they were for the most part blunt sort of men, every one devoted to the business of the hour, each after his own fashion. One of them, however, I must distinguish from the rest—a serious but very worthy man, of a kind frequently met with among the Prussian military at that time; more æsthetic than philosophical; earnest, with a slight touch of melancholy; quietly absorbed in his own thoughts, and disposed to beneficence, together with a touch of sentimentality.

As we thus proceeded onward in our course, we came upon a sight which was as singular as it was pleasing, and excited general interest. Two hussars had brought a one-horsed, two-wheeled car up the hill; and when we inquired what was under the canvas-covering, a boy of about twelve years of age, who drove the horse, made his appearance from beneath, as also a beautiful girl, or young wife, who leant forward out of the corner to look at the numerous cavalcade which encircled her two-wheeled screen. There was nobody who did not feel interested in her; but we had to leave the actual intercession in favour of the pretty girl to our beneficent friend, who from the moment that he had examined the humble vehicle more closely felt himself uneasy till he had effected its rescue. We retired into the background; he, however, inquired particularly into all the circumstances; it turned out that the young person, who belonged to Samogneux, had wished to avoid the impending confusion, by going to some friends who lived at a distance, but had flown straight into the jaws of danger. In cases of anxiety people are apt to fancy that any place is better than the one where they happen to be. In the kindest way possible it was made known to her that she must go back. Our captain, who at first suspected some espionage, allowed himself at length to be persuaded by the rhetoric of our benevolent comrade, who thereupon, accompanied by two hussars, conducted her, now less frightened, to her home. Shortly afterwards, when we passed through the place in military order, we saw her seated upon a low wall among her relations, and she saluted us gayly, and hopefully too, as her first adventure had ended so well.

Incidents of this kind sometimes occur in campaigns, when it is endeavoured to inspire confidence by means of temporary discipline, and a kind of compulsory peace is proclaimed in the midst of the confusion. These moments are invaluable both for the townspeople and the peasantry, and, indeed, for every one from whom the horrors of war have not robbed all belief in humanity.

A camp was formed on this side of Verdun, and we counted on a few days' rest.

On the morning of the 31st I was lying in the sleeping-carriage, certainly the driest, warmest, and most cheerful resting-place, half awake, when I heard something rustling against the leather curtains, and on opening them I perceived the Duke of Weimar, who introduced an unexpected stranger to me. I recognised at once the adventure-loving Grothhus, who, was even here inclined to sustain his character as partisan, and had come here in order to undertake the dubious task of summoning Verdun to surrender. In pursuance of which he had come to ask our Prince for a staff-trumpeter, who, rejoiced at this particular mark of distinction, was at once ordered to undertake the charge. We saluted each other very heartily in remembrance of old frolics, and Grothhus hastened to his task; which was afterwards the cause of many a jest. It was said that he had ridden down the high-road in front of the trumpeter, with the hussars behind him; that the Verdun people, however, in their character of *Sansculottes*, not knowing, or despising the law of nations, had fired upon him; that he had tied a white handkerchief to the trumpet, ordering it to be sounded louder and louder; that he had been met by a detachment, and led blindfolded and alone into the fortress, where he made some fine speeches, but effected nothing; and other things to a like effect; whereby, according to the world's way, they succeeded in throwing disparagement upon services performed, and diminishing the credit of him who had undertaken them.

Now as the fortress, as might have been expected, had refused to surrender on the first summons, it was necessary to proceed with the preparations for the bombardment. The day passed thus; meanwhile I transacted another little piece of business, the beneficial consequences of which extend to the present day. In Mainz, Herr von Stein had furnished me with Jäger's atlas, which exhibited, in a number of sheets, the present and, it was to be hoped, also the immediately succeeding "Theatre of the War." I took out one of them, the forty-eighth, within the area of which I had entered at

Longwy, and as there happened at the time to be an embosser among the Duke's people, it was cut out and mounted on canvas; it serves me still as a remembrance of those days, so full of importance for the world and for myself.

After these preparations for future advantage and present comfort, I went to have a look at the meadow on which we were encamped, and whence the tents extended as far as the hill. On the spacious green carpet before me a curious spectacle attracted my attention. A number of soldiers had formed themselves into a circle, and seemed to be engaged with something in the middle. On closer examination I found they had stationed themselves round a funnel-shaped depression in the ground, which was filled with the purest spring water, and might be about thirty feet in diameter at the top. It turned out that the soldiers were angling for a small kind of fish which abounded in the hole; they had brought tackle with them, together with their other baggage. The water was the clearest in the world, and the sport amusing enough to look at. But I had not been watching it long, before I remarked that there was a play of colours on the fish when in motion. At first, I took this appearance to be the changing colours of the movable little bodies; but a welcome explanation soon disclosed itself to me. A piece of earthenware had fallen into the hole, and from the depths the most beautiful prismatic colours presented themselves to my eye. Being clearer than the bottom, and brought closer to the eye, the edge furthest from me exhibited a blue and a violet colour; the nearest, a red and a yellow. When afterwards I moved round the spring, the phenomenon, of course in an experiment of this subjective description, followed me, and the colours appeared relatively always the same.

Being passionately attached to this subject, it gave me the greatest pleasure to see a phenomenon here, so vivid and natural in the open air, to observe which teachers of natural philosophy had, for nearly a hundred years, been in the habit of watching with their pupils in a dark room. I procured some more pieces of earthenware, which I threw in, and I could easily remark, that the appearance under the surface of the water commenced very soon, increased as the piece was sinking, and at last reached the bottom, a small white body coloured all over, and like a little flame. I then remembered that Agricola had already mentioned this appearance, and had been induced to class it among the fiery phenomena.

After dinner we rode up the hill which concealed the view of Verdun from our tents. We found the position of the town very pleasant, surrounded by meadows and gardens, in a cheerful plain, several branches of the Meuse flowing through it, and lying among hills both near and distant; as a fortress, it is exposed to a bombardment on every side. The afternoon was passed in erecting batteries, as the town had refused to surrender. With good telescopes, meanwhile, we inspected it, and could see distinctly what was going on on the rampart opposite to us, and noticed a number of people moving about, who appeared very busy at one particular place.

About midnight the bombardment commenced, both from the battery on the right bank and from the one on the left, which as it was the nearest, and made use of rockets, produced most effect. These tailed fire-meteors we quietly watched shooting through the air, and shortly afterwards saw part of the town in flames. Our telescopes, pointed in that direction, enabled us to observe these disasters in detail; we were able to see the people on the top of the walls exerting themselves actively to extinguish the flames; we could see the timbers that were still standing, and could distinguish them from those falling in. All this took place in the company both of acquaintances and of strangers; and all manner of unspeakable, often contradictory, observations were made, and widely different opinions were expressed. I had entered a battery which was hard at work, but the frightful thundering noise produced by the discharge of howitzers was intolerable to my peaceful ears, and I was soon obliged to retire. I then met Prince Reuss XIII., who had always been kind and gracious to me. We walked up and down behind some vineyard walls, protected by them from the balls which the besieged were incessantly hurling at us. After discussing sundry political matters, which only entangled us in a labyrinth of hopes and cares, the Prince asked me what I was busy with at present, and was much surprised when, instead of speaking of tragedies and novels, I began—excited by the phenomenon of the morning—to speak, with great animation, about the theory of colours. For it was the same with my investigations of natural phenomena as with my poems; I did not make them, but they made me.* The interest once excited maintained its sway; production took its own course, without allowing itself in the slightest degree to be interrupted by cannon-balls and balls of fire. The Prince requested me to inform him how I had come to take an interest in this subject, and herein the occurrence of the morning did me good service.

With such a man it did not require many words to show him that a lover of nature who is in the habit of passing his time in the open air, whether it be in a garden, in hunting, travelling, or campaigning, always finds leisure and opportunity sufficient to observe nature as a whole, and to make himself acquainted with phenomena of every kind. Now, the atmospheric air, vapours, rain, water, and the earth, present to us ever-varying appearances of colour, and this under such different conditions and circumstances, that one feels a desire to know them more accurately, to separate them from each other, to bring them under certain rubrics, and to search out their approximate and more distant relationship. By this means, I said, one gains new views in every department, totally different from the learning of schools and of printed traditions; our ancestors, with their senses highly cultivated, had observed things excellently, but had not inquired into them further or completed their observations; and had been still less successful in placing the phenomena in proper order, and bringing them under fitting rubrics.

These things were discussed while we walked up and down the wet grass: I was proceeding with my theory,

* This coincides with a remark of Goethe's mentioned by Eckermann in his 'Conversations with Goethe:' "All my poems are 'occasional' poems, suggested by real life, and have therein a firm foundation. I attach no value to poems snatched out of the air."

excited by the questions and remarks of the Prince, when the cold of the day-break drove us towards a bivouac of the Austrians, which had been kept up the whole night, and we found an enormous round fire, which was very acceptable under the circumstances. Engrossed with my subject, which I had been studying for the last two years, and which, therefore, was still fermenting in me in an immature state, I should scarcely have known whether the Prince was listening to me or not, if he had not occasionally interrupted me with some intelligent remarks, and in the end taken up my discourse, and encouraged me by approving of what I had said.

Indeed, I have always remarked that business men and men of the world, who have many things laid before them extempore, and consequently are always on their guard against being deceived, are much easier to talk to even on scientific matters than other men, because they keep their minds free, and listen to the person speaking without any other interest than a desire to get information; learned people generally will not listen to anything except what they have themselves learnt and taught, and about which they have become agreed with those of their own set. The subject is usurped by some word-credo, by which it is as well to abide as any other.

The morning was fresh but dry; we walked up and down, either being roasted or frozen, when all at once we saw something moving on the vineyard walls. It was a picket of riflemen, who had passed the night there, but now took up their muskets and knapsacks again, and were about to march down into the burnt suburbs, in order to annoy the ramparts from thence. They were, in all probability, about to encounter death, and yet kept singing very libertine songs, which were perhaps excusable in such a situation.

Scarcely had they left the place when I thought I remarked a very striking geological phenomenon on the wall where they had been stationed. I saw on the little limestone wall a cornice of bright green stones, exactly the colour of jasper, and was very much puzzled as to how such a remarkable kind of stone came to exist in such quantities in the middle of these limestone strata. I was undeceived, however, in a very peculiar way, for when approaching the spectre, I found it to be mouldy bread, which, being unfit for food, the riflemen had, in fun, cut down and spread out as an ornament upon the wall.

This immediately led us to talk about poisoning, which, ever since we had entered France, had been a subject of conversation; it had created a panic in the army, seeing that not only every piece of meat, but even the bread they baked themselves was suspected, although the fact of its becoming rapidly mouldy might be ascribed to natural causes.

It was the 1st of September, at eight o'clock in the morning, when the bombardment ceased, although balls still continued to be exchanged on both sides. The besieged had turned a twenty-four pounder against us, the shots from which were becoming unfrequent and fired more in jest than earnest.

Upon the open rising ground at the side of the vineyard, exactly in front of this enormous gun, two hussars were stationed on horseback, to observe attentively the town and the intermediate space. They remained at their post without being once attacked. As, however, on relieving guard, not only the number of men was increased, but, at the same moment, a number of lookers-on came running up, and a considerable knot of people was thus collected, the enemy held themselves ready to fire. I was standing at the moment with my back turned to the troop of hussars and people, about a hundred yards from them, talking to a friend, when all at once a dreadful, whistling, crashing sound came upon me from behind, which made me turn quickly round on my heel, without being able to say whether the movement was produced by the sound, the vibration of the air, or some inward psychical or moral cause. I saw the ball, a long way behind the crowd, which it had dispersed, rebounding through some hedges. With loud cries the people ran after it when it had ceased to be dangerous; nobody was hit; and those fortunate enough to get possession of this round lump of iron, carried it about in triumph.

Towards noon the town was summoned for the second time, and obtained twenty-four hours' respite. Of this we also availed ourselves to make our quarters somewhat more comfortable, to obtain provisions, and to have a ride about the country. I did not fail to return to the instructive spring, where I could now make my observations more quietly and deliberately; for the water had been quite emptied of fish; and was perfectly clear and undisturbed, allowing the play of the falling flames to be renewed at pleasure; and I was in the most pleasant mood. Some unlucky accidents happened shortly afterwards, and changed our condition, again giving it a warlike aspect. An officer of the artillery wished to water his horse; a want of water was general in the district; and my spring, which he passed, not being level enough, he proceeded to the Meuse which flowed close by, and there fell from a sloping bank and was drowned. His horse was saved, but he was carried past us dead.

Shortly after this a loud explosion was both seen and heard in the Austrian camp, on the hill before us; the report and the smoke recurred two or three times. In charging a bomb, through some carelessness, fire had broken out, and the greatest danger was apprehended; it had come in contact with some bombs already charged, and it was feared that all of them might explode. These apprehensions, however, were soon removed by the brave conduct of some of the imperial soldiers, who, disdaining the threatening danger, dragged out the powder and the filled bombs beyond the reach of the tents.

Thus passed another day; the following morning the town surrendered, and fell into our hands; but at the same time a trait of a republican character was presented to us. Commandant Beaurepaire, pressed by the distressed townspeople, who saw that their whole town would be in flames and in ruins with the continuance of the bombardment, could no longer refuse to surrender; but immediately after giving his vote for it in the town-hall, he drew out a pistol and shot himself, thus giving one more example of the highest patriotic devotion.

After this speedy capture of Verdun nobody doubted any longer that we should soon leave it behind, and compensate ourselves for our previous sufferings with the good wine of Châlons and Epernay. I, therefore, got my Jäger maps which showed the road to Paris cut out without delay, and carefully mounted upon canvas, with white paper pasted upon the back of them, as I had done with the first; this enabled me to consult them from day to day.

3rd September.

In the morning a party met to ride into the town, and I joined them. We found upon entering it the signs of great preparations that had been made early during the siege, and which seemed to indicate a more protracted resistance; the causeway had been dug up and heaped up against the houses, the wet weather making the streets therefore most unpleasant for walking. We visited the shops particularly celebrated for the sale of the best liqueurs of all kinds. We tried them all, and provided ourselves with a variety of sorts. There was one called *Baume humain*, less sweet, but stronger than the rest, and which had a peculiarly refreshing effect. The *dragées* also, small sugar-plums in neat cylindrical boxes, were not refused. Amidst such a profusion of good things, one naturally thought of the loved ones at home, to whom they would, no doubt, be a great treat on the peaceful banks of the Ilm. Small boxes were packed; some good-natured couriers, employed in carrying intelligence to Germany of the successes of the army up to that time, willingly took charge of some of these packages; thus the ladies at home might in all tranquillity satisfy themselves that we were pilgrims in a country where *esprit* and sweetness will never become extinct.

When, thereupon, we surveyed the half-ruined and desolate city, we were induced to repeat the observation that in cases of misfortune like those which man inflicts upon his fellow-man, as well as those which nature lays upon us, there are isolated cases which appear to be destiny—the intervention of some kind providence. We saw in the lower story of a corner house in the market-place a porcelain shop with a number of windows, and our attention was directed to the fact that a bomb, which had rebounded from the ground in the square, had struck the stone door-post, but had recoiled from it again, and taken another direction. The door-post, of course, was injured, but it had acted as a good defence. The brilliant rows of fragile porcelain were still standing in glittering splendour behind the clean bright windows.

At dinner, at the table-d'hôte, we were treated with good legs of mutton and wine from Bar, which must be drunk in the country itself, as it does not bear transporting. At these table-d'hôtes it is the custom to furnish spoons, but you get neither knives nor forks, which therefore one has to provide oneself with. Aware of this custom of the country, we had procured these articles in cases, flat and with ornamental workmanship on them. Some lively, active servant-girls waited on us, just as they had done a few days before on their own garrison.

At the capture of Verdun an occurrence happened, which, although an isolated case, created a great sensation, and excited general interest. Whilst the Prussians were marching in, a musket-shot was fired from the midst of a crowd of French people, which hurt nobody, but which daring act a French grenadier, who was accused of it, neither could nor wished to deny. At the guard-house to which he was brought I saw him myself; he was a very handsome, well-made young man, with a firm look and composed demeanour. Until his fate was decided he was allowed to stand free. Close to the guard-house was a bridge, under which flowed a branch of the Meuse; he mounted the parapet, remained quiet for a time, and then threw himself backwards into the abyss, and was taken out of the water dead.

This second heroic, ominous deed excited passionate hatred among the new Emigrants; and I heard otherwise sensible people declaring that honourable burial should not be granted either to this man or the commandant. They had expected a different state of feeling, and there did not appear as yet the slightest movement amongst the French troops to go over to us.

A better spirit, however, was aroused by the description of the King's reception in Verdun; fourteen of the most beautiful and accomplished young women had welcomed his Majesty with graceful speeches, flowers and fruit. His attendants, however, fearing poison, dissuaded him from tasting it; but the magnanimous monarch graciously accepted the welcome gifts, and unsuspectingly partook of the fruit. These charming children appeared to have inspired our young officers, too, with some degree of confidence; those among them who had had the good luck to be present at the ball, at all events could not cease talking of their amiability, grace, and good manners.

But for more solid enjoyments provision had likewise been made; for, as had been hoped and expected, excellent and abundant supplies were found in the fortress, and great despatch (perhaps too great) was manifested in making use of them. I could easily see that the men were not sufficiently frugal with the smoked bacon and beef, with the rice and lentils, and other good and necessary things, which seemed imprudent in our situation. It was amusing, also, to see how coolly an armoury or arsenal was plundered. Into one of the monasteries had been conveyed all kinds of armour, more of the ancient sort than modern, and many other curious things, with which man, when put upon his defence, wards off his assailant, or slays him.

This mild kind of plundering can be accounted for in the following way: after the capture of the town, the chief military people wished to satisfy themselves as to what supplies there were of all kinds, and repaired, amongst others, to this collection of arms, and while they claimed it for the general purposes of war, they found many other curious things which, very likely, took the fancy of the individual man, and no one could well be employed in the inspection of these weapons without being tempted to pick out something for himself. Now, this mode of procedure went through all ranks, till at last the collection was open almost to every one. Everybody gave the sentry stationed at the gate a small gratuity to be allowed to see the collection, and at the same time carried off anything that took his fancy. My servant, in this way, appropriated a long, flat stick, strongly and skilfully wound round with string, which at the first glance gave no indication of anything further; its weight, however, indicated more dangerous contents, and it proved to contain a very broad sword-blade four feet long, with which a strong hand could have done wonders.

Thus, between order and disorder, preserving things and destroying them, between plundering and paying, our time passed; and this may be one reason why war is so peculiarly injurious to the mind. One is daring and destructive one day, and humane and creative the next; one accustoms oneself to phrases adapted to excite and keep alive hope in the midst of the most desperate circumstances; this produces a kind of hypocrisy of an unusual character, and perfectly distinct from priestly, courtly hypocrisy, or whatever else it may be called.

A remarkable person I must mention, whom I saw at a distance behind the prison-railings; it was the postmaster of St. Menehould, who had been stupid enough to allow himself to be captured by the Prussians. He did not in any way avoid the looks of the curious, and appeared quite composed, notwithstanding the uncertainty of his fate. The Emigrants declared that he deserved a thousand deaths, and kept urging the highest authorities to that effect; to their credit, however, we must add, that in this as in other cases, they conducted themselves with becoming and dignified self-possession and equanimity.

4th September.

The many persons who kept going and coming enlivened our tents during the whole day; many things were related, discussed, and criticised, and the state of affairs was becoming more intelligible than before. It was the unanimous opinion that we must advance towards Paris as fast as possible. The fortresses of Montmedy and Sedan had been left unreduced on our flank, and little fear seemed to be entertained of the army stationed in that quarter.

La Fayette, who possessed the confidence of the soldiers, had been obliged to abandon the cause; he found himself forced to go over to the enemy, and to be treated as one. Dumourier, although as minister he had displayed insight in military affairs, had not distinguished himself in any campaign; and being promoted from a government office to the command-in-chief of the army, he appeared to evince the inconsistency and embarrassment to be expected at the moment. From the other side news of the melancholy occurrences, which had taken place in Paris in the middle of August, was brought to us, where, in defiance of the Brunswick manifesto, the King had been taken prisoner, dethroned, and treated as a criminal. The most detailed discussions, however, treated of what was most critical in the immediately impending military operations.

The forest-clad ridge of mountains, which forces the Aire to flow in a direction parallel to it from south to north, and is called the Forêt d'Argonne, lay immediately in our front, and checked our movements. Mention was often made of the Islettes, the important pass between Verdun and St. Menehould. No one could understand why it was not taken possession of, and why it had not been occupied before. The Emigrants were said to have taken it for a moment, without having been able to hold it. The garrison retreating from Longwy had, so much was known, retired into it; Dumourier also, whilst we were on the march to Verdun, and engaged with the bombardment of the town, had sent troops across the country, in order to strengthen this post, and to cover the right wing of his position behind Grandpré, in fact, to plant a second Thermopylæ in the way of the Prussians, Austrians, and Emigrants.

We confessed to one another the unsatisfactory nature of our situation, but had to reconcile ourselves to the dispositions made for marching the army, which was to have advanced straight forwards, without stopping, along the Aire in order to try its fortune upon the entrenched mountain defiles; and considering this state of things it was thought highly advantageous that Clermont had been wrested from the French, and was now occupied by Hessians, who, operating against the Islettes, would be able to annoy it, if not to carry it.

6th to 10th September.

In accordance with this view, the position of the camp was now changed, and was set behind Verdun. The head-quarters of the King, called Glorieux, and of the Duke of Brunswick, Regrets, gave occasion to some curious observations. I arrived myself at the first place by an unpleasant accident. The Duke of Weimar's regiment was to be stationed at Jardin Fontaine, near the town and the Meuse; we got safely out of the town by smuggling ourselves in among the string of vehicles of some unknown regiment and allowing ourselves to be carried along by it, although it was evident we were going too far. But, in fact, we should not have been able to get out of the line, without falling irrecoverably into the ditch. We looked right and left without discovering anything; we asked also, but received no answer, for all were strangers like ourselves, and full of ill humour at the situation. At length, having reached the top of a gentle eminence, I saw on the left, down below in a valley—which at a more favourable season would be pleasant enough— a pretty village, with castellated buildings, down to which luckily a smooth green strip of ground promised us an easy descent. I was all the more ready to leave the frightful track downhill, as I saw officers and men galloping about below, and baggage-waggons and carriages coming up. I suspected it to be one of the head-quarters, and so it turned out; it was Glorieux, the quarters of the King. But here also my question, as to where Jardin Fontaine lay, was made in vain. At last I fell in with a very messenger from heaven, with Herr von Alvensleben, who had previously shown me some kindness, and now directed me to follow the village road, which was unobstructed by carriages, along the valley to the town, then to make my way onwards to the left ; saying, that thus I should very soon discover Jardin Fontaine.

I succeeded in both, and found our tents pitched, but in the most dreadful situation; everything was sunk in bottomless mud, the rotten ropes of the tents giving way one after the other, and the canvas flapping about the shoulders and heads of those who thought of seeking shelter under them. For a time this was endured; however, at last it was decided that we should repair to the little town itself. We found the proprietor of a well-arranged house, with a court-yard, to be a good, facetious kind of man, who had formerly been a cook in Germany. He received us good-humouredly. There were some handsome cheerful rooms on the ground-floor, with a good fireplace, and everything else that was necessary for our comfort.

The suite of the Duke of Weimar was supplied from the royal kitchen; but our landlord begged that I would taste a specimen of his skill. He did, in fact, prepare a very savoury meal for me, which, however, made me very ill. Hence I too might have suspected poison, had it not occurred to me soon enough that it was garlic that had been used to make the dishes so tasty, a herb which, even in the smallest quantity, had generally the most powerful effect upon me. The mischief soon passed away, and I resolved all the more willingly to keep to German cooking as long as there was the smallest supply.

When we were about to depart, the good-humoured host gave my servant a letter, which he had previously spoken of, addressed to his sister in Paris, whom he wished particularly to recommend; but added good-naturedly, after some other observations: "You will, however, probably never get there."

11th September.

After several days of kind treatment we were again driven out into the most terrible weather; our way lay along the mountain ridge, which separated the waters of the Meuse and the Aire, and compels both to flow northwards. After great sufferings we arrived at Malancour, where we found empty cellars and kitchens untenanted, and were forced to content ourselves with being able to enjoy, under cover and on dry benches, the scanty provisions we had brought along with us. The arrangement of the dwellings themselves pleased me; it indicated the existence of quiet domestic comfort; everything was simple, natural, and adapted to meet the most immediate necessities. All this we had disturbed and were disturbing; for from the neighbourhood a cry of distress resounded against plunderers, whereupon, on hastening to the spot, we succeeded in quieting the disturbance, but not without some danger. It was strange enough to listen to the complaints of the poor, unclad delinquents, from whom we had torn cloaks and shirts, accusing us of barbarous cruelty, for not allowing them to cover their nakedness at the expense of the enemy.

We were, however, about to experience a still stranger reproach. On our return to our first quarters, we found a distinguished Emigrant whom we had formerly known. He was welcomed kindly, and did not despise our frugal meal; but some inward emotion was visible in him; he had evidently something at heart which he sought to give vent to by exclamations. When, for old acquaintanceship's sake, we tried to inspire him with some confidence in us, he denounced bitterly the cruelty of the King of Prussia to the French Princes.* Startled, almost confounded by this, we demanded some further explanation. Then we learnt that the King, on leaving Glorieux, in spite of the drenching rain, had put on no great coat or anything in the shape of a cloak, and consequently the Royal Princes had also been obliged to do without their weather-proof garments. Our Marquis could not bear to see these illustrious persons lightly clad, wet through and through, and dripping with rain; it put him in the greatest distress; indeed, if it would have been of any avail, he would have laid down his life to see them riding in a dry carriage—they, upon whom rested the hopes and happiness of the whole country, who were accustomed to such a different style of life.

We, of course, had nothing to reply to this; for to him there would have been no consolation in the reflection, that war, as a foretaste of death, makes all men equal, abolishes all property, and threatens even the most exalted personages with pain and danger.

12th September.

The next morning, however, I resolved, in respect of such distinguished examples, to leave my carriage, which,

* The French princes here referred to are the brothers of Louis XVI., the Duke of Provence, and the Count d'Artois: since the spring of 1791 they generally resided at Coblenz, and were now taking part in the campaign.

although a light one, was drawn by four requisitioned horses, under the protection of the trusty Chamberlain Wagner, who was ordered to bring the equipage and the very necessary ready money after us. I leaped upon my horse, joined some pleasant companions, and thus we betook ourselves on the march to Landres. We found on the way some bundles of faggots, from a small birchwood that had been cut down, the internal dryness of which soon overcame the outward moisture, and supplied us speedily with a blazing fire, and fuel sufficient both for warming ourselves and for cooking. But the good arrangements of a regimental mess were not visible; tables, chairs, and benches were wanting; and one had to shift for oneself standing, perhaps leaning against something, as best one could. However, the camp was safely reached towards the evening; we encamped not far from Landres, exactly opposite Grandpré, but knew very well how strongly and advantageously the pass was guarded. It rained incessantly, with occasional gusts of wind, the tent-coverings affording but little protection.

Happy is he, however, whose bosom is filled with some higher passion! The colour phenomenon at the spring had never for a moment left my thoughts during the last few days; I thought of it over and over again, in order that I might succeed in making some experiments with it. So I dictated a short account of it to Vogel, who in this case also proved himself a good secretary; I then sketched the figures beside it myself. These papers I possess still, with all the marks of the rainy weather, which are witnesses of my faithful study in the dubious path I had entered. The road to truth has this advantage, that we always like looking back to the uncertain steps we took, the circuitous paths we pursued, nay, even to our false steps.

The weather got worse, and became so bad during the night, that one felt oneself most fortunate in being able to spend it under cover of the regimental carriage. How fearful was our situation, considering that we were encamped in face of the enemy, and exposed to an attack at any point from the mountain and forest entrenchments!

From 13th till 17th September.

Wagner the Chamberlain, with the poodle, and the baggage, arrived in good time at our quarters. He had passed a fearful night; and after a thousand other hindrances had fallen away from the army in the dark, deceived by the sleepy and drunken servants of a General whom he had followed. They reached a village, and imagined the French quite near. Tormented by all kinds of alarms, and left without horses, which did not return after being taken to the water, he, nevertheless, contrived to get away from the ill-starred village; thus we found ourselves together again with all our movable goods and chattels.

At length we felt a kind of trembling sensation, which at the same time aroused a feeling of hope. A loud cannonade was heard on our right wing, and it was said that General Clairfayt had arrived from the Netherlands, and attacked the French on their left flank. There was the greatest anxiety everywhere to learn the result.

I rode to head-quarters to learn more accurately what the cannonade meant, and what, in fact, was to be looked for. Nothing was known there for certain, except that it must be General Clairfayt engaged with the French. I met Major von Weyrach, who, from impatience and ennui, was just mounting his horse to ride to the outposts; I accompanied him, and we soon reached a height where we had an extensive view. We came upon an outpost of hussars, and spoke to the officer, a young, goodlooking man. The cannonade was at a great distance, on the other side of Grandpré, and he had orders not to advance, as this might occasion some movement. We had not been speaking long before Prince Louis Ferdinand[*] came up with several attendants, and after a hasty salute, and some little talk with the officer, desired him to make an advance. The latter protested strongly against this; but the Prince paid no attention, and rode forwards, and we had all to follow. We had not gone far before a French rifleman was seen in the distance; he ran up to

---

[*] Son of Prince Ferdinand of Prussia, who was brother of Frederick the Great.

within musket-shot, and then, turning round, disappeared as fast as he had come. After him came a second, then a third, and in the same way disappeared again. The fourth, however, who was the same probably as the first, fired his musket very deliberately at us, and we could distinctly hear the ball whistle past us. The Prince was not to be deterred, and the riflemen, too, continued their operations, so that several shots were fired whilst we pursued our way. I had often looked at the officer, who hesitated between his duty and the respect due to a Royal Prince. No doubt he noticed some sympathy in my looks, and rode up to me and said : " If you have any influence with the Prince, beseech him to turn back ! He is putting me in the most difficult position. I have the strictest orders not to leave my appointed post; and nothing can be more reasonable that we should not provoke the enemy, encamped, as he is, in a strong position behind Grandpré. If the Prince does not turn, the whole chain of outposts will soon be alarmed; at head-quarters no one will know what it means, and the blame will all fall upon me, without my being at fault." I rode up to the Prince, and said: " The honour has just been done me of being supposed to have some influence with your Highness, hence I beg a gracious hearing." I laid the whole affair clearly before him, which seemed scarcely necessary, for he saw it himself, and was good-natured enough to turn back immediately with some kind words; whereupon the riflemen also disappeared, and ceased firing. The officer thanked me most cordially, showing that a mediator is welcome everywhere.

The situation gradually became intelligible. The position of Dumourier at Grandpré was exceedingly strong and advantageous; that he could not be attacked on his right wing was well known; on his left were two important passes—La Croix aux Bois, and Le Chesne le Populeux, both of them well barricaded, and considered inaccessible; but Le Chesne was entrusted to an officer who was either unfit for such a post, or neglected his duty. The Austrians attacked him. At the first charge the Prince de Ligne, the son, was killed, but the attack was successful; the post was overpowered, and Dumourier's great plan frustrated. He was forced to abandon his position, and to march up the Aisne; Prussian hussars were now able to advance through the pass and pursue him on the other side of the forest of Argonne. This caused such a panic in the French army, that ten thousand men fled before five hundred, and were with difficulty made to halt and rally again. The regiment Chamborand particularly distinguished itself here, and checked the further advance of our troops; they had been sent out only for the purpose of reconnoitering, and returned in high spirits, as they had succeeded in capturing several waggon-loads of good booty. Things for ordinary use, such as money and clothes, they had divided among themselves; the papers, however, fell to my share, as a literary man; among them I found some previous orders of Lafayette, and several very fairly written lists. But what most of all surprised me was, a pretty recent number of the *Moniteur*. The type and form of this paper, with which I had been acquainted for several years past uninterruptedly, and which I had now not seen for some weeks, greeted me in a somewhat unpleasant way, for in a laconic article under 3rd September, were the menacing words: " *Les Prussiens pourront venir à Paris ; mais ils n'en sortiront pas.*" Hence, Paris, it seemed, did consider it possible that we might get there; but as to our return, some higher power would have to manage that.

The frightful condition in which we found ourselves, between sky and earth, was in some degree alleviated when we saw the army in motion, and one division of the avant-guard after the other marching forwards. At length our time came also ; we marched over hills, through valleys, and past vineyards where we found something to revive us. Then, with better weather, we got into more open country, and saw, in a cheerful part of the Aire valley, the castle of Grandpré, finely situated on a height, at the point where this river forces its way westwards between the hills, and on the other side of the mountain joins the Aisne, whose waters, flowing westwards, finally, fall into the Seine with the Oise. From this it is evident that the mountain ridge which separated us from the Meuse, although not of any considerable height, exercised a decisive influence upon the water courses, and brought us into the region of other rivers.

On this march I got accidentally among the attendants of the King, afterwards of those of the Duke of Brunswick; I conversed with Prince Reuss and other diplomatico-military acquaintances. The masses of horsemen formed a rich decoration to the pleasing landscape; one could have wished a Van der Meulen* had been there to immortalise the march; all was cheerful, lively, full of confidence, and heroic. Some villages in front were indeed in flames; but in a war picture smoke has not a bad effect. The people, it was said, had fired out of the houses on the advanced guard, and they, in accordance with the laws of war, had exercised their right to avenge themselves. They were blamed, but things could not be altered; on the other hand, the vineyards were protected; but there was no prospect of a good vintage to the proprietors. And thus, among peaceful and warlike occurrences, we pursued our onward course. Leaving Grandpré behind us, we reached and crossed the Aisne, and encamped near Vaux les Mourons; here we were in the much-abused Champagne, but, as yet, things did not look so very bad. Over the water, on the sunny side, lay some well-cultivated vineyards; and, on inspecting the villages and barns, sufficient provision was found both for men and beasts; unfortunately, however, the wheat was not threshed out, nor was there a sufficient number of mills. Ovens for baking were also rare; and thus our situation began really to resemble that of Tantalus.

———

18th September.

A large party assembled to discuss the state of affairs, in fact, they generally met when there was a halt, and always in a friendly sort of way, particularly when coffee was served after dinner. The party consisted of a number of curious elements: Germans and Frenchmen, military

* Anton Franz van der Meulen (1634-1690), a somewhat important painter of battle-pieces, accompanied Louis XIV. on his campaigns. Two of his most famous paintings are his " Entry of Louis XIV. into Arras " and his " Siege of Maestricht."

men and diplomatists, all persons of some note, experienced, shrewd, clever, and excited by the importance of the moment; all men of character and weight, but still not admitted into the privy councils, and consequently all the more anxious to ascertain what had been decided upon, and what was likely to happen.

Dumourier, when he could no longer maintain the pass of Grandpré, had marched up the Aisne, and as his rear was secured by the Islettes, he took up a position on the heights of St. Menehould, fronting France. We had advanced through the narrow pass, and had in our rear and on our flank the uncaptured fortresses of Sedan, Montmedy, and Stenay, which could intercept all access to us according to their pleasure.

We were entering a singular kind of country, the inhospitable chalk soil of which afforded only a scanty subsistence to some widely-scattered villages. Rheims, Châlons, and their rich environs, were not far off, it is true; and abundance of good things could be hoped for in our front; our party, therefore, was almost unanimously of opinion that we must march upon Rheims, and take possession of Châlons; Dumourier would then be unable to remain in his advantageous position, a battle would be inevitable somewhere; in fact, the victory was already considered certain.

19th September.

Many doubts, therefore, were felt when, on the 19th, we were ordered to direct our march upon Massiges, to follow the course of the Aisne upwards, and to keep this stream as well as the forest-clad mountains on our left, either near or at a distance.

We cast off these critical reflections by interesting ourselves in the numerous accidents and occurrences which happened on the way. A singular phenomenon engrossed my attention completely. In order to push forward several columns together, one of them was led right across some fields, over low-lying hills; and when they were about to descend into the valley again, they found a steep declivity in their way. This was immediately made as level as possible, but remained steep enough still. At noon the sun shone brightly forth and was reflected upon all the arms. I kept upon a hill, and saw this glittering river of arms advancing, glistening in the sunlight; the effect was quite surprising when the column reached the steep declivity, for the hitherto closed ranks here separated at a bound, and each man made his way to the bottom singly as best he could. This confusion created a spectacle exactly like a waterfall; innumerable bayonets intermingled, flashing to and fro, presented the liveliest commotion. And when they formed again at the bottom into rank and file, and marched forwards into the valley, in the same order as they had arrived at the top, the resemblance to a river became more vivid still. The sight was rendered the more pleasing as it was favoured by uninterrupted bright sunshine throughout; we learnt its value in critical circumstances, after the late long-continued rains.

In the afternoon we arrived at Massiges, only a few leagues' distance from the enemy; the camp was marked out, and we occupied the place assigned to us. Stakes were already stuck in the ground, the horses tied to them, a fire was lit and the cooking-carriages opened, when, quite unexpectedly, the report was spread that no encampment was to be made there. Information had arrived that the French army was marching from St. Menehould upon Châlons; that the King intended to prevent their escape, and had given orders to break up. I inquired about the truth of this at the proper quarter, and heard what I had already been told, with this in addition: that, upon receiving this uncertain and improbable intelligence, the Duke of Weimar and General Heymann had gone to the front with the hussars who had raised the report. After some time the Generals came back, and assured us that there was not the slightest movement to be observed; and the patrols were obliged to confess that they had inferred rather than seen what they had reported.

The movement, however, had commenced, and the order was for the army to advance, but without the smallest portion of the baggage; vehicles of every description were to return to Maison Champagne, to form a waggon-bulwark, and await the presumed successful issue of a battle.

Without a moment's hesitation as to what I should do, I committed carriage, baggage, and horses, to my resolute servant, and forthwith started off on horseback with my military comrades. It had often been the subject of conversation, that any one who joins a campaign should remain throughout with the regular troops, with whichever division he may have attached himself, and shun no danger; for whatever may happen is honourable, whereas to remain with the baggage is both dangerous and contemptible; hence I had arranged with the officers of the regiment that I should always accompany them, and, if possible, the first squadron, and thus kept on the best terms with them. Our way led through the most melancholy of valleys, up the little stream La Tourbe, between some low-lying hills, without a tree or a bush: orders and injunctions were given to march with as little noise as possible, as if we were going to surprise the enemy; who, however, from his position, was no doubt able to observe the approach of a mass of fifty thousand men. Night came on; neither moon nor stars were shining in the heavens, the wind was howling dismally; the silent movement of so large a body of men in profound darkness had a most singular effect.

In riding alongside the column, one met occasionally officers of one's acquaintance, galloping to and fro, sometimes to accelerate the movement of the troops, at others to retard it. Words were exchanged, horses brought to a stand, and sometimes several collected together. In this way a circle of perhaps twelve, partly acquaintances and partly strangers, would come together. All sorts of questions, complaints, and expressions of surprise would be uttered, together with grumblings and reasonings; the General was not to be forgiven the interruption of the dinner. One facetious fellow expressed a wish to have sausages and bread, another immediately raised his wishes to venison and anchovy salad; as, however, all this was done without any paying, there was no want of orders for tarts and other dainties, nor for expensive wines; and such a perfect meal was thus arranged, that at last one of the party, whose appetite had been excited beyond all bounds, began to swear at the whole party, and declared the torment of an excited imagination as insupportable in contrast with the scarcity that prevailed. After a while all were scattered again, and each singly was no better off than they had been altogether.

19th September, at night.

Thus we arrived at Somme Tourbe, where a halt was called; the King had retired to an hotel, before the door of which the Duke of Brunswick had established his headquarters and offices in a kind of shed. The ground was spacious; several fires were burning, fed by large bundles of vine-stakes. The Prince Field-marshal complained several times that the flames were made to blaze up too much; we talked the matter over, and nobody could bring himself to believe that our presence had remained a secret to the French.

I had arrived late, and, wherever I looked I found everything already appropriated, if not consumed. While I was thus searching about, I saw a sight which showed me what clever cooks the Emigrants were; they were sitting round a large circular, flat heap of smouldering ashes, in which many a vine-stake had been burnt; they had cleverly and quickly got possession of all the eggs in the village, and it was really a tempting sight to see the eggs standing upright in the ashes, and taken out one after the other, when ready to be eaten.

I knew none of the noble assistants in the cooking, and unknown I did not like to address them ; as, however, at the moment I met a favourite acquaintance, who was suffering like myself from hunger and thirst, I bethought me of a plan which had been suggested by an observation made during my short military career. I had remarked that whilst foraging in the villages, the men generally went very clumsily to work; those who came first fell to, plundered, destroyed, demolished ; the next comers found less and less, and what was lost was of no use to anybody. I had already thought that a more skilful plan might be adopted, and when the crowd was pressing forward in front a search might be made in an opposite direction. This could scarcely be done here, for every place was overflowing; but the village was a very long one, and lay chiefly on one side of the street by which we had entered. I asked my friend to go down the long street with me. Out of the last house but one came a soldier swearing that everything was consumed, and not a thing more to be had. We looked through the window and saw some riflemen sitting within very composedly; we entered, in order that we might have, at all events, a bench to sit upon and be under cover; we saluted them as comrades, and complained of course of the general scarcity. After some conversation, they asked us if we would promise to keep a secret, which we did by giving them our hands; whereupon they told us that they had found in the house a capital well-filled cellar, the entrance into which they had themselves concealed, but that they had no wish to refuse us a share of the supply. One of them drew out a key, and, on removing some obstructions, a cellar-door was found. On descending, we found several casks on the floor; but what was of more interest to us, there were various partitions full of bottles filled and laid in sand, where our good-natured comrade, who had already tried them all, pointed out the best sort. I took two bottles between the fingers of each hand, and drew them under my cloak; my friend did the same; and thus in hopes of soon getting something to refresh us, we strode up the street again.

Now close to the large watch-fire I saw a heavy, strong harrow, and sat down upon it, pushing the bottles under my cloak between its spikes. After a little while I brought out one bottle, which caused exclamations from my neighbours, to whom I offered a share. They took good pulls at it, the last one somewhat modestly, as he saw very well that there was but little left for me. I hid the bottle beside me, and soon afterwards brought out.
second, drank to my friends, who were well pleased to taste it again, but did not at first observe the seeming miracle; at the third bottle, however, loud were their exclamations about the conjuror; and in our melancholy situation the joke was welcome in every respect.

Among the numerous persons whose figures and faces were lit up by the fire, I perceived an elderly man whom I thought I knew. Upon inquiring, and approaching him, he was not a little astonished to find me here. It was the Marquis de Bombelles, whom I had met two years before in Venice, when there with the Duchess Amalia; he had been residing there as French Ambassador, and had done everything in his power to make the visit of this excellent Princess as pleasant as possible. Exclamations of surprise on both sides, joy at meeting again, and recollections of former times enlivened the present solemn moment. His splendid residence on the grand canal became the subject of conversation, and mention was made of the very hospitable reception he gave us, when we visited him in gondolas, and of his having contributed so much to the entertainment of the lady and her friends, by the little fêtes he gave, which were quite in keeping with the taste and fancy of one who was a lover both of Nature and of Art, of cheerfulness and decorum; and further, of his having procured for them the enjoyment of things from which visitors to Venice were usually excluded.

How surprised I was, however, when I heard the man, whom I supposed would be over-joyed by my genuine panegyric, exclaim sorrowfully: "Let us be silent about these things! those times lie too far in the past; for even when I was entertaining my noble guests with apparent cheerfulness the worm was gnawing at my heart; I foresaw the consequences of what was taking place in my native land. I admired the lightness of heart which prevented you from having any forebodings of the danger which was impending over you as well; I was preparing myself in silence for a change in my condition. Soon afterwards I was obliged to abandon my honourable post, to leave Venice, and to commence my wanderings, which have at length led me here."

The air of secrecy which, from time to time, it was endeavoured to give to this uncovered march, made us suspect that, before the night was over, we should break up and go forward; but the dawn came, and with it a drizzling rain began to fall; it was quite daylight before we were in motion. As the Duke of Weimar's regiment formed the vanguard, some hussars, who were acquainted with the road to our destination, were made to accompany the first squadron as the foremost of the whole column. We now advanced, sometimes at a sharp trot, over fields and hills without a bush or tree; in the distance only, to our left, we saw the Argonne forest; the drizzling rain struck more sharply in our faces; but shortly afterwards we perceived an avenue of very fine poplars, which lay directly across our path. It was the high road from Châlons to St. Menehould, being the way from Paris to Germany; we were led across it, and away into unknown regions.

Some time before this we had seen the enemy, encamped and drawn up in front of the forest, and could also perceive that fresh troops were arriving; it was Kellermann, who was just about to join Dumourier, in order to form his left wing. Our troops were most eager to pounce upon the French, officers as well as men were most ardent in their desire that the General should instantly make the attack; our rapid advance, too, seemed to indicate that such was his intention. But Kellermann had placed himself in too favourable a position; thereupon commenced the cannonade of which so much has been spoken, but the violence of which at the time it is impossible to describe, or even to recall in the imagination.

The high road was already a long way behind us, and we kept storming towards the west, when all at once an adjutant came galloping up, ordering us to go back again; we had been led too far, and were now ordered to recross the road, and to draw up with our right flank close upon the left side of it. This was done, and we thus made front against the outwork La Lune, which was seen on a hill, about a mile before us, close to the road. Our commander came up to us, bringing with him the half of a horse-battery; we received orders to go forwards under cover of it, and came upon an old driver of the baggage-waggons, lying stretched upon the ground, the first victim of the day. We rode on unconcerned, and had a nearer view of the outwork, the battery erected there was firing away fiercely.

Soon, however, we found ourselves in a curious situation;

cannon-balls were flying wildly amongst us, without our being able to make out whence they came; for we were advancing behind a friendly battery, and the hostile guns on the opposite hills were much too distant to be able to reach us. I kept to one side of the front, and had the most extraordinary view: balls were falling by dozens in front of the squadron, not rebounding, luckily, for they sank into the soft ground; but mud and dirt bespattered man and horse; the black horses, admirably held together by their gallant riders, snorted and plunged; the whole mass, without separating or falling into confusion, fluctuated to and fro.

A curious sight brought other times to my remembrance. In the first rank of the squadron the standard was waving to and fro in the hands of a handsome boy;* he held it firmly, but was being unwillingly shaken by his furious horse; his sweet face, singularly but naturally enough, even at this fearful moment, brought the still sweeter face of his mother up before me; and I could not help thinking of the peaceful moments I had spent in her presence.

At length came the command to go back, and down the hill: this was done by all the cavalry regiments with great order and steadiness; only a single horse, Von Lottum's, was killed, although the rest of us, particularly those on the outside of the right wing, ought all, properly speaking, to have been killed.

After we had withdrawn out of the range of the inexplicable fire, and had recovered from our surprise and astonishment, the riddle was solved: we found the half battery, under whose cover we fancied we were marching, far down in a hollow, of which there are a great many in this district. It had been dislodged from above, and had gone down into a ravine on the other side of the road, and thus we had not remarked its retreat. Hostile guns took its place; and what was intended for our protection, very nearly became the means of our destruction. The fellows only laughed at us when we

* This was Emil von Bechtoldsheim. See Düntzer's *Goethe und Karl August.*

reproached them, and assured us, jestingly, that it was much better down here in the penthouse.

When, however, we afterwards saw with our eyes how this horse-battery had had wearily to be dragged across terrible marshy hills, we could not but again reflect upon the critical situation into which we had brought ourselves.

Meanwhile the cannonade continued without interruption. Kellermann occupied a dangerous post at a mill by Valmy, at which point the fire was principally directed; a powder-waggon exploded there, and we rejoiced in the mischief which was thus probably caused to the enemy. Hence all those who were exposed to the fire and those who were not, remained, properly speaking, merely spectators and listeners. We kept upon the road from Châlons, and halted near a signpost which pointed out the road to Paris.

This city, therefore, we now had in our rear, and the French army stood between us and our native land. Stronger barricades were, perhaps, never placed in any path, and they caused the greatest apprehension to one who had been for four weeks incessantly studying a map of the theatre of the war.

However, the necessities of the moment make good their claims even in spite of dangers that might be impending. Our hussars had been lucky enough to capture several waggons of bread, which were on their way from Châlons to the army, and brought them up along the high road. Now, in the same way, as it appeared strange to us to be posted between Paris and St. Menehould, the people at Châlons could never imagine that the enemy would be found on the road leading to their army. For a few pieces of money the hussars gave up a part of the bread; it was of the finest white kind; a Frenchman is terrified at a morsel of black. I distributed more than one loaf among my immediate followers, upon condition that they would keep a share for me during the ensuing days. I found occasion for another piece of foresight. A rifleman belonging to the retinue had likewise purchased of these hussars a thick woollen blanket; I came to an agreement with him, that he should let me have it for three consecutive nights, every night for eight pence, and that he should have it during the daytime. He considered the bargain a very advantageous one; the blanket had cost him a florin, and in a short time he would have it back again with interest. However, I had also reason to be satisfied; my precious woollen coverings from Longwy had remained behind with the baggage; and now, amid the general want of shelter and covering, I had obtained a second protection besides my cloak.

All·this took place with the uninterrupted accompaniment of the thundering of the cannons on each side; this day ten thousand shots were fired, by which, on our side, only twelve hundred men fell, and these, moreover, to no purpose. The sky was cleared by the tremendous concussion; for the cannon were fired exactly as if it had been platoon firing, irregularly, stopping, and then commencing again. At one o'clock, at noon, after a pause of some duration, the cannonading was at its height; the earth literally trembled, and still there was not the slightest change in the positions. Nobody knew what would be the result.

I had heard so much about cannon-fever, that I wanted to know what kind of thing it was. Ennui, and a spirit which danger of any kind excites to daring, nay, even to rashness, induced me to ride up composedly to the outwork of La Lune. This was again occupied by our people; but it presented the wildest aspect. The roofs were shot to pieces, stacks of corn scattered about, men mortally wounded lay stretched upon them here and there, and occasionally a spent cannon-ball fell and rattled among the ruins of the roofs.

Being quite alone, and left to myself, I rode away along the heights to the left, and could plainly survey the favourable position of the French; they were standing in the form of a semicircle, in the greatest composure and security; Kellermann, on the left wing, was the easiest to reach.

I fell in with good company on the way; officers of my acquaintance, belonging to the general staff and the regiment, and greatly surprised to find me here. They wanted to take me back with them; but I told them I had a special object in view, and they left me, without further discussion, to my well-known but strange caprices.

I had now got right into the region where the balls came playing across: the sound of them is curious enough, and seemed composed of the buzz of humming-tops, the gurgling of water, and the whistling of birds. The balls were less dangerous by reason of the wetness of the ground; wherever one fell it stuck fast. And thus my fool-hardy ride in search of experience was secured at least against the danger of the balls rebounding.

In the midst of these circumstances, I soon remarked that something unusual was affecting me; I paid close attention to it, and still the sensation can be described only by similitude. It seemed as if I were in some extremely hot place, and quite penetrated by the heat of it, and felt as it were altogether one with the element in which I was. My eyes lost nothing of their strength or clearness of sight, but it seemed to me as if the world had a kind of brown-red tint, which made the situation, as well as the surrounding objects, look more terrible. I was unable to perceive any agitation of my blood; but everything seemed rather to be swallowed up in the glow of which I speak. From this it is clear in what sense the condition can be called a fever. It is remarkable, however, that the feeling of horror and anxiety arising from it is produced in us solely through the ears. For the thunder of the cannons, the howling, whistling, and crashing of the balls through the air, is the actual cause of these sensations.

After I had ridden back, and was again in perfect security, I remarked with surprise that the glow in me was completely extinguished, and not the slightest feverish agitation was left. This condition is moreover one of the least desirable; and, indeed, among my dear and noble comrades, there was scarcely one who expressed a sincere wish for it.

Thus the day had passed away; the French stood immovable, Kellermann* having acquired a more advantageous position. Our people were withdrawn from the fire, and it was exactly as if nothing had happened. The greatest consternation was diffused amid the army.

* During the night Kellermann had occupied the heights south of the Aire, and hence there was no possibility of the Prussians being able to make a successful attack.

That very morning they had thought of nothing short of spitting all the French, and of devouring them; nay, I myself had been tempted to take part in this dangerous expedition from the unbounded confidence I felt in our army and in the Duke of Brunswick. Now, every one went about solitarily, no one looked at his neighbour, or if it did happen, it was but to curse, or to swear. Just as night was coming on, we had accidentally formed ourselves into a circle, in the middle of which not even the usual fire could be kindled; most were silent, only a few conversed, in fact, the power of reflection and judgment seemed to be wanting in every one. At last I was called upon to say what I thought of the state of affairs; for I had been in the habit of enlivening and amusing the party with brief remarks. This time I said: "From this place and from this day forth commences a new era in the world's history, and you can all say that you were present at its birth."*

At such times, when nobody had anything to eat, I claimed a morsel of the bread captured in the morning; there was also remaining about as much as would fill a brandy-bottle of the wine so freely used the day before; and I had, therefore, completely to abandon the part of conjuror so boldly played while seated at the fire the night before.

The cannonade had scarcely ceased when rain and wind again commenced, and made our condition most uncomfortable on the spongy clay soil, exposed as we were to the weather. However, as a natural result of long watching and agitation of mind and body, sleep asserted her empire as night drew near. We had lain down behind an elevated part of the ground, which protected us from the cutting wind, when it occurred to somebody that for this night we should bury ourselves in the earth, and cover ourselves with our cloaks. Preparations were immediately made for this, and several holes were dug with implements supplied by the horse artillery. The Duke of Weimar even did not despise this kind of premature burial.

* "Goethe," says Hempel, "no doubt meant by this that as the Allies had not been victorious, the real power of the Revolution would now begin in good earnest, and moreover try its influence upon the other countries of Europe."

I now demanded, on payment of eight pence, the blanket mentioned above, wrapped myself in it, and spread my cloak over me, without feeling its dampness much. Ulysses,* I am sure, did not repose with greater comfort and satisfaction in the cloak which he obtained in a similar way.

All these preparations were made contrary to the wish of the Colonel, who called our attention to the fact that the French had a battery upon the opposite hill, behind a copsewood, with which they could bury us in real earnest, and annihilate us at their pleasure. But we were loath to abandon the sheltered spot and our sagaciously invented snuggery; and this was not the last time I had occasion to remark that people do not avoid danger to put themselves to inconvenience.

21st September.

The salutations exchanged by the awakened sleepers were by no means joyous or cheerful; for all were conscious of being in a disgraceful and hopeless situation. We found ourselves stationed on the edge of a huge amphitheatre, on the other side of which the enemy formed a semicircle, extending farther than the eye could reach, upon heights which were secured by rivers, ponds, brooks, and morasses, at their feet. We, on our side, stood exactly as we did the day before, lighter by ten thousand cannonballs, but not a whit better for the attack; we looked down into a wide arena, where the hussars of both armies kept chasing each other about among the cottages and gardens, and in their skirmishes, hour after hour, contrived to engage the attention of the spectators. But from this galloping to and fro, and popping at each other, there was no result except that one of our people, who had ventured too boldly within the enclosures, was surrounded and shot, as he obstinately refused to surrender.

This was the only victim of this day's operations; but our uncomfortable, oppressive, and helpless situation was

---

* This can only refer to the meeting of Odysseus with Nausikaa, although the comparison does not quite tally; for in the Odyssey, Odysseus receives the mantle from Nausikaa as a gift, and he does not lie down under it, but, adorned with it, proceeds to the palace of Alkinoos.

rendered more melancholy and frightful still by the prevailing sickness.*

However venturesome and ready for battle all had been the day before, it was now confessed that a suspension of hostilities was desirable; for, on reflection, even the boldest and most passionate were obliged to declare that an attack would be the greatest possible madness. Opinions wavered throughout the day, during which, to save appearances, the same position was maintained as during the time of the cannonade; towards evening, however, it was slightly changed, the head-quarters being ultimately established at Hans, and the baggage carried there. We now heard of the alarm, the danger, and the destruction which had nearly befallen our servants and effects.

The wooded heights of Argonne, from St. Menehould to Grandpré, were occupied by the French; from whence their hussars carried on a most daring and annoying little warfare. We had learnt yesterday that a secretary of the Duke of Brunswick, and some other followers of the Prince, had been taken prisoners between the army and the bulwark of waggons. The latter, however, did not in the least deserve the name of a bulwark, for it was badly constructed, was not enclosed, and had not a sufficient escort. They had been alarmed by one unaccountable noise after the other, as well as by the cannonade, which was not far distant. Afterwards they were deceived by the report, or fact, that the French troops had come down from the forests, and been on the way to seize the whole of the baggage; and General Kalkreuth's runner, who had been taken prisoner and again liberated, took great credit to himself for what he had done, declaring that he had prevented an attack from the enemy by some successful lies he had invented about numerous escorts, mounted batteries, and the like. Possibly enough! Who is there that has not done something, or has not something to do, in moments of such importance?

Tents, carriages, and horses we now had; but not a bit of

* Recent accounts agree in thinking that the indecision of the Duke of Brunswick, and the feeling of discouragement in the army, to which the disappointment gave rise, were greater evils than the unfortunate position of the moment, from which successful enterprises might nevertheless have been made.

food for any living thing. Although the rain was falling, we were in want of water; and some of the ponds were polluted by the bodies of dead horses which had fallen into them. All this together made the situation most frightful. I could not understand what he meant when I saw my faithful pupil, servant, and companion, Paul Götze, busily baling off the water collected on the leather covering of the travelling carriage; he then told me he wanted it for preparing some chocolate, a supply of which he had luckily brought along with him. In fact, I have seen some persons scooping out the water from the horses' footmarks to quench their burning thirst. Bread was bought from the older soldiers, who were accustomed to fasting, and were laying by money, in order to cheer themselves with brandy, if any again were to be had.

22nd September.

We heard that Generals Manstein and Heymann were at Dampiere, at the head-quarters of Kellermann, where Dumourier also was expected. Their apparent object was, to effect an exchange of prisoners, and make proper provision for the sick and wounded; but they really expected to effect an entire change in the present disastrous state of affairs. Since the tenth of August the King of France had been taken prisoner, and innumerable massacres had taken place in September. It was known that Dumourier was in favour of the King and Constitution; he would therefore be obliged, for his own safety and security, to oppose the present state of things; and a great event, indeed, it would have been if he had joined the Allies and advanced upon Paris.

Since the arrival of the equipage the quarters of the Duke of Weimar were much improved, for it must be acknowledged that the chamberlain, the cook, and other household officials, never were without provisions, and even during the greatest scarcity always supplied us with some kind of warm food. Refreshed by it, I rode about the country, in order to make myself acquainted with it, but without success; those flat hills possessed no striking characteristics, not any one object seemed to be in any way distinguished from the rest. To ascertain, however, whereabouts I was, I looked for the long avenue of tall poplars, which had been a striking object the day before; not finding it, I thought I had wandered far out of my way; but on closer examination I found that it had been cut down, carried away, and was, no doubt, already burnt.

The places within the cannons' range presented a horrible aspect. Men were lying unburied, and beasts writhing in pain and unable to die. I saw one horse whose fore-feet had become entangled in its own entrails that projected from its body, and was limping about in this awful manner.

In riding back, I met Prince Louis Ferdinand in the open field, sitting upon a wooden chair, which had been brought up from a village in the plain; at the same time some of his people were dragging up a kitchen cupboard, containing, they asserted, something that rattled, and they were in hopes of having captured a rich prize. They broke it open eagerly, but found only a thick cookery-book; and thereupon, while the shattered cupboard was blazing in the fire, they read aloud the precious cookery receipts, which so excited their imaginations, that hunger and want were again raised to the pitch of desperation.

24th September.

The worst possible weather was rendered, in some measure, less dismal by the news that a suspension of hostilities was decided upon, and that there was the prospect of being able to suffer and starve at least in some tranquillity. But this served only partially to console us, for we soon heard that the agreement was merely that the outposts should cease fighting, and that, with this exception, it was not forbidden to prosecute the operations at pleasure. This condition was properly in favour of the French, who could change their position in all directions round about, and hem us in more closely; whereas we, in the centre, were compelled to keep stationary, and remain in our position. The outposts, however, gladly availed themselves of this order. At first they agreed among one another that whichever side had the wind and weather in their faces should be entitled to turn round, and, wrapped

in their cloaks, have nothing to fear from the other.
They went even further; the French had still some
small supply of food, whereas the Germans were in want of
everything; the former, therefore, bestowed a portion of
theirs upon the latter, and they grew more friendly every
moment. At length printed papers were handed about
good-naturedly on the part of the French, proclaiming the
blessings of freedom and equality to the good Germans,
in two languages; the French imitating the manifesto
of the Duke of Brunswick in an inverted sense, offered
good will and hospitality; and as greater numbers had
taken the field than they knew how to manage, this proclamation, at least for the present, tended more to weaken
the enemy than strengthen themselves.

24th September.

As companions in distress at this time, I could not help
pitying two handsome boys of about fourteen or fifteen
years of age. They had been put in requisition with four
light horses to drag my little carriage, and suffered in
silence more for their horses than themselves; but it was
as difficult to help them as the rest of us. As they were
enduring all these hardships on my account, I felt bound
to do something for them, and wished to divide the commissariat bread before mentioned with them; but they
refused it, and assured me that they could not eat that
kind of bread; and when I asked what they ate in ordinary times, they replied: " *Du bon pain, de la bonne soupe, de
la bonne viande, de la bonne bière.*" So, as everything with
them was good, and everything with us was bad, I forgave
them freely, but they shortly afterwards made their escape,
leaving their horses behind. They had endured much
misery; but I think it was the commissariat bread, like
a frightful spectre, which induced them, to take the last
decisive step. White and black bread is properly the
shibboleth, the battle-cry, between Germans and French.

One observation I must not omit here. We came
at an unfavourable season into a country unblessed by
nature, but which, at all events, supports its scattered,
industrious, orderly, and contented population. Richer and

more favoured districts may look down upon it; but it was not by any means wretchedness and beggary that met me there. The houses are well built, and covered with tiles, and sufficient signs of industry everywhere. The really poor district, too, is, at the most, from sixteen to twenty miles broad; and, in the direction of the Argonne mountains as well as towards Rheims and Châlons, has a more favoured region close at hand. Children who had been picked up in the first good village, spoke contentedly of the way in which they were fed; and I had only to recollect the cellar at Somme Tourbe and the white bread which had fallen into our hands fresh from Châlons, to perceive that, in a time of peace, hunger and misery were not exactly at home here.

25th September.

That during the suspension of hostilities the French would be active, was to be expected and could be observed. They were trying to re-establish the broken communication with Châlons, and to push the Emigrants upon us, or rather, drive them upon our rear; but our greatest misfortune for the moment was, that they could obstruct, if not completely destroy, our communication both from the Argonne mountains and from Sedan and Montmedy.

26th September.

As I was known to take an interest in various things, the men brought me everything that appeared in any way extraordinary. Amongst other things they brought a cannon-ball, seemingly about four pounds weight, the extraordinary thing about which, however, was, that the whole of its surface was covered with little crystallised pyramids. Balls enough had been shot that day, and it was not wonderful if one of them had made its way over here. I made all kinds of hypotheses to account for the peculiar shape of the ball, whether it had arisen in the casting of the metal or afterwards; an accident explained the matter to me. Upon returning to my tent after a short absence, I inquired for the ball, but it could not be found. Persevering in my demand, the men confessed it had burst, after all kinds of experiments had been made upon it. I asked for the fragments, and found, to my great astonishment, crystallisation at the centre which, commencing there, radiated towards the surface. It was pyrites, and must have been formed in some open place. This discovery led further; more of this kind of pyrites was found, but smaller, in the shape of balls and kidneys, and in other less regular shapes, all, however, alike in this, that they had not become fixed there from without, and that the crystallisation could always be traced to some centre; they were not rounded off either, but freshly and plainly crystallised on the surface. Can it be that they had been produced spontaneously in the earth, and are other things of the kind to be found in the fields?

But it was not I alone that had my attention directed to the minerals of the district; the fine white chalk which was found everywhere appeared decidedly valuable. The soldiers had, in fact, only to dig a hole to come upon the finest white chalk, a very necessary article to them for keeping their accoutrements white and trim. An order was actually issued that the soldiers were to provide themselves with as much as possible of this necessary commodity, which was here to be had for nothing. This order was somewhat laughed at, for although trudging through the deepest mud, they were ordered to load themselves with materials for cleanliness and ornament; while languishing for bread they were to content themselves with dust. The officers, too, were not a little annoyed on being ill-received at head-quarters, because they did not appear as clean and well-dressed as when on parade in Berlin or Potsdam. The commanders could not mend matters, so it was thought they ought not to have grumbled.

27th September.*

A somewhat singular expedient for meeting the pressing hunger was also announced to the army; they were

---

* A letter to Knebel bears the same date as this, and the situation of the Allies is there also briefly described; Goethe ends by saying: "I am very glad to have witnessed all with my own eyes, and that when this important time is spoken of I shall be able to say *et quorum pars minima fui.* Æneus, of course, used the words *pars magna.*"

ordered to thresh out as best they could the whole of the barley sheaves in their possession, to boil the grain thus obtained in hot water till it burst, and endeavour to appease their hunger with this food!

Our immediate neighbourhood, however, was destined to have better succour afforded to it. Two carts were seen at a distance sticking fast in the mud, to which assistance was willingly conveyed, as they contained provisions and other necessaries. Von Seebach, Master of the Horse, immediately sent horses to them, and they were moved off, but conducted to the Duke's regiment; the drivers protested against this as they were destined for the Austrian army, to which, indeed, their passports bore witness. But, nevertheless, they were taken, and in order to keep off the crowd, and at the same time to retain possession of the carts, sentinels were placed by them; and as the drivers were paid all that they demanded, they were obliged to submit to see the things pass into our hands.

First of all, the stewards and cooks pressed forward with their assistants, and took possession of the butter-vats, hams, and other good things. The crowd increased, the greater number calling for tobacco, which was given out likewise in great quantities at a high price. The carts, however, were so hemmed in, that at last nobody could get near them, and I was most earnestly entreated by our people and troopers to assist them in procuring some of this most necessary of all commodities.

I ordered some soldiers to make way for me, and immediately mounted the nearest cart, in order not to be entangled in the crowd; here I purchased and filled my pockets to their utmost with tobacco; and when I descended again, and freely dispensed it among the people, I was praised as the greatest benefactor that had ever taken pity on suffering humanity. Brandy also was there, and was welcome to many, who were glad to pay a French crown for a bottle.

27th September.

At head-quarters, to which access was sometimes obtained, as well as of all those who were met coming thence, inquiries were made as to the state of affairs, which could not be more alarming. More and more was heard of the horrors that had occurred in Paris; and what was at first considered as fable, appeared at last as veritable truth of the most fearful kind. The King and his family were prisoners, his dethronement already spoken of; hatred of royalty in general was gaining ground every day, and in fact, it was now expected that judicial proceedings would be commenced against the unhappy monarch. Our nearest antagonist in the war had again opened up a communication with Châlons; here Luckner was stationed, in order to form the crowds of volunteers streaming out from Paris into military corps; but these men, who came from the capital during those first fearful September days from amid the wild and fierce streams of blood, brought with them a taste for murder and robbery rather than for legitimate warfare. Following the example of the savage population of Paris they selected their own victims, to rob them of all they possessed, whether of authority, property, or life. To let them loose, undisciplined as they were, would have been to complete our ruin.

The Emigrants had been driven upon us, and we were told of many a danger that threatened both our rear and flanks. In the neighbourhood of Rheims twenty thousand peasants were said to have gathered together in bands, armed with agricultural implements, and other rural weapons, snatched up wildly at the moment; and there was great fear lest these also might fall upon us.

These matters were discussed in the evening in the Duke's tent, by some of the distinguished commanders in the army; each one offered his share of information, conjecture, and anxiety, to this helpless counsel, and it seemed as if only a miracle could save us. However, it occurred to me, that, in time of misfortune, people are fond in general of drawing comparisons between themselves and persons in an exalted station, especially if they happen to be in a worse plight; hence I felt induced, as a diversion, to recount some of the terrible incidents in the history of St. Louis. This King, during his crusade, first undertook to humble the Sultan of Egypt, for the Holy Land was then an appendage of his. Damietta fell without a siege into the hands of the Christians. Spurred on by his brother, the Count d'Artois, the King undertook a march to Babylon-Cairo, up the right bank of the Nile. They succeeded in filling up one of the canals which drew water from it. The army marched over this; but they now found themselves hemmed in between the Nile and its larger and smaller canals, whereas the Saracens were advantageously posted on both sides of the river. To get over the larger watercourses became a matter of difficulty. Blockhouses were built, and opposed to those of the enemy; but the latter had the advantage of Greek fire. With this they spread havoc among the wooden bulwarks, buildings, and men. Of what use to the Christians was their unwavering battle array, whilst continually provoked, insulted, and attacked by the Saracens, and involved in confusion by the perpetual attacks of their skirmishers? Isolated cases of daring and hand-to-hand encounters produced an animating and spirit-stirring effect; but the heroes, and even the King himself, were cut off from the main body. The bravest amongst them, indeed, forced their way through, but the confusion increased. The Count d'Artois got into danger, and the King risked everything for his rescue. His brother was already dead, and the danger rose to the highest pitch. During this awful day everything depended upon the defence of a bridge over a side stream, in order to keep off the Saracens from the rear of the main battle. The few warriors posted there were reinforced, as much as possible, with guns by the soldiers, with stones and mud by the soldiers' boys. In the midst of all this havoc the Count de Soissons said, jestingly, to the Duke of Joinville: "Seneschal, let the hounds bellow and bark! by God's throne (this was his usual oath), of this day we shall yet speak in our homes to our ladies."

They smiled, received the story as a good omen, and discussed the probabilities of the case, more particularly gave reasons why the French were more likely to spare us than to destroy us. The long unbroken truce, and their hitherto unaggressive demeanour, gave some hope. To increase this feeling I ventured upon another historical narrative, and, producing the particular maps, brought to their remembrance that eight miles to the westwards of us lay the famous Devil's field, to which Attila, King of the Huns, in the year 451, had advanced with his countless hords, but was there routed by the Burgundian princes, as-isted by the Roman General Ætius; that, had they followed up their victory, Attila, together with all his people, would have been utterly destroyed. But the Roman general, desirous that the Burgundian princes should not be altogether free from this powerful enemy, as in that case they might turn against the Romans, persuaded them, one after the other, to return home; and that thus the King of the Huns escaped with the remains of his countless host.

At this moment news was brought that the expected supply of bread had arrived from Grandpré; this doubly and trebly cheered the hearts of all; they parted in better spirits, and I was able to read to the Duke till late in the night, out of an amusing French book, which had fallen into my hands in a very curious way. Amidst the audacious, outrageous jokes, which aroused our laughter in spite of our precarious position, I thought of the lively riflemen at Verdun, who marched into the jaws of death singing frivolous songs. One must not be too particular about the means, when wishing to escape the bitterness of one's fate.

28th September.

The bread had arrived, but not without difficulty and loss; several of the carts had stuck fast in the wretched roads on their way to us from Grandpré, where it was baked; others had fallen into the hands of the enemy, and a portion of the supply was unfit for use; for, from having been too wet and too quickly baked, the crumb had separated from the crust, and become mouldy. As there was again a fear of poison, they brought me some of the loaves, which this time had a high orange colour in the inside, indicating arsenic, and sulphur, as those at Verdun had shown signs of verdigris. But supposing even that the bread was not poisoned, the look of it excited disgust and loathing; hunger became keener, being balked of a supply; sickness, wretchedness, and discontent pressed heavily on the large mass of brave men.

K

In the midst of these distresses our surprise and uneasiness were increased by an incredible piece of intelligence. The Duke of Brunswick, it was said, had sent his former manifesto to Dumourier, who, astonished and enraged, immediately proclaimed the truce at an end, and commanded a renewal of hostilities. In spite of the greatness of the dilemma in which we were, and foreseeing a still greater before us, we could not refrain from laughing and jeering; here was an instance, we said, of the misery which authorship draws upon itself! Every poet or writer is fond of showing people his works, without inquiring whether it be the right time for it or not; and this was precisely what the Duke of Brunswick was doing; for, in order to enjoy the pleasures of authorship, he was producing his unlucky manifesto at the wrong time.

We now expected to see the advanced posts popping at each other again, and looked towards the hills for an enemy to make his appearance, but all was as quiet and tranquil as if nothing had happened. In the meantime we lived in the most painful state of uncertainty and insecurity, for everybody was aware that, from a strategical point of view, we were lost if the enemy should take the slightest fancy to annoy us or press us. But in the midst of this uncertainty many things already indicated a better understanding and more peaceful disposition; for instance, the postmaster of St. Menehould had been delivered up, free and unhurt, in exchange for the persons belonging to the King's suite, who had been taken prisoners on the twentieth between the bulwark of waggons and the army.

29th September.

Towards evening, according to the orders given, the baggage was put in motion. It was to go forward under the escort of the Duke of Brunswick's regiment, and the army to follow at midnight. All bestirred themselves, but uneasily and slowly; for even with the best will they slipped on the splashy ground, and sank into it before they were aware. These hours also passed away; time runs its course, even on the roughest day.

Night had come on; and this also we had to pass sleepless. The weather was not unfavourable, the full moon was shining, but had nothing to illuminate. The tents had vanished; waggons, carriages, and horses, were all away, and our little party in particular was in a curious state. We had appointed the place where we were for the horses to meet us, but they did not come. As far as we could see round about by the pale light, everything appeared desolate and dreary; we listened in vain; neither shape nor sound could be seen or heard. Our minds wavered, doubtful and uncertain; we were more inclined not to leave the appointed place than to put our people in the same dilemma, and miss them altogether. Yet it was terrible, thus in the enemy's country, after such events, to stand isolated and abandoned, or, at least, to appear so for the moment. We watched to see whether any hostile demonstration might be a-foot; but nothing was stirring, either for or against us.

We collected all the tent-straw which had been left behind in the neighbourhood, and burned it, not without fear. Allured by the flame, an old female sutler approached us; she had apparently made good use of her time in remote places in which she had loitered on her way back, for she carried a pretty large bundle under her arm. After greeting us and warming herself, she first of all began to praise Frederick the Great to the skies, and extolled the Seven Years' War, in which, she said, she had been present; then she fiercely abused the present princes and generals, who had brought the large army into a country where the sutlers could not drive their trade, which, according to her, was the main point. It was pleasant and amusing enough, for the moment, to look at the affair from her point of view; however, the horses were exceedingly welcome when they arrived at length, for then, together with the Weimar regiment, we commenced our ominous retreat.

The measures of precaution taken, and the significant orders issued, gave us reason to fear that the enemy would not look quietly on our retreat. We had observed, with apprehension, even while it was still daylight, all the vehicles sunk in the miry ground, moving with difficulty along; and this particularly alarmed us in the case of the artillery. What might not be our fate when night came on! It was mournful to see the baggage-waggons, overturned and broken, lying in the brooks, and deplorable to leave the sick lying helpless behind us. When those who were in any way acquainted with the country looked around them, they confessed that nothing could save us here, if the enemy, who was known to be on both our flanks and rear, was inclined to attack us. As this, however, did not take place during the first few hours our hopeful minds again took courage, and, owing to a tendency to assign a rational cause to everything that happened, we took comfort in believing that the negotiations between the head-quarters of Hans and St. Menehould had been successfully concluded in our favour. From hour to hour this belief increased; and when I saw a halt made, and the whole of the waggons moving along in good order above the village of St. Jean, I felt quite certain that we should reach home, and, surrounded by good society, be able to recount our past sufferings, *devant les dames*. I now again imparted my belief to my friends and acquaintances; and we already began to endure our present difficulties with cheerfulness.

No encampment was made, but our people struck a large tent, and spread wheat-sheaves about, both inside and outside, for sleeping on. The moon was shining clear through the calm air, only a thin streak of light cloud was perceptible; the whole country round about being almost as visible and distinct as in the daytime. The moon shone upon the men sleeping, and upon the horses, which were kept awake by a want of food; many white ones were among them, and the light was strongly reflected from them; the white waggon-coverings, and even the white wheat-sheaves, used as layers, shed light and cheerfulness over this imposing scene. Truly the greatest artist would have considered himself fortunate if he could have painted it!

Not till late did I lie down in my tent, hoping to enjoy the soundest sleep; but Nature has interposed many discomforts between her richest gifts; and one of the most unsocial habits of man is, that, whilst asleep, and himself enjoying the most profound repose, he is wont to keep his fellows awake by violent snoring. Head to head, I within the tent, the other outside, I found myself lying beside a man who was perseveringly disturbing my needful rest by his abominable grunting. I untied the rope of the tent-stake to see who was my foe, and found it was one of the servants, a brave and worthy man, who was lying in the moonlight as sound asleep as if he had been Endymion himself. The impossibility of obtaining any rest in such neighbourhood excited a mischievous spirit within me; I took up an ear of corn, and drew it lightly over his forehead and nose. Thus disturbed in his rest, he rubbed his hand several times across his face; and as soon as he again sank into sleep I renewed my game, he being, no doubt, unable to understand from whence a gad-fly came at this time of the year. This went on till at last, quite awakened, the man decided to get up. Meanwhile, all tendency to sleep had left me also. I went out in front of the tent, and, in the scarcely altered picture, looked wonderingly upon the infinite stillness, so close upon the existing danger; and as, in such moments, anxiety and hope, apprehension and confidence, alternate in the mind, a thrill of horror ran through me, when I thought that if the enemy should fall upon us at this moment, neither the spoke of a wheel nor a human limb would be able to escape.

Daybreak soon changed the aspect of things; for many a strange sight was to be seen. Two old women, camp-followers, had tied several silk petticoats of various colours round their bodies and shoulders, the chief of them having in addition a kind of cape round her throat and head. In this garb they strutted about, looking most comic, but asserted that they had obtained the things all by fair purchase and exchange.

30th September.

Notwithstanding that the waggons were put in motion as soon as the day broke, we made but little way; for, as early as nine o'clock, we stopped between Laval and Varge Moulin. Men and cattle took what refreshment they could find; but we did not encamp. The army also arrived, and took up its post upon a hill; the greatest quiet and order being maintained throughout. It could easily be perceived, by different precautionary measures being put in force, that all danger was not yet considered at an end; reconnoitering parties were sent out, and secret interviews were held with strangers, and preparations made for breaking up again.

1st October.

The Duke of Weimar led the vanguard at the same time, and covered the retreat of the baggage. Order and quiet prevailed during the night, and our spirits were becoming more composed, when, about twelve o'clock, we were ordered to break up. It was now evident, from everything we saw, that this march was not considered quite safe, owing to the predatory bands which, it was feared, might attack us from the forest of Argonne. For even supposing, what was by no means certain, that an agreement had been entered into with Dumourier and the higher powers, still there was so little subordination at the time, that a mountain force might easily have declared itself independent, and made an attempt to destroy us, which, if successful, would have been sanctioned. This day's march also did not extend far; it was intended that the baggage and the army should proceed together, should keep up with the Austrians and Emigrants, who were on our left flank, and parallel to us, and had likewise commenced their retreat.

And here I may as well mention that, in the midst of all this wretchedness, I made this whimsical vow: that, if we escaped, and I reached home in safety, nobody should ever hear me again complain of the obstruction to the view from my chamber-window caused by the projecting gable of the next house, which, in fact, I now ardently longed to behold; further, that I would never again complain of want of comfort or of ennui in a German theatre, where, thank God, one is at least always under cover, whatever may be taking place on the stage. I made a third vow—which, however, I have forgotten.

It was sufficient still for every one to provide for himself in this way; and cattle and waggons, man and horse, remained together, according to their regular divisions. We also again found tables covered, and benches and chairs in readiness, when we halted or encamped. It struck us that we got rather short allowance, but knowing the general scarcity, we submitted cheerfully to our fate.

Fortune, however, gave me an opportunity of enjoying a better meal. It had grown dark early, and everybody had lain down upon the straw prepared for them. I, too, had fallen asleep, but was awakened by a lively and pleasant dream; for I fancied that I smelt, in fact, that I was eating, the most delicious morsels; this woke me, and on rising up, I found my tent full of a glorious smell of bacon, frying and frizzling, which greatly excited my appetite. In the wild kind of life we were leading, we might surely be excused for considering swine-herds divine,* and pork as inestimably good. I stood up and saw a fire at some little distance, luckily in the direction whence the wind was blowing, which brought me an abundance of the pleasant odour. Hastening to the spot, I found all the servants engaged round a smouldering fire, the back of the sow nearly roasted, the rest of it cut up, and ready for packing, and every one busy, and giving a hand to the rapid preparation of the sausages. Not far from the fire lay the trunks of some large trees, upon one of which, after a friendly salutation of the party, I sat down, and looked on with pleasure and in silence at their work. Some of the good people were kindly disposed towards me, others felt that they could not with propriety exclude the unexpected guest; so when it came to making a division, they bestowed a goodly share upon me. Bread also was not wanting, and a drop of brandy besides; in fact, there was no want of any good thing.

A large piece of sausage was also presented to me when we mounted our horses amid the darkness and fog of midnight; I stuck it in my pistol holsters. Thus the favour of the night-wind had done me good service.

* In allusion apparently to Homer's Eumaios, the divine swine-herd.

2nd October.

Although refreshed by having partaken of food and drink, and our minds appeased by consolatory reasonings, still hope and anxiety, chagrin and a feeling of disgrace, alternated within us; we were glad to be still alive, yet we abjured a life passed under the present conditions. About two o'clock in the morning we broke up, marched cautiously past a wood, and traversed at Vaux the scene of our late encampment, and soon afterwards arrived at Aisne. Here we found two bridges, which enabled us to cross over to the right bank. We halted for the present between the two, within sight of both, upon a sandy willow-bank, and kindled a blazing fire to cook with. The tenderest of lentils I ever tasted, and long, red potatoes of good flavour were soon prepared. And when the hams which had been conveyed by the Austrian drivers, but which had hitherto been kept secret, were served up, there was an abundant supply for all.

The baggage had already come across; but soon a spectacle both splendid and melancholy presented itself. The army was coming up; the infantry and artillery marching across the bridges, the cavalry through a ford; all faces were downcast, and every mouth silent, indicative of gloomy reflections. When a regiment arrived in which acquaintances and friends were known to be, we hastened towards them, embraced them, and conversed; but what questions these were, and amid what mortification and shame, and even tears, it took place!

Nevertheless, we rejoiced in having managed to be able to accommodate both high and low so well. At first, the drum of a picquet which had been posted there served as a table; afterwards, chairs and tables were brought from some neighbouring villages, and guests of every degree were made as comfortable as possible. The Crown Prince and Prince Louis did not despise the lentils; and we were joined by several generals, who were attracted from a distance by the smoke. But good as was our supply, what could it avail among so many! A second and a third party had to be served, and our supply was diminishing every moment.

Our Prince being in the habit of dispensing liberally to all, his people followed his example; and it would be difficult to mention every case in which chamberlain and cook furnished refreshments to the numerous invalids who went by.

This continued during the whole day, and thus the retreat presented itself to me not merely in detail and by comparison, but in its full reality; and the painfulness of it was renewed and increased by every new uniform. The truly melancholy spectacle was destined to end in a way worthy of it; the King and his staff rode up from a distance, remained some time stationary upon the bridge, as if to survey and reconsider the whole matter again; but at last he, too, followed his discomfited army. In the same way the Duke of Brunswick appeared on the other bridge, hesitated, and then rode across.

The night set in windy but dry, and was passed on the gloomy willow-bank by most without sleep.

3rd October.

Next morning, at six o'clock, we left this place, marched over a hill to Grandpré, and joined the army encamped there. Fresh evils and anxieties awaited us; the castle had been turned into a hospital, and was already filled with several hundred sick, for whose assistance and support it was impossible to make any provision. We passed them, not without some qualms of conscience, but were obliged to abandon them to the mercy of the enemy.

Here we again encountered fearful rains, which impeded all our movements.

4th October.

The difficulty of moving on increased more and more; as the high roads were impassable, an attempt was made to cross the fields. The soil, of a reddish colour, which was more clammy even than the chalk soil we had passed, obstructed us at every step. The four small horses were scarcely able to drag my little carriage along, so I thought it would be as well to relieve them of the weight of my person at least. The riding-horses were nowhere to be seen; but the large kitchen-waggon, drawn by six strong horses, came up to me. I mounted it; it was not quite empty of victuals, but the kitchen-maid was sitting peevishly in the corner. I devoted myself to my studies. I had taken out of my portmanteau the third volume of Fischer's Lexicon of Natural Philosophy, a dictionary being in such times the best of all companions, as at every moment an interruption may occur, and our attention is diverted by being led from one thing to the other.

We had, in our dilemma, imprudently entered a tough, spongy, red-clay field, and in the fallow ground even the strength of the strong team that drew the cooking-waggon gave way. Seated there I seemed to myself like a parody on Pharaoh in the Red Sea; for around me horse and foot were about to sink in an element of similar colour, and in a similar way. I looked wistfully towards all the neighbouring heights, and at length espied the riding-horses, and amongst them the gray one destined for myself. I beckoned them eagerly to approach, and delivered up my Natural Philosophy to the poor dispirited kitchen-maid, commending it to her care. I leaped upon my horse, and firmly resolved not readily to take such a drive again. I was now more independent certainly, but did not get on either better or faster.

Grandpré, which was now to be described as a place of pestilence and death, we gladly left behind us. Several friends and comrades met, and formed a circle round a fire; we held our horses by the bridle behind us. I was told that this was the only time that I had shown a gloomy face, and had neither fortified them with wise words, nor entertained them with witty ones.

4th and 5th October.

The road the army had taken led towards Busancy, as it was their intention to cross the Meuse above Dun. We encamped close to Sivry, and found that everything had not yet been consumed in that neighbourhood. The soldiers rushed into the first gardens that came in their way, and destroyed much that would have been of use to others. I set our cook and his people upon a more skilful plan of foraging; we went round the whole village, and found some gardens still quite untouched, and a rich undisputed harvest. There was abundance of cabbages, onions, radishes, and other good vegetables; we took no more than we required, moderately and sparingly. The garden was not large, but was well kept; and as we crept back to the hedge again, I began to speculate as to how it had happened that, in a vegetable-garden like this, not a trace was to be discovered of any door into the adjoining house. On returning, well laden with kitchen-booty, we heard a great uproar in front of the regiment. A horse, which had been put in requisition about twenty days before, had escaped, carrying away the stake to which it had been tied; the trooper, who was in very bad odour with his officers, was being ordered, with threats, to regain possession of his horse.

As it was decided that we should pass the fifth in this neighbourhood, we took up our quarters in Sivry, and after so many hardships greatly enjoyed domestic life again, and were glad of the opportunity thus presented of observing idyllic Homeric country-life in France. The houses were not entered immediately from the street, but first there was a small, open square space, the entrance-door forming one side of the square; one then passed through what was properly the house-door, and entered a spacious lofty room, appropriated to the common uses of the family; it was paved with tiles, and on the left, in the middle of a long wall, stood a fire-place; above it was a flue which carried away the smoke. After saluting our hosts, we approached the fire, observing that regular fixed places were assigned to whoever might be in the room, according to their respective ranks. On the right of the fire-place stood a large box, with a lid, which also served for a chair; it contained the salt, a supply of which was stored up, and had to be kept in a dry place. This was the seat of honour, and was immediately assigned to the most distinguished of the strangers; the other visitors seated themselves upon wooden chairs, as did also the people of the house. The cooking apparatus, peculiar to the district, a *pot au feu*, I had an opportunity of examining for the first time. A large iron kettle was suspended above the fire from a hook, which could be raised or lowered by means of indentations; in this a goodly piece of beef was boiling, with water and salt, together with white and yellow turnips, leeks, cabbages, and other vegetable ingredients.

Whilst conversing in a friendly way with the good people, I perceived with what architectural skill the dresser, sink, and plate-rack had been arranged in the room. These occupied the oblong space formed at the side by the open square entrance. The dishes were neatly ranged in order; a girl, either a servant or one of the family, attended to every one in the prettiest way. The mother of the family was sitting by the fire, with a boy standing at her knee, and two little girls pressing close up to her. The table was covered with a cloth, a large earthen bowl was placed upon it, some small slices of fine white bread thrown into it, the hot broth poured over these, and recommended to a *bon appétit.* The boys who had so despised my commissariat bread might have referred me to this as a sample of "*bon pain*" and "*bonne soupe.*" The vegetables, which had been prepared at the same time, now followed, together with the meat, and anybody might have been satisfied with this simple specimen of culinary skill.

We inquired kindly about the state of their affairs. It seemed that when we were first at Landres they had suffered severely, and now, scarcely recovered from their former fears, they apprehended total ruin from the retreating hostile army. We sympathized with them in their anxiety, and comforted them by assuring them that the danger would now soon be over, as, with the exception of the rear-guard, we were the last of the army; and gave them advice and directions as to how they should behave to marauders. With wind and rain alternating every moment, we passed the day principally under cover before the fire, thinking over the past, and contemplating what might immediately be awaiting us, not without anxiety. Since we had left Grandpré I had seen neither carriage, portmanteau, nor servants, and hope and fear by turns took possession of my mind. Night had come on, and the

OCTOBER 1792.

children had to go to bed; they approached their father and mother respectfully, made a bow, kissed their parents' hands, and said: "*Bon soir, papa! bon soir, mama!*" with becoming grace. Soon after this we heard that the Prince of Brunswick* was lying dangerously ill in our vicinity, and went to inquire for him. We were not admitted to his presence, but were assured that he was so much better as to intend proceeding on the march next morning.

Scarcely had we got under shelter again from the dreadful rain, and were seated by the fire, when a young man came in, whom we immediately recognised as our landlord's younger brother. He was a handsome young man, dressed in the usual fashion of the country-people in France. Looking very grim, and with a wild, discontented look, he sat down beside us at the fire without saying a word; but, as soon as he had warmed himself, he rose, and walked up and down the room with his brother, and then both went into the other room. They conversed in a very animated yet confidential tone. He then went out into the drenching rain, our host not seeking to detain him.

But we, too, were soon called out into the stormy night by loud cries of distress. Under the pretext of searching for forage in the fields, our soldiers had commenced plundering, and in the most absurd fashion, for they had robbed a weaver of his loom—a thing of no use in the world to them. With a little severity and good advice we put matters to rights again; for it was only a few of the men who had ventured upon such proceedings. How easily, however, this might have become infectious, and brought everything into confusion!

A considerable number of persons had collected, and a Weimar hussar, a butcher by trade, came up to me and confided to me that he had discovered a fatted sow in a house close by, for which he had tried to bargain, but could not obtain it from its owner, and now wished some measures to be taken to get possession of it, for there would be a great scarcity of everything during the ensuing days. It was curious enough that we, who had just put

* The fourth son of the then reigning duke; subsequently he became famous for his military exploits, and as "Brunswick's fated chieftain," whose death at Quatre Bras is celebrated by Byron.

down plundering, should be called upon to do the same ourselves. However, as hunger acknowledges no law, we went with the hussar into the house indicated, found a large fire burning, saluted the people, and sat down beside them. Another Weimar hussar, called Liseur, had come with us, and to his ingenuity we confided the management of the affair. He began, in French, fluently to speak of the virtues of the regular troops, and praised those who sought, in fair exchange for ready money, to obtain merely the most necessary articles; on the other hand, he abused marauders, baggage-servants, and sutlers, who, with violence and force, were in the habit of seizing everything they could lay their hands on, and did not leave a scrap of anything behind. He wished, he added, to give them his friendly piece of advice, and to consider whether it was not more to their interest to sell what they possessed, seeing that gold was less difficult to conceal than beasts, which were always easily discovered. His arguments, however, appeared to be making no great impression, when the negotiation was interrupted in a curious way.

A violent knocking was heard at the outer door, which was locked; to this no attention was paid, as they had no desire to admit more visitors; the knocking continued, a plaintive female voice kept calling out, and beseeching clamorously that the door might be opened. Softened at length they unlocked the door, and an old woman, one of the camp-followers, rushed in, carrying something in her arms wrapped up in a cloth; behind her was a young woman, not bad-looking, but pale and debilitated, and scarcely able to stand on her legs. In a few words, and with great energy, the old crone explained the state of the case, displaying a naked infant, of which the woman had been delivered on her flight. They had been left behind, ill treated by the peasants, and this night at last reached our door. The mother, as her milk had left her, had not been able to give the child any nourishment since its birth. The old woman now clamoured for meal, milk, and a pan, and linen to wrap the child in. As she did not know French, we had to ask for her; but her imperious and passionate gestures gave sufficient pantomimic weight and emphasis to what we said. What she demanded could not be got very quickly; and when it was brought, it was not good enough for her. It was curious, too, to notice her alertness in going to work; she soon drove us back from the fire, the best place being immediately engaged for the young mother, she herself sitting upon a stool with as confident an air as if the house had been her own. In a twinkling the child was washed and wrapped up, the pap boiled; she fed the little creature first, then the mother, paying little attention to herself. Afterwards she asked for clean clothes for the sick woman, whilst the old ones were drying. We looked at her in amazement; she clearly understood how to make requisitions.

The rain ceased; we went back to our former quarters, and shortly afterwards the hussars brought in the sow. We paid what seemed a reasonable price for it. It had now to be slaughtered; this was done, and a staple being found in the beam of the adjoining room, it was hung up. there to be properly cut up and prepared.

That our hosts, on this occasion, manifested no ill-nature, but displayed rather a desire to help us, appeared somewhat singular to us, as they had good reason to consider our conduct both barbarous and inconsiderate. In the same room in which we were carrying on the operation the children were lying in their clean beds, and being awakened by the noise we made, they peered out prettily from among the blankets, with frightened faces. The sow was hanging close to a large double marriage-bed, closed in carefully with green serge, the curtains constituting a picturesque back-ground to the illuminated carcase. It was a night-piece without its like. But the inmates could not indulge in such reflections; we remarked that they had some grudge against the people from whom the sow had been taken, and felt a certain malicious pleasure about it. We had moreover promised them some of the meat and sausages; and this was advantageous to us in the operation, which had to be completed in a few hours. Our hussar now showed himself as active and clever in this business as the gipsy over the way was in hers; and we enjoyed, in anticipation, the good sausages and joints of meat which were to fall to us as our share of booty. To await this, we lay down in the smithy belonging to our host upon some delicious sheaves of corn, and slept soundly till the day broke. Meanwhile our hussar had finished his business in the house; breakfast was ready waiting for us, and the remainder of the beast packed up, our hosts having first obtained their share, not without some signs of discontent on the part of our people, who maintained that kindness was ill bestowed upon them, as they doubtless had both meat and other good things concealed which we had not yet succeeded in ferreting out.

On looking round about in the back room I found a door barred, which, from its position, evidently led into a garden. Through a small window at the side, I could see that I had guessed rightly; the garden lay rather higher than the house, and I recognised it plainly as the same from which, in the morning, we had supplied ourselves with the kitchen-stuff. The door was blocked up, and covered so skilfully with earth heaped up against it that I could now easily understand why I had been unable to discover it in the morning. Thus it had stood written in the stars, that we were to enter the house in spite of all their precautions.

6th October, morning.

In our present circumstances we could never calculate on a moment's rest, or expect that the same state of things would continue for an instant. With the break of day, the whole place was suddenly put into a great state of excitement; the affair of the horse which had escaped again became the subject of conversation. Its anxious rider, who had either to regain possession of it or suffer punishment and march on foot, had been running about the nearest villages, when at last the people, in order to rid themselves of the hubbub, assured him that the horse must be hid in Sivry; that some weeks before, they had seen a black horse like the one he described, taken from that town; that it was close to Sivry where it had made its escape—and added other things which they thought might make this more probable. He now came, accompanied by a non-commissioned officer, who, by threatening the whole place, at last found a solution of the mystery. The horse

ι to Sivry, to its former master; the joy
ιey said, had been boundless on finding
mpanion of the house and stable—univer-
athy of the neighbours. Artfully enough
the horse into a hay-loft, and concealed it
y; nobody divulged the secret. It was
:th amidst lamentations and grief; and
ιr mounted it and followed the sergeant,
the whole of the little community. No-
his own troubles, or of the general and
isfactory state of things; the horse and
ιcated out of it for a second time, were
interested the assembled throng.
ray of hope appeared; the Crown Prince
ιp, and whilst seeking to learn what had
wd together, the good people went up to
ιd him to give them back the horse. This
ι power to do; for the necessities of war
n kings; and they were left disconsolate,
ιim depart without making any reply.
n talked over with our good hosts the
practised against marauders; for already
ιre prowling about. We advised them,
ιe, maid and serving-man, all to stand in
ide the small entrance hall, and, in case
out a morsel of bread, or a glass of wine,
fii mly to withstand any attempt to enter.
dom invaded a house by force; but once
impossible to control them. The good
us to stop some time longer, but we had
ves; the regiment of the Duke had already
ιnd the Crown Prince was off; this was
:mine our departure.
this determination was became clearer
ng the column, we heard that yesterday
the French princes, immediately after
ιf Chesne le Populeux and the Aisne behind
.ttacked by peasants, between the Graudes
ses; one of the officers was said to have
lled under him, and the servant of the
hat pierced by a bullet. It now occurred

L

to me that, on the preceding night, when the quarrelsome brother-in-law entered the house, I had had some foreboding of this.

6th October.

We had now got over the worst of the mess; but our retreat was still difficult and hazardous, and the transport of our goods and chattels became day by day more troublesome; we carried about, it is true, a complete set of furniture with us, and besides the kitchen-utensils we had some tables and benches, trunks, boxes, and chairs, and even a couple of tin stoves. How were we to transport the waggons, when the horses were diminishing in number every day! Some of them fell down, and others were greatly exhausted.* There was nothing to be done but to leave one waggon behind, and to bring the others along. A council was now held to determine what could most easily be spared; and the result was, that we abandoned a waggon, filled with all sorts of things, in order not to lose everything. This operation had to be repeated several times; our train became much smaller; but we had soon to bethink us of another reduction, when crawling with the greatest difficulty along the low banks of the Meuse.

But what at this time grieved and vexed me most was, that I had been without my carriage for several days. I could only account for this by supposing that my servant, who had always hitherto displayed such energy, must have got into some scrape, have lost his horses, and been unable to obtain others. In this melancholy picture, which my imagination drew, I saw my costly Bohemian phaeton, the gift of my Prince, which had carried me pretty well about the world already, sunk in the mud, perhaps overturned and broken; and as I sat on my horse, imagined myself now as possessing nothing but what I had about me. The portmanteau, with my clothes, all kinds of manuscripts, and many other things, which, by long habit, had become valuable to me, all seemed lost and scattered about at random.

What had become of my pocket book, with the money

* The march from Sivry to Buzancy had been continued, and the Prussian troops were not pursued.

and important documents, and of the many other little things which one carries about with one? After I had speculated in a sorrowful way about all this, my mind cast off these intolerable thoughts. I felt my confidence in my servant reviving; and as the moment before I had been thinking of all that I had lost, I now began to fancy that everything must have been rescued by his activity, and rejoiced in this thought as if I had had the things beside me.

7th October.

Whilst we were marching up the left bank of the Meuse, to get to the place where we were to cross and reach the high-road on the other side, and just as we had reached a very swampy part of the ground, we heard that the Duke of Brunswick was coming up behind us. We stopped, and saluted him respectfully; he drew up quite close to us, and said to me, "I am sorry indeed to see you in this unpleasant situation; but it is an advantage to me in one respect, I have one more intelligent and honourable man who can testify that we have been defeated not so much by the enemy, as by the elements."

He had seen me at head-quarters in Hans, in passing by, and knew that I had been present during the whole melancholy march. I made some suitable reply, and expressed, finally, my sorrow that, after so much suffering and anxiety, he had been rendered uneasy besides by the sickness of his son the Prince, with whom, the night before, in Sivry, we had sincerely sympathized. He seemed pleased at this allusion, for the Prince was his favourite son, and pointed him out to us as riding close by, and we made our obeisance to him. The Duke wished us patience and perseverance; and, in return, I wished him uninterrupted good health, adding that nothing else was wanting to enable him to save us and the good cause. He had in truth never liked me; this I had to put up with; he made no secret of it, and that I could forgive him. Misfortune now proved herself a kind mediatrix, and brought about this sympathetic meeting between us.

7th and 8th October.

We crossed the Meuse, and struck out, upon the road which leads from the Netherlands to Verdun; the weather was more frightful than ever, and we encamped at Consenvoye.

Our discomfort and wretchedness reached its highest pitch; the tents were wet through and through, and there was no other cover or protection from the weather; we did not know where to turn to; my carriage was still missing, and I was in want of everything. Even supposing one tried to get shelter under a tent, there was nothing to lie down upon. How we longed for some straw, and even for the smallest bit of dry board! In the end, there was nothing for it but to lie down upon the cold, wet ground.

I had previously in cases of a similar description, discovered an expedient for enduring this kind of misery; I stood as long as I could upon my legs, till my knees gave way; I then sat down upon a camp stool, where I continued to sit till I felt as if I should fall, so that any place where I could stretch myself out in a horizontal position was a perfect relief. And, thus as hunger is always the best sauce, fatigue is the best sleeping draught.

Two days and nights we had passed in this way, when the melancholy condition of some of the sick was destined to benefit some of those enjoying good health. The valet of the Duke had fallen ill of the general sickness, and a young gentleman, belonging to the regiment, rescued by the Prince from the hospital at Grandpré, it had been resolved to send on to Verdun, about eight miles distant. The Chamberlain Wagner was sent in charge of them; and I did not hesitate, on receiving a kind and gracious hint, to accept the fourth seat. We were dismissed with letters of recommendation to the Commandant; and as, in taking our places, the poodle could not be left behind, the sleeping-carriage, so favourite a place at other times, became in some sort a hospital and menagerie combined.

Liseur, the hussar, was given to us as our escort, and as a fit person to provide quarters and provisions for us; being a native of Luxembourg, he was acquainted with the

country, and united in his person all the qualities of a
freebooter—skill, dexterity, and daring. He seated himself with evident satisfaction in front, and made a good
addition to the appearance of the carriage, which was
drawn by six strong greys.

Although I was squeezed in between persons with infectious diseases, I felt no apprehension. If true to oneself, one can always find some helpful maxim in whatever
situation one may be placed: thus whenever any great
danger threatened me, the blindest fatalism came to my
assistance; and I have observed that people, who are constantly exposed to great danger, feel themselves steeled
and strengthened by the same belief. The Mahomedan
religion furnishes the best proof of this.

7th October.

We moved along on our melancholy journey with the
invalids, and had cause for serious reflections, for we had
come upon the same high-road by which, in such good
spirits, and so full of hope, we had entered the country.
Here we were in the district where the first shot had been
fired from the vineyard, and upon the same highway where
the pretty woman fell into our hands, and was taken back
to her home; here we had passed the low wall from which
she, with her relations, saluted us, and wished us good
speed. How different all this seemed now! And how
doubly disastrous appeared the result of the fruitless
campaign, when seen through the melancholy veil of the
continuous rains!

However, in the midst of these troubles, I was destined
to fall in with the very thing which, of all others, I wished
to meet. We overtook a vehicle, driving along before us,
drawn by four wretched little horses; what a joyful shout
of recognition was raised, when I saw that it was my own
carriage, and my own servant! "Paul, you rascal," I
called out, " is it you? Where do you come from?" The
portmanteau was lying quietly packed up in its old place;
what a joyful sight! And whilst I was inquiring hastily
for the portfolio and other things, two friends jumped
out of the carriage, Weyland the Private Secretary, and

Captain Vent. It was indeed a joyful meeting; and I now learnt the whole history of their journey.

Since the flight of the peasant-boys my servant had succeeded in bringing along the horses, and had managed not only to get from Hans to Grandpré, but afterwards, on losing sight of me, across the Aisne; and from thence had made good his way by questioning, entreating, foraging, and exacting, till, at last, we had got happily together again. And now, in the highest spirits, we were on our way to Verdun, where we hoped to find rest and comfort. Our hussar, with great prudence and foresight, had made admirable arrangements for ensuring this; he had ridden on before into the town, and had very soon become persuaded, that, owing to the greatness of the confusion, nothing was to be expected in the regular way from the exertions and assistance of the Commandant. Luckily, however, he saw, in the courtyard of a fine house, preparations for an approaching departure, and galloped back, telling us which way to go. He then hastened, as soon as the other people had left, to occupy the gate and prevent its being shut, and joyfully received us when we arrived. We drove in and descended from the carriage, under the loud protestations of an old housekeeper, who, just freed from one party that had been quartered upon her, had no desire to receive another. In the meanwhile the horses had been taken out of the carriage and put in the stable, whilst we took possession of the upper rooms. The master of the house, an elderly nobleman, and Knight of St. Louis, did not interfere, neither he nor his family wishing to have anything to do with the guests, and least of all with Prussians on their retreat.

10th October.

A boy, who conducted us round the desolate town, asked us, with a significant look, if we had tasted the incomparable Verdun tarts? He, thereupon, conducted us to the most celebrated master of this art. We entered a large room, round which some large and small ovens were ranged, and in the centre were placed a table and chairs, to enable the visitors to partake of the new-baked tarts. The artist made his appearance, but in a state of the utmost despair declared that he could not oblige us, as he had no butter. He showed us a splendid supply of very fine flour; but of what use was this to him without milk and butter! He praised his own talent; said that the inhabitants and all travellers approved of his tarts; and deplored his bad luck in being without the most necessary ingredients at a time when he had an opportunity of showing his ability to such distinguished visitors, and of spreading his reputation. He besought us, therefore, to procure him some butter; and gave us to understand, if we would only take a little trouble about it, that it would be forthcoming. He was satisfied at last when we promised him, if we remained long enough, to fetch some from Jardin Fontaine.*

We asked our young guide, who accompanied us round some other parts of the town, and who seemed to be a connoisseur of pretty women as well as of tarts, to tell us the name of a beautiful girl whom we saw leaning out of the window of one of the better class of houses. "Ay," he cried, after naming her, " she had better take care of her pretty head, she is one of those who presented flowers and fruits to the King of Prussia. Her family and relations thought the Prussians would be uppermost again; the tables are turned, however; and I would not change places with her now." He said this with peculiar composure, as if it were quite a matter of course, and could not, and never would be, otherwise.

My servant had returned from Jardin Fontaine, where he had gone to visit our former host, and to give him back the letter to his sister in Paris. The facetious man received him good-naturedly, entertained him most hospitably, and asked him to bring his master and friends, whom he likewise promised to entertain.

We were not destined, however, to be so fortunate; for we had scarcely hung the kettle over the fire, with the usual ingredients and ceremonies, when an orderly entered, and, in the name of the Commandant Corbière, civilly informed us that it would be necessary to prepare for leaving Verdun the following morning at eight o'clock.

* The head-quarters of the Duke of Weimar and his regiment, from the 6th to the 10th of September.

Greatly annoyed at being obliged so hastily to leave our quarters and our newly-acquired home, before we had in any measure recovered from our fatigue, and at again being driven out into the wild and dirty world, we appealed to the illness of the young gentleman and the valet as a reason for stopping, whereupon he gave us to understand that we must manage to get these conveyed away as fast as possible, as the hospital was to be emptied during the night, and only those who were unfit to travel were to be left behind. Upon this, terror and alarm took possession of us; for nobody had doubted that the Allies would retain possession of Verdun, and perhaps capture some other fortified places, and prepare safe winter-quarters. We could not at once bid adieu to these hopes; it seemed to us, that it was only a pretext for ridding the fortresses of the crowds of sick and camp-followers, in order to put sufficient garrisons into them. Wagner the Chamberlain, however, who had delivered the Duke's letter to the Commandant, saw in these measures reason to fear the most alarming state of things. But whatever might be the upshot of it all, we had nothing left but again to submit to our fate, and were tranquilly and slowly consuming our simple meal, when another orderly entered and told us that we must endeavour, without fail, to get away from Verdun the following morning at three o'clock. Chamberlain Wagner, who thought he knew what the letter to the Commandant contained, saw in this a decided proof that the fortress was immediately to be given up again to the French. We then thought of the boy's threats, and of the beautiful, gaily-dressed lady, and of the fruits and flowers; and now, in right good earnest, did we deplore the complete failure of so great an enterprise.

Although I had found some genuine and valuable friends amongst the diplomatic corps, I could not refrain, as often as I saw them in the midst of these great movements, from making some odd comparisons that forced themselves irresistibly on my mind. They appeared to me like so many playhouse directors, who choose the pieces, distribute the parts, and move about unseen; whilst the actors, doing their best, and well prompted, have to leave the result of their exertions to fortune and the humour of the public.

OCTOBER 1792.

Baron Breteuil lived opposite to us; since the affair of the diamond necklace I had never forgotten him. His hatred of Cardinal de Rohan caused him to precipitate matters fearfully. The shock caused by this trial made the State tremble to its very foundation, and annihilated all respect for the Queen and for the higher ranks in general; for, unfortunately, everything that came to light made it only too evident in what depravity the Court and the upper classes were sunk.

At present it was believed that he was the author of the strange convention which occasioned our retreat, and to excuse which it was supposed that some very advantageous conditions were made in our favour; we were assured that the King, the Queen, and their family were to be liberated, and many other advantages obtained. But the question, as to how all these great diplomatic triumphs could be reconciled with what was already known to us, excited many misgivings in our minds.

The rooms we inhabited were respectably furnished; a bookcase attracted my attention, through the glass-door of which I saw a number of pamphlets regularly cut into the same form of quarto. To my astonishment I then discovered that our landlord had been one of the Notables in Paris in the year 1787; in these pamphlets his instructions were printed. The moderation of the people's demand at that time, and the modesty with which they were put forward, formed a striking contrast to the violence, insolence, and desperation of the present state of things. I read the papers with genuine emotion, and took some copies of them with me.

11th October.

Without having obtained any sleep during the night, we were just on the point of entering our carriage, which was drawn up before the gate of the courtyard, when we perceived an insuperable obstacle to our progress. An uninterrupted line of sick-waggons was moving along between the pavement-stones that were heaped up on either side, through the town, which had become a perfect bog. Whilst we stood waiting to see what could be done, our landlord, the Knight of St. Louis, brushed past us, without saluting. But our astonishment, at his sudden appearance and discourteous behaviour, was soon turned into pity; for his servant, who followed him, carried a small bundle on his stick; it became only too evident that, after returning to his house and home only four weeks ago, he was now compelled to leave it again, as we had had to leave our conquests.

But my attention was soon turned to the improved appearance of the horses attached to my carriage; and the servants confessed that they had exchanged the old ones, which were done-up and useless, for a supply of sugar and coffee, but at the same time had been lucky in putting others in requisition. The activity of our dexterous Liseur had been conspicuous in this; through him also we got out of our present difficulty; for he made a dash into a gap in the string of carriages, and kept the advancing team back long enough to allow our two teams of six and four horses to get in. Thus I was again able to enjoy the fresh air in my light little carriage.

We now moved along at a funeral pace, but still we moved; the day broke, and we found ourselves on the outskirts of the town, in the midst of boundless tumult and confusion. All sorts of vehicles, a few horsemen, and countless pedestrians, were going to and fro on the great open space before the gate. We turned to the right with our column towards Etain, upon a narrow road, with ditches at each side. Self-preservation in so tremendous a pressure knew no pity, had no regard for others; not far before us a horse fell down in front of an ammunition-waggon; they cut the traces and left it lying. But as the three that remained were unable to drag the vehicle further, they were cut loose also, the heavy-laden waggon tumbled into the ditch, and with but little delay we drove on right over the horse, which was just going to rise again; I saw its limbs crushed and quivering under the wheels.

The horsemen and pedestrians endeavoured to escape from the narrow impracticable high-road into the fields; but they were ruined by the rains, inundated by the overflowing of the ditches, and the connection of the foot-paths was everywhere interrupted. Four respectable, handsome, well-dressed French soldiers waded for some time close to our carriages; they were very trim and clean, and succeeded so well in picking their steps that no mud was to be seen on them higher than their ankles, in spite of the dirty pilgrimage which the good fellows were making.

That, under such circumstances, dead horses were often to be seen lying in the ditches, meadows, fields, and pastures, was a natural consequence of the state of things; but we soon saw instances where the skins had been cut off, and even the fleshy parts taken—a melancholy evidence of the universal distress.

Thus we moved along, every moment in danger, on the slightest stoppage of our own carriage, of being ourselves thrown off; under which circumstances the exertions of our guide were beyond all praise. These he again displayed at Etain, where we arrived about noon, and witnessed around and beside us a bewildering tumult throughout the streets and squares of the handsome, well-built little town; the crowd swayed to and fro, and as all were pressing forwards, each hindered the other. Unexpectedly our guide ordered the carriages to stop in front of a good house in the market-place, which we entered, the master and mistress saluting us at a respectful distance.

We were conducted into a wainscotted room on the ground-floor, where, in the black marble fire-place, a comfortable fire was burning. We saw ourselves in the large mirror above it, by no means an agreeable sight; for I could not make up my mind to have my hair cut short, and it was now hanging like tangled hemp about my head; my bristly beard also gave additional ferocity to my personal appearance.

From the low windows which overlooked the whole market-place, we could almost touch the immense throng. All sorts of pedestrians, soldiers in uniform, marauders, sturdy but dejected citizens and country people, women and children, pressed and jostled each other amid vehicles of all descriptions; ammunition and baggage-waggons, carriages with teams of every variety, numbers of horses of all kinds, requisitioned and lawfully owned, jostling, pushing, and making way for each other, swaying to the right and the left. Droves of horned cattle also were moving along, which had probably been captured and driven away on the march. Few horsemen were to be seen, but the elegant carriages of the Emigrants were conspicuous, painted in all colours, and adorned with gold and silver, which I had already admired in Grevenmachern. The greatest crush, however, arose when the crowd, which filled the market-place, had to push their way into a street, straight indeed and handsome, but proportionately much too narrow. I never in my life saw anything like it; the scene might be compared to a stream which had first overflowed the fields and meadows, and was again compelled to force its way through the narrow arches of a bridge, and flow onwards in its limited channel.

Throughout the long street, which was overlooked by our windows, the strangest tide seemed swelling and heaving; a lofty double-seated travelling-carriage towered above the flood; we thought it might be the pretty Frenchwomen; it was not they, however, but Count Haugwitz,* whom, with a sort of malicious pleasure, I now saw slowly advancing, and being rocked to and fro.

11th October.

A good dinner was prepared for us, a delicious leg of mutton being particularly acceptable; there was no want of good wine and bread; and thus, on the verge of the wildest tumult, we were enjoying ourselves in the greatest tranquillity; like a man seated on the rocks of a lighthouse may look out upon the raging billows of a stormy sea, and every now and again see a ship abandoned to its fury. But a truly pathetic family-scene awaited us in this hospitable mansion.

The son, a handsome young man, carried away by the

* Goethe had been acquainted with Count Haugwitz since 1775, and in his *Autobiography* and the *Tag- und Jahresheften* always speaks leniently of him. The "malicious pleasure" here spoken of must therefore have proceeded from Goethe's dissatisfaction at the issue of the Campaign, for which Haugwitz's policy was doubtless somewhat to blame.

general feelings of the day, had joined the national troops in Paris, and had distinguished himself there. But when the Prussians entered the country, and the Emigrants arrived, in proud confidence of certain victory, the parents who believed in this also, implored their son to give up his situation, which must now be odious to him, to return home, and to fight for the good cause. The son, against his inclination, and out of respect for his parents, had returned just when the Prussians, Austrians, and Emigrants were retreating. In a state of desperation he pressed through the crowd to his father's house. What would he do now? And how would they receive him? Joy filled their hearts at seeing him again; but great was their grief at losing him the moment afterwards; in a state of distraction also from fear of losing both house and home in the storm. Attached, as most young men were, to the new order of things, he was compelled to join the party which he abhorred, and no sooner has he done this than he sees this party overwhelmed in ruin.

As he had run away from Paris, he knew very well that he must already be inscribed in the list of traitors, and condemned to death; and now, in an instant, he was to be banished from his country, and driven from his father's house. The parents, whose inclination it was to load him with caresses, are themselves obliged to drive him forth, and he, amid his tears of joy, at seeing them again, could hardly tear himself away; their embraces seemed reproaches; and the parting, which took place before our eyes, was terrible.

All this occurred in the entrance-hall, just before the door of our room. Scarcely had quiet been restored, and the parents retired weeping, when another scene, almost more wonderful and striking, occurred, in which we were ourselves interested, and which caused us some embarrassment, but about which, although touching enough, we could not in the end help smiling. Several of the country people, men, women, and children, rushed into our room, and threw themselves, yelling and screaming, at my feet. With the burning eloquence with which their grief and affliction inspired them, they complained that the soldiers were driving away their cattle; they appeared to be farm people of some large estate. They said if I would only look out of the window, I could see them that instant being driven past—the Prussians had seized them—and they begged me to help them, and order them to be restored. On this I went to the window, to consider what I should do, when our cunning hussar got behind me, and said: "I beg your pardon, but I have given you out as the brother-in-law of the King of Prussia, as a means of getting a hearty reception and good treatment. The peasants, indeed, ought not to have come in; but just refer the good people to me, and with some kind words make it appear as if you were convinced by my proposals."

What could I do? Surprised and displeased, I tried to gather my thoughts, and appeared as if I were considering the circumstances, silently saying to myself, Are not cunning and deceit allowable in war? He who is served by rogues, is in danger of being led astray by them. A useless and shameful piece of business had here to be avoided; therefore, like the physician who in desperate cases continues to hold out hope, and writes his prescriptions, I dismissed the good people, more with pantomimic gestures than otherwise; then, to ease my conscience, I again said to myself, if the true heir to the throne at Sivry was unable to promise the clamorous people their horse, then, surely, the spurious brother-in-law of the King may well be excused for seeking to rid himself of these unfortunates with some well-turned excuse.

Amid the darkness of night we rearched Sebincourt; all of the windows were lit up, as a sign that the rooms were already all occupied. At every door we were refused admittance; first by the inmates themselves who wanted no new visitors; then by those who were quartered on them, and who wished no new companions. Without much ceremony, however, our hussar made his way into a house, and finding some French soldiers sitting at a fire in the hall, he requested them earnestly to make room beside it for a distinguished gentleman. We entered and found them very civil; they made room for us, but resumed their singular attitude—holding their feet up before the fire. They also occasionally took a turn up and down the hall, and then returned to their former position; whereupon I observed, that their chief object was to dry the under part of their gaiters.

Very soon, however, I found them to be people I had seen before; they were, in truth, the very same who, in the morning, had walked so skilfully in the mud beside our carriage. Having arrived before us, they had already washed the lower parts at a spring, brushed them, and were now drying them, to be able the following morning gallantly to front the mud and dirt of another day. It was an example worth following, and which one ought to remember in various emergencies of life. It reminded me also of my good comrades, who had received the order about cleanliness with such grumblings.

But to have got us established thus far, was not enough for our clever untiring Liseur; the fiction of the preceding day, which had been so successful, was boldly repeated; the name of the great General, brother-in-law of the King, had a powerful effect, and banished a whole crowd of worthy Emigrants from one of the double-bedded rooms. To make up the number, we brought in two officers, named Von Köhler; I betook myself outside to the well-tried sleeping-carriage, the pole of which, pointing to Germany, suggested very peculiar reflections, which were, however, very soon cut short by my falling asleep.

12th October.

To-day's march was even more melancholy than yesterday's; the exhausted horses kept falling more frequently, and lay in greater numbers among the overturned carriages in the fields beside the road. Some smart portmanteaux, belonging to the Emigrant corps, had fallen through the torn coverings from the roofs of the waggons; the ornamental, decorated appearance of these abandoned, unclaimed articles, tempted passers-by to appropriate them, and some picked them up—a load which they were very soon obliged to throw down again. This probably gave rise to the accusation made against the Prussians of having plundered the Emigrants on the retreat.

Some good stories were told of occurrences of this sort;

a heavily-laden Emigrant waggon had stuck fast ascending a hill, and had been abandoned. The troops that came up behind searched it; found some boxes of moderate dimensions, but of a weight that surprised them; joining forces, they carried them with unspeakable difficulty to the top. They then proceeded to make a division of the booty and burden. What a sight was presented! Out of each of the boxes, when broken open, tumbled innumerable packs of cards; and the money-seekers had to console themselves with bantering and laughing at each other.

We proceeded on our march through Longuion to Longwy; and here I must observe, that it is most fortunate for us that in the same way as many important and joyful occurrences vanish from the memory, scenes of horror likewise become blunted in the imagination. Why, therefore, repeat that the roads became no better; that now, as before, we shuddered, again and again, at the sight of horses flayed, with the flesh freshly cut from their bones, lying about on all sides among the overturned waggons? Naked bodies of men also, from which the clothes had been stripped, were frequently seen at times, but barely concealed under bushes, and at others lying exposed to view, close to the road.

Rest and refreshment, however, again awaited us, in a place removed from the common route; but we had occasion also to make sad reflections on the condition of well-to-do and worthy citizens amidst the fearful horrors of war, which had, this time, come upon them quite unexpectedly.

13th October.

Our guide, wishing to show us that he had not falsely boasted of his good, well-to-do relations in this quarter, brought us, by a circuitous route, through Arlon, where, in the handsome little town, we were most kindly received by some honest people, to whom he had announced our visit; they seemed to hold a respectable position, and inhabited a good, well-furnished house. The worthy persons seemed rejoiced to see their cousin, and thought they saw certain improvement and rapid advancement in prospect for him in the commission with which he had been entrusted of extricating us, our two carriages and numerous horses, and, as he had given them to believe, large sums of money and jewels besides, from the prevailing confusion. We were also able to bear testimony to his good conduct hitherto; and although we had no great belief in the conversion of this prodigal son, he had been of so much service to us hitherto that we could not avoid having some confidence in his future behaviour also. The rascal did not fail, in his fawning way, to act his part, and actually received from the excellent people, in secret, a handsome present in gold.

We, for our part, refreshed ourselves with a cold breakfast which was laid out for us, and some very excellent wine; and replied, as comfortingly as possible, to the questions of the honest people, who were in a state of great bewilderment about the probabilities of the immediate future.

We had observed before the house some singular-looking waggons, longer, and higher in some cases, than ordinary baggage-waggons, and with curious projections at the sides. Out of curiosity I made inquiries about these singular vehicles, and was told in a confidential, cautious way, that they had contained the Emigrants' assignat machinery; and also heard of the boundless misery the things had caused in the district. For some time past the people had found it almost impossible to protect themselves from the genuine assignats, and now, since the inroad of the Emigrants, had, in addition, to submit to false ones being thrust into circulation. Some prudent tradespeople had immediately sent several of these suspicious pieces of paper to Paris, and had succeeded in obtaining from thence an official declaration of their spuriousness; but the things were causing infinite confusion to trade and commerce. With the genuine assignats they were, of course, only cheated of a part, but with the spurious ones, on the other hand, they were sure of being cheated of everything. And as it was impossible at a first glance to distinguish the one from the other, nobody any longer knew what to give and what to take; and so much uncertainty, suspicion, and apprehension were thus spread abroad, even as far as Luxembourg and Trèves, that a more wretched state of things could not be imagined than now existed throughout the country.

In the midst of all these already existing miseries, and others that were still impending, the people maintained a citizen dignity, kindliness, and polish of manners, which excited our astonishment—a reflex of which is to be found in the serious French plays of former and recent times. Of such a state of society no conception can be formed from the condition of our own country, or its attempts to imitate its neighbour. The *petite ville* * may be laughable, but the burghers of small German towns are ridiculous.

14th October.

We were very agreeably surprised in driving from Arlon to Luxembourg to find an excellent high-road, and were admitted into this fortress, at other times so important and well-guarded, as we had been into every village and town on the road. Without being stopped or questioned anywhere, we went leisurely looking about us within the outworks, ramparts, ditches, drawbridges, walls, and gates, trusting the rest to our guide, who said he wanted to go and find out his father and mother. The town was crowded both with wounded and sick, and with vigorous and healthy, who were doing their best to restore their own and their horses' strength, and to get their vehicles repaired.

Our party, which had hitherto kept together, was now obliged to separate; our clever quarter-master procured a good room for me, overlooking a very small court, not much larger than a chimney, but as the room had very high windows there was sufficient light. He managed to establish me there very comfortably with my baggage and other things, and to supply all my wants; he described what sort of people were in the house, and assured me that

---

* Hempel thinks it difficult to say what French dramas Goethe can have referred to here. And even Kotzebue's *Kleinstädter*, which did not appear till 1803, was an imitation of the French, which, therefore, makes even the French provincialist ridiculous. It was taken from Picard's *Petite Ville*.

some small gift would ensure me from being driven out again, and procure me good treatment.

Here, for the first time, I was able to open my portmanteau again, and to assure myself that I had lost none of my travelling effects, money, or manuscripts. The bundle containing my notes relating to my theory of colours I arranged first; my first maxim as usual, always being to enlarge my experience, and improve my method. My notes of the war, and my own adventures, I felt no inclination to meddle with. The unfortunate result of the expedition gave me reason to fear that greater evils might come, and lead to new vexations and fresh anxieties springing up in the mind. My quiet abode, from which was shut out every noise, like a cloister-cell, allowed me opportunity enough for the quietest reflections; whereas, as soon as I set my foot beyond the door of the house, I found myself in a warlike tumult of the liveliest description, and could wander at my pleasure about one of the most singular places perhaps to be found in the whole world.

15th October.

He who has not seen Luxembourg himself will be unable to form any conception of this fortress. The imagination becomes bewildered when endeavouring to recall the strange variety, with which the eye found it difficult to become familiar, even when in the midst of it. A map and plan would be requisite, to make what I am going to say in any measure intelligible.

A brook called the Petrus, at first alone, and afterwards in conjunction with the river which meets it, the Elze, winds meandering round about the place between and around the rocks, sometimes in its natural channel, sometimes in an artificial one. On the left bank, high up and on a flat, lies the old town; this, with its fortifications towards the open country, resembles most other fortified towns. When, however, provision for its security towards the west was contemplated, it was evident that it would also have to be protected on the side of the chasm where the water flowed; with the continued improvement of military science even this was insufficient, and it became necessary to erect new redoubts on the right bank of the stream, towards the south, east, and north, on the salient points and recesses of the irregular rocks, the one for the protection of the other. This caused an innumerable series of bastions, redoubts, half-moons, *tenailles*, and other works of the kind, which the art of defence requires only in the most extraordinary cases.

Nothing can be more singular than the aspect of the narrow valley which stretches itself along the river through the midst of all this; the few level places, both where it is merely sloping or abruptly precipitous, are laid out in gardens, cut into terraces, and enlivened with pleasure-houses; and from there, one looks to the right and left upon the steepest rocks, and upon walls towering upwards. Here one finds so much sublimity united with beauty, so much solemnity with loveliness, that one cannot help wishing that Poussin had exercised his glorious talent in such a place.

The parents of our roguish guide owned a house in the *Pfaffenthal* (priest's valley), with a pretty sloping garden, and very kindly allowed me to enjoy it. The church and monastery, not far off, justified the name given to this Elysium, and where the ecclesiastical neighbourhood would seem to promise the lay inhabitants peace and tranquillity, every glance directed towards the heights would remind them of war, violence, and destruction.

Meanwhile it was most refreshing to me to get out of the town, where the miserable sequels of war were being enacted; hospitals, maimed soldiers, broken weapons, axletrees out of repair, wheels, and gun-carriages, together with all the other evidences of the ravages of war. To escape from the streets, where wheelwrights, smiths, and other workmen were unweariedly and noisily carrying on their operations, and to conceal myself in the little garden in the priestly valley was indeed most agreeable. Here, one, who had been longing for rest and reflection, found the most welcome asylum.

16th October.

The inconceivable variety of the warlike structures which towered up and joined each other, presented a different view at every step one took, forwards or backwards, up or down, and excited in me a wish to make a sketch of, at least, a portion of them. This wish, indeed, was easily aroused in me here, seeing that for many weeks past my eyes had beheld scarcely a single object calculated to awaken it. Amongst the other singular effects noticed here was that produced by many of the rocks, fronting each other, and the walls and other defensive works connected up on high by drawbridges, galleries, and other curious contrivances. A professional eye would have surveyed it all from a scientific point of view, and enjoyed the skill displayed in the secure arrangement; I, however, could only profit by the picturesque effect, and should have been only too glad to have exercised my imitative powers upon it, had not drawing been strictly forbidden in fortresses.

19th October.

For several days I had thus wandered about, solitary enough—but with many thoughts and reflections—among these labyrinths, where the natural rock and the warlike erections towered up, one by the side of the other, vying with the singularly steep defiles, where however, on the other hand, trees and ornamental shrubs were not excluded. On returning to the house, I thereupon endeavoured to put upon paper the views, as they had gradually impressed themselves upon my imagination; imperfectly this was done, no doubt, but still sufficiently well to preserve the recollection of an extremely singular state of things.

20th October.

I had had time to reflect upon the immediate past; but the more one reflected, the more confused and uncertain did everything appear. I saw also that probably the most necessary thing to be done was, to prepare for what was next to come. The few remaining miles to Trèves had to be got over; and what confusion might we not expect to find there, seeing that the upper classes were now pressing forwards among the other fugitives!

The most painful intelligence that reached us, and

which could not be concealed, and filled every one with rage and fury, however resigned he might hitherto have been, was, that our Commanders-in-chief had been obliged to come to terms with the accursed insurgents, although, in their manifesto, they had doomed them to destruction —wretches debased by the most frightful crimes; that, moreover, the fortresses had been delivered up to them, as the only means of securing a retreat of themselves and their troops. The effect of the news upon some of our people made us fear they would lose their reason.

22nd October.

At Grevenmachern, on our road to Trèves, nothing more was to be seen of the gallant bulwark of a carriage which we had noticed there on our first visit; the fields lay desolate and deserted, and cut up by wheels; and the prospect, far and near, bore witness to our late, fleeting visit. I drove this time past the post-office in perfect silence, with requisitioned horses; the letter-box was still standing in its old place, but no crowd was pressing round it; I could not refrain from making the strangest reflections.

But a glorious gleam of sunshine lit up the landscape just as the monument at Ygel came in sight, and this cheered me as a lighthouse does the sailor at night.

Perhaps the power of antiquity was never so much felt as in this contrast; it is a monument of warlike times, but still of prosperous, victorious days, and of an enduring, healthy state of existence, of a stirring race of men in this part of the country.

Although built in later times, under the Antonines, it has retained, nevertheless, so many qualities of the highest kind of art, that it impresses one with a feeling of pleasing solemnity, and bears witness, in its different parts, to the existence of a joyous, active mode of life. It detained me a long time; I made some notes upon it, and left it unwillingly, as afterwards I felt more acutely still the wretchedness of my present condition.

But even then more joyful thoughts suggested themselves to my mind, which were destined, soon afterwards, to be realised.

Trèves, 23rd October.

We brought our friend, Lieutenant von Fritsch, whom, much against his inclination, we had left behind at his post, the welcome intelligence that he had received the order of merit for good military service; an honour justly bestowed as a reward for a brave action; and he was the more favoured by fortune as he had had no share in our sufferings. The story of the matter is as follows.

The French, when they knew us to have marched sufficiently forward into the country, in great difficulties, and at a distance, tried to play us an unexpected trick in our rear; they advanced close to Trèves in considerable numbers, and even with guns. Lieutenant von Fritsch heard of it, and with a small body of troops went out to meet the enemy, who, startled by this display of vigilance, and fearing that more troops might be advancing, retired to Merzig, after a slight skirmish, and appeared no more. Our friend's horse was wounded, and his boot grazed by the same ball; but he was rewarded with a most distinguished reception on his return as the victor. The magistrates and burgesses showed him the greatest attention; the ladies, too, who had hitherto known him only as a handsome young man, were doubly loud in his praise now as a hero.

He informed his commanding officer of the occurrence, which, as a matter of course, was also told to the King, and the blue cross and star was the result. The joy of the brave youth, and his supreme delight, afforded me the greatest pleasure; Fortune who had shunned us, had sought him out in our rear; and he found himself rewarded for his obedience to military discipline, which had appeared at first to chain him down to a position of inactivity.

24th October.

My friend obtained quarters for me in the house of the same Canon with whom I had lodged before. I had not altogether escaped from the general sickness, and stood in need of some medicine and rest.

During these tranquil hours I again took up the notes I had jotted down before about the monument at Ygel.

If we are to say what is the most general impression it produces, it may be said that we here find face to face, life and death, the Present and Future, and both merged in each other in an æsthetic sense. This was the glorious manner of the ancients, which was preserved for long in the world of art.

The height of the monument may be about seventy feet; it rises, in the manner of an obelisk, in several architectural divisions; first the basis, above that a socle, then the chief mass of the structure, above this an attic, then a frontal; and last of all a curious pinnacle, winding upwards, and displaying the remains of a ball and an eagle. Each of these divisions, together with the parts of which it is composed, is adorned all over with figures and ornamentations.

This peculiarity proves it to be the work of later times; for things of this kind are introduced, as soon as the pure proportion is lost in the whole; in connection with which many other points might be noticed.

Nevertheless, it must be acknowledged that this work is based upon a higher style of art than had existed but a short time previously. Thus the antique spirit prevails through the whole of it, inasmuch as actual life is represented, seasoned allegorically with mythological allusions.

In the principal space are a man and a woman of colossal size, joining hands, and united by a third figure, now missing, as of one giving the blessing. They stand between two highly-ornamented pilasters, decorated with dancing children ranged one above another. All of the flat surfaces then depict the happiest family relations, representing the cordial union of kinsmen, and a life of social, honest industry and enjoyment.

But active life is the chief characteristic everywhere, although I cannot trust myself to explain it all. In one of the spaces some merchants appear as if assembled to discuss some piece of business; but there are evidently ships laden with merchandise, with dolphins for ornaments, beasts of burden conveying goods from place to place, the arrival of commodities, an examination of these, and other things likely to occur in the lives of mankind.

Then also in the zodiac is a horse in rapid motion, that,

perhaps, in former times had a carriage and driver behind it; in the friezes and other spaces are Bacchus, Fauns, Sol, and Luna, and other objects pertaining to the miraculous, embellish, or have embellished, the ball and summit.

The whole has a most pleasing effect, and considering the stage now attained by architecture and sculpture, a noble monument to the most distinguished individuals might be erected in this style, depicting their enjoyments and good deeds. And while occupied with these reflections, I was, in a silent way, celebrating the birthday of our revered Duchess Amalia, and recalling her life, her noble works, and beneficence; and thus I was very naturally led, in imagination, to erect a similar obelisk to her, and characteristically to embellish all the monumental fields with her individual actions and virtues.

Trèves, 25th October.

The quiet and leisure I was now enjoying, I made use of further in arranging and working out many things which I had commenced in days of the wildest confusion. I read over and revised my chromatic papers; drew various diagrams for my colour-tables, which I altered repeatedly, in order to make clearer what I wished to represent and maintain. This reminded me to try and recover the third part of Fischer's Lexicon of Natural Philosophy. Inquiring and searching, I at last found the kitchen-maid in the hospital, which had been established comfortably enough in one of the convents. She was suffering from the general complaint; the rooms, however, were airy and clean, and she recognised me, but could not speak; took out the volume from below her pillow, and delivered it to me as clean and in as good a condition as I had given it to her; and I hope that the attention which I ordered the people to bestow on her has been of service to her.

A young schoolmaster * who visited me, and brought me some of the latest numbers of the newspapers, gave me an opportunity for some pleasant conversation. He was astonished, like many others, that I had no wish to

* Wyttenbach, who was then only twenty-five; he was afterwards appointed director of the Gymnasium in Trèves.

converse about poetry, but rather seemed to throw myself with all my energy into the study of Nature. He knew the philosophy of Kant, and I could therefore point out to him the path I had entered. When Kant, in his 'Critique of Pure Reason' places teleologic judgment side by side with the æsthetic, it is evident that he wishes to show that a work of art should be treated in the same way as a work of Nature, and a work of Nature in the same way as a work of art; and that the worth of each should be developed out of itself, and considered by itself. About such things I could be very eloquent; and I believe I was of some use to the worthy young man. It is wonderful what a mixture of truth and error every period carries and drags about with it, inherited from days but recently passed, or even from days long gone by; whilst enterprising spirits cut out a new path for themselves, where, for the most part, they have to go alone, or find a companion only for some short distance of the way.

Trèves, 26th October.

One could not leave these peaceful surroundings without finding oneself, as it were, in the Middle Ages, where convent-walls, and the wildest, most irregular, and warlike condition of things, might be constantly contrasted with each other. The great subject of complaint, which was felt both by the citizens of the place and by the returning Emigrants, was the frightful misery caused both to town and country by the false assignats. Some of the mercantile houses had sent these to Paris, and had been informed from thence of their spuriousness, complete worthlessness, and of the great danger of having anything to do with them. Further, that the genuine ones likewise were falling into discredit; and it was feared by everyone that, owing to the complete up-turn of everything in the State, all these papers would be destroyed. This terrible evil was now being followed by others; so that altogether the troubles appeared quite endless to the imagination and the feelings. A desperate state of things, like that upon seeing a town burnt down before one's very eyes.

Trèves, 28th October.

The table d'hôte, which was, on the whole, well served, presented a bewildering spectacle; there were soldiers and civilians, in all sorts of uniforms, colours, and costumes. Some were sitting in moody silence, others giving vent to passionate expressions; but all of them appeared to fancy themselves confined in the same common hell.

Here, a truly affecting incident occurred to me. An old hussar officer, of middle size, with grey beard and hair, and sparkling eyes, came up to me after dinner, seized hold of me by the hand, and asked if I had actually been obliged to endure what all the rest had had to undergo? I told him something about what occurred at Valmy and Hans, from which he could easily imagine the rest. On this he began to express the warmest sympathy, and addressed enthusiastic speeches to me, which I scarcely like to repeat. It was, he said, wrong, that those even whose profession and duty it was to suffer hardships and to risk their lives, had been led into such unheard-of troubles; but that I (expressing at the same time his high opinion both of myself and my works) should have been obliged to endure them, appeared to him quite inexcusable. I represented the matter to him from the brighter point of view, and spoke as if it had been good experience for me to have suffered for a few weeks along with my Prince, and with the many brave soldiers, to some of whom I had not been altogether useless. But he continued in the same strain; meanwhile civilians came up, and said that they owed me thanks for having gone to witness it all, as they might now expect to get from my practised pen a description and explanation of the campaign. The old warrior would not listen to this either and exclaimed, "Do not fancy that; he has too much sense. What he would be allowed to write, he can have no wish to write; and what he would like to write, he will not write!"

One felt scarcely any further wish to hear what was going on, boundless mortification was for ever the subject of conversation. And in the same way as it excites an uncomfortable feeling when happy persons are incessantly proclaiming their happiness, it becomes even more intolerable when misfortunes, which we would gladly drive out of our minds, are talked of again and again. To have been driven out of the country by the French whom they hated, to have been obliged to make terms with them, to have had to come to terms with the men of the tenth of August—was as severe an infliction for the mind and spirit, as the previous sufferings had been for the body. The Commanders-in-chief were not spared; and the confidence which had been reposed for so many years in the renowned generals, seemed to have vanished for ever.

Trèves, 29th October.

Now, when again upon German ground, and we might thus hope to be able to disentangle ourselves from the dreadful confusion, information reached us of Custine's audacious and successful exploits. The large magazine at Spires had fallen into his hands, and he had thereupon been able to effect the surrender of Mainz. These advances appeared to be dragging boundless evils in their train; they bore witness to an extraordinary genius, as sagacious as it was daring, and therefore everything in that quarter was given up for lost. It appeared highly probable and likely that Coblentz was already occupied by the French, and how in that case were we to undertake our retreat! Frankfort * also we gave up in imagination; Hanau and Aschaffenburg on one side, Cassel on the other, we saw threatened; and, altogether, what might not be apprehended! The neighbouring Princes were paralysed by the wretched neutrality system; this made the general mass more zealous and active in support of the revolutionary sentiments with which they were filled. Might they not introduce a change of sentiment in the country around, and in the adjacent provinces, as had been done in Mainz, and make

* On the same day that Mainz surrendered to the French some two thousand men were sent on to Frankfort, and the city was called upon to pay a contribution of two millions of crowns. One million was paid before the 31st of October; but, before the arrangements about the second installment had been made, Mainz had been recaptured by the Hessians.

rapid use of the converts they had already gained? This had all to be thought of and to be discussed.

I often heard such observations as: Were the French likely to have taken such important steps without great consideration and circumspection, and without a large army to support them? Custine's actions seemed as bold as they were cautious; he, his subordinates, and superiors, were described as prudent, energetic, sagacious men. The present troubles were great and bewildering—of all the sufferings and anxieties hitherto endured, unquestionably the greatest.

In the midst of this misery and confusion a stray letter from my mother found me, and, in a strange manner, called up to my mind the peaceful days of my youth, and many circumstances connected with my family and native town. My uncle, the Alderman Textor,* had died; it was my near relationship to him that had excluded me during his lifetime from holding the honourable and useful post of a Frankfort Councillor; and now, in accordance with an established and laudable custom, they thought of me, I being pretty far advanced among the Frankfort graduates.

My mother had been commissioned to ask me whether I would accept the office of Councillor if I were chosen one of those to be balloted for, and the golden ball should fall to me? Such a question could not, perhaps, have arrived at a more singular time than the present; I was taken by surprise, and thrown back upon myself; a thousand images started up before me, and prevented me from forming any definite conclusion. But as a sick person or prisoner forgets his pains and troubles whilst listening to some tale, so I was carried back to other spheres and other times.

I fancied myself in my grandfather's garden, where the espaliers, richly laden with nectarines, were wont to arouse the grandson's longing appetite; and only the fear of being

* The only brother of Goethe's mother, Johann J. Textor, died on the 24th of October 1792. Goethe's remark about being excluded from the post of Councillor refers to the Imperial Resolution of 1725, which maintains that a candidate for the office must not have any near relative in the Council.

banished from this paradise, only the hope of receiving from the good old grandfather's own hand the red-cheeked fruit when ripe, could in some measure restrain this longing, till the proper time at length arrived. Thereupon I saw the venerable old man busied with his roses, and carefully protecting his hands from the thorns with the old-fashioned gloves, presented to him as tribute by toll-freed cities; like noble Laertes—all but in his longings and his sorrows. Then I saw him in his Mayor's robes, and gold chain, seated upon the throne under the Emperor's portrait; then, alas! in his dotage as he had been for several years in his sick chair, and, finally—in his grave!

On my last journey through Frankfort, I had found my uncle in possession of the house, court, and garden, he, as a worthy son of such a father, had likewise been appointed to some of the highest offices in the government of the free city. Here amid the family circle, in the unchanged, well-known old place, these boyhood recollections were vividly called up, and were now again brought before me with new emphasis. They were united with other youthful feelings, which I must not conceal. What burgher of a free city will deny that he has been ambitious of, sooner or later, rising to the dignity of councillor, alderman, or burgomaster; and has industriously and carefully striven, to the best of his ability, to obtain these, or perhaps other less important offices? The pleasing thought of one day filling some post in the government is awakened early in the breast of every republican, and is liveliest and proudest in the soul of a boy.

I could not, however, abandon myself long to these pleasing dreams of my childhood. Too soon aroused from them, I surveyed the ominous locality around me, the melancholy circumstances which hemmed me in, and, at the same time, the obscure, nay, dark prospect of affairs in the direction of my native town. I saw Mainz in the hands of the French; Frankfort threatened, if not already taken; the way to it obstructed; and within its walls, streets, squares, dwellings, the friends of my youth and my relations, overtaken, perhaps, by the same misfortune which I had seen the people in Longwy and Verdun so cruelly called upon to suffer. Who would have dared to rush headlong into the midst of such a state of things!

But even in the happiest days of that venerable corporation, it would have been impossible for me to agree to this proposal; my reasons could be easily explained. For twelve * years past I had been enjoying singular good fortune—the confidence as well as the indulgence of the Duke of Weimar. This highly-gifted and cultivated prince was pleased to approve of my inadequate services, and gave me facilities for developing myself, which would not have been possible under any other conditions in my native country. My gratitude was boundless, as was also my attachment to his august consort and mother, to his young family, and to a province which might be said to be in some little way indebted to me. Was it not my duty to think of that circle of newly-acquired, highly-cultivated friends, and of the many other domestic enjoyments and advantages which had sprung from my fortunate and settled position? These images and feelings, which were excited in me anew by this occurrence, had a sudden and cheering effect upon me at this moment of deepest depression; for one already feels half rescued, even amid the most mournful circumstances in a foreign country, when one can cast a hopeful glance towards the security of home. Thus, here upon earth, we enjoy what is promised us beyond the spheres.

In this mood I began my letter to my mother; † and if the reasons I gave seemed to have reference principally to my own feelings, personal comfort, and individual advantage, I was able also to add others which showed my consideration for my native town, and were sufficiently weighty to convince my well-wishers there. For how could I expect to work effectually in so peculiar a sphere,

---

* Hempel says that there must be a mistake in this number, for Goethe had been in Weimar since November 1775, and cannot possibly mean to say that he had lived there five years without having won the Duke's confidence.

† It seems strange that Goethe's letter to his mother in answer to her inquiry should bear the date of the 24th of December, fully two months after having received her letter. This letter of Goethe's is published in Reimer's *Mittheilungen über Goethe*.

where a careful previous education perhaps is more necessary than for any other? I had been accustomed, for many years, to occupation adapted to my capacity, and which was of such a nature as could scarcely be required for the aims and objects of a town. Nay, I could add, that only those who were properly citizens of the town ought to be admitted into the Council, and that I had become so much a stranger as to consider myself altogether an outsider.

All this I graciously made known to my mother who, no doubt, did not expect any other answer. Late enough, truly, it must have been before this letter reached her

Trèves, 29*th October*.

My young friend, with whom I had many pleasant talks on scientific and literary subjects, was also very well informed about the history of the town and neighbourhood. Our walks, therefore, when the weather was tolerable, were always instructive, and I was able to note what was of principal importance in the neighbourhood. The city itself is striking; it lays claim to possessing more ecclesiastical buildings than any other town of the same size; this it would be difficult to deny, for inside the walls it is crowded, nay, overwhelmed, with churches, chapels, monasteries, convents, colleges, and other buildings for knightly orders and fraternities to meet; outside it is beset by abbeys, institutions, and Carthusian monasteries.

All these bear testimony to a widely-extended ecclesiastical jurisdiction, over which, in former times, the Archbishop ruled; his diocese reached from here as far as Metz, Toul, and Verdun. The civil government also is not without important possessions: the Elector of Trèves rules over a magnificent country on both sides of the Moselle; and thus palaces are not wanting in Trèves, to prove that, at different periods, she claimed sovereignty over a very extensive territory.

The origin of the town dates back to legendary times, and its favourable position is likely to have early attracted settlers. The inhabitants of Trèves were included in the Roman Empire, were first heathens, then Christians, and were subdued by the Normans and the

Franks; finally, the beautiful country was incorporated with the German-Roman Empire.

I should have liked to have seen the town at a more favourable season, and to have become better acquainted with its inhabitants, who have always had the reputation of being good-natured and cheerful. Of the first quality some traces are still met with, scarcely any of the other; but how could cheerfulness be expected in the midst of such a state of things!

When we look back in the annals of the city we find repeated mention made of warlike devastations committed in this region; the valley of the Mosello, and even the river itself, being favourable for the movements of armies. Attila, from the far East, and his countless host, like ourselves, made both his advance and retreat through the region bordering on this river. What sufferings the inhabitants endured during the Thirty Years' War, till the end of the seventeenth century; and their Prince, who had allied himself with France, as his nearest neighbour, had to suffer a tedious imprisonment in Austria! The city had also more than once suffered from civil wars; this has ever been the case in episcopal cities, where the citizens are not always able to agree with the ecclesiastico-secular authorities.

My guide, whilst communicating the historical details, drew my attention to buildings of very different periods, most of which were curious, and therefore worthy of observation; but few of them afforded pleasure to a cultivated taste, like that derived from the monument at Ygol.

The remains of the Roman amphitheatre I found remarkable enough; but as the building had fallen in, and had, in all probability, served for several centuries as a quarry, nothing could be deciphered. We admired, however, the way in which the ancients, in their wisdom, accomplished great results with moderate means; and how they had made use of the natural advantages offered by a site between two hills, to lighten the work both of excavating and building.

After ascending the first slopes of the Martisberg, with its ruins, and mounting a little higher, we had a view of the Apolloberg over the tops of all the relics of the saints,

N

over cupolas and roofs; and thus the two gods, with Mercury at their side, make good the remembrance of their names; the monuments were destined to perish, but not the genius of the place.

Trèves possesses some remarkable specimens of architecture belonging to the earlier period of the Middle Ages; I have little knowledge of such things,* and they have no attraction to a cultivated mind. After a superficial inspection I found that they confused me; many of them are mere heaps of rubbish, altogether ruins, or turned to other uses.

I was conducted across the large bridge, which was also erected in the Middle Ages, just as everything was enlivened by a glimpse of bright sunshine. Here we could plainly survey the position of the town, which is built upon a flat projecting piece of land, causing the river to bend to the left. The eye could here range from the foot of the Apolloberg, over river, bridge, mills, town, and country; the vineyards—not yet quite leafless—both beneath our feet and opposite us on the first slopes of the Martisberg, displayed themselves in pleasant relief; we felt what a blessed region we were in, and became conscious of a feeling of happiness and pleasure, which seems to pervade the atmosphere in countries where the vines grow. The best Moselle wine, which fell to our lot here, appeared to taste even better after the lovely view we had enjoyed.

Trèves, 29th October.

Our princely chief arrived, and took up his quarters in the Monastery of St. Maximin. The rich and otherwise prosperous occupants had for some time past been in great distress; the brother of the King had been quartered upon them, and the building had never been free since. An establishment of this kind, which originated from a desire for tranquillity and peace, and was arranged for tranquillity

* Goethe somewhat incorrectly calls these remains early medieval, whereas, in fact, they belong to the preceding period of the Roman Empire. Goethe's interest in medieval art was stimulated through his acquaintance and intercourse with Sulpiz Boisserée, and belongs to a later period. (See the Rhine Tour.)

and peace, had a curious aspect under the altered circumstances, for, with every possible forbearance, a violent contrast was evident between knighthood and monkdom. But the Duke, here, as everywhere else, succeeded, even as an unbidden guest, in making himself and his attendants welcome, by his liberality and good nature.

But I was destined here again to be persecuted by the evil demon of war. Our good Colonel Gotsch was also quartered in the monastery; I found him at night watching and nursing his son, who was suffering severely from the ill-fated sickness. I was obliged once more to listen to lamentations and maledictions about our campaign, from the mouth of an old soldier and father, who was well entitled vehemently to denounce the whole string of errors, which were manifest to him as a soldier, and detestable to him as a father. The Islettes* also were talked of again; and, in fact, anybody who had made this fatal point clear to himself, could not help feeling quite desperate about it.

I enjoyed the opportunity of looking at the abbey, and found it an extensive and truly noble building; the rooms were large and lofty, and the floors inlaid, adorned with velvet and damask tapestry, stucco-work, and there was no want of gilding and carving, and other things such as one finds in this sort of palace; and everything was reflected over and over again in large mirrors.

The persons quartered here were also very well provided for; but there was not room for all of the horses, and they were obliged to remain in the open air, without stalls, racks, or mangers. Unfortunately the nose-bags had become rotten, so the oats had to be snuffed up from the ground.

But if the stabling was insignificant, this was made up for by the largeness of the cellars. Besides their own vineyards, the monastery enjoyed the receipt of a number of tithes. Many a cask seemed to have been emptied during the last few months, as numbers of them were lying in the courtyard.

---

* The mountain pass near St. Menehould, mentioned under the date of September 18th. The Allies had never been able to gain possession of it.

30th October.

Our Prince had a large party at dinner; three of the chief ecclesiastics were invited; they had provided some fine table-linen for the occasion, and a very beautiful service of porcelain; there was not much silver, all their plate and valuables had been removed to Ehrenbreitstein. The dishes were deliciously prepared by the Prince's cooks; the wine, which was to have followed us to France, had been brought back from Luxembourg, and was now drunk here; but what was most deserving of praise was some delicious white bread, which reminded us by contrast of the commissariat bread at Hans.

In my investigations into the history of Tròves, during the last few days, I had necessarily to make some inquiry about the Abbey of St. Maximin; I was, therefore, able to carry on a learned conversation with my clerical neighbour. The great antiquity of the foundation was taken for granted; then its manifold and various fortunes were dwelt upon, and its close proximity to the town, which was alike dangerous to both; it had, in fact, been burnt down and completely destroyed in the year 1674. I had also informed myself as to when it was rebuilt, and of its gradual restoration to its present state. Much could be said in its praise, as well as of all the arrangements, and this my clerical friend heard with great pleasure. But he would not listen to anything in praise of the present times; the French Princes had been quartered there for long, and he made sad complaints of their mischief, insolence, and waste.

The conversation, thereupon, again turned to historical subjects; but when I mentioned the time when the abbey had set itself up as equal to the archbishop, and the abbot held rank in the German-Roman Empire, he smiled, and changed the subject, as if he thought such recollections had something suspicious in them at the present time.

The solicitude of the Duke about his regiment now became active and manifest; it was impossible to transport the sick in waggons, hence the Prince ordered a boat to be hired to convey them to Coblenz.

But other soldiers now arrived, who had become disabled in a peculiar way. On the retreat it had very soon been observed that the cannon could not be transported. The artillery-horses perished one after the other, and only a few fresh ones could be found; the horses put in requisition on the march into the country had run away on the retreat, and were scarce everywhere. As a last resource, it was ordered that a large number of the troopers of each regiment should dismount and march on foot, in order that the guns might be saved. Owing to their stiff boots, which at last went to pieces, these brave fellows suffered severely from the wretched state of the roads. A better time was now coming for them, for preparations were made for enabling them to go to Coblenz by water.

November.

My Prince had commissioned me to wait upon the Marquis Lucchesini,* to deliver some complimentary farewell message, and to make some other inquiries. It was late in the evening, and with some difficulty, that I gained admission to the presence of this distinguished man, who in former times was favourably disposed towards me. The gracious and kind way in which he received me was most agreeable; not so his answers to my questions or his attention to my wishes; he dismissed me without having been of the slightest use to me; and I may safely say that I was prepared for this.

When I saw the busy preparations for the departure of the sick and exhausted troopers, it struck me that the best thing I could do would be to make my escape likewise by water. I was very sorry to leave my carriage behind, but they promised to send it after me to Coblenz. I hired a boat with one man, into which all my goods and chattels were conveyed; and as they were put in one by one, they made a very pleasant impression on me, for I had more than once given them up for lost. On this

---

* Goethe had become acquainted with Lucchesini in 1787 in Naples. He is frequently mentioned in the *Italienische Reise*, and his correspondence and dispatches are an important source for information relating to this campaign.

expedition I was joined by a Prussian officer, an old acquaintance, whom I well remembered as a page, and he too had a vivid recollection of his period of court-service, for he insisted that he had usually handed me my coffee.

The weather was tolerable, the passage peaceful, and the agreeable nature of the change in our mode of travelling was manifest, when we saw with what difficulty the columns were marching along the road, which occasionally approached the river; from time to time they were even seen to halt and remain at a stand-still. Even in Trèves, complaints had been made that, in so hurried a retreat, one of our greatest difficulties was to find quarters, as the places assigned to a regiment were very often found to be already occupied, and this occasioned great annoyance and confusion.

The views along the banks of the Moselle were extremely varied during this passage; for although the main direction of the stream is always from south-west to north-east, still, as it flows through rugged and mountainous country, with projecting angles at both sides, which make it bend sometimes to the right, and sometimes to the left, it is forced to flow onwards in a very circuitous course. An experienced boatman is therefore highly necessary; ours displayed both strength and skill, contriving, at one time, to avoid the gravel-banks which obstructed the passage, and then boldly taking advantage, for greater speed, of the rapid current which flowed between the rocky walls. The numerous villages on both sides greatly enlivened the scene; the cultivation of the vine, which appeared everywhere to be carefully attended to, gave indication of a prosperous population, who spared themselves no trouble in the production of the precious juice. Every sunny hill was made use of; but we were also struck by seeing that on the narrow projecting ledges of the precipitous rocks overhanging the stream, as well as on natural terraces, accidentally formed, the vines seemed to thrive the best.

We landed at a pretty inn, and were well received by the old landlady, who complained to us of the many evils she had lately suffered, but gave the Emigrants credit for most of the mischief. She said, that she had often seen, with dismay, these godless people making little balls of the precious bread, and throwing them at each other's heads, and that she and her maids, with tears in their eyes, had afterwards gathered them up again.

And thus we glided down the stream, in good spirits and without any accident, till twilight, when we found ourselves amid the windings of the meandering river, just where it rushes towards the heights of Montreal. Night overtook us before we could reach Trarbach or even got in sight of it. It was pitch dark; we knew we were confined between more or less precipitous banks; when a storm, which had already announced itself from behind, broke upon us with tremendous violence. The stream was soon lashed into billows by the force of the wind, the blasts coming down upon us with a furious roar; one wave after the other washed over the little boat, and we felt wet to the skin. The boatman made no attempt to conceal his uneasiness; the danger appeared the greater the longer it lasted; and our anxiety had risen to the highest pitch, when the honest fellow assured us, that he neither knew where he was, nor in what direction he should steer.

Our companion did not utter a word, on we went in the blackest darkness; sometimes it appeared to me as if I could see dark masses above me, blacker even than the black sky; this did not give much consolation or hope, for to be hemmed in between the land and rocks made our situation more perilous still. We were thus being tossed to and fro in total darkness, when at length a light was seen in the distance, and hope was again awakened within us. We now steered as straight as possible towards it, Paul lending all the assistance in his power.

At last we reached Trarbach in safety, and upon landing found a tolerable inn, and were soon provided with a fowl and some rice. A merchant,[*] who had heard of the arrival of strangers in the dark and stormy night, insisted upon our going to his house, where, in handsomely fur-

[*] The merchant here mentioned was the father of Böcking, the lawyer, who was born in Trarbach in 1802 and died in Bonn in 1870 (Düntzer, *Goethe und Carl August*).

nished rooms, lit up with wax candles, we saw some dark English prints, hung up in pretty glass frames upon the wall. These awakened a cheerful feeling in us, and even some emotion, contrasting, as they did, with the black dangers to which we had just been exposed. The gentleman and his wife, still young people, exerted themselves in showing us every kindness; they gave us some exquisite Moselle wine, of which my companion, who stood most in need of restoration, made particularly good use.

Paul confessed that he had taken off his coat and boots, in order to take to swimming, if the boat had been upset; in which case, indeed, he could have saved nobody but himself.

Scarcely had we dried and refreshed ourselves when I began to feel restless again, and wished to get away. Our kind host wanted to prevent our leaving, and wished us to remain the following day also; and promised us that, from a neighbouring height, he would show us a most extensive and beautiful view over a fine country, and much besides that would have contributed to our restoration and amusement. But it is a singular fact that, in the same way as persons may become habituated to a state of rest and find pleasure in continuing in this state, there is also such a thing as being habituated to a state of restlessness; thus I felt a constant irritation to be on the move, which I could not control.

When we were on the point of hastening away, the good man pressed us to take a couple of mattresses with us, that we might be able, at all events, to make our boat a little more comfortable; the lady did not seem to like giving them, and as they were very good and new, we could hardly blame her. Thus it happens, when quartered in a house, that it is sometimes the husband, and sometimes the wife, who is the more or less kind to the intruding guest.

Without further hinderance we glided down to Coblenz; and the only thing I distinctly remember is, that, at the end of the voyage, I saw the most beautiful view that, perhaps, I have ever seen in my life. When we approached the bridge over the Moselle, this enormous black structure stood out in bold relief before us; through the arches we saw the stately buildings which covered the valley, and above the line of the bridge rose the castle of Ehrenbreitstein, peering through the blue mist which enveloped it. On the right, the town, which joins the bridge, forms a good foreground; this view was a great but only a momentary enjoyment, for we landed immediately, and conscientiously sent the mattresses unharmed to the commercial house to which our worthy friends at Trarbach had directed us.

The Duke of Weimar had excellent quarters assigned to him, in which I also found good accommodation; the army marched in by degrees; the servants of our Prince and General arrived, and never ceased talking of the sufferings they had endured. We rejoiced in having made the passage by water; and even the storm we had successfully encountered seemed a small evil in comparison with all the obstructions and obstacles of a journey by land.

The Prince himself had arrived. A number of generals had assembled round the King; and I, on my solitary rambles along the banks of the Rhine, recalled the strange occurrences of the last few weeks :—

"A French general, La Fayette, the head of a large party—and shortly before the idol of his nation, enjoying the entire confidence of the soldiers—rebels against the supreme authority, which, after the imprisonment of the King, is the sole representative of the nation; he takes to flight, and his army, not stronger than 23,000 men, is now left without a general or superior officer, is disorganised and panic-stricken.

"At the same time, a powerful King, with an allied army of 80,000 men, sets foot upon the French soil, and, after a short delay, two fortified towns surrender.

"A general now appears, of no reputation—Dumourier; without ever having held a superior command; he, with great sagacity and rapidity, makes himself master of a very strong position; this is destroyed, but he obtains a second, where he is again surrounded, and in such a way that the enemy gets between him and Paris.

"But a strange and complicated state of things is produced by uninterrupted rains and frightful weather; the formidable allied army, when not more than six leagues from Châlons, and ten from Rheims, finds itself prevented from reaching either of these places, is forced to retreat, abandons the two places it had captured, loses a third of its numbers, of which, at the utmost, two thousand perished by the sword, and now again finds itself on the banks of the Rhine." All these events, which border on the miraculous, have happened in less than six weeks, and France is saved from the greatest danger that has ever been recorded in her annals.

When one thinks of the many thousand sufferers from this unfortunate expedition, and of their fearful sufferings both of mind and body, which gave them some right to complain, it can easily be imagined that this was not done in silence, and that, in spite of everything, grumblings were still heard from many whose hearts were full to overflowing.

In connection with this I may mention, that I was one day sitting at a large dinner-party, next an excellent old general, and made some allusion to late events, when he interrupted me, and said, very kindly indeed, but with a certain degree of sternness, "Do me the honour to wait upon me to-morrow morning, and then we can speak about these things freely and fairly." I acted as if I meant to agree to the proposal, but remained away, inwardly vowing that I would not again break my customary silence.

Both upon the journey down the river, as well as in Coblenz, I had made many observations relating to my chromatic studies, and obtained a new insight more particularly into epoptic colours; I had always increasing hopes of being able to connect the physical phenomena, and separate them from others with which they seemed to stand in more distant relationship. The diary of Chamberlain Wagner was of much use to me as a supplement to my own, which I had altogether neglected for some time past.

The Duke's regiment had arrived, and went into cantonments in the villages towards Neuwied. Here our Prince showed the most fatherly solicitude for his people; each had only to make known any cause of complaint, and, if possible, redress and assistance were given him. Lieutenant von Flotow, who held command in the town, and stood next to our benefactor, was active in giving assistance to all who required it. The chief want, that of shoes, was provided for by buying leather, and making the shoemakers of the regiment work under the master-shoemakers in the town. Provision was also made for cleanliness and the good appearance of the troops; yellow chalk was procured, jackets were cleaned and coloured, and our troopers trotted about quite smart again.

My studies, and also the conversations I had both with my companions in the household and with the official people, were greatly enlivened by the wine which was presented to our Prince by the town-council; it was the best kind of Moselle, and we had permission to drink it as the Prince generally dined out.

On finding an opportunity for complimenting and thanking one of the donors for it, adding, at the same time, that they must have robbed themselves of many a good bottle, the answer was, that we were welcome to this, and a great deal more; and that they only regretted the casks which they had been obliged to bestow upon the Emigrants, who had, it is true, brought a good deal of money, but also much mischief into the town; in fact, had turned it topsy-turvy. Complaints were made particularly of their conduct to the Duke, whose place they had, to a certain extent, usurped, and had committed many daring and lawless acts in defiance of him.

During the late threatening times he had set out for Ratisbon; and I slipped away one fine morning to his castle, which stood upon the left bank of the Rhine, beautifully situated, somewhat above the town, and which had sprung up, as it were, since I had last been in that part of the country. There it stood solitary, the latest wreck, to speak in a political, if not an architectural, sense; and I had not the courage to ask the warden, who was walking about, for permission to enter. How beautiful was the surrounding country, both far and near! How richly cultivated, and like a garden, the space between the palace and the town! The view up the Rhine was peaceful and calm; but towards the town and fortress, gorgeous and animated.

With the view of crossing the river, I proceeded towards

the flying-bridge; but was soon stopped, or rather stopped of my own accord, to watch the passage of some Austrian waggons, which were being conveyed across one by one. Here a dispute arose between a Prussian and an Austrian non-commissioned officer, which brought out the character of the two nations.

The Austrian, who was posted here to see that the column of waggons was conveyed over with all practical speed, and to prevent confusion by keeping any other vehicle from getting into the line, was imperiously demanded by the Prussian to make an exception in favour of his little car, containing his wife and child, and some baggage. With great composure the Austrian said that he could not comply with the request and appealed to the order, which expressly forbade him to do so; upon this the Prussian became more violent, the Austrian, if possible, more cool; the one would not allow any gap to be made in the column entrusted to his charge, and the other could find no place to enter it. At last the Prussian put his hand to his sword, and challenged his antagonist to fight him; with threats and abuse he tried to inveigle him into the nearest alley, to settle the affair there; but the Austrian, with imperturbable coolness and good sense, and knowing very well that he had right on his side, refused to stir, and went on keeping order as before.

I would have liked this scene to have been witnessed by some caricaturist; for the two men were as different in figure as in behaviour; the calm man was sturdy and strong; the furious man, for so he seemed at last, lean, tall, lanky, and nimble.

The time at my disposal for my little excursion was now nearly over, and the fear of being again delayed in the same way on my return determined me not to visit the valley, formerly such a favourite scene, but which now would only have excited painful feelings and fruitless broodings over earlier years. However, I stood for some time gazing over towards it, mindful of those peaceful times amid the bewildering change of earthly events.

And thus it accidentally happened that I became further instructed about the measures taken for prosecuting the campaign. The Duke's regiment was preparing to cross over; the Prince, with all his retinue, was to follow. I dreaded any continuation of the war, and the desire for flight took possession of me again. This might be called home-sickness in an inverted sense—a longing for the wide world instead of a confined home. There I stood; the glorious river lay before me, gliding down softly and sweetly through the broad extensive landscape; it was flowing towards friends to whom, in spite of many changes, I had always remained faithfully attached. I longed to escape from the strange and fierce world around me, and again to be among friends; and, therefore, on obtaining leave of absence, I hired, with all speed, a boat to take me to Düsseldorf, entrusting my still missing carriage to the care of some Coblenz friends, with a request that they would send it after me.

When I found myself with my baggage on board, and floating down the stream, accompanied by my faithful Paul and a blind passenger, who had been engaged to row occasionally, I congratulated myself on my good luck, and thought I had now escaped from all misfortunes.

However, some other adventures awaited us still. We had not been rowing down the river very long when it became evident that the boat leaked very much, for the boatman, from time to time, kept busily baling out the water. And now we discovered that, in our hurry to get away, we had not observed that the boatmen are in the habit, on the long passage from Coblenz to Düsseldorf, of taking an old worthless boat, and, at the end of the passage, of selling it for firewood; then, with their money in their pockets, and unencumbered, they travel homewards again, comfortably.

However, we went on our course without fear. A clear starry night, but very cold, favoured our voyage; suddenly, the strange oarsman requested to be put on shore, and began to dispute with the boatman as to where was the best place for him to land, about which they could come to no agreement.

In the midst of this dispute, which was carried on with great vehemence, our boatman tumbled into the water, and was with difficulty helped out again. He could not now endure the cold of the bright clear night, and anxiously requested to be put ashore at Bonn, in order to dry and to warm himself. My servant went with him to a public-house frequented by the boatmen; I preferred remaining in the open air, and got a sleeping-place prepared for me with the help of my portmanteau and portfolio. Such is the force of habit, that, having passed the last six weeks almost always in the open air, I had now a sort of aversion to being confined in a room, and to being under cover. On this occasion a new kind of evil arose, which might, indeed, have been foreseen; the boat had been drawn up as far as possible on the shore but not far enough to prevent the water coming in through the leak.

After a deep slumber I found myself more than merely refreshed, for the water had made its way up to my sleeping-place, and had drenched both myself and my effects. I was therefore obliged to rise and find the inn, and to dry myself as well as I could in the midst of a crowd of people smoking tobacco and drinking mulled wine; meanwhile the morning had pretty far advanced, and our voyage was resumed, the boatman doing his best to make up for the lost time by increased exertions at the oar.

DIGRESSION.*

When I look back to the time when I was thus sailing down the Rhine, it seems difficult to say what my feelings were then. The sight of the peaceful expanse of water, and the pleasure derived from the comfortable mode of travelling, made me regard my late experiences as a painful dream, from which I had just awakened; and I abandoned myself to the brightest hopes of a speedy and joyful meeting with my friends.

But, if I am to continue my narrative, I must adopt a mode of treatment which would not have suited my previous record as well. For when the most important events take place daily before our eyes, when our time is passed in suffering and fear amidst thousands in the same

* The *Digression* was not written at the time when Goethe was keeping his diary, but somewhat later, when he was revising his notes on the campaign.

state, and when even our hopes are tinged with apprehension, the Present assumes an aspect of paramount importance, and, by being depicted step by step, renews the Past, whilst it points to the Future. What occurs in social life, on the other hand, can be treated only as a series of representations of inward occurrences; reflection is here in its place; the Present will not speak for itself; the remembrance of the Past, and subsequent speculations, must act as its interpreters.

I had got into the habit of being engrossed by the business and occurrences of the moment, and had of late years, in particular, reason to be satisfied with this kind of life; this led to a peculiarity in me of never forming any conception before-hand of persons whom I expected to meet, or of places I intended to visit, but allowed them to produce their effect upon me without being previously prepared for them.

The advantage that arises from this is great; one does not require to come back from a previously-conceived idea, or to blot out a picture arbitrarily painted by ourselves, and painfully to accept the reality in its place. The disadvantage, on the other hand, that may arise, is, that we are unprepared in moments of importance, and are at a loss how to act in unforeseen emergencies.

For the same reason, too, I never paid any attention to the effect which my presence or the temper of my mind produced upon others; for I often found, quite unexpectedly, that I had inspired affection or repugnance, and frequently even both at the same time.

Whatever may be said respecting this manner of behaviour, whether, as an individual peculiarity, it can neither be praised nor censured, it must be added, that in the present case it produced some very curious phenomena, and these not always of the most agreeable description.

I had not met the friends whom I was about to visit for many years;* they had kept steadily to their old course of life; whereas it had been my strange lot to undergo many trials, and to pass through various kinds of occupations and endurances. Hence, although the same person,

* The family Jacobi, Plessing, and the Countess Gallitzin.

I had become quite a different being, and almost unrecognisable to my old friends.

It is difficult, even in maturer years when we have a freer survey of life, to give an accurate account of those transitions in it, which sometimes appear as an advance, sometimes as a retrogression, but all of which, nevertheless, prove of use and advantage to a God-fearing man. Notwithstanding these difficulties, I will endeavour to oblige my friends, and to note down a few points.

A virtuous man inspires affection and love only in so far as we discover longing in him; this expresses both possession and desire—the possession of a tender heart, and the desire of finding the same in others; with the former we attract others to us, with the latter we give up ourselves to them.

Whatever of this quality lay in me, which in earlier years I had encouraged, perhaps too much, but which as I grew older, I energetically sought to overcome, was no longer in keeping with the man, no longer satisfied him, and he sought, therefore, for full and final contentment.

The object of my most ardent longing, a pain which filled my very soul, was Italy, the image of which had floated before my mind for many years in vain, till at length I formed the bold determination of beholding the reality face to face. To that glorious land my friends gladly followed me in thought, they accompanied me on my way thither, and on my return. Would that they may affectionately share a longer residence there with me, and accompany me back again, for many a problem will be more intelligibly solved!

In Italy I felt myself gradually freed from petty conception, and from false wishes; in place of the longing for the land of the fine arts, there arose in me a longing for art itself; I had beheld it, and now wished to penetrate into, and comprehend, it.

The study of art, like that of the ancient authors, gives us a certain stability, a sort of satisfaction in ourselves; it fills our souls with great objects and ideas, it takes possession of every wish that struggles outwardly, but nourishes every worthy aspiration in the tranquil breast; the need of communicating our thoughts to others becomes less and less; and the amateur becomes like painter, sculptor, and architect—he works in solitude for enjoyments which he seldom is called upon to share with others.

But I was, at the same time, destined to be estranged from the world by another cause, and thrown in the most emphatic way upon Nature, to which instinctively I had a great leaning. Here I found neither masters nor companions, and was obliged everywhere to trust to myself. In the solitude of the woods and gardens, in the obscurity of the dark apartments, I should have remained quite alone, had not a happy domestic connection at this strange period of my existence come to rescue and cheer my heart. The "Roman Elegies," the "Venetian Epigrams," date from this period.

But I was also to have a taste of warlike events; for I was ordered to be present during the campaign in Silesia,* which came to an end with the Congress of Reichenbach, and obtained, in this new and important part of the world, additional experience and information, and some good diversion as well. The horrors of the French Revolution, which meanwhile spread farther and farther, drew the attention of every one, whatever might be his thoughts or studies, to the surface of the European world, and forced the most terrible realities upon his mind.

Then duty called me to accompany my Prince and master, to face with him the dangers and disasters of the day, and manfully to endure the sufferings of which I have ventured to give the reader but a faint picture; it can easily be conceived, that then whatever of tenderness and warmth lurked still in my inward being vanished altogether.

If all this be taken into consideration, the state of things which follows, roughly sketched as it is, will not appear altogether enigmatical. This I am the more anxious about, as I feel greatly inclined to rewrite these pages, which were written carelessly many years ago, and to offer them from my present point of view and my present convictions.

* Goethe's sojourn in Silesia, which lasted from the 2nd of August to the 17th of September, 1790, is most graphically described by H. Wenzel in his *Goethe in Silesia*, Leipzig, 1867.

Pempelfort, November 1792.

It was dark when I landed in Düsseldorf, and I had therefore to be conducted with lanterns, to Pempelfort, where, after the sudden surprise which my arrival caused, I received the most hearty welcome; the usual amount of talking to and fro, which is a necessary consequence of such meetings, ran away with the greater part of the night.

The next day I soon felt at home again in the midst of questions, answers, and anecdotes. The unfortunate campaign offered sufficient materials for conversation, and nobody was prepared for so melancholy a result. But neither could any one describe the dreadful effect of the ominous silence, which had lasted nearly three weeks; and the feeling of the uncertainty had gone on increasing from the entire want of intelligence. For all that was known of the allied army it might have been swallowed up; every one looking at the frightful void was tortured with fear and anxiety, and now military operations were again expected with terror in the Netherlands, and both banks of the Rhine appeared to be threatened.

We banished these reflections from our minds as well as we could by discussing moral and literary subjects; and as my realism showed itself here, the subject seemed to afford but little edification to my friends.

Since the Revolution, and in order to divert my attention from the wild confusion of things, I had begun a curious work, "The Journeyings of Seven Brothers," * of different capacities, each of whom served the covenant in his own way—a very Quixotic intricate thing, concealing both its aim and object; in fact, a sort of picture of our own condition. I was asked to read it aloud; this I readily agreed to and brought out my manuscripts, but soon perceived that nobody was edified by it. I therefore left my travelling family in some safe haven, and the remainder of my manuscript to take care of itself.

My friends, however, who found it difficult to acquiesce in this change of sentiment, made many attempts to show me what had been my former ideas by referring to my

* This refers to Goethe's *Reise der Söhne Megaprazon's*.

earlier works, and gave me my *Iphigenia* to read aloud to them in the evening. This, however, I could not endure; its tender strain was foreign to me now, and even when read by others, the sound of it was painful to me. This piece was very soon laid aside; but they were determined apparently to try me by a more severe test: *Œdipus auf Kolonos* was thereupon produced; but its lofty sanctity was intolerable to my mind, turned as it now was to Art, Nature and Life, and hardened by the events of the late dreadful campaign. I could not read a hundred lines of it. They then gave in to the humour of their altered friend, and other subjects of conversation presented themselves in abundance.

From the earlier period of German literature many single pieces were brought forward with happy effect; but no very close examination was entered upon, in order to avoid all differences of opinion. If I am to mention anything here of a general nature, it may be added that the last twenty years were really a remarkable period, in which many eminent persons were brought into contact with others whose views were widely different; every one carried with him into society a high opinion of himself, and mutual respect and forbearance were willingly practised by all.

Men of talent succeeded in maintaining the position they had acquired in the general esteem, and in their social relations assisted and supported each other; the advantages thus acquired were no longer preserved only by single individuals, but by an unanimous majority. That some degree of intentionality was necessary here, was to be expected; like other children of the world, they contrived to introduce a certain kind of art into their relations; the peculiarities of each were excused; the sensitiveness of the one counterbalanced that of the other; and mutual misunderstandings remained long in the background.

In the midst of all this, I myself occupied a singular position; my talents gave me an honourable place in society, but my warm enthusiasm for what I perceived to be true and natural made me use many hateful utterances in combating what appeared to me to be false tendencies; so that, at times, I fell out with the members of this circle;

we became reconciled again, wholly or partially, but I always proceeded in my usual course, fully persuaded of being in the right. With all this I retained something of the ingenuousness of Voltaire's Hurons * even at a more advanced age, so that 1 could be both insufferable and very amiable at the same time.

There was one province, however, which we could enter with more freedom and harmony—a western one, if not exactly French literature. Jacobi, whilst going his own course, allowed nothing of importance to escape him; and the vicinity of the Netherlands contributed much towards drawing him into that sphere, not only in a literary sense, but personally as well. He was a man singularly well formed, with very agreeable features and manners, which, although stiff, were very pleasant; in fact, a man sure to shine in all cultivated circles.

It was a wonderful time, which it is difficult to recall again. Voltaire had completely broken the old fetters that chained society; and this gave rise among men of intellect, to a feeling of scepticism towards all that had hitherto been held in veneration. While the philosopher of Ferney was exerting all his energies to diminish and weaken the influence of the priesthood, with Europe principally in view, De Pauw † was extending his spirit of conquest over more remote regions of the world; he would not grant either to the Chinese or the Egyptians the honour which the accumulated prejudices of centuries had heaped upon them. He was a Canon of Xante, in the neighbourhood of Düsseldorf, and kept up a friendly correspondence with Jacobi ; ‡ how many others might not be mentioned here ! We may at least mention Hemsterhuis,§ who, owing

* The chief character of Voltaire's *L'Ingenu* is a Huron.

† Cornelis de Pauw was at the Court of Frederick the Great between 1767 and 1770. His most celebrated work bears the title of *Recherches Philosophiques sur les Grecs*.

‡ F. H. Jacobi, a younger brother of the poet, distinguished himself in literature as a philosopher, writer, and novelist. His correspondence with Goethe shows the intimate relation that existed between them.

§ Franz Hemsterhuis, the philosopher and archæologist, was highly esteemed by many of the eminent persons of the day for his extensive knowledge, natural appreciation of the Beautiful, and kindliness of disposition.

to his attachment to the Princess Gallitzin, passed much of his time in the neighbourhood of Münster. He, with others of a kindred mind, devoted himself to studies of a milder and more ideal description, and, while imbued with Platonic sentiments, devoted himself to religion.

Amid these fragmentary recollections I must also mention Diderot, the vehement dialectician, who had been on a visit to Pempelfort, apparently much to his satisfaction, and where he maintained his paradoxes with great courageousness.

Rousseau's views, on Nature were likewise not unknown to this circle, which, in fact, excluded nothing, and hence not even myself, although it would be truer to say that it only tolerated me.

What effect external literature had upon me in my earlier years has already been indicated in various places. I could make use of it for my own purposes, but could not adopt it, and was therefore unable to come to any agreement about it with others. I was equally peculiar in regard to composition; this always went step by step with the course of my life; and as the latter, for the most part, remained a secret even to my most intimate friends, people found it difficult to befriend any new production of mine, as they expected something similar to what they already knew of mine.

If I had succeeded but badly with my *Seven Brothers* on account of their total dissimilarity to their sister *Iphigenia*, I could easily perceive that my *Gross-Kophta*, which had been printed long ago, had even given offence; nothing was said about it, and I was on my guard not to call their attention to it. However, it will be acknowledged that an author who is so placed as to be unable to read his works to others, or to hear them spoken of, must feel in as painful a situation as a composer who is kept from playing his newest melodies.

I was equally unfortunate with my views on Natural Philosophy; the enthusiastic earnestness with which I pursued the subject seemed unintelligible to every one, no one perceived that it was part and parcel of my inward being; they considered this laudable endeavour a whimsical mistake; in their opinion I might have done something better, and allowed my talents to pursue their old course. They felt the more entitled to say this, as my way of thinking did not at all agree with theirs, and, in fact, in most points, maintained exactly the contrary. There was not a more isolated being than I was then, and for a long time afterwards. The Hylozoism, or whatever it may be called, to which I was attached, and the deep foundation of which I left untouched in all its dignity and sanctity, made me unsympathetic, nay, intolerant towards that way of thinking, which set up, as an article of its faith, the existence of matter as a dead thing, in whatever way it might be supposed to be stirred up and put in motion.

It had not escaped me, in my study of Kant's Natural Philosophy, that attraction and repulsion belong to the nature of matter, and that the one cannot be separated from the other in the conception of matter; this appeared to me to result in the primary polarity of all beings, which penetrates and animates the infinite variety of phenomena.

During a former visit of the Princess Gallitzin to Weimar, with Fürstenberg and Hemsterhuis, I had advanced these views; but I was always set down as giving utterance to blasphemous opinions.

No circle can be found fault with for shutting itself up within itself; and this my friends at Pempelfort did most religiously. They had taken little notice of my *Metamorphoses of Plants*, which had been printed a year ago; and when I endeavoured to explain my morphological views —familiar as they were to me and in the best order, and moreover in a way that I imagined must necessarily produce conviction—I could not help remarking that a barren way of viewing things, namely, that nothing can come into existence which is not already there, had taken possession of all minds. Whereupon I was again told that every living thing comes from an egg; this made me, with bitter irony, raise the old question, whether the hen or the egg existed first? It seemed so plausible a doctrine to shut Nature up in a box, and so edifying to contemplate her in company with Bonnet.*

* Charles Bonnet, the eminent naturalist, was also a philosophical writer; Goethe here finds fault with his teleological opinions.

They had heard something about my *Contributions to the Science of Optics*, and I readily agreed to entertain them with some phenomena and experiments. I had no difficulty in producing something new, for every one, however well educated, had been taught the doctrine of the division of light, and unfortunately wished to see that which, in itself, was full of life, and which afforded them so much enjoyment, traced back to some dead hypothesis.

I let them have their way for a time, for a discussion of this kind was always of use to me; generally, while conversing, I obtained some new insight into the subject, and in the flow of conversation invention came most quickly.

In this, it is true, I could proceed only in a didactical and dogmatical way; for a gift for dialectics and conversation I never actually possessed. I must also confess to have acquired a bad habit which frequently manifested itself: ordinary conversation was excessively tiresome to me, as nothing but narrow individual views were expressed, so I was in the habit of stirring up the narrow discussions that usually spring up in the course of conversation, by violent paradoxes, and of exciting the disputants to the utmost. The assembled company would thereupon feel hurt and annoyed in more senses than one; for often, in order to attain my object, I was obliged to play the evil spirit; and as people wished to be agreeable, and desired that others should be so too, they would not let this pass; they would not allow it to be earnestly meant, because it was not well-grounded, and not jest either, because it was too bitter. At last they dubbed me a hypocrite in the inverted sense, and were soon reconciled to me again. However, I cannot deny that this bad habit has alienated many persons from me, and made many others my enemies.

But, as with an enchanter's rod, I could immediately drive from me all evil spirits when I began to talk about Italy. Thither I had also gone unprepared and without premeditation; of adventures there was no lack; the country itself, its beauty and splendour, had been fully impressed on my memory; the form, colour, and character of the landscape, in the light of its beautiful sky, were still vividly present to me. The poor attempts which I had made to sketch it had sharpened my memory, and I could describe it as if it were still actually before me. I could fill it with a multitude of figures, and thus every one was pleased and often charmed with my descriptions.

In order to give a complete picture of the pleasure of a residence at Pempelfort, it will now be as well to describe the locality in which all this took place.* The house was large, and stood in an open space near extensive and well-kept gardens—a very paradise in summer, and very agreeable in winter. Every ray of sunlight was enjoyed amid neatness and freedom. In the evening, or in bad weather, we assembled in the large, handsome rooms, which, although comfortable, were not luxuriously furnished, yet well adapted for social entertainments. In the large dining-room, which was cheerful and comfortable, and spacious enough for the numerous family and their never-failing guests, all were invited to take their seats at a long table, on which was placed an abundance of good things. Here the company all met; the host was always in good spirits and encouraging, the sisters good-natured and sensible, the son earnest and hopeful, the daughter good-looking, hearty, frank, and amiable, reminding us of her late mother, and of the days which, twenty years before, we had spent with her in Frankfort. Heinze, who belonged to the family, could reply to all sorts of jokes; there were evenings when the laughter scarcely ceased.

The few hours I had to myself in this most hospitable of mansions I devoted to a singular work. During the campaign, in addition to my diary, I had written some satirical *ordres du jour*, and I now set about revising them. I soon perceived that, with short-sighted presumption, I had seen many things in a false light, and had judged them incorrectly; and as one is never more severe than against errors that have been abandoned, and it seemed unwise to expose such papers to accidents of any kind, I threw the whole bundle into the fire. This I am sorry for

* The residence of the Jacobi family so frequently spoken of in the 14th book of Goethe's *Dichtung und Wahrheit*. The son mentioned here studied medicine in Jena in 1793, and afterwards settled in Düsseldorf.

now, as they would have furnished me with very valuable information about the course which events took, and my reflections upon them.

Many visits were made to Düsseldorf, which was at no great distance, to see persons belonging to the Pempelfort circle, and the Gallery was our usual place of meeting. Here, decided favour seemed to be shown to the Italian school, and great injustice towards the Netherland school; the lofty character of the former was, indeed, more attractive to elevated minds. On one occasion we remained a long time in the hall of Rubens and the most distinguished masters of the Netherland school; on coming out again, the Ascension of Guido * hung directly in front of us, and one of our party exclaimed, enthusiastically, "Is it not exactly as if we had come out of a pothouse into good society?" I was not ill-pleased to find that the masters who, a short time before, had enchanted me on the other side of the Alps, should appear so glorious here, and excite such admiration. However, I endeavoured also to become acquainted with the Netherland masters, whose merits and excellences were here displayed in the highest perfection; and this has been a gain to me for the rest of my life.

But what struck me still more was, that a certain spirit of liberalism, a tendency towards democracy, had spread amongst the higher ranks; they did not seem to feel how much would have first to be lost, before they could attain to any kind of even doubtful advantage. Lafayette's and Mirabeau's busts, by Houdon, were very good and natural likenesses. These men I found worshipped here as something god-like; the former on account of his chivalrous and civil virtues, the latter for his abilities and his oratorical power.

Thus oddly enough, even at this time, the opinions of the Germans wavered; some had even been in Paris, where they had seen the distinguished men speaking and at work, and had, after our unfortunate German fashion, been excited to imitate them; and this, too, at a time when anxiety for the left bank of the Rhine was rapidly changing into actual fear.

* This picture of Guido's, and Rubens' *Last Judgment* were removed to Munich in 1805.

The danger seemed imminent; Düsseldorf was crowded with Emigrants; even the King's brothers had arrived, and every one hastened to see them. I met them in the Gallery, and recollected how I had last seen them dripping with rain on the march out of Glorieux. Herr von Grimm and Frau von Bouil appeared at the same time. Owing to the crowded state of the town, they had taken up their quarters at an apothecary's, his cabinet of natural curiosities serving as their bedroom; monkeys, parrots, and other animals, watched over the morning slumbers of this most lovable of women; shells and corals encumbered her toilet-table; and thus the evil of demanding quarters, which we had before carried with us into France, was now being borne back to ourselves again.

Frau von Coudenhofen, a handsome, clever woman, formerly the ornament of the Mainz Court, had also taken refuge here. Herr and Frau von Dohm arrived from the interior of Germany, in order to obtain more exact intelligence of the state of affairs. Frankfort was still occupied by the French, and military operations were being carried on between the Lahn and the Taunus mountains. Owing to the constantly varying intelligence which arrived day by day, first reassuring, then uncertain as ever, the conversation proved animated and instructive; but, on the other hand, owing to the conflicting interests and opinions, it was not always of the most enjoyable description. I could not come to any serious conclusion from such a problematical and uncertain state of things, which seemed to depend upon mere accident, so I kept up my paradoxical jokes which sometimes caused amusement and sometimes vexation.

Thus, I remember once, at supper, the citizens of Frankfort being praised for their manly and proper behaviour to Custine; their conduct and disposition, it was said, contrasted strongly with the unjustifiable manner in which the people of Mainz had conducted themselves, and still continued to act. Frau von Coudenhofen, with an enthusiasm which became her well, exclaimed, that she would give a great deal to be a citizen of Frankfort, whereupon I replied, that that could easily be managed, that I knew a means, but meant to keep the secret to myself. All then urged me, with ever-increasing eagerness, to tell them what this was; whereupon I at last explained, that the excellent lady had only to marry me to become a Frankfort citizen on the spot. General laughter!

It would be difficult to say what was not talked about. Once, when the unlucky campaign, and the cannonade at Valmy in particular, was the subject of conversation, Herr von Grimm assured the company, that my strange ride in among the cannon-balls had been spoken of at the King's table. Probably the officers, whom I encountered on the occasion, had mentioned it; they came to the conclusion that it was useless being surprised at such a proceeding, as it was impossible to say what such a paradoxical being might do next.

A very able and clever physician took part in our semi-saturnalia; and I had no idea, in the midst of my mad jokes, that I should so soon stand in need of his assistance. He broke out into a loud laugh one day when he found me in bed, confined there almost without the power of moving, by a violent rheumatic attack that I had brought upon myself by exposure to the cold. He was a pupil of Hoffmann, whose specifics had met with such success, first in Mainz and the Electoral Court, and afterwards all along the Rhine; he first used camphor, which was looked upon as the universal remedy. Blotting-paper, with chalk rubbed upon it and a sprinkling of camphor, was employed outwardly, and camphor also, in small doses, inwardly. Whether it was this that cured me or not, I cannot say; but I was quite well in a few days.

The tedium of my sufferings, however, led to many reflections; the debility which so readily follows confinement to bed, depressed my spirits. The French were making considerable progress in the Netherlands, which was exaggerated by rumour; and new arrivals of Emigrants were constantly announced.

My sojourn in Pempelfort had now been sufficiently long, and but for the cordial hospitality of the family one would have feared to have been troublesome; my stay had, moreover, been prolonged accidentally. I expected my

Bohemian carriage daily and hourly, and did not like to leave without it; it had arrived at Coblenz from Trèves, and was to be forwarded from thence down the river. However, as it did not make its appearance, and the impatience which had taken possession of me for the last few days increased, Jacobi offered me a travelling-carriage, which was very comfortable although rather heavy, from the quantity of iron about it. All, it was said, were on their way to Westphalia; and the King's brothers intended to establish themselves there.

Thus I took my departure in the most curious state of perplexity; my inclination would have led me to remain with my friends, who were just then in a state of the greatest alarm, and yet I had to leave these most excellent people in trouble and anxiety, and to start forth again into the wild world, carried along by the stream of hurrying fugitives, and with the feelings of a fugitive myself.

I had, however, the prospect of a very agreeable visit on the way, for I was to pass so close to Münster, and could not avoid paying my respects to the Princess Gallitzin.

Duisburg, End of November.

Thus, after the lapse of four weeks, I found myself many miles distant from the theatre of our first misfortunes, but again amid the same company, amid the same crowd of Emigrants, who, now finally driven out of France, were streaming into Germany without hopeful prospects of any kind.

At dinner, in the inn, I sat at the end of the long table, having arrived rather late; the host and hostess, who had expressed to me, as a German, their aversion to the French, apologised that all the best places were already occupied by these unwelcome guests. It was observed, that, in spite of their degradation, misery, and impending beggary, the same jealousy was still to be found amongst them about precedence and rank.

On looking up the table I perceived, at the other end opposite to me, first of all, a small but well-built old man, of quiet, almost insignificant presence. He seemed a man of importance, for the two persons who sat next him were paying him the greatest attention, and picking out the choicest bits to put before him, it might almost be said, putting them into his mouth. I soon perceived that he was in his dotage, and, like a wretched automaton, was miserably dragging about the shadow of his former substantial and honourable life, while his two devoted attendants were trying to recall to him the dream of his former condition.

I then looked at the rest; the most melancholy fate seemed legible on the brows of all. Soldiers, commissaries, adventurers, might perhaps be distinguished; all were silent, for each had his own particular misery to endure, and boundless wretchedness stared them in the face.

When the dinner was about half over, a young, good-looking man came in, without anything distinguished in his appearance, or decoration of any kind, and bearing unmistakable marks of being a traveller on foot. He sat down in silence opposite to me, and after civilly asking the landlord to order some dinner for him, quietly ate what was fetched and placed before him. After dinner, as I was exchanging a few words with the landlord, he whispered into my ear, "Your neighbour shall not be charged much in his bill." I did not understand what he meant by this; but when the young man came up, and asked what he had to pay, the host, after looking round the table, replied that the bill amounted to a *Kopfstück*.* The stranger seemed surprised, and said, it must be a mistake; for he had not only had a good dinner, but also a pint of wine, which must amount to more. The landlord thereupon said, in a serious tone, that he was in the habit of making out his own bills, and expected his guests to pay what he demanded. The young man paid his bill, and retired modestly and astonished. The landlord then explained the mystery to me. "He is the first of that cursed set of people," he exclaimed, "who has eaten the black bread given him, and he deserved something for that."

In Duisburg I know of but one old acquaintance, whom I did not delay to visit; this was Professor Plessing, between whom and myself a sort of romantic and sentimental relation had sprung up many years before. I

* *Kopfstück*, a coin of about the value of eightpence.

shall describe this visit more fully as our evening's conversation carried us back from the most turbulent to the most peaceful times.

Werther, when it first appeared in Germany, did not by any means create a disease, or excite a fever, as it had been accused of doing, but only exposed the malady which lay concealed in youthful minds. During the course of a long and happy time of peace the literary and æsthetic culture of the Germans had developed most promisingly within the limits of their own country and their native language; but as this related only to the mind, independently of its relation to external nature, it was followed by a kind of sentimentality, in the origin and progress of which the influence of Yorick Sterne * cannot but be recognised. And even though his spirit did not affect the Germans, the more decidedly were they imbued with his sentiments. From this arose a kind of sentimental asceticism, which, as the humorous irony of the Briton was wanting to us, necessarily degenerated into a miserable species of self-torture. I had endeavoured to free myself from this malady, and strove, according to my conviction, to assist others; this, however, was more difficult than can well be imagined; for what was really required was, to assist everybody against himself; and therefore any assistance which might be expected from the outward world, whether in the way of information, instruction, occupation, or favour, could not come into question.

We must here pass over in silence many co-operating agencies whose united influence was felt at that time; but it is necessary for our purpose to consider closely another great agent, which operated independently.

Lavater's *Physiognomics* had given an entirely different direction to ethical and social interests. He felt himself possessed of the power of indicating, in the clearest way, the impressions which the human face and form produce upon us all, without being able to account for this to himself; and as he was not able to follow out any

* Laurence Sterne (1713-1768), the author of *The Sentimental Journey through France and Italy*, and of *The Letters from Yorick to Eliza*. The name Yorick is first met with in the title of the German translations, the earliest of which appeared in 1768.

abstract question methodically, he confined himself to single cases, and, consequently, to the individual.

Heinrich Lips,* a clever young artist, particularly as a portrait-painter, attached himself closely to Lavater, and, both at home as well as on the tour which they made together on the Rhine, never left his patron's side. Now Lavater, partly from an insatiable desire for boundless experience, partly to familiarise and obtain the co-operation of a number of notable men in his future work, had portraits taken of every person he met in any way distinguished by station or talent, character or action.

In this way many an individual was brought prominently forward, and became more highly esteemed, from having been admitted into this distinguished circle; peculiarities were pointed out by the master; and people fancied they got to know each other better. Thus it happened most curiously, that many an individual who had previously passed unnoticed in the every-day life of society, now had his personal value brought prominently forward.

The effect of all this was stronger and greater than may be imagined; every one claimed the right to form a high opinion of himself as a distinct complete being, and, relying on this individuality, considered himself entitled to adopt all sorts of peculiarities, absurdities, and defects, into the complex of his precious existence. This ensued the more easily, as, in this procedure, the particular nature of the individual alone came into question, without reference to reason in general, which latter, however, must govern all nature. On the other hand, the religious element in which Lavater lived and moved was unable to keep in check the egoism that was every day becoming more marked; and seemed among piously-disposed persons, to give rise to a species of spiritual pride of a more presumptuous character than even the ordinary kind.†

Another remarkable consequence of this was, the con-

---

* J. H. Lips was, through Goethe's influence, appointed Professor of drawing at the Academy in Weimar in 1789.

† This appears to be the main reason of the impossibility of any agreement between Goethe and Lavater. Their correspondence ceases with the year 1783.

sideration in which individuals were held by each other. Notable old men were honoured, if not personally, at least in their portraits; and a young man had only to come forward prominently in some way, to make people wish to become personally acquainted with him, and if this could not be accomplished, contented themselves by obtaining his portrait. For this purpose profiles drawn from the shadow thrown on a wall were found very useful, and when carefully and well done, furnished an exact likeness. Everybody was a practised hand at this, and no stranger passed by without having himself inscribed on the wall. Of an evening, pantographs were not allowed any rest.

Knowledge of mankind, and love of mankind, were promised us from this mode of procedure. Mutual sympathy had certainly been excited, but mutual knowledge and understanding were not so easily acquired. There was, however, an active tendency towards both objects, and it would be pleasant here to relate what was done to encourage and promote this, both far and near, by a splendidly-gifted young prince, and the genial, intellectually active men he had collected about him, were it not advisable to consign to a venerable obscurity the beginnings of such important affairs. Perhaps the cotyledons of that seed-time looked somewhat strange; the harvest, however, of which our own native land and foreign countries joyfully accepted their share, will not fail to be gratefully remembered in all days to come.

If what I have just said be kept in view, and thoroughly understood, the following adventure, which at supper was the cause of lively and pleasant recollections to both parties concerned, will not be found either improbable or absurd.

Among a host of importunities, addressed to me, both by letter and in person, I received, in the middle of the year 1777,* a paper, or rather a pamphlet, dated Wernigerode, and subscribed Plessing, the most wonderful production of the self-torturing kind that I ever beheld. It was plainly from a young man filled with all knowledge of school and

* The date 1776, which is given in all the earlier editions, can only be a mistake in memory on Goethe's part.

University; but whose learning, nevertheless, did not contribute in the least to his own inward moral tranquillity. His handwriting was good, and pleasant to read; his style clever and flowing; and, although a tendency to pulpit oratory could at once be perceived, still everything seemed so fresh, and written so from the heart, that one could not help sympathising with him. But when one's sympathy was allowed to become active, and an endeavour was made to get a clearer understanding of the condition of the sufferer, it seemed as if there was in him more of wilfulness than of patience, more of obstinacy than submission, and more of pure selfishness than of ardent longing. In accordance with the propensity of the time, which I have described above, I felt a great desire to see the young man face to face; but considered it inadvisable to ask him to come to me. I had already, under circumstances which are known, burdened myself with a number of young men,* who, instead of accompanying me on my road towards a purer and higher culture, had lingered on their own path, deriving no benefit themselves, and obstructing me in my progress. Hence I allowed the matter to rest, till some opportunity should occur for effecting my object. Whereupon I received a second letter, short, but more passionate than the first, in which the writer pressed for an answer and explanation, and implored me most earnestly not to refuse them to him.

But even this renewal of the storm did not trouble me; the second paper affected me just as little as the first; but the habit I had acquired of assisting young men of my own age in affairs of mind or heart, did not allow me to forget him altogether.

The party assembled in Weimar around the excellent young Prince did not readily separate from one another; their occupations and enterprises, amusements, joys and sorrows were all shared in common. But about the end of November, a hunting-party was got up to hunt wild boar in the Eisenach district, in order to satisfy the urgent and repeated complaints of the country people; and as I

* Lenz, Klinger, and others, whose presence in Weimar not unfrequently put Goethe to some inconvenience and unpleasantness.

happened to be on a visit there, I was to be of the party, but obtained permission to join them after making a slight detour.

I had a curious, secret journey in view. I frequently heard a strong desire expressed that the Ilmenau mines should be worked again, not only by men of business, but also by persons in Weimar interested about the matter in a general way. Now, although possessing only the most general ideas about mining, I was required, not indeed to give my advice or opinion, but to take an interest in it; and this could not be excited in me in the case of any subject, except by a direct examination of it. I considered it indispensable above all things to get some general understanding, if only superficially, of the nature of mining; in fact, to see things with my own eyes, and to grasp them with my mind; then only could I hope to enter further into the details. I had, therefore, for some time contemplated a journey to the Harz, and as this time of the year was usually passed in the open air, in the pleasures of the chase, I felt myself attracted towards it. The winter season had besides, at that time, a great charm for me; and as far as the mines were concerned, neither winter nor summer would be perceptible there. But I must confess, that my wish to see my singular correspondent face to face, and to test him, contributed in no small degree, too, of my forming this resolution.

Therefore, whilst the hunting-party went in another direction, I rode off alone towards the Ettersberg, and began the ode, which, under the title of "A Winter's Journey in the Harz," so long remained a riddle among my smaller poems. In the sombre snowclouds, rolling up from the north, and high up in the air, a hawk soared above me. I remained over night in Sondershausen, and reached Nordhausen so early next day, that I determined to proceed on my journey immediately after dinner; but it was late at night before I reached Ilfeld, and this was only accomplished with the assistance of guides and lanterns, and not without some risks.

I found a respectable looking inn brilliantly lit up, and some special festivity was apparently being celebrated. At first the landlord did not want to take me in. The commissioners of the supreme courts, I was told, had been busy here for some time past in making arrangements of importance, and reconciling various interests; and as this had now been brought to a successful termination, the matter was being concluded with a general feast. But on being urgently remonstrated with, and on some hints being given by my guide that it would be advisable to treat me well, the man offered to give me the room partitioned off from the dining-room, his own special abode, and likewise his large double bed, with white hangings. He led me through the spacious brilliantly lighted dining-room, and I had an opportunity of glancing at the merry party.

I had a better opportunity, however, of examining them closely through a hole in the boards of the partition, which had often doubtless furnished the landlord a means for watching his guests. I was greatly amused, and looked right up the long well-lighted table, surveying it, as one might have the marriage feast at Cana represented in a picture; I had a comfortable view of them from one end to the other: presidents, councillors, and others connected with them, and then, secretaries, clerks and assistants. The successful termination of a troublesome affair appeared to produce an equality amongst all those who had taken an active part in it; they were chatting very freely, and drinking healths; jokes were bandied about, and some of the guests seemed to be the butts for sallies of wit and jest; in short, it was a high and joyous feast, which I could quietly observe in all its peculiarities by the brilliant light of the wax candles, just as if the devil himself had been standing at my side, and treating me with a direct view and insight into some strange state of things. How charming this was to me after the gloomiest of rides among the Harz mountains, will be readily understood by lovers of such adventures. It struck me at times as something ghost-like, as if I were looking at a party of merry spectres amusing themselves in some mountain cavern.

After a good sleep, I hastened early next morning, again accompanied by a guide, to the miners' cavern, crept into it, and closely examined the incessant working of the natural phenomenon. Masses of black marble broken down and restored to white crystalline pillars and flat slabs, showed me the never-resting activity of Nature. Whilst quietly contemplating the scene, all the miraculous images which a gloomy imagination is so fond of conjuring up out of formless appearances vanished, it is true, but in their place the particular truth stood out all the more purely, and I felt myself greatly enriched by it.

On again reaching daylight, I wrote down what seemed the most necessary observations, and, likewise, while fresh in my mind, the first stanzas of the poem which, under the title of "A Winter's Journey in the Harz," has attracted the attention of many of my friends down to the present day. It may be as well to insert the stanzas that refer to the singular man who is soon to be presented to the reader, as they are better adapted than anything else that I could say to describe the sympathetic state of my mind at that time.

> But who is this who walks aside,
> His path in tangled thickets lost?
> Behind his wayward heel
> The twining branches close;
> Up comes the grass again;
> The waste devours his track.
>
> Ah! who shall soothe his woe, who drinks
> But poison from the balm,
> And from love's cup distils
> Black hatred of all his kind?
> At first despised, now a despiser,
> He lives apart, wasting in selfish dreams
> The glory of his prime.
>
> Father of love! if there
> Live in Thy sacred lyre
> One tone to touch his ear,
> Oh, gladden Thou his heart!
> And let his clouded eyes
> The thousand springs behold,
> That, ever welling, ever shining, cheer
> The thirsty waste.

On arriving at the inn in Wernigerode,* I entered into conversation with the waiter, and found him a sensible

* The details of the story given here do not quite tally with those given in Goethe's letters to Frau von Stein, where on one occasion he says: "I went out for a walk with P. up the hill." In the present case it would seem as if we had an account of one evening only.

person, who seemed to be pretty well acquainted with his fellow-townsmen. I then told him that it was my custom, on arriving at a place where I had no particular introductions, to seek out such young persons as might in any way be distinguished for learning and science; and thereupon asked him to do me the favour to name somebody of this description, with whom I might hope to pass the evening pleasantly. Without hesitation the waiter replied, that no doubt I should find what I desired in Herr Plessing, the son of the Superintendent; that as a boy even he had been distinguished at school, and still maintained his reputation for diligence and ability; that people now found fault with his gloomy disposition, and did not like him on account of unsociable behaviour which led him to shut himself out from society. But that towards strangers he was always polite, as examples could prove, and if I wished an introduction, it could be got immediately.

The waiter soon brought me word that I might pay Plessing a visit, and conducted me to his residence. The evening had already set in, when I entered a large room on the ground-floor, the usual style in ecclesiastical houses, and although it was twilight I could distinguish the young man tolerably well. I observed some signs of the parents having hastily left the room, to make place for the unexpected visitor.

When the lights were brought in, I had a distinct view of the young man, and he was exactly what his letter had led me to expect; and, like it, he excited one's interest without being exactly attractive.

In order to lead to a more intimate conversation, I described myself as an artist from Gotha, and said that, on account of some family matters, I was about to visit a sister and brother-in-law in Brunswick at this unfavourable season.

With great animation he thereupon exclaimed, scarcely allowing me to finish my sentence. "As you live so near Weimar, you have no doubt frequently visited that place, which has become so celebrated?" I answered, with perfect simplicity, in the affirmative, and began to speak of Counsellor Kraus, and the Drawing Academy; of Bertuch, Counsellor of Legation, and his unwearying assiduity; I did not omit either Musäus or Jagemann; spoke of Wolf, the band-master; and some ladies; described the circle in which these worthy people moved, and said they were always glad to see strangers amongst them, who were sure to be well received.

At last he exclaimed, somewhat impatiently: "But why do not you mention Goethe?" I replied, that I had seen him in the aforesaid circle as a welcome guest, and had even been myself personally well received and kindly treated by him as an artist, but that I could not say much further about him, partly because he lived alone, and partly because he belonged to other circles.

The young man, who had listened with restless attention, now demanded me, with some impetuosity, to describe this strange individual, who had created such a sensation in the world. Whereupon, with great ingenuity, I gave him a description, which it was not difficult to do, as the strange person happened to be before me in the strangest of situations; and if Nature had only favoured him with a little more sagacity of heart, he could hardly have failed to perceive that his visitor was describing himself.

He had walked up and down the room two or three times, when the maid-servant entered, and placed a bottle of wine and some cold supper on the table; he filled both our glasses, touched my glass with his, and drank it off excitedly. Scarcely had I, with somewhat less eagerness, emptied mine, when he seized me by the arm with great vehemence, and exclaimed: "Oh, excuse my singular behaviour! But you have inspired me with such confidence, that I cannot help telling you all. This man, from your description of him, ought certainly to have answered me; I sent him a detailed, affectionate letter, describing my condition, my sufferings, and begged him to interest himself in me, to advise me, to help me; and now months have passed, and I have no reply. The very least he could do, was to have sent me a refusal, in return for such unbounded confidence."

In reply to this, I said that such conduct I could neither explain nor excuse; but this much I knew from my own experience, that owing to a heavy pressure of things both ideal and real, this, otherwise well-meaning, good-natured, and helpful young man, was often unable to do as he pleased, much less to act for others.

"As we have accidentally got so far," he now added, with somewhat more composure, "I must read the letter to you; and you can then judge whether it did not deserve some answer, some reply."

I walked up and down the room waiting for him to read it, knowing, of course, what effect it would produce, and therefore had no fear of making a false step in so delicate an affair. He sat down opposite to me, and began to read the papers, which I knew as well as himself; and nothing, perhaps, ever convinced me more of the truth of the assertion made by physiognomists: that a living being, in all its actions and conduct, is in complete accordance with itself, and that every monad, when once it has entered the world of reality, manifests itself in complete unity with its characteristics. The reader was an exact counterpart of what he read; and as the letter had not attracted me at first, it did not attract me now in his presence. One could not, indeed, deny the young man one's respect, one's sympathy; in fact, it was this which had induced me to make this curious journey; for an earnest will was visible in him, a noble tendency and aim; but although the tenderest feelings were in question, his manner of reading was without grace, and a peculiar, narrow kind of selfishness was strongly apparent throughout. When he had finished, he asked hastily what I now thought, and whether such a paper did not deserve, nay, demand, an answer?

Meanwhile I had obtained a clearer insight into the young man's deplorable state of mind; he had never taken cognisance of the outward world, but had, on the contrary, cultivated his mind by multifarious reading, and directed all his powers and interests inwards; and, not finding any productive talent in the depths of his being, he had gone far to ruin himself altogether. And even the occupation and consolation so gloriously offered us by a study of the ancient languages, seemed to be completely wanting to him.

As I had already proved, both in myself and others, that the best remedy in such cases is to throw ourselves with energy and faith upon Nature and her infinite variety, I made an attempt to apply it in this case also. After a little reflection I answered him in the following way:—

"I think I can understand why the young man, in whom you have placed so much confidence, has remained silent towards you. His present way of thinking is doubtless too different from yours to allow of any hope that you could come to any agreement with each other. I have been present during some conversations in the circle spoken of, and have heard it maintained, that the only way in which a person can escape and save himself from a painful, self-torturing, gloomy state of mind, is by a contemplation of Nature, and a heartfelt sympathy with the outward world. Even a most general acquaintance with Nature, no matter in what way, in fact any active communication with it, either in gardening or farming, hunting or mining, draws us out of ourselves; the employment of our mental energies upon real, actual phenomena, affords, by degrees, the greatest satisfaction, clearness of mind, and instruction; in the same way as the artist who keeps true to Nature, while cultivating his mind, is certain to succeed the best."

My young friend appeared to get very restless and impatient at this, just as one does when listening to some foreign or confused language, the meaning of which one cannot understand. However, although there seemed but little hope of a successful result, I proceeded more for the sake of saying something, and added that: "To me, as a landscape painter, this appeared very evident, as my particular department of art was in direct communication with Nature. But since that time, I have observed things with more assiduity and eagerness than I had previously done, and not merely noted uncommon and remarkable natural objects and phenomena, but felt myself more full of love for all things and all men." In order not to lose myself in the abstract, I thereupon told him that even this necessary winter excursion, instead of being irksome, had furnished me with lasting enjoyment. I described to him the course of my journey artistically and poetically, and yet as truly and naturally as I could; I spoke of the snow-clouds which I had that morning seen rolling over the mountains, and the various other appearances that had struck me during the day; I then revealed to his imagination the curious turreted and walled fortifications of Nordhausen, as seen in the twilight; and further, at night, the torrents rushing down the mountain ravines, their waters lighted up now and then, and glistening in the flickering light of the guide's lantern; and, last of all, the miners' caverns.

Here he interrupted me with warmth, and assured me that he heartily regretted the trouble he had taken in going to see the latter, short as the distance was; it had not at all come up to the picture he had formed of it in his imagination. After what had passed between us, such morbid symptoms did not annoy me; often had I seen how men throw away the valuable possession of a clear reality for a dismal phantom of their gloomy imaginations! Just as little did it astonish me, when, in answer to my question, "How he had pictured the caverns to himself?" he described them in such a way as the boldest scene-painter would scarcely have ventured to do in depicting the fore-courts of Pluto's kingdom.

Upon this I tried other propædeutic suggestions as expedients for effecting a cure. But these were rejected so emphatically with the assurance that nothing in this world ever could or should content him, that my heart closed itself against him; and I felt my conscience completely freed from the necessity of taking any further trouble about him, considering the fatiguing journey I had undertaken on his account, and the best intentions I had had towards him.

It was already pretty late, when he spoke of reading to me his second still more passionate letter, which was, of course, likewise not unknown to me; he accepted my apology for not wishing to hear it then, owing to my being too tired, but invited me, in the name of his family, to dine with them the following day; I told him I would let him know early next morning if I could come.* We parted peaceably and

* Schaefer's assertion that Goethe, in taking leave of Plessing, admitted who he was, and that, in this case as in his *Wahrheit und Dichtung*, Goethe has described his adventure very freely, has been disputed by Düntzer in his work: *Aus Goethe's Freundekreis*.

becomingly. His person left a peculiar impression upon me; he was of middle height, his features had nothing attractive, but neither had they anything repulsive in them; his gloomy presence had nothing uncourteous about it; and he might, in fact, have passed for a well-educated young man, preparing himself quietly in schools and academies, for the pulpit or a professorial chair.

On going out, I found the sky clear and bright with stars, the streets and squares covered with snow; I stopped on a narrow bridge, and stood quietly looking at the surrounding objects in the wintry night. At the same time I thought over the adventure, and felt quite resolved not to see the young man again; hence I ordered my horse at daybreak, gave the waiter an anonymous note containing my apologies and, at the same time, said many things in praise of the young person to whom he had introduced me, which were true enough, and of which, no doubt, the dexterous fellow made good use for his own purposes.

I now rode along the north-east slopes of the Harz amid wild stormy weather, with the snow-flakes drifting around me, on to Goslar, after having first seen the Rammelsberg, the brass foundry, and other establishments of that kind, and obtained an insight into their working. Of Goslar I shall say nothing further at present, as I hope to entertain my readers with a more detailed account of it on a future occasion.

I cannot say how long it was since I heard anything of my young friend when, quite unexpectedly, one morning a note was delivered to me in my Summer-house at Weimar, in which he introduced himself to me. I wrote him a few words to say that I would be glad to see him. I expected a singular scene of recognition; but on coming in he said quietly: "I am not surprised to find you here, the handwriting of your note brought so vividly to my recollection the lines which you left me on leaving for Wernigerode, that I never for a moment doubted that I should here find the mysterious traveller again."

This was a good beginning, and we began talking very cordially together; he endeavoured to describe his condition to me, and I, in no way, concealed my opinion from him. I am unable to say now whether I found his mind in a more healthy state or not; but it cannot have appeared very bad, for we parted after a good deal of conversation, on good terms; but I could not reciprocate the vehement desire he manifested for passionate friendship and the closest intimacy between us.

For sometime we kept up a correspondence; I was able to be of some real service to him, which, at our present meeting, he gratefully remembered, and altogether, the recollection of former times filled up a few hours very pleasantly for both of us. He was still, as he had always been, occupied with himself, and had a great deal to relate and communicate. He had in the course of time acquired a reputation as an author, by applying himself earnestly to the history of ancient philosophy, particularly to that part of it which deals with the mysterious, from which he endeavoured to deduce the origin and primal condition of man. His books, which he always sent me as soon as they were published, I had not read; the subjects were too far removed from what had any interest for me.

His present condition I found by no means satisfactory; the study of languages and history, which he had so long neglected, he had at length taken up, as if by storm, with frantic exertions, but the excessive strain on his mind, had destroyed his health. His economical circumstances moreover did not appear to be in a very flourishing state, his moderate income did not allow of his taking proper care of himself; his youthful gloomy tendencies, too, did not seem to have altogether disappeared; he still seemed always to be aspiring after something unattainable, and after we had exhausted the remembrance of former relations, it seemed impossible to bring the conversation into any really pleasant channel. My present manner of life might be considered as almost further removed from his than ever. We parted, however, on very friendly terms; but him, too, I left in apprehension and anxiety about the pressure of the times.

I also paid a visit to worthy Merrem* whose distinguished attainments in Natural History immediately gave occasion to more cheerful talk. He showed me many

* Blassius Merrem, afterwards Professor in Marburg.

remarkable objects, and presented me with his work on snakes; I became interested in his future career; it proved of use to me in many ways. One great advantage of travelling is, that we never lose our interest in persons and places we have once become acquainted with.

Münster, November, 1792.

Having informed the Princess of my arrival I had the immediate prospect of a very pleasant time. But I was destined first to undergo a trial characteristic of the times, for I had been delayed on the road by various hinderances, and it was late at night before I arrived in the town. I did not think it right to put my friend's hospitality to so severe a test at the very outset by making an inroad at that late hour; I therefore drove to an inn, where, however, I could get neither bed nor quarters of any kind; the Emigrants had come in *en masse*, and filled every corner. In these circumstances I did not hesitate long, and passed the night on a chair in the dining-room, where, at all events, I was more comfortable than I had been a short time before, when no shelter, or covering of any kind, could be found even from the heaviest rains.

After this slight privation I received the next morning the most welcome intelligence. The Princess was coming to meet me; and I found in her house everything prepared for my reception. My relation to her was unembarrassed. I was sufficiently well acquainted with the members of the circle, and knew that I was joining pious, virtuous people, and conducted myself accordingly. They, on their part, were sociable, and not at all narrow-minded.

The Princess had visited us in Weimar some years before with Von Fürstenberg and Hemsterhuis; her children also were of the party. In those days we had compared notes on various topics, and had separated on the best terms, each side making concessions. She was one of those individuals of whom no idea can be conceived without actually seeing her, and of whose individuality no proper judgment can be formed, without taking it in connection as well as in conflict, with the circumstances of the time. Von Fürstenberg and Hemsterhuis, two very superior men, were her faithful attendants, and in such society there was always scope for the display of the Good as well as the Beautiful. The latter had since died; the former, now by so many years older, I found the same intelligent, noble, composed man; and what a singular position he occupied amongst his contemporaries! a clergyman, statesman, and close upon ascending a prince's throne.

At first our conversation, after some slight allusions to former times, turned upon Hamann,* whose grave in the corner of the leafless garden soon caught my eye.

His great incomparable qualities gave rise to many splendid reflections; his last days, however, were not spoken of. The man who had been of so much importance, and contributed so much to the enjoyment of this circle, which was his own choice, was in death the cause of some inconvenience to his friends; one might speak of his burial as one pleased, it was out of rule.

The position of the Princess, when closely observed, could not be considered as anything but pleasing; she had early been impressed with the feeling that the world can give us nothing; that we must withdraw into ourselves, and within a limited circle, in order to devote ourselves to the affairs of time and eternity. She had comprehended both; the highest temporal blessings she found in what was natural, and here Rousseau's maxims concerning civil life and the training of children will be brought to mind. In everything she strove to return to what was simple and true; stays and high-heeled boots and shoes vanished; hair-powder disappeared, and her hair allowed to fall in natural locks again. Her children were taught to swim and run, perhaps also to box and wrestle. I scarcely recognised her daughter; she had grown taller and stouter; I found her intelligent, amiable, a good housewife, and devoting herself without any signs of displeasure to the half-

* J. G. Hamann, studied first theology then law. He is spoken of highly by Goethe, who was, in fact, the first to recognise the full value of his influence, and even thought of editing his works. Hamann seems to have lacked fixity of purpose, and in spite of eminent talent has left only smaller works which, however, have had their influence. His great idea was " a return to the simple forms of the earlier style of poetry, a return to the childhood of nations, a return to the simplicity of a child's faith, which alone could give rise to a new era of poetry."

monastic kind of life. Thus it was with the Present and Temporal; the Future and Eternal they had found in a religion which solemnly asserts and promises as certain, that which the teaching of others holds out only as a hope.

The fairest means of uniting the two worlds, gave rise to beneficence, as the mildest effect of an earnest asceticism; their life was devoted to the exercises of religion and benevolence; temperance and frugality were expressed in all their domestic arrangements; their daily wants were supplied plentifully and plainly, but the house itself, the furniture, and other common necessary articles of an establishment, were neither elegant nor costly; it had the appearance of a well-furnished house that had been taken for a time. The same could be said of Von Fürstenberg also; he inhabited a palace, but one that did not belong to himself, and which would not be left to his children. In everything he displayed great plainness, temperance, and frugality; relying upon inward dignity, rejecting every thing external, as did the Princess herself.

Within this sphere the most intellectual and cordial intercourse was kept up, rendered earnest by philosophy, and enlivened by art; if, in the former study different persons seldom proceed from the same principles it is all the more pleasant to find that people generally agree about the latter.

Hemsterhuis, a native of the Netherlands, a man of refined mind, and trained from youth upwards by the study of the ancient authors, had dedicated his life as well as his writings to the Princess; his writings bear throughout incontestable evidence of their mutual confidence in each other, and of the similarity of their progress in intellectual attainments.

With peculiarly acute delicacy of feeling, this estimable man was led unweariedly to strive after the intellectual and moral, as well as the sensuous and æsthetical. If we are to be imbued with the former, we ought constantly to be surrounded by the latter. To a private person, whose movements are confined within a narrow sphere, and who, even when travelling, finds it difficult to dispense with an habitual enjoyment of art, a collection of carved gems is a great boon; he is accompanied everywhere by what gives him the highest enjoyment, and is a valuable means of instruction without being cumbersome; and he can continually enjoy a very precious possession.

But in order to obtain the enjoyment, it is not enough merely to wish for it; to accomplish this, one must, above all things, be favoured by circumstances. These were not wanting to our friend; he lived on the high-road between England and Holland, and had before him the continued activity of commercial transactions, and the treasures of art which floated backwards and forwards with it, and gradually, by purchase and exchange, became possessed of a fine collection of about seventy pieces. The advice and instructions of the excellent lapidary Natter * had moreover been of the greatest service to him.

This collection the Princess had, in a great measure, seen growing to its present dimensions; she had acquired an insight, a taste, and a love for the subject. She possessed it now as the bequest of a departed friend, who seemed always present to her in these treasures.

Hemsterhuis' philosophy, the basis of it and the course of his thoughts, I could not make my own, except by translating them into my own language. The Beautiful, and the Enjoyable—he thus expressed himself—is to be able readily to perceive and to comprehend the greatest number of conceptions at one and the same moment. But I was obliged to reply: The Beautiful is to behold what is living and conformable to law, in its full activity and completeness, whereby we are excited to reproduction, and feel that we ourselves are living, and placed in the highest state of activity. Properly speaking, both mean the same thing, only expressed by different persons—and I refrain from saying more; for the Beautiful does not so much fulfil our expectations as it excites our hopes; whereas the Ugly, inasmuch as it springs from stagnation, creates stagnation, and leaves us nothing to hope for, to desire, or to expect.

I thought I could explain his 'Letter on Sculpture,' according to my definition; and his little book 'On Desire,'

* Johann Lorenz Natter is also spoken of by Meyer in his *Winckelmann und sein Jahrhundert* as an excellent artist, and specially praised for a very finely-cut portrait of Cardinal Albani.

also appeared clear to me in this way; for when the coveted beautiful object comes into our possession, it does not always give us in detail what it promised as a whole; and thus it is evident, that what attracted us as a whole does not invariably satisfy us in particulars.

These remarks were the more important, as the Princess had seen her friend grow cold over the possession of works of art, which he had so greatly coveted; this he has himself cleverly and pleasantly shown at length in the above-mentioned little book. No doubt, one point to be considered is, whether the object be worthy of the enthusiasm felt for it, or not? If it is, the pleasure and admiration which it excites will always increase, and be renewed; if it is not, then the thermometer falls a few degrees, and we gain in insight what we lost by prejudice. It is therefore quite right that we should buy works of art, in order to get acquainted with them; in this way the desire for them will cease, and their true value will be established. However, in this case also, longing and satisfaction must alternate in a pulsating life, must mutually meet and separate again, in order that he who has once been deceived may not cease to desire again.

He who has looked into Hemsterhuis' works will best judge how interesting conversations of this nature were to the society in which I was now living, for they originated in this circle, and received life and nourishment from it.

An inspection of the carved gems was often highly delightful; it was certainly a coincidence most singular that the flower of heathenism was destined to be preserved and cherished in a Christian family. I did not omit to descant upon some of the charming subjects which caught the eye in these little artistic works. It could not be denied that imitations of larger and more valuable ancient works, which would otherwise have been lost to us for ever, were preserved like jewels, in this narrow compass; and there was scarcely any one species wanting. The brawniest Hercules, crowned with ivy, could not deny his colossal origin; a severe Medusa head; a Bacchus, formerly preserved in the Medicean cabinet; charming Sacrifices and Bacchanalia; and, in addition to all this, valuable portraits of personages, known and unknown, repeatedly excited our admiration.

From these conversations, which, notwithstanding their elevation and depth, ran no danger of losing themselves in the abstruse, there seemed to arise a kind of agreement; for reverence for a worthy object is always accompanied by a religious feeling. Still it could not be concealed, that the purest form of Christian religion is always at variance with true plastic art, because the former strives to avoid all mere sensuality, whereas the latter regards the sensual element as its proper sphere of action, within which it must abide. In this spirit I wrote down, on the spur of the moment, the following lines:

> Amor, not the child, but the youth, the lover of Psyche,
> Over Olympus walked, conqueror frequent and bold;
> Gazing, a goddess he spies, the fairest of all the immortals,
> Venus Urania named; fiercely he burned for her charms;
> Nor she, the heavenly fair, resisted his passionate pleading.
> Soon the amorous youth held her in closest embrace.
> From them sprang a son, a new and lovelier Amor;
> Sense, to his father he owes, feeling his mother bestows;
> Always thou'lt find him haunting the paths of the beautiful Muses,
> And his magical shaft awakening the love of the arts.

With this allegorical profession of faith they did not seem altogether dissatisfied, but the subject was allowed to drop, both sides considering it their duty to bring forward only so much of their feelings and convictions as were held in common, and could tend, without opposition, to our mutual instruction and enjoyment.

But the carved gems were always at hand, as a delightful resource, whenever the conversation threatened to come to a stand-still. I, for my part, could appreciate only what was poetical about them, and criticised and praised, in a general way, the subjects themselves, the composition and execution; whereas my friends were accustomed to indulge in entirely different reflections. For the amateur who collects such gems, and wishes to form a valuable collection, does not find it enough merely to comprehend and enjoy the spirit and meaning of the admirable works of art; to assure himself of their value, he also appeals to their outward characteristics, which it must be very difficult for those to detect who have not

Q

the technical knowledge of artists in the same department. Hemsterhuis had kept up a correspondence for many years with Natter on this subject, and some important letters were found. The different kinds of stones employed were taken into account, since some kinds were used in earlier, others in later, times. Then, above all things, the greater degree of detail displayed in the execution was kept in view; for, in this way, periods of importance were detected, and earlier or later epochs were recognised in the superficial workmanship in so far as it showed talent, or incapacity, or carelessness. Particular weight was attached to the polish of the hollow parts, as this was thought unquestionable evidence as yielding the best epochs. But as to whether a carved gem was decidedly antique or modern, no absolute rule for judging was given; Hemsterhuis himself, it was said, determined such points only upon obtaining the assent of the excellent artist above mentioned.

I could not conceal the fact that I had here entered quite a new field, which interested me exceedingly; and only regretted the shortness of my sojourn, which would deprive me of the opportunity of examining this new class of objects more closely. On one of these occasions, the Princess said, with animation, that she would like me to take the collection away with me, that I might study it at home with my friends and others who had a scientific knowledge of such things, and, with the assistance of paste, gain new insight in this important branch of art. This offer, which I could not consider as an empty compliment, and which was most tempting to me, I declined, however, with the expression of my grateful thanks; yet, I confess, I felt the greatest anxiety about the way in which this treasure was kept. The rings were in separate cases, sometimes one by itself, or two and three together, as the case might be; it was impossible, after showing them, to notice whether any one of them was wanting or not; indeed, the Princess herself confessed, that once, when shown to the best company, a Hercules had disappeared, which was missed only sometime afterwards. Moreover it seemed rather hazardous in those agitated times to burden oneself with property of so much value, and to expose oneself to so much anxiety and responsibility. I endeavoured, therefore, with my best thanks, to give some plausible reasons for refusing it, which my friend seemed good-naturedly to take into consideration; and, without going beyond the bounds of propriety, I also endeavoured to turn her attention to these points.

Of my studies in Natural Philosophy, which I kept somewhat in the back ground, from having little hope of advancing them in this place, I was, however, also obliged to give some account. Von Fürstenberg said, that he had heard in various quarters, with surprise, that I studied osteology as a means of acquiring a knowledge of physiognomy, and seemed to think that little assistance could be expected from that quarter in judging of the countenances of men. In order to excuse my study of osteology,* which was considered quite out of place in a poet, and, perhaps, to bring the subject into notice, I might indeed have informed these friends that, as was actually the case, Lavater's work on physiognomy, had induced me to take up this subject, my first acquaintance with which had been acquired at the University. Lavater himself, the most successful investigator of the superficial organs, perceived that the form of the muscles and skin, and the effect produced by them, must entirely depend upon the definite structure of the bones beneath; the skulls of several animals were given as illustrations in his work, and he advised me to bestow a glance at them. But whatever I might have said to this effect in explanation of my proceduro would have availed but little here. At that time, such scientific reasons were too deep for those who were wholly occupied with the concerns of social life of the moment, where the movable features alone were regarded as of any real importance, and even these, perhaps, only in moments of passion; it was not considered that a mere uncontrolled appearance might have produced the effect, and that the external, movable and changeable form must be viewed as a decided result of an inward determinate Life.

* As early as 1784 Goethe had sent the Dutch naturalist Camper a treatise on the *Os intermaxillare;* for the further results of his studies in osteology we refer the reader to R. Virchow's pamphlet, *Goethe als Naturforscher und in besonderer Beziehung auf Schiller.* Berlin, 1861.

I was more successful in my attempts to entertain larger parties of people than in discussions on these subjects; we had some clever men among us, men of sense and understanding, and rising young men, of good presence and good education, and of much promise, both in respect of mind and general character. With them I voluntarily chose the Romish Church festivals, Passion-week and Easter, Corpus Christi, the feasts of Saints Peter and Paul, as subjects for discussion; then, for their amusement, the blessing of the horses, in which other domestic animals likewise participate.* These festivals were, at that time, vividly present to my mind, with all their characteristic peculiarities, for I was about to write an account of a year in Rome, with its series of ecclesiastical and lay ceremonies. I was thus enabled to describe them from the clear and direct impression that had been produced on my mind, and saw that my pious Catholic circle were as well satisfied with the pictures I presented to them, as the worldlings were with my accounts of the carnival. Indeed, one of those present, not well acquainted with all the circumstances, asked, in an under tone, whether I was really a Catholic. When the Princess told me this, she related another fact: somebody had written to her, before my arrival, that she must beware of me, as I could feign piety so well that I might be regarded as religious, and even pass for a Catholic.

"Pardon me, my esteemed friend," I exclaimed; "I do not feign piety, I am pious at the proper season; it is not difficult for me to take note of the different forms of belief with a clear and innocent glance, and to describe them again as clearly. Every sort of grotesque distortion, by which presumptuous men sin against the subject, according to their own humour, was always hateful to me. From what is distasteful to me I turn away my eyes; but many a thing, of which I do not altogether approve, I like to take cognisance of in its own peculiar mode of existence. It then appears, generally, that the others have just as much right to live after their own peculiar fashion, as I have to live after mine." By this means an important

* Of these festivals we have a detailed description by Goethe in his *Italienische Reise*.

point was cleared up, and thus a secret, and by no means commendable, interference with our relations, instead of exciting suspicion, had, on the contrary, produced confidence.

In the midst of such an amiable circle, it would have been impossible to be either harsh or disagreeable; I felt myself in a gentler mood than for a long time past, and nothing could have been more fortunate for me than thus again to feel the influence of pious, friendly persons upon me, after the frightful events of the war and the disastrous retreat.

In one point, however, I failed in proper deference to my excellent and worthy friends, without myself knowing how it occurred. I was celebrated for my felicitous, free, and emphatic style of reading: they wished to hear me, and as they knew that I had enthusiastically admired Voss's "Louise," when it appeared in the November number of the *Mercury* of 1784,* they manœuvred to get me to read it, without being too importunate about it: they laid the number of the *Mercury* below the mirror, and left me to act as I chose. It would be difficult to say now what it was that kept me from complying; I felt as if mind and lips were sealed; I could not take up the book, and could not resolve to make use of the pause which occurred in the conversation for my own pleasure and that of my friends; the time passed away, and I am still astonished when I think of my inexplicable obduracy.

The day of my departure approached; sooner or later, we had to part. "Now," said the Princess, " no objections will avail any longer; you must take the carved gems with you, I desire it." When, as courteously as possible, I still persevered in my refusal, she at last said: " I must, then, disclose to you why I demand it. I have been advised not to trust you with this treasure, and for this very reason I will do it, must do it; it has been represented to me that I do not know you well enough to be quite sure of you in such a case. My reply to this," she continued, " was, do you believe that the opinion I have of him is not dearer to

---

* The beginning of Voss's idyl appeared in the *Musen-Almanach* of 1784; it was the continuation of it that appeared in the *Mercur*, as hero stated by Goethe.

me than these stones? If I am to lose my opinion of him, then this treasure may go, too." To this I could make no further reply, since by such a declaration she laid me under as great an obligation as she did me honour. Every other obstacle was set aside; sulphur casts were at hand, catalogued, and ready for use if required, packed up in a neat box with the originals, and a very small space contained this costly treasure, which could thus be easily carried about from place to place.

In this friendly way we took leave of each other, but did not part immediately; the Princess informed me that she intended to accompany me as far as the first stage, got into the carriage beside me, and ordered her own to follow. The important points in life and doctrines were again discussed; I repeated my usual credo quietly and mildly, and she remained stedfast to hers. Both of us then wended our way homewards; she expressing, as her last wish, that she might see me again, if not in this world, in the next.

This farewell formula of well-meaning, friendly Catholics was neither strange nor distasteful to me; it had often been said to me, by casual acquaintances at watering-places and elsewhere, generally by priests I had met, and who had become attached to me. I see no reason why I should object to any one wishing to draw me into his sphere, where alone, according to his convictions, it is possible to live in tranquillity, and, sure of eternal salvation, to die in peace.

Weimar, from December 1792 *to April* 1793.

With the utmost kindness and attention, my excellent friend had not only urged the postmaster to exercise all despatch in forwarding me, but even horses were bespoke, this was both very agreeable and highly necessary. For, amid the cultivated and peaceful society of my friends, I had forgotten that the fugitives from the scene of war were still crowding up behind; and I found hosts of Emigrants upon the road, pressing onwards into the heart of Germany, towards whom the postilions here showed as little favour as those on the Rhine had done. Very often

there was no actual road, the vehicles were driven first in one
direction, then in another, encountering and crossing each
other. Furze bushes and underwood, stumps of trees, sand,
bogs, and rushes, lay in our way, each more annoying than
the other. And there was no want of passionate scenes.

One of the vehicles stuck fast, and Paul immediately
jumped down to lend a helping hand; he perhaps thought
the pretty Frenchwomen, whom he had again met in
Düsseldorf, were once more in need of his assistance. The
lady had not yet found her husband, but borne along by
the fearful current, and in the greatest alarm, had at last
been cast across the Rhine.

It was not she, however, who appeared amid the confusion here; some venerable old ladies claimed our aid. But
when we asked the postilion to stop, and to allow his
horses to assist in moving the carriage, he refused saucily,
and said: "We had better look to our own coach with
its burden of gold and silver, and see that it did not stick
fast somewhere, or get overturned; for although he meant
honestly by us, he would not answer for anything in
such a wilderness."

Luckily, to quiet our consciences, a number of West-
phalian peasants had collected round the unfortunate
carriage, and, on being promised a handsome reward,
they helped to get it upon a better piece of road.

What made our coach so heavy was, the quantity of
iron about it; the costly prize we carried with us was
so light, that, if the carriage had been a light one, no
additional weight would have been perceived. How I
longed for my little Bohemian carriage! The general
belief, that we had something valuable with us, occasioned
me some uneasiness. We had observed, that every pos-
tillion told the other that our coach was too heavy, and
gave him to understand that there must be gold and other
valuables in it. Orders having been sent on before for
fresh horses, we were forwarded at every stage with great
speed; on one occasion we were literally driven out
into the night, when the awkward case hinted at by the
postilion actually occurred. In the midst of a gloomy
night, he swore that he could not move the thing any
further, and stopped in a wood before a lonely house, the

situation, aspect, and inhabitants of which would have raised a shudder even in broad daylight.

The dawn, although one of the greyest, brought some comfort; I thought of the friends with whom I had, shortly before, passed such a happy time; they came up before me one by one, and I dwelt with pleasure on their good qualities and peculiarities. But as soon as night again set in, I found myself filled with fresh cares and anxieties. Gloomy, however, as my thoughts had been in the last and darkest of the nights, they as suddenly brightened up as I drove into Cassel, lit up by its myriads of lamps. At this sight my mind was vividly impressed with a sense of the advantages possessed by the inhabitants of large towns; I saw the comfort enjoyed by each individual citizen in his own well-lit dwelling, and the commodious establishments for the reception of strangers. The cheerfulness produced by the scene was disturbed, for a moment when we drew up at the well-known inn in the splendidly-illuminated Königsplatz, where it was as light as day. The servant who announced our arrival returned with the answer that there was no room for us. Upon seeing that I did not mean to go away, a butler stepped very civilly up to the carriage-window, and, with some fine phrases in French, begged me to excuse them, as it was quite impossible to take me in. I replied, in good German, that I could not help being surprised, that in so large a building, the extent of which was well known to me, a stranger should be refused admittance in the middle of the night. "Ah! you are a German!" he exclaimed, "that is quite a different thing;" and he immediately told the postilion to drive into the courtyard. After showing me a good room, he added, that he was quite determined not to admit any more of the Emigrants. Their behaviour was most arrogant, and their pay niggardly; for, in spite of their wretched plight, and not knowing where to turn, they conducted themselves as if they had taken possession of a conquered country. We parted good friends; and on the way to Eisenach I found the crowds of these numerous fugitives and unwelcome guests less frequent.

My arrival in Weimar had also something adventurous

about it; it took place after midnight, and occasioned a family scene, which would have enlivened and brightened the darkest scene in any novel.*

I found the house, which had been assigned to me by my Prince, repaired and newly fitted up, and almost wholly in order, but was not quite deprived of the pleasure of co-operating in its completion. My family met me in good health and spirits; and when we began mutually to relate what had happened meanwhile, a striking contrast was presented between those who had enjoyed the sweet-meats sent from Verdun in peace and tranquillity, and ourselves, whom they fancied had been luxuriating in a kind of paradise, while in reality we had been struggling against every imaginable difficulty.

Our quiet domestic circle I found enriched and enlivened by the presence of Heinrich Meyer, an artist, a patron of art, and fellow-worker, who took an active interest in all our studies and labours.

The Weimar theatre had existed since May 1791. The company had acted during the summer of that and the following year in Lauchstädt, and had succeeded tolerably in the representation of the well-known and standard pieces of the day. A remnant of the Bellamo company, hence persons accustomed to each other, had formed the foundation; and some others, who had already shown considerable talent, and gave promise of more, filled up the gaps.

Acting may be said to have been still a trade; the members who had graduated in it, although belonging to the different theatres scattered over the country, willingly co-operated with each other, particularly when they were fortunate enough to obtain Low Germans for the acting, and High Germans for the singing; hence, for a beginning, the public had good reason to be satisfied.

As I had taken part in the management I endeavoured to discover how the undertaking could best be carried out. I very soon saw, that a certain technical proficiency and routine were easily acquired, by imitating and

* What took place upon his return home on this occasion, says Hempel, is not stated anywhere. In no *Life of Goethe*, as far as we know, is there any explanation of it. His arrival, according to the text here, must have taken place on the 16th or 17th.

copying others; but that there was an entire want of what may be called grammar—which must form the foundation, before rhetoric and poetry can be attained. As I intend to return to this subject, and do not wish to give it piece-meal, I will, for the present, merely say, that I applied myself to study the technical part, which seemed altogether made up of tradition, and to reduce it to its elements, and further to take note of what had become clear to me in detail, without reference to the subject in general.

I was greatly assisted in this undertaking by the natural tone that began to be adopted in conversation, which is indeed very agreeable and acceptable when it appears as the perfection of art—as second nature—but not when each one thinks that he has only to exhibit his own naked being to perform a service worthy of all praise. I made use of this tendency for my own purposes, and was well satisfied to see the natural faculties freely display themselves, in order, by certain rules and regulations, to be gradually conducted towards a higher culture. But I must not say anything further about this, because what has been achieved, developed only by degrees, and must therefore be represented historically.

Some circumstances, which were very favourable for the new theatre, I must, however, shortly notice. Iffland and Kotzebue were at the height of their fame; their pieces, written in a simple and popular style, were directed on one hand against the self-indulgences of social life; on the other, against the excesses of immorality. This style of writing was in accordance with the feelings of the time, and received hearty sympathy; several of the pieces, even when read as manuscripts, excited pleasure, from the lively aroma of the moment represented. Schroeder, Babo, Ziegler, men of activity and felicitous talent, rendered important assistance. Bretzner and Jünger, also contemporaries, came forward with an easy, light style of gaiety, without any pretence. Hagemann and Hagemeister, whose reputations were not destined to be of long duration, likwise worked for the day, and were noticed and welcomed, if not admired.

Greater elevation was sought for from the influence of

Shakespeare, Gozzi, and Schiller; the old custom of constantly learning new pieces which were shortly to be thrown aside again, was given up; a more careful choice was made, and a repertory was prepared, which lasted for many years. We must not forget gratefully to remember the man who helped us to establish this. It was F. J. Fischer, an actor of many years' standing, who understood his business, a temperate man, without strong passions, content with his condition, and with representing unimportant characters. He brought several actors with him from Prague, who worked in the same spirit, and succeeded in winning the good-will of the inhabitants; and a good understanding was thus kept up between all.

In regard to the opera, those from Dittersdorf* were most serviceable to us. He had ability and humour, and as he had worked for a private princely theatre, his productions acquired a certain easy grace, which was useful to us as well, for we had been wise enough to regard our new theatre as an amateur one. Much attention was bestowed upon the librettos, both the rhythmical and prosaical parts, in order to adapt them to the upper Saxon taste; and thus this light commodity obtained both approbation and sale.

Our friends who had been in Italy brought back with them the lighter Italian operas of the time, of Paiesiello, Cimarosa, Guglielmi, and others; and the effects of Mozart's genius also began to be felt. When it is considered that, of all these productions, very few were known, and that none of them were hackneyed, it will be acknowledged that the origin of the Weimar theatre was contemporaneous with the youthful times of the German theatres in general, and enjoyed advantages which necessarily led to its development and success.

In order to facilitate and secure my enjoyment and study of the collection of gems entrusted to me, I ordered two neat ring-cases to be made, in which the stones could be surveyed at a glance, side by side, and any blank at

* Of the many operas written by Carl Ditters, of Dittersdorf, two had been performed in Weimar.

once be observed; several sulphur and plaster casts were also made, and examined with powerful magnifying glasses, and existing casts of older collections were procured, and compared with them. We soon perceived that our studies in this department were at the very beginning, and the extent of our obligation to the Princess manifested itself only by degrees.

The result of several years' study may therefore be inserted here, as it is not likely that we shall soon have our attention directed to this point again.

From certain internal reasons, we thought ourselves justified in considering the greater number, if not the whole of these carved gems as genuine antiques; and several of them, we thought, might be regarded as among the most exquisite specimens of this kind of workmanship. Some of them were found to be actually identical with older sulphur casts; several were found to coincide with other antique gems, but which might be considered as original. In the largest collections duplicates frequently occur; and it would be a great mistake to declare the one original, and the other modern copies.

We must not forget the faithful way in which the ancient artists adhered to what had once been successfully executed, frequently repeating the representation of it. They thought themselves original enough if they were able to comprehend an original conception, and possessed of capacity and skill sufficient to represent it in their own way.

Several of the stones had the artists' names engraved upon them, and much value had been set upon this for many years past. An addition of this kind is certainly always worthy of remark, but is generally of mere problematical importance; for it is possible that the stone may be old, and that the name newly carved upon it, in order to give additional value to an exquisite piece of workmanship.

Although, as may be supposed, I do not intend here to give any detailed catalogue of the gems, as a description of such things, without copies, give but a poor idea of them, still I think it right to mention the most remarkable among them in a general way.

A head of Hercules.—Distinguished for the exquisite taste displayed in the execution, and still more to be admired in respect of the beautiful ideal form, which does not correspond exactly with any of the known Hercules' heads; it is this that renders the precious gem more remarkable than it would otherwise be.

A bust of Bacchus.—A work which looks as if it had been breathed upon the stone; and in regard to its ideal form is one of the noblest works of antiquity. Several similar pieces are to be found in other collections, if I remember rightly, both in relief and carved into stone; however, I know of none superior to this one.

A Faun about to snatch the dress from a Bacchante.— An excellent piece of composition, frequently found upon old monuments; likewise very well executed.

An overturned Lyre—the horns of which represent two dolphins; the body, or, if preferred, the foot, the head of Cupid, with a garland of roses; prettily grouped to this is the panther of Bacchus, holding the thyrsus in its forepaw. The execution of this gem would satisfy the connoisseur, and those fond of subtle allusions would also find their account in it.

A Mask—with a long beard, and wide open mouth; a sprig of ivy encircles the bald forehead. This stone is probably one of the most exquisite of its kind; equally valuable is also

Another Mask—with a large beard, and the hair gracefully tied up. This is engraved much deeper than usual.

Venus giving suck to Cupid.—One of the most charming groups to be seen; executed with great talent, but without much expense of labour.

Cybele riding on the lion—deeply cut; a work, the excellence of which is sufficiently known to amateurs by means of casts, and are to be found in almost all pastecollections.

A giant pulling a griffin from its hole in a rock.—A work of great artistic merit, and perhaps unique as a composition. An enlarged copy of it will be found by our readers prefixed to the programme of the Jena A. L. Z., 1804, vol. iv.

The profile of a head with a helmet and a large beard.

It is perhaps a mask; it has, however, nothing whatever of a caricature about it, but is a firm, heroic countenance, and beautifully worked.

Homer as Hermes—represented almost full front, and very deeply cut. The poet is here depicted younger than usual, scarcely on the verge of old age; consequently this piece is valuable, not only as a work of art, but for the sake of the subject.

In collections of casts of carved gems, the head of a venerable aged man, with long beard and hair, is frequently met with, which (without any good reasons being given) is said to represent Aristophanes. A head of this kind, differing from the above one only in insignificant points, is to be found in our collection, and is, in fact, one of the best pieces.

The profile of some unknown person—was probably found broken off above the eyebrows, and at a later period recut for a ring. Nobler and more lifelike we never saw the human form represented on the small space of a gem, and seldom a case in which the artist showed such unlimited ability. Of equal merit is

The portrait of another person unknown, clothed in a lion's skin—this, like the preceding one, has also been broken off above the eyes, but the missing part is restored with gold.

The head of a man advanced in years—firm and strong in character, with short hair; it is executed with remarkable intelligence and ability; the bold treatment of the beard is particularly to be admired, and perhaps unique of its kind.

A man's head or bust—without a beard, and with a band round the hair; the drapery attached in rich folds to the shoulder. There is a grand powerful expression in this work, and the features are such as are usually attributed to Julius Cæsar.

A man's head—likewise without a beard; the toga, as was the custom with victims, drawn over the head. There is a wonderful degree of truth and character in this face; and there is no doubt that the work is a genuine antique, belonging to the times of the first Roman emperors.

The bust of a Roman lady—the hair wound round the head in double braids; the whole finished with wonderful care, and, in regard to character, full of truth, ease, naïveté, and life.

A small head with a helmet—thick beard, and energetic character, represented full front, and of exquisite workmanship.

In conclusion we will mention a beautiful modern gem —the head of Medusa, in a splendid carnelian. It is exactly like the well-known Medusa of Sosikles, the slight differences between them being scarcely perceptible. Without doubt, one of the best imitations of antiquity; for an imitation it must be considered to be, notwithstanding its great merit, as the work is somewhat wanting in freedom; and besides this, an N engraved upon the neck, is a good reason for supposing it to be of a work of Natter himself.

Even from the little we have said, connoisseurs will recognise the great value of the collection. I do not know where it is at present to be found; perhaps information might be obtained about it, and some rich lover of art, if it were for sale, obtain possession of it.

The Weimar patrons of art took all possible advantage of the collection, so long as it remained in their hands. During the current winter, it furnished the intellectual society which usually gathered round the Duchess Amalia, with admirable entertainment. They were induced to cultivate the study of carved gems; and the favour of the excellent lady who owned them proved of the greatest service, for she allowed us to keep them for several years. Shortly before her death, she was enabled to enjoy them more than she had ever done before, arranged as they now were in the two cases, and thus had every reason to rejoice in the confidence she had reposed in us.

Our art studies extended in another direction. I had made sufficient observations on colours in various circumstances, and hoped now at last to discover their art harmony (*Kunstharmonie*) as well. My friend Meyer drew up a number of tables, where they could be seen as a series, and also in contrast, and could thus easily be reviewed and compared.

This harmony was perceived most readily in simple rural objects, where the light side always comprises the yellow and yellow-red; and the shaded side, the blue and blue-red; but owing to the variety of natural objects, these may very easily be blended by the brown-green and blue-green. Of this, many great masters have given us examples; in landscapes more frequently than in historical subjects, where the artist has to trust to himself in the choice of colours for his drapery, and, when in doubt, snatches at any assistance which custom or tradition may afford him; and also allows himself to be led astray by wrong directions from others, and frequently, therefore, diverted from a true harmonious representation of his subject. These studies in plastic art, I feel compelled to leave, and to return to the theatre, to make some observations on my own relation to it, which at first I intended to have avoided. One would think it offered me the best opportunity of giving my assistance, as an author, to the new theatre, and to the German stage in general; for there were many gaps to be filled up between the works of the authors mentioned above; there was plenty of material at hand, ready for natural and simple treatment.

But to make myself quite intelligible, I may mention that my earliest dramatic works, relating to history, were too diffuse to be fitted for the stage; my later ones, addressed as they are to the deepest inward feelings, made but little impression when played, by reason of their too great conciseness. I had, however, trained myself to an intermediate kind of work, by which I might have produced something sufficiently well adapted for the stage; but I fell upon wrong subjects, or rather the subjects overpowered my inward moral nature, and thus became quite unmanageable as subjects for dramatic treatment.

In the year 1785, the affair of the diamond necklace had startled me like the head of the Gorgon. By this unheard-of wickedness, I saw the dignity of royalty undermined, annihilated as it were in anticipation; and subsequent events only too completely confirmed my fearful forebodings. I carried these forebodings with me to Italy, and brought them back with me increased in intensity. Fortunately I got my *Tasso* finished; but after that my mind became absorbed in the great occurrences of the day.

For many years I had had occasion to denounce the treacherous doings of bold fantastical men and interested enthusiasts, and had been amazed at the incomprehensible shortsightedness of many superior men, who allowed themselves to be led astray by these bold importunities. The direct and indirect consequences of these follies now lay clearly before me in the form of crimes against royalty, which, if united, were sufficient to shake the most splendid throne in the world to its foundations.

In order to divert my mind from these horrors, I endeavoured to look upon them from a cheerful point of view; and the form of comic opera, which had appeared to me for some time past as one of the best modes of dramatic representation, seemed not altogether unadapted to such serious subjects, as had been shown in *King Theodore*. Hence this subject was treated rhythmically, the musical part being discussed with Reichardt, of which some rough sketches of bass arias have been made public; other portions of the music, which had no meaning beyond the context, were not published, and the passage from which the greatest effect was expected was likewise never completed. The apparitions in the crystal ball, seen by the sleeping clairvoyant Cophta, were intended to be a dazzling *finale* to the whole.

But there was no joyous spirit in it, and it came to a stand-still; in order not to lose all the labour I had expended on it, I wrote a piece in prose, and representatives for the principal characters were found among the new company of actors, who performed their parts admirably, when it was brought upon the stage.

But from the very fact of the piece having been excellently acted, the more repulsive was its effect. A frightful, and at the same time an absurd subject, boldly and unsparingly handled, startled every one, and aroused no sympathy; the proximity in time and place of the subject represented, made the impression more keenly felt; and as secret connections believed themselves harshly treated, a large and respectable portion of the public felt alienated, while female delicacy was alarmed at the audacious love adventure.

I had been always indifferent to the effect produced by my works, and was not at all disturbed by seeing that this, the last of them, on which I had expended so many years' labour, met with no sympathy; nay I felt a malicious kind of pleasure, when I heard certain persons, whom I had often enough seen deceived, asserting that nobody could be deceived by such clumsiness.

From this occurrence, however, I did not draw any lesson; that which occupied my mind appeared to me constantly in dramatic form; and as the necklace affair had taken possession of me as a dismal omen, the revolution itself appeared to me as its most dreadful fulfilment; a throne I saw overthrown and shattered; a great nation cast out of its groove, and, considering our unfortunate campaign, the world itself out of joint.

Oppressed and tormented by such reflections, I had occasion, unhappily, to observe that my own countrymen were also dallying with sentiments which were preparing a like fate for us. I knew many noble spirits who fantastically gave themselves up to certain views and hopes, without understanding either themselves or the matter; while unprincipled men were striving to excite bitter discontent, and to increase it for their own advantage.

As an evidence of my irritated good-humour, I produced the *Bürger-General*; I was induced to do this by an actor named Beck, who acted the part of Schnaps in the *Two Billets*, in imitation of Florian, with characteristic excellence, his very faults being of service to him. As this character suited him so well, the first part of the continuation of this small and favourite afterpiece, called the *Stammbaum*, by Anton Wall, was produced; and as I bestowed the greatest care upon the rehearsals, preparation, and representations of this trifle, I became so engrossed with the comical Schnaps, that I was tempted to reproduce him. This I did both with good-will and in detail; for the capacious carpet-bag was a real French one which Paul had hastily snatched up during our flight. In the principal scene Malcolmi appeared as an old, well-to do, good-natured countryman, who at times enjoyed an outrageous piece of impudence as a good joke, in a way not to be surpassed, and vied with

Beck in his natural rendering of the character. But it was all in vain; the piece produced the most unfavourable effect, even with my friends and well-wishers, who, to excuse me and themselves, obstinately maintained that I was not the author, but had only, from some odd caprice, given my name and some touches of my pen to a very indifferent production.

As, however, nothing external was ever able to estrange me from myself, but rather threw me back upon myself, these representations of contemporary events formed a kind of consolatory occupation for me.

The *Unterhaltungen der Ausgewanderten*,* a fragment, and an unfinished piece called the *Aufgeregten*, are so many confessions of what was passing in my own breast at the time; *Hermann und Dorothea*, at a later period, flowed from the same spring, which, it is true, dried up altogether at last. The poet could not keep pace with the rapid course of events, and was obliged to remain indebted to himself and others for the conclusion, when he saw the problem solved in a way that was as decisive as it was unexpected.

Amid these constellations nobody could have readily felt more oppressed than I did, away so far from the actual scene of the mischief; the world appeared to me bloodier and bloodthirstier than ever; and if, as has been said, the blood of a king slain in battle is equal to that of a thousand ordinary men, it is more significant still in a contest with the Law. The trial of a king for his life puts thoughts in circulation, and brings relations into dispute, that, to prevent them ever arising, *kingship* had been firmly established centuries before.

But I tried to save myself from these horrors also, by declaring the whole world worthless, and by a curious coincidence *Reinecke Fuchs* fell into my hands. Tired and disgusted as I was of scenes arising from mob insurrections and street encounters, it was quite refreshing to cast a glance into a glass reflecting courts and princes; for

---

* The separate stories contained in this work appeared almost immediately after they were written in Schiller's periodical *Die Horen*, and are frequently referred to the Schiller and Goethe correspondence.

although here also the animal nature of man is displayed naturally enough, and without disguise, still everything is represented in a cheerful, if not an exemplary way, and one's good humour is never disturbed.

In order thoroughly to enjoy the delightful work, I at once commenced a faithful imitation of it; and from what follows it will be seen why I wrote it in hexameters.

For many years past, pretty tolerable hexameters had been written in Germany after Klopstock's example; Voss, although he himself made use of them, showed that he thought there was room for improvement in this department, and did not even spare his own works and translations, notwithstanding the favour with which they were received by the public. I had a desire to learn this, but could not manage it. Herder and Wieland were latitudinarians in this respect; and Voss's works one scarcely dared mention, as they were gradually becoming more severe and inappropriate for the moment. The public valued his earlier works more than his later ones; but I had always a silent confidence in Voss, whose earnestness was not to be mistaken; and had I been younger, or had circumstances been different, I would have gone to Eutin, in order to learn his secret. For, owing to an honourable regard for Klopstock, he did not wish, in the lifetime of the worthy poet whose renown filled the whole world, to tell him to his face, that a stricter observance of rules must be introduced into German rhyme, if any hope was to be held out of its ever being established on a sure basis. His utterances, meanwhile, were like sibylline leaves to me. The trouble I took with the preface to the Georgics I still remember with pleasure, for the sake of my honest intention, not for any advantage I gained from it.

As I was quite conscious that, in my case, culture could be acquired only in a practical way, I took the opportunity of writing down several thousand hexameters, which were likely to meet with a good reception and be of some lasting value owing to the delightful subject, whatever might be the defects in the technical construction. What might prove faulty in them, I thought, would show itself in the end; I devoted every hour I could dispose of to

this work, and found my reward in the actual effort.
I built and furnished away, without thinking of what
else was to happen to me, although I might easily have
foreseen the consequences.

Notwithstanding our being far to the east of the great
events that were taking place, there appeared among us this
winter outrunners of those of our neighbours who had been
driven from the west; it seemed as if they were searching
for some civilised place, in which to find protection and
shelter. Although only temporary visitors, they conducted
themselves so well and patiently, and showed themselves
so ready to submit to their fate, to maintain themselves
by some kind of labour, that every body became pre-
possessed in their favour; the faults of the general mass
were forgotten in the merits of these few, and the
aversion which had been felt for their class was changed
into a feeling of good-will for them. This was of service
to those who arrived later, and settled in Thuringia,
among whom I need only mention Mounier and Camille
Jourdan to justify a feeling that had been formed for the
whole colony which showed itself, if not quite equal in all
respects to those I have named, at all events by no means
unworthy of them.

I may here observe, that in all important political emergencies, those spectators are most fortunate who join one
of the contending parties; what is really favourable to
them they joyfully lay hold of, what is unfavourable
they keep out of sight, reject, or turn it to their advantage.
But the poet, who from his very nature is and must
remain free from party feelings, seeks to comprehend the
state of the case from both points of view, and, if an
adjustment is impossible, he must decide to make the
end tragical. And with what a cycle of tragedies were
we not ourselves threatened by the raging commotion
in the world!

Who is there that has not been horrified from youth
upwards by the history of the year 1649; who has not
shuddered at the execution of Charles I., and taken some
comfort in the hope, that such scenes of party rancour could
never be renewed? But they were now being repeated, more
frightfully and terribly than ever, by the most civilised of

the neighbouring nations, and before our very eyes, as it were, day by day and step by step. Think what a January and December had been passed by those who had taken the field to save the King, and who were now unable to stop the proceedings, or hinder the execution of the sentence against him.

Frankfort was again in possession of the Germans, and active preparations were being made to recapture Mainz. The German troops had advanced towards it, and occupied Hochheim; Königstein had been forced to surrender. But the first thing necessary was to free their rear; they therefore marched by the Taunus mountains to Idstein, and proceeded past the Benedictine convent Schönau to Caub, then across a strong bridge of boats to Bacharach; from thence an almost uninterrupted series of skirmishes took place between the outposts of both armies, and the enemy was forced to retreat. Our troops left the Hundsrück hills to the right, and marched to Stromberg, where General Neubinger was taken prisoner. They then reached Kreuznach, and cleared the angle lying between the Nahe and the Rhine, and were able to move towards the latter river in safety. The Imperialists had crossed the Rhine at Spires, and had been able to complete the investment of Mainz on the 14th April, and to threaten the inhabitants with scarcity, as the forerunner of still greater evils.

This intelligence I received accompanied with a request to join the army and take part in the stationary dangers and sufferings of a siege, as I had done formerly in the active ones of the campaign. The investment had been completed, and the siege could not be long delayed. With what reluctance I again approached the theatre of the war may be seen in the second etching from my sketches.* It is copied from a very exact pen-and-ink

* This sketch represents the back or garden view of Goethe's house in Weimar. A simple wooden staircase, entwined by a vine plant, leads from the central door into the garden; at the foot of the steps is a bench with two orange trees on either side. Through the open door is seen a youthful female figure (Goethe's wife, Christiana Vulpius) looking down with evident joy at a little boy (her son) sitting on the staircase. (Hempel's edition of Goethe's works.)

sketch, which I had very carefully made a few days before my departure—with what feelings, may be seen in the few lines appended to it—

> Here, at home, the toilsome march is o'er,
> And kindly faces smile from door to door;
> Here the glad artist seeks repose from strife,
> And leads again his old familiar life;
> And, weary of long wandering to and fro,
> Muses at ease on life's continuous flow;
> For, e'en venturous hearts that farthest roam,
> Return at last for happiness to home.

THE SIEGE OF MAINZ.

SIEGE OF MAINZ.

MONDAY, the 26th of May, 1793, I left Frankfort for Höchst and Flörsheim. Here, I found a quantity of heavy artillery for the siege. The old road to Mainz was blocked, and I had to cross the bridge of boats at Rüsselsheim; we stopped to feed the horses in Ginsheim; this place was much injured by shot; thence, by the bridge of boats, to the Nonnenau, where numbers of trees, that had been cut down, lay strewn about; by the second half of the bridge of boats, we crossed the larger arm of the Rhine. Thence on to Bodenheim and Oberolm, where 1 took up my quarters in a cantonment, and then rode off with Captain Vent to the right wing of the army past Hochtsheim, and examined the positions of Mainz, Castel, Kostheim, Hochheim, Weissenau, the Maine, and the islands in the Rhine. The French had seized one of these, and entrenched themselves on it; I passed the night in Oberolm.

Tuesday, the 27th of May, I hastened to present myself to my Prince at Marienborn, where I had also the good fortune to wait upon Prince Maximilian of Zweibrücken, who had always been very gracious to me.* I then exchanged my indifferent quarters in the cantonment for a large tent in front of the regiment. I was desirous of becoming acquainted with the centre of the semicircle formed by the blockading troops, and rode to the entrenchments in front of the Toll-house, surveyed the position of the town, the new French entrenchment at Zahlbach, and the singularly dangerous position of the

* Great-grandfather of the present King of Bavaria; he was made king in 1806.

village of Bretzenheim. I then returned to the regiment, and made some careful sketches, in order the better to impress on my mind the relative positions and distances of the different objects.

I waited upon General Count Kalkreuth in Marienborn, and passed the evening with him. There was a great deal of talk about some report that had been raised the previous night at the other end of the camp, of a German general who was said to have gone over to the French; the watchword, it was said, had been changed, and several battalions had taken up arms.

We also discussed the details of the position, the blockade, and the impending siege. Much was said about personal influence, which often produced great effects without being much heard of. This showed how little history can be relied upon; as, in fact, no one can tell why or wherefore one thing or another is done.

Wednesday, the 28th of May, I was with Colonel von Stein, at the Ranger's house, which is beautifully situated —a delightful residence. One felt what a pleasant post that of Forest Ranger to the Elector of Mainz must be. From thence is seen the large caldron-shaped piece of country which stretches across to Hochheim, where, in primeval times, the united waters of the Rhine and Maine, whirling and restagnating, produced the fertile soil found here, and thence forced a clear passage at Biberich to flow westwards.

I dined at head-quarters; the retreat from Champagne was discussed; Count Kalkreuth gave free vent to his sarcastic humour against the theorists.

After dinner, a clergyman was brought in, suspected of revolutionary opinions. He was either really mad, or pretended to be so; he believed he had been Turenne and Condé, and that he had never been born of woman, —that by the Word all things were made! He was very merry, and, in the midst of his madness, displayed great consistency and presence of mind.

I asked permission to pay a visit to Lieutenant von Itzenplitz, who had been wounded both by a sabre and a ball on the 9th of May in a skirmish before Mainz, and afterwards made prisoner. He had been very kindly treated by the enemy, and soon delivered up again. He was not yet allowed to speak, but the presence of an old comrade, who had much to relate, had a cheering effect upon him.

In the evening, the officers of the regiment assembled in the quarters of the commissary, where things were done with rather more spirit than the previous year in Champagne; for we were now able to drink its sparkling wine, in beautiful weather, without being drenched with rain. A former prophecy of mine was recalled; they repeated my very words: "From this place and from this day forth commences a new era in the world's history; and you can all say that you were present at its birth."* Wonderfully enough did this prophecy seem to have been fulfilled, not only in a general sense, but even to the very letter, as the French date their calendar from those days.

But man at all times, and particularly in war, easily reconciles himself to what is inevitable, and endeavours to fill up the intervals between danger, difficulty and vexation, with amusements and pleasures; and so it was here; the Thadden hautboys played the Ça ira, and the Marseillaise; and bottle after bottle of Champagne was emptied.

In the evening, at eight o'clock, a loud cannonade was heard from the batteries on the right wing.

Thursday, the 29th of May, in the morning, at nine o'clock, a general salute of the guns in honour of the victory of the Austrians at Famars. This general firing of the guns enabled me to become acquainted with the position of the batteries and the troops; at the same time, a serious affair was going on at Bretzenheim; and the French certainly had good reason for wishing to drive us out of this village, which lay so near them. Meanwhile, we learnt how the story got afloat about the desertion the day before; a strange series of accidental coincidences, as absurd as possible, but still current for a time.

I accompanied my gracious Prince to the left wing, and

* See p. 81.

waited on the Landgrave of Darmstadt; the whole of his camp was prettily decorated with twigs of pine, but his own tent surpassed everything of the kind I had ever seen; well designed and beautifully executed, comfortable and splendid.

Towards evening, a most pleasant spectacle awaited us all, but particularly myself; the Princesses of Mecklenburg* had been dining with His Majesty, at head-quarters, in Bodenheim, and after dinner came to visit the camp. I crept into my tent, and could thus closely observe the great ladies, who walked up and down in front of it, quite unconscious of being observed. And, truly, amidst all the hurly-burly of war, the two young ladies might have been taken for heavenly apparitions, and the impression they made will never vanish from my mind.

Friday, the 30th of May. In the morning we heard the firing of musketry at the back of the camp, which caused some alarm. It was afterwards explained to have been some peasants celebrating Corpus-Christi day. A general salute was fired later, both from the cannons and small guns in honour of the happy event which had just occurred in the Netherlands; a sharp fire, too, was kept up between the besiegers and besieged. In the afternoon a thunderstorm.

The Dutch artillery flotilla has arrived, and is lying at Ebenheim.

In the night between the 30th and 31st of May, I was sleeping quietly in my tent as usual, with all my clothes on, when I was awakened by an explosion of musketry, which seemed at no great distance. I jumped up, went outside, and found everything in commotion; it was plain that Marienborn had been attacked. Shortly afterwards our cannon on the battery at the Toll-house began to fire, which could be explained only by the approach of the enemy. The Duke's regiment, one of the squadrons of which was encamped behind the Toll-house, moved out; the affair was inexplicable for the moment. The firing of

* These were Louise, afterwards Queen of Prussia and mother of the present Emperor of Germany, and her sister Fredericke, who married the King of Hanover. The princesses had been brought up at the Court of their grandmother, the Landgravine of Hesse-Darmstadt.

the musketry in Marienborn, in the rear of our batteries, continued, and our batteries fired also. I mounted my horse and rode forwards, where, although it was dark, I could still recognise the positions owing to the survey I had previously made. I expected every moment to see Marienborn in flames, and rode back to our tents, where I found the Duke's people busy packing up to be ready for any emergency. I gave my portmanteau and portfolio into their charge, and arranged about our retreat. They were going towards Oppenheim; I could easily follow them, as the footpath through the orchards was well known to me, but determined first to ascertain the result, and not to retire till the village was on fire and the struggle extended farther up behind it.

In this state of uncertainty I waited and watched; the firing of the musketry soon ceased, the cannon ceased thundering, the day began to dawn, and the village lay perfectly quiet before me. I rode down. The sun rose, but shed a gloomy light, and I saw the victims of the night lying there together. Our gigantic well-dressed cuirassiers contrasted strangely with the dwarfish, ragged *sansculottes*; death had cut them all down without distinction. Our good Captain La Viere was among the first killed; Captain von Voss, an adjutant of Count Kalkreuth's, was shot through the breast and not expected to live. I was induced to write a short account* of this curious and unpleasant occurrence, which I insert here, together with some other particulars relating to it.

Account of the sortie of the French upon Marienborn during the night.

The head-quarters of Marienborn are situated in the centre of the semicircle of camps and batteries which commence on the left bank of the Rhine above Mainz, begird the town at a distance of not quite two miles, and end below it at the river again. The chapel of the Holy Cross, the villages of Weissenau, Hechtsheim, Marienborn,

* This same report Goethe forwarded to Herder on the 2nd of June and to Jacobi on the 15th, but differs somewhat in the details.

Drais, Gunzenheim, Mombach, all either touch upon this circle, or are not far beyond it. Both wings, Weissenau and Mombach, were frequently attacked by the French from the commencement of the blockade, and the first mentioned village was burnt down; the centre, however, was not disturbed. Nobody imagined that the French would direct an attack upon it, because they would thereby incur the risk of being attacked on all sides, and cut off, without effecting anything of importance. However, the foreposts around Bretzenheim and Dalheim, places which lie in a hollow extending towards the town, were always at each other; and Bretzenheim was looked to the more jealously by us, as the French had erected a battery at Zahlbach, a convent near Dalheim, which commanded the open country and the high road.

A design, which the enemy had not suspected, induced him at last to make an attack upon our head-quarters. The French, it was ascertained from the prisoners, intended either to capture and carry off General Kalkreuth, who was quartered in Marienborn, together with Prince Louis, Ferdinand's son, who was stationed at the Toll-house a few hundred yards from the village, or to leave them dead behind them. They chose the night between the 30th and the 31st; about 3000 men advanced from the hollow at Zahlbach, crossed the high road, and wound their way through some hollows till they again reached the road, crossed it once more, and dashed upon Marienborn. They were ably led, and made their way between the Austrian and Prussian patrols, who, unfortunately, owing to the slight · undulation of the ground, were not in contact with each other. Another circumstance was also in their favour.

The day before, the peasants had been ordered to cut down the corn in the neighbourhood of the town; when they had finished their work, and were returning home, the French followed them, and some of the patrols were mistaken as to who they were. The French got a considerable way forward without being discovered; and when at last they were observed and fired upon, they pressed on in the greatest haste towards Marienborn, and reached the village about one o'clock when all were either asleep or quite unaware of an attack. They at once fired upon the houses where they saw lights, rushed through the streets, and surrounded the place and the convent in which the General was. The confusion was great; the batteries fired; the Wegner infantry immediately advanced; a squadron belonging to the Duke of Weimar, which was posted behind the village, was at hand, as were also the Saxon hussars. A confused skirmish took place.

At the same time the firing of feigned attacks was heard round the whole circuit of the blockading camp; all were apprehensive of an attack upon themselves, and none ventured to go to the others' assistance.

The waning moon was in the heavens, and shed a dim light. The Duke of Weimar brought up the remaining portion of his regiment, which was lying on the heights about a mile behind Marienborn, and hastened to the scene of action. Prince Louis led the Wegner and Thadden regiments; and after a battle, which lasted an hour and a half, the French were driven back to the town. They left thirty dead and wounded behind them; how many they carried away with them is unknown.

The loss of the Prussians in dead and wounded might be about ninety men. Major La Viere, of Weimar, was killed; Adjutant von Voss mortally wounded. An unfortunate accident increased the loss on our side; for when the pickets were retiring from Bretzenheim towards Marienborn, they got among the French and were fired at by our batteries.

When day broke, wisps of pitch and birch fagots covered with pitch, were found strewed in all directions about the village; if the sortie had proved successful they meant to have set fire to the place.

It was ascertained that the French had also attempted to throw a bridge over from one of the islands in the Rhine off the Maine promontory, upon which they had for some time been ensconced, to the one next it, probably with a view of having something to compete with the boat-bridges at Ginsheim. The second link of the chain had been brought nearer the first, and the Duke's regiment is now stationed near Marienborn.

It is known that in the sortie, national troops formed the van, troops of the line then followed, and national

s

troops again brought up the rear; this may have given rise to the report that the French marched out in three columns.

On the 1st of June, the regiment moved closer to Marienborn; the day was spent in moving the camp; the infantry also changed their position, and various defensive measures were taken.

I visited Captain von Voss, whom I found in a hopeless state; he was sitting up in bed, and appeared to recognise his friends, but he could not speak. At a hint from the surgeon we left. A friend told me on our way back, that, some days before, a warm dispute had taken place in that same room, some one having obstinately maintained, against a number of others, that Marienborn lay much too near the town for head-quarters, and that greater precautions should be taken against a sortie. But as it seemed to be the order of the day to be constantly complaining about all orders and arrangements from high-quarters, no notice had been taken of it, and this warning, like so many others, had been neglected.

On the 2nd of June, a peasant from Oberolm, who had acted as guide to the French in the sortie, was hanged; the circuitous course they had taken would not have been possible without the most accurate knowledge of the ground. Unfortunately for him, he was not able to reach the town with the retiring troops, and was taken prisoner by the patrols sent out, and who made a keen search round about.

Major La Viere was buried in front of the standards, with all military honours. Captain von Voss died. Prince Louis, General Kalkreuth, and several others, dined with the Duke. In the evening there was firing on the Rhine point.

On the 3rd of June, Herr von Stein gave a large dinner party at the Ranger's house. Glorious weather; incomparable view; enjoyment of the landscape saddened by scenes of death and destruction. In the evening Captain von Voss was buried close to Major La Viere.

5th June. Continued preparations for the intrenchment of the camp.

Great attack and cannonade on the Maine promontory.

SIEGE OF MAINZ.

On the 6th of June the Prussian and Austrian Generals dined with the Serenissimo in a large wooden hall, constructed for such feasts. A Lieutenant-colonel of the Wegner regiment, who sat opposite to me, stared at me rather more than was pleasant.

The 7th of June. In the morning I wrote a number of letters.* During dinner at head-quarters, a Major blustered a great deal about the future bombardment, and spoke very freely about our proceedings hitherto.

In the evening a friend took me to the Lieutenant-colonel who had stared so at me the day before, as he wished to make my acquaintance. No special reception had been prepared for us; it was already dark, but no candles were brought in. Of seltzer-water and wine, which it was the custom to offer to all visitors, there was no sign, and the conversation was null. My friend attributed this ill-humour of the Colonel's to our having come too late; when we had gone a few paces on our way back to our quarters, we returned to make an apology, but the Colonel quietly replied that it was of no consequence, that he had seen by my face yesterday, at dinner, that I was not at all the kind of man he had imagined me to be. We laughed heartily over this unsuccessful attempt at making a new acquaintance.

The 8th of June. I worked industriously at *Reinecke Fuchs;* rode with my gracious Prince to the Darmstadt camp, where I paid my respects to the Landgrave, who for many years had been most kind to me.

In the evening, Prince Maximilian of Zweibrücken came with Colonel von Stein to Serenissimo; many things were discussed; and last of all came the open secret of the siege, which was just about to commence.

On the 9th of June the French made a successful sortie upon Holy Cross; they succeeded in setting fire to the church and village in the very face of the Austrian batteries; took some prisoners, but then retired with considerable loss.

* Of these two were addressed to Herder and Jacobi, in which he speaks of his *Bürger-General* and *Reinecke Fuchs;* Goethe had asked Herder to look through the latter. The letters also contain characteristic remarks on Kant and Lavater.

On the 10th of June the French ventured an attack in the daytime upon Gunzenheim, which was repulsed; but, for a time, our left wing was in some danger, and particularly the Darmstadt camp.

The 11th of June. The camp of his Majesty the King was now established about a thousand paces above Marienborn, on the incline at the end of the hollow in which Mainz lies and the clay cliffs and hills commence; this was taken advantage of for making some very pleasing arrangements. The ground which was easy to handle, the gardeners turned into a kind of park with but little trouble; the steep incline was levelled, and covered with turf; arbours were erected; walks cut out on the side of the hill, and large flat districts turned to account, where the military could display themselves in all their elegance and splendour. Some neighbouring woods and thickets were taken in as well, so that, if the whole district had been laid out in the same way, we should have possessed one of the finest parks in the world, with the most glorious of views. Krause* drew a careful sketch of the scene, with all its present peculiarities.

The 14th of June. A small redoubt, which the French had erected and occupied below Weissenau, stood in the way of the opening of the parallels; it was to be attacked during the night, and several persons, who were informed of this, proceeded to the entrenchments on our right wing, from whence the whole position could be surveyed. The night was very dark, and as we knew the point to which our troops had been sent, we expected to witness an imposing spectacle when the attack commenced and resistance was made under heavy fire. We waited long and waited in vain; however, we witnessed a much livelier scene. All the posts of our position must have been attacked; for round the whole circuit we perceived sharp firing, without having the slightest idea what could have caused it; yet at the point where an attack was expected, everything remained motionless and silent. We returned disappointed, particularly Mr. Gore, who was the most interested of our party in such explosions and night battles.

* Krause, and an Englishman, Gore, had joined the camp with the object of making sketches of military life and actions.

The next day the mystery was solved. The French had fixed on this night for an attack upon all our posts, and had drawn the whole of their troops from the entrenchments, and collected them for the attack. Our attacking party, on approaching the entrenchment with the greatest caution, found therefore neither firing nor resistance of any kind; they got into the redoubt, and found it unoccupied, except by a single cannonier, who was greatly astonished at their visit. During the general discharge of the guns, when they alone were left unmolested, they had plenty of time to destroy the walls and retire. This general attack had no further effect; and the lines which had been taken by surprise recovered their composure when day broke.

The 16th of June. The long-talked-of siege, which had been kept secret from the enemy, was approaching at last; it was rumoured that the trenches were to be opened tonight. It was very dark, and some of us rode along the well-known path to the redoubt at Weissenau. We saw nothing, heard nothing; but our horses suddenly started, and we perceived directly in front of us a scarcely distinguishable column of troops. Austrian soldiers, dressed in grey, with grey fascines on their shoulders, were marching along silently, the rattling of their shovels and hatchets against one another, alone intimating that something was moving near us. A more extraordinary and ghost-like scene can scarcely be conceived; they seemed to appear for a moment, then to vanish, but appeared again when looked at attentively, yet never became any more distinct.

We remained on the spot till they had passed, for we could at all events see the point where they were to commence operations in the dark. As undertakings of this kind are always in danger of being discovered by the enemy, it was to be expected that they would fire from the ramparts in this direction, were it only at random. In this expectation we did not wait long, for exactly at the spot where the trenches were to be commenced, a discharge of musketry was heard, which no one could understand. Could the French have made a sortie, and ventured up to, or even beyond, our outposts? We could not comprehend it. The firing ceased, and everything sank into profound silence. Not till next morning was it explained that our own outposts had fired upon the advancing column, as they believed it to be one of the enemy's; the column was startled and confused, each man threw away his fascine, but shovels and hatchets were saved. The French upon the ramparts having thus had their attention attracted, were upon their guard; our men returned without effecting their object, and the whole besieging army was in a state of alarm.

The 17th of June. The French are erecting a battery on the high road. At night a dreadful storm of wind and rain.

The 18th of June. When the late unsuccessful attempt to open the trenches came to be discussed by those who had a knowledge of such matters, it appeared as if the point fixed upon had been much too far from the fortress; it was therefore decided that the third parallel should be brought nearer, and a decided advantage thus obtained from the failure of the first attempt. It was tried, and was successful.

The 24th of June. The French and the Clubbists seeing that things were becoming serious, and in order to stop the rapid diminution of their supplies, determined pitilessly upon expelling all the old men and invalids, women and children, and sending them over to Castel; they were, however, as pitilessly driven away again. The misery of these unarmed and helpless wretches, between foes within and without, was indescribable.

We did not omit to go and hear the Austrian tattoo, which excelled all the others in the allied army.

The 25th of June. In the afternoon a violent cannonade was heard at the extremity of our left wing, which nobody could account for. At last it was explained that the firing came from the Rhine, where the Dutch flotilla was manœuvring before his Majesty, for which purpose he had gone to Ellfeld.

The 27th of June. Commencement of the bombardment, and immediately the Deanery went on fire.

In the night our troops succeeded in storming Weissenau, and the entrenchment above the Carthusian monastery—

indispensable points for securing the right wing of the second parallel.

The 28th of June, at night. Continuance of the bombardment, the firing directed against the cathedral; the tower and roof, and a number of houses near it, are in flames. After midnight the church of the Jesuits caught fire.

We surveyed this fearful spectacle from the entrenchment in front of Marienborn; it was a very clear starry night, and the bombs seemed to vie with the heavenly luminaries, there being moments when it was impossible to distinguish the one from the other. It was a new sight to us, this rising and falling of fireballs; they rose, making an arch across the sky, and when they had reached a certain height and, as it were, about to strike the firmament, they broke with a crash, and the flames that soon burst forth announced that they had done their work.

Gore and Krause treated the events artistically, and made so many studies of it that they succeeded afterwards in preparing a transparent night-piece, which is still in existence, and, if properly lit up, would furnish a much better representation than any written account of the pitiable scene presented by the burning of one of our country's chief cities.

And what an indication it was of our condition, that we had to resort to such means in order to save ourselves, and to restore the country to some degree of security!

The 29th of June. For some time past a great deal had been said about a floating battery, which had been constructed at Ginsheim, and which was intended to command and operate against the Maine promontory, and the islands and fields adjoining. It had been so long talked of, that it had been forgotten. On riding, as usual, after dinner to our entrenchment above Weissenau, I had scarcely reached it, when I perceived a great commotion on the river; numbers of French boats were busily rowing towards the islands, and the Austrian battery, which commanded that part of the river, kept up a constant ricochet fire upon the water—quite a new spectacle to me. When the balls first struck the movable element, a column of water shot up many feet into the air; this had scarcely fallen, when a second column was shot up, as distinct as the first, but not quite so high; then a third and a fourth followed, and so on, always diminishing in height, till the ball got nearer the boats, skimming along the surface, and occasionally proving dangerous to them.

I could not feast my eyes enough upon this spectacle; for shot followed shot, and at every moment new fountains leapt up into the air before the others had quite disappeared.

Suddenly, on the other side of the river, a curious-looking machine was let loose; and moved out from among the bushes and trees. It was a large square object made of beams, and to my great astonishment, and to my great delight also, away it floated, for I found I was to be an eye-witness of this much-talked-of expedition. My wishes for its success, however, seemed destined to be disappointed, and my hopes were but of short duration; very soon the thing began to wheel round about, and it was evident that it did not obey the rudder; it continued to whirl round, and was borne away by the current. On the Rhine redoubt above Castel, and before it, everything was in motion; hundreds of French were running up the banks of the stream, and raising loud huzzas, when this Trojan sea-horse, in place of reaching the intended point of land, was caught by the waters of the Maine, and carried away by the current of the united rivers. At length the stream carried the unwieldy machine towards Castel, where it stranded, not far from the boat-bridge, upon a flat piece of ground which was still flooded. The French gathered round it; I had been able hitherto, with my excellent field glass, to watch the whole occurrence, and now, unfortunately, saw the trap-door opened and the soldiers confined in it come out to be made prisoners. It was a mortifying sight; the draw-bridge did not reach the shore, and the small garrison had to wade through the water before they got among their enemies. There were sixty-four men, two officers, and two cannon; they were kindly received, taken to Mainz, and afterwards conveyed to the Prussian camp, to be exchanged for other prisoners.

On my return I did not omit to give information of this unexpected occurrence. Nobody would believe it, and, indeed, I had scarcely been able to trust my own eyes. His Royal Highness the Crown Prince happened to be in the Duke of Weimar's tent at the time; I was called in, and had to relate what I had seen; I told them exactly what had occurred, but did so somewhat unwillingly, knowing very well that Job's messenger generally comes in for his share of the blame, in return for the bad news he brings.

Amongst the deceptive appearances which present themselves under unusual circumstances, there are very many against which we can guard ourselves only at the moment of their occurrence. Towards evening, I rode along the usual footpath, to the redoubt at Weissenau, without meeting with the slightest inconvenience; the road crossed a slightly hollow part of the ground, where neither water, swamp, nor ditch of any kind was to be seen. On my return, night had set in, and just as I was going to ride into the hollow, I saw directly in front of me a black line perfectly distinct against the dark brown ground. I at once thought it must be a ditch; but yet, how a ditch could have been dug across my path in so short a time was inconceivable. There was nothing to be done but to ride up to it.

On approaching it, the black streak, it is true, remained unchanged, but it seemed to me as if something were moving up and down in front of it; I was soon challenged to halt, and found myself among well-known cavalry officers. It was the Duke of Weimar's regiment, that had been drawn up in the hollow; for what reason I know not; the long line of black horses had looked like a cutting in the ground that intercepted my path. After mutual salutations I hastened, without further hindrance, to the tents.

The same causes which were producing boundless suffering within the town, had gradually come to be the means of affording pleasure to those on the outside. The redoubt above Weissenau, from which there was a glorious view, and which was visited daily by those who wished to make themselves acquainted with the positions, and to observe what was passing within the wide circuit, was the rendezvous, on Sundays and holidays, of an immense number of country-people from the neighbourhood. The French could do little harm to this entrenchment; shots fired high were very uncertain, and generally went beyond it. When the sentry, who paced up and down on the breastwork, noticed that the French were going to fire in that direction, he called out, Down! and it was understood by all inside the battery that they were to fall on their knees in order to be protected by the breastwork from a low-flying ball.

It was an amusing sight on Sundays and holidays, when a large crowd of well-dressed country-people on their way from church, many of them with prayer-books and rosaries in their hands, filled the entrenchment; they looked about them, chatted and joked, when all at once the sentry would call, Down! and all of them instantly fell down before the revered and dangerous object, as if it were some divinity flying past, and which they fell down to worship; when the danger was over, up they rose again, joked at each other, and then again, if it so pleased the besieged, had to fall down on their knees again. The best way to watch this scene was to mount the nearest height, a little to one side, out of the direction of the balls, from there one could look down upon the singular throng of people, and listen to the balls whizzing past.

But although the balls missed the entrenchment, they were not fired without an object. The road from Frankfort ran along the ridge of these heights, so that the procession of carriages, horsemen, and pedestrians, could be plainly seen by the occupants of Mainz, who could thus threaten the entrenchment and the travellers on the road at the same time. Upon the military authorities observing this, the gathering of large crowds was very soon forbidden, and the Frankfort people had to take a circuitous route, by which they arrived at head-quarters unperceived, and out of reach of the guns.

The end of June. One night, when very restless, I amused myself by listening to the multifarious sounds that reached me, both from a distance and near at hand, and was able plainly to distinguish the following—

The " Who goes there ?" from the sentry before the tent.
The " Who goes there ?" from the infantry posts.
The " Who goes there ?" at every round.
The walking up and down of the sentries.
The rattling of the sabres against the spurs.
The barking of dogs at a distance.

The howling of dogs near at hand.
The crowing of cocks.
The pawing of horses upon the ground.
The snorting of horses.
The chopping of straw.
The singing, disputing and squabbling of the men.
The thunder of the guns.
The lowing of cows.
The braying of mules.

AN INTERVAL.

That this should occur here is no wonder. Every hour was pregnant with disasters; every moment we thought of our honoured Prince, of our dear friends, and forgot to think of our own safety. Attracted by the wild and terrible danger, as by the glance of a rattlesnake, we rushed unbidden into places where death was strewing his victims around; walked and rode through the trenches, allowed the grenades to boom and burst above our heads, and the fragments to fall at our feet; many a severely wounded man we prayed might speedily be freed from frightful sufferings, and the dead we would not have recalled to life.

The respective positions of the besiegers and besieged may be described in a general way, thus—The French, on the approach of danger, had taken early precautions, and had erected smaller redoubts in front of the principal works, according to the rules of military science, in order to keep the enemy at a certain distance, and to render the siege more difficult. These obstacles would have all to be removed, if the opening and completion of the third parallel was to be effected; and will be described in detail in what follows.

Whilst this was going on, we with some friends, but without orders or permission, proceeded to the most dangerous outposts. Weissenau was in the hands of the Germans, and the entrenchment farther down the river had been already captured; we visited the ruined place in the charnel-house, and made a collection of diseased bones, the best of which had probably already fallen into the hands of the surgeons. As the balls from the Carl fort kept dashing in among the ruined roofs and walls, we bribed one of the men posted there to conduct us to a well-known and important point, where, with a little care, a great deal might be seen. We proceeded cautiously through the wreck and ruins, and were at length conducted up a winding staircase that was still standing, to the bow-window in an open gable, which, in peaceful times, must have afforded its owner a glorious view. Here we saw the confluence of the Maine and Rhine, the Maine and Rhine promontories, the Bleiau, the fortifications of Castel, the boat-bridge, and then, on the left bank, the beautiful city with its spires shattered to pieces, its roofs full of holes, and all around a melancholy display of smoking ruins.

Our guide warned us to be cautious, and to look out of the window one at a time; as, if we were observed, we should immediately be fired upon from the Carl fort, and the blame would fall upon him.

Not content with this, we crept on towards the convent, where it looked wild enough, and where, down below, in the vaults, wine was to be had at a moderate price. From time to time, the balls kept rattling upon the roofs, and riddling them with holes.

Our inconsiderate curiosity led us even farther; we crept into the last entrenchment of the right wing, which had been dug deep into the glacis of the fortress, directly above the ruins of the Favorite and the Carthusian monastery; and where our men, from behind the gabions, were exchanging fire with the enemy at the distance of a few hundred yards; here, of course, everything depended upon which side was first able to silence his antagonist.

To confess the truth, I found it hot enough; and one could hardly be surprised that some symptoms of the cannon-fever began to manifest themselves. We retreated by the same way we had come, but when opportunity and occasion offered, returned to scenes of equal danger.

When it is considered what our condition was, that we

tried to deaden our fear by exposing ourselves to all kinds of danger, and that this lasted three weeks, I may be forgiven for having hurried over those terrible days, as over burning ground.

The 1st of July. The third parallel was put in action, and the Bock battery bombarded.

The 2nd of July. Bombardment of the citadel and Carl's fort.

The 3rd of July. St. Sebastian's chapel again set fire to; the neighbouring houses and palaces in flames.

The 6th of July. The so-called Clubbist entrenchment, which hindered the right wing of the third parallel from being completed, had to be captured; but the men sent against it missed it, and attacked the outer redoubts of the main line of fortifications, from which they were of course driven back.

The 7th of July. Ultimate capture of this position: Kostheim was attacked, and the French have abandoned it.

The 13th of July, at night. The town-hall and several public buildings are burning.

The 14th of July. The firing ceased; a day of rejoicing and festivity on both sides; on the French side, owing to the conclusion of the National Confederation;* on the German side, owing to the capture of Condé; the latter celebrated it by a discharge of cannon and musketry; the former by a theatrical and liberty fête, about which there was a great deal of talk.

At night between the 14th and 15th of July. The French are being driven out of a battery in front of the Carl fort; a frightful bombardment. The Benedictine monastery upon the citadel was set on fire by the battery on the Maine promontory. On the opposite side, the laboratory is seen to catch fire and explode. The windows, shutters and chimneys on this side of the town are all broken and falling in.

On the 15th of July we visited Mr. Gore in Klein-Wintersheim, and found Councillor Krause engaged in painting the portrait of our worthy friend, and was succeed-

* The French were celebrating the anniversary of the Destruction of the Bastille; the town of Condé had been captured on the 10th.

ing admirably. Mr. Gore was splendidly dressed, for he was going to appear at the Prince's table, after taking another look round the country. Here he was in a peasant's cottage in a German village sitting on a box surrounded by all kinds of household and agricultural implements, with a loaf of sugar standing by his side; he was holding a coffee-cup in one hand, a silver pencilcase, instead of a spoon, in the other. Our English friend was thus, even amid our wretched cantonment quarters, depicted in that very pleasant and respectable appearance in which we now daily see him before us in the pleasant momento.

Having mentioned this gentleman once or twice, it may be as well to give some further account of him. He was very successful in taking sketches with his camera obscura; and in his travels, both by land and sea, had collected many beautiful views. He took up his residence in Weimar, but being accustomed to move about, could not refrain from making occasionally little excursions, in which he was generally accompanied by Councillor Krause, a very successful landscape painter; and they worked away in emulation of each other.

The siege of Mainz, which promised to be an extraordinary and important occurrence, where even misfortune might be found to be picturesque, had attracted the two friends to the Rhine, where they found occupation for every moment of their time.

They accompanied us on a second dangerous expedition to Weissenau, which delighted Mr. Gore in particular. We visited the churchyard again in search of pathological bones; a part of the wall on the Mainz side had been broken down by the cannon, and through it we could overlook the open fields towards the town. But no sooner did the French on the ramparts perceive something moving, than they commenced a ricochet fire at the gap; we saw the balls coming, bounding several times from the ground, and raising the dust, and protected ourselves behind the part of the wall left standing, or in the vaults, and amused ourselves by looking at the balls rolling through the churchyard.

The continuance of this amusement appeared hazardous to the valet, who, apprehending danger to his old master, appealed to our consciences, and induced the venturesome party to retire.

The 16th of July was an anxious day; and I dreaded what might happen to my friends in the ensuing night; for one of the small hostile redoubts, which had been pushed forward in front of the so-called French fort, had effected its object; it presented the greatest obstruction to our foremost parallel, and was to be captured at any price. Nothing, could be said against this, but still it was an anxious proceeding. Upon information, or rather a suspicion that the French had stationed cavalry behind this redoubt, under cover of the fortress, it was decided that cavalry too were to be employed in the attack upon it. The nature of such an undertaking may easily be conceived: cavalry were to be taken beyond the trenches, and to act directly in front of the cannon of the redoubt and of the fortress, and to fight in the middle of the night, on the glacis of the fortress occupied by the enemy. My unusual anxiety arose from knowing that Herr von Oppen, my best friend in the regiment, had been ordered to take the command. When night came, we bade each other adieu; I then hastened to the entrenchment No. 4, from whence a tolerably good view of that part of the ground was to be had. That the attack was made, and that a struggle was taking place could easily be seen, and it was but too evident also that many a brave fellow would never return.

The morning told us that the undertaking had been successful; the redoubt had been taken and demolished, and our troops had entrenched themselves opposite to it in so strong a position, that its restoration by the enemy was impossible. My friend Oppen returned unhurt, the missing men we lost I did not know very well; we were sorry for Prince Louis Ferdinand, who, after bravely leading on his men, had been severely wounded, and was obliged unwillingly to leave the field of battle at an important moment.

On the 17th of July he was taken by ship to Mannheim; the Duke of Weimar moved to his quarters at the Toll-house; no pleasanter residence could well be imagined.

With my customary love of order and cleanliness, I got the beautiful court in front of it swept and cleared; from the change of occupants, it had become strewn with straw and all kinds of refuse.

On the 18th of July, in the afternoon, after intolerable heat, we had a thunderstorm and heavy rain, which was refreshing to most, but of course excessively uncomfortable to those in the entrenchments.

The Commandant sent in proposals for treating with us, which were refused.

The 19th of July. The bombardment continued, and the mills on the Rhine were damaged, and rendered useless.

The 20th of July. The Commandant, General d'Oyre, sent in a proposal, which is being discussed.

At night between the 21st and the 22nd of July. Tremendous bombardment; the church of the Dominicans is in flames, and a Prussian powder-magazine exploded on our side.

The 22nd of July. When we heard that a truce had been actually concluded, we hastened to headquarters to await the arrival of the French Commandant, d'Oyre. He soon came—a tall, well-built, slim man, of middle age, very natural in his bearing and demeanour. Whilst the discussion was going on inside, we were all in a state of expectancy, and full of hope; and when it was announced that it had been settled, and the town was to be delivered up the next morning, there arose in the minds of many that singular feeling which is provided by the near prospect of being freed from former sufferings, anxiety, and fear; and some, in their excitement, could not refrain from mounting their horses and riding off towards Mainz. We overtook Sömmering on our way, who was likewise bound for Mainz, for more important reasons certainly than ourselves, but, like us, heedless of the danger of such an undertaking. We saw from a distance the barrier of the outer gate-way, and behind it a concourse of people, crowding and pressing round it. We also came across some covered pits; but our horses were accustomed to them, and brought us across without danger. We rode straight up to the barrier, the people calling out and demanding what news we brought. There were but few soldiers among the crowd, nearly all of them being townfolk—men and women. Our answer, that we could promise a cessation of hostilities and liberation, probably next morning, was received with shouts of joy. We exchanged such information as each side thought it prudent to give; and just as we were going to turn back, accompanied by the good wishes of the crowd, Sömmering arrived, and added his news to ours. He discovered well-known faces, entered into a more familiar conversation, and at last disappeared among the people before we were aware of it: we, however, thought it time to go back.

A number of the persons who had voluntarily quitted the town, seemed to be filled with similar curiosity and restlessness, and, having provided themselves with supplies of provisions, had succeeded in pushing their way into the outworks, and then into the fortress itself, in order to embrace and comfort the friends they had left behind. We met several of these wanderers, and they became so numerous, that at last the posts had to be doubled, and it was strictly forbidden to approach the ramparts; the communication was suddenly stopped.

The 23rd of July. This day was passed in taking possession of the outworks both of Mainz and Castel. I procured a light carriage, and drove as close up to the town as the sentries would permit. We visited the trenches, and other earthworks, which were now useless since they had effected their object.

When driving back, I was addressed by a middle-aged man, who begged me to give his boy of about eight years of age, whom he was leading by the hand, a seat in my carriage. He was a native of Mainz, who had left it in great haste to enjoy the sight of the enemy marching out, and swore deadly vengeance against the Clubbists who were left behind. I advised him to use milder language, and represented to him that the return to a peaceful and domestic state of things should not be destroyed by a new war between fellow-citizens, and by feelings of hatred and revenge, as otherwise our misfortunes would never end; that the punishment of such guilty persons must be left to the Allies and the true ruler of the country, upon his return.

T

Other things were said that I thought likely to pacify him, and to bring him to a more sober way of thinking. This I had a good right to do, for I took the boy into my carriage, and refreshed them both with a glass of good wine and some biscuits. At the place appointed, I set the boy down again, the father, at a distance, stood waving me a thousand thanks, hat in hand.

The 24th of July. The morning was passed without much disturbance, the evacuation having been deferred on account, it was said, of some money-matters, which could not be immediately settled. At length, about noon, when every one was at dinner, and perfect stillness reigned throughout the camp and upon the road, several carriages were seen driving past. They had each three horses, and proceeded at great speed at some distance from each other, but nothing particular was thought of this; however the report was soon spread that it was several of the Clubbists, who had got off in this daring and dexterous manner. Some excited persons declared that they ought to be pursued; others were satisfied with the expression of their discontent; others again, expressed their surprise that on no part of the road was a trace to be seen of sentry, picket, or watch of any kind; they maintained that it was clear from this that the proceeding was winked at by the higher powers, who were inclined to leave everything to accident.

These reflections were interrupted, and the attention of all attracted by the actual evacuation. The windows of the Toll-house were here of good service to myself and friends. We saw the procession approach in all its solemnity. Led by Prussian cavalry, the French garrison came first. A more singular sight it was impossible to behold; a column of Marseillaise, short, black-looking men, dressed in rags of all colours, came tramping along, as if King Edwin had opened his mountain, and sent out his lively host of dwarfs. Regular troops followed, grave and sullen, but neither downcast nor ashamed. The most remarkable sight, however, and which struck everybody, was when the *chasseurs à cheval* came riding up; they had come close up, to where we were, in perfect silence, when, all at once, their band struck up the Marseillaise hymn. This revolutionary Te Deum has at all times something melancholy and ominous about it, however briskly it may be played; they, however, played it quite slow, in keeping with the sluggish pace at which they were riding. It was impressive and fearful, and a solemn sight when the troopers themselves approached, long, lanky men of advanced years, whose mien accorded well with the solemn music; singly you might have compared them to Don Quixote; together they looked very venerable.

A remarkable group now appeared—the French commissaries. Merlin of Thionville, in hussar uniform, conspicuous by his long beard and fierce look; by his side was another figure in a similar costume;* the populace, in wrath, called out the name of one of the Clubbists, and moved as if to attack him. Merlin stopped, appealed to the respect due to the dignity of a French representative, reminded the people of the vengeance which would follow any insult, and advised them to be quiet, for it was not the last time that they would see him there. The crowd seemed awe struck, and nobody ventured to advance. He had addressed some of our officers who were near, and appealed to the promise of the King; thereupon no one seemed inclined either to venture an attack, or make any reply, and the procession advanced unmolested.

The 25th of July. On the morning of this day, I remarked that no preparations had yet been made to prevent confusion, either upon the high-road, or in the neighbourhood of it. This seemed more necessary to-day than ever, as the poor Mainz people, who had left the town during the siege, and had since been suffering boundless misery, had now collected from distant places, and were beleaguering the road in crowds, relieving their overburdened hearts with oaths and threats of vengeance. The stratagems by which some had succeeded in getting off the day before were of no use now. Single travelling-carriages at times again rattled along the road; but the Mainz people had stationed themselves in the ditches by the side of the road, and if the fugitives managed to escape one ambuscade, they soon afterwards fell into another.

* In a letter to Jacobi, Goethe gives fuller particulars of what occurred on that day.

T 2

Every carriage was stopped; if the occupants were Frenchmen or Frenchwomen, they were allowed to proceed, but Clubbists on no condition whatever. A very handsome travelling-carriage, with a team of three horses, came rolling along, a pretty young girl looked out of the window, and bowed to everybody right and left; but the people seized hold of the reins, the hood was thrown back, and one of the chief Clubbists found seated by her side. There could be no mistake about him; he was a short, thick man, with a big face marked with the small-pox. They dragged him out by the heels, pulled up the hood, and wished the beauty a pleasant journey. The man they took into the nearest field, and kicked and beat him unmercifully; every bone of his body must have been bruised, and his face disfigured. One of the sentries took pity on him, and got him carried into a cottage, where he was laid upon straw, and saved from the violence of his fellow-townsmen, but still exposed to the sneers, deridings, and contempt of the bystanders. This, however, was carried so far, that in the end the officer would allow no one to enter; and begged me, whom, as an aquaintance, he would not have refused, to give up all thoughts of witnessing this most melancholy and disgusting of spectacles.

On the 25th of July we were occupied with watching the continued and regular march of the French out of the town. I stood with Mr. Gore at the window of the Toll-house, and a large crowd had collected below; the space in front, however, was large, and nothing could escape our observation.

Infantry—active, good-looking troops of the line—came along; many of the girls of Mainz accompanied them, sometimes at the side of the column, sometimes within the ranks. Their acquaintances in the crowd greeted them, shook their heads at them, and addressed them in contemptuous phrases: "Ay, Miss Lizzy, so you want to see a little of the world, do you?" and then : "It looks all very fine just now, but wait a little!" Further: "You've been learning French too! Well, a pleasant journey!" and so on. The girls, however, seemed all in good spirits, and did not mind them; some of them called out a good-bye to their female neighbours, the most remained silent, and looked at their lovers. Meanwhile the people were becoming very angry, and abused and threatened the girls. The women reproved the men for allowing these hussies to pass, who doubtless carried away the property of many an honest citizen in their bundles. It was only the steady march of the troops, and the strict order maintained by the officers, that prevented an outbreak; the excitement was fearful.

At this most dangerous moment there appeared a party, who no doubt wished themselves anywhere rather than where they were. Without any special escort, a good-looking man came up on horseback, dressed in a uniform somewhat different from that of a soldier; at his side, in male costume, rode a very handsome woman, and some carriages drawn by four horses followed, covered with boxes and trunks; the silence was ominous. There was a sudden movement among the people, followed by cries of, "Stop him! kill him! That is the scoundrel of an architect who first plundered the Deanery, and afterwards set fire to it with his own hand!" Had there been one determined man among them, he would not have escaped.

Without further consideration than that the peace must not be broken before the Duke's quarters which was followed with the rapidity of lightning by the thought of what the Duke would say were he to find the entrance to his own quarters obstructed by the havoc of such a scene, I sprang down-stairs, ran out among the crowd, and called out with a loud voice: "Hold!"

The people had already approached the man; nobody, indeed, had dared to close the barrier, but the road was obstructed by the crowd. I repeated my "Hold!" and a dead silence followed. I continued to harangue the crowd with a loud voice and with great vehemence. "Here," I said, " were the quarters of the Duke of Weimar; it was sacred ground; if they wanted to commit mischief and exercise their vengeance, they could find abundant space for that elsewhere. The King had granted free egress to all; had he wished to make any conditions or exceptions, he would have appointed officers to turn back the guilty, or to make them prisoners; nothing, however, had been heard of this, and no patrols were to be seen; that they, who or whatever they might be, had here amidst the German army, nothing to do but to remain peaceful spectators of what passed; that their misfortunes and their hatred gave them no rights: and that, once and for all, I would tolerate no violence on this spot."

The people seemed amazed, and remained silent, but soon began to mutter and grumble; some became violent, and two men pressed forward to take hold of the horses' reins. Curiously enough, one of them was the hairdresser whom I had warned the day before, while showing him some kindness. "How!" I exclaimed, addressing myself to him, "have you already forgotten our conversation of yesterday? Have you not considered what I told you, that it is a crime to exercise self-revenge; that we should leave the punishment of the guilty to God and to the established authorities, as we have to leave the termination of all this wretchedness and misery to them?" These and other such brief and convincing observations, as occurred to me at the moment, I made, and spoke in a loud and vehement tone. The man, who recognised me at once, stepped back; the child clung close to his father, and smiled across to me; the people had moved back, and left the place free, and the passage through the barrier was again unobstructed. The two persons on horseback scarcely knew how to act. I had advanced a considerable way among the crowd; the man rode up to me, and said he wished to know my name, and to whom he was indebted for such an important service; that he would never forget it, and only regretted he could make me no return. His pretty companion also approached me, and warmly thanked me. I answered that I had done nothing but my duty, and maintained the peace and sacredness of the place; I gave them a hint, and they moved on. The crowd, who had thus been diverted from their thoughts of vengeance, remained quiet; had this occurred thirty paces farther on, nobody could have held them in check. It is always the case, that when one difficulty has been overcome, others vanish likewise. *Chi scampa d'un punto, scampa di mille.*

On returning to my friend Gore after my adventure, he exclaimed, in broken French: "What, in the name of wonder, made you do this? you might easily have got the worst of it." "I had no such fear," I replied; "and do you not think it well that order has been kept before the house? How would it have been, if everything were in confusion before us, evil passions excited and of no good to anybody; even supposing the fellow has carried away what does not belong to him?"

Meanwhile, the French continued to march quietly past beneath our windows; the crowd, who had lost their interest in the sight, were dispersing; those who could find a way, stole into the town to seek out the friends they had left behind, and to collect their goods and chattels. A more powerful motive, however, was the very pardonable desire to punish their hated enemies, the Clubbists and Committee-men, against whom they kept uttering threats of vengeance as they went along.

My good friend Gore could not yet understand how I cared to risk so much for an unknown and perhaps criminal person. I, jocosely, pointed always to the clear space before the house, and said, at last, rather impatiently: "The fact is, it is part of my nature; I would rather commit an injustice than suffer disorder."

The 26th and 27th of July. On the 26th we were able, with some friends, to ride on horseback into the town. Here we found the most lamentable state of things. Ashes and ruins were all that was left of what it had taken centuries to build. Occupying as it does one of the finest situations in the world, this city had been the receptacle of the wealth of provinces, and here the Church had sought to secure and to increase what her servants already possessed. The mind became distracted at the sight—a much more melancholy scene than that of a town burnt down by accident.

Owing to the absence of all police regulations, a collection of all kinds of filth and offal was mingled with the ruins; traces of pillage were perceptible everywhere as the miserable consequence of enmity among fellow-townsmen. High walls and spires stood threatening to topple over. But why need I give any further description of this after having already named the different buildings as they successively exploded? From old predilection, I hastened to the Deanery, which had always hovered before my mind as a little architectural paradise; the portico was still standing entire, but only too soon I came upon the ruins of the beautiful vaulted roofs, which had fallen in; the wire gratings of the skylight windows lay strewn about; here and there some remnant of old splendour and beauty was to be seen, but this model of architecture was destroyed for ever. All the buildings in the square had met the same fate; it was the night of the 27th of June in which the destruction of these splendid edifices had illuminated the district.

I then proceeded to the neighbourhood of the castle, to which all access was forbidden. Wooden erections, built up against the walls, indicated the desecration of this royal residence; in the square, in front of it—a confused heap of cannon were standing, which had been disabled partly by the enemy, and partly by too great a strain upon their own power.

As many a noble building, with all its contents, had been destroyed by hostile violence from without, much destruction had likewise ensued from the violence, barbarity and wantonness of internal foes. The Ostheim Palace was still standing entire, but it had been turned into a tailor's workshop, and soldiers and sentries had taken up their quarters in it—a detestable spectacle. The halls were strewn with rags and tatters, and the marble walls defaced with hooks and nails, upon which arms were hanging, and others stood up round about.

The Academy looked unchanged from without, except that a bullet had broken the windows of Sömmering's lodgings. I found him there, not exactly comfortably settled, for the handsome apartments had been shamefully treated by their wild occupants. They had not been content with destroying the clean blue wall-paper, as high as they could reach, but must have used ladders, or tables and chairs placed above one another, to soil the walls, for lard and other greasy stains reached up to the ceiling. These were the same rooms in which we had sat together so happily the year before, mutually instructing and entertaining each other. Sömmering was somewhat consoled for what he had lost, by finding his cellar unopened, and his preparations, which had been placed there for security, uninjured. We visited them, and had thus an opportunity for some instructive conversation.

A proclamation of the new Governor had been published; and I found that it spoke the same sentiments, and almost the same words, as I had used to the hairdresser. All self-revenge was forbidden; the right to distinguish between good citizens and bad, belonged exclusively to the Sovereign of the country on his return. This order was very necessary; for, owing to the momentary dissolution of authority caused by the truce a few days before, the most daring of the citizens, who had left the town, pressed back again, led on attacks against the Clubbists' houses, and excited the newly-arrived soldiers to plunder. The order was very properly couched in the mildest terms, in order to conciliate the justly exasperated feelings of the deeply-injured inhabitants.

How difficult it is to quieten a mob that has once been excited! Even in our own presence irregularities took place. A soldier would go into a shop, demand tobacco, and, whilst it was weighed, seize upon the whole supply. Our officers had to go to the rescue of the distressed citizens, and gradually succeeded in repressing the disorder and confusion.

During one of our rambles, we found an old woman standing at the door of a mean house, which seemed almost buried in the earth. We expressed our surprise that she had returned so soon, and were told that she had never gone away, although she had been ordered to leave the town. "The jackanapes came to me too," she said, "with their gaudy scarfs, ordering and threatening me; but I told them the truth to their faces; God, I said, will preserve me, poor woman as I am, in life and honour, in my hut, long after I have seen you people overwhelmed with disgrace and shame. I told them to go elsewhere with their buffooneries. They were afraid my cries might raise the neighbours, and left me in peace. And so I have remained here the whole time, partly in the cellar, and partly in the open air; supporting myself upon the little I could get, and am still alive to praise God, whilst they will now fare badly enough."

She then pointed to a house at the corner of the street, to show how near the danger had been. It was one of the better class of houses, and we could see into the corner room on the ground-floor; a strange sight it was! Here, for many years, had stood an old collection of curiosities, consisting of figures in porcelain and figure-stone, Chinese cups, plates, dishes, and all kinds of vessels; works in amber and ivory, and other carved objects and turnery ware; articles formed of moss and straw, and other things usually found in such collections. These could now be recognised only by the fragments which were strewn about ; for a bomb, which had forced its way downwards through all the upper stories, had burst in this room; the terrific explosion, which had upset everything in the room, drove out the windows; the wire screen, which had been on the inside, was likewise driven outwards, and could now be seen bulging through the iron stanchions. The good woman assured us, that when this explosion took place, she had given herself up for lost.

We dined at a large table-d'hôte, where, amid all the confusion and hubbub, we thought it best to keep quiet. It was strange to hear the musicians requested to play the Marseillaise and the *Ça ira;* all the guests seemed to join in it, and to enjoy it.

In strolling further about the town, we could scarcely recognise the place where the *Favorite* had stood. In August of last year, a splendid garden was to be seen there; terraces, orangeries, and fountains, formed a delightful retreat, close to the waters of the Rhine. Here were the green avenues, where, as the gardener related, the Elector had entertained the great generals and their suites, at tables of immense length with endless quantities of damask table-linen and silver plate. · Such recollections only increased the melancholy feeling excited by its present aspect.

The neighbouring Carthusian monastery had also well nigh disappeared from sight; the walls of the buildings had been speedily destroyed in order that the stones might be used for the construction of the Weissenau redoubt. The convent was still recognisable in its ruins, but too much damaged to be again restored.

I accompanied my friends Gore and Krause to the citadel. Here stood Drusus' monument, very much in the same state as when I had sketched it in my boyish days; it was uninjured, in spite of the fire-balls that must have whistled past or struck it.

Mr. Gore immediately placed his portable camera upon the ramparts, with the view of obtaining a picture of the town, disfigured as it was by the siege. He succeeded perfectly with the central part, where the cathedral stood, and the adjacent parts, but not so well with the sides; this may be seen from his beautifully arranged posthumous papers.

We then turned our steps towards Castel. On the Rhine bridge we could breathe freely, as in days of old, and for a moment fancied that those times might return. During the siege, operations had been ceaselessly carried on to strengthen the fortifications of Castel;* we found a trough of fresh lime, also bricks, and an unfinished work; after the proclamation of the truce and surrender of the town, everything had been left standing as it was.

A singular as well as a melancholy spectacle was presented by the abattis round the Castel entrenchments; it was constructed of fruit-trees from the neighbourhood, which had all been cut down for the purpose. They had been sawed off at the roots, the tender outer branches lopped off, and the summits dove-tailed into each other; this formed an impenetrable outer bulwark. They appeared to be trees which had been planted at the same time, to have flourished under like favourable circumstances, and had now been used for hostile purposes and given over to destruction.

We could not long give ourselves up to these melancholy reflections, for the landlord of the inn and his wife, in fact, every person we met, forgetful, apparently, of their

* This had been done by the French Commandant, General Meynier, who was mortally wounded during the siege. He had rendered good service to his country as an engineer in connection with the fortifications of Cherbourg.

own sorrows, assailed us with endless details of the sufferings of the citizens of Mainz, who had been driven from their homes, and tossed about between foes within and without. For it was not the war alone, but the madness and folly of some of the citizens themselves, that had brought about this state of things.

It was a relief to us to listen to the accounts of the many heroic actions that were related of the brave townspeople. At first the bombardment had been regarded as an unavoidable evil; and the destructive power of the combustible balls seemed too great, the impending destruction too certain, to allow of any hope of successfully opposing it; but, when better acquainted with the danger, they at last resolved to encounter it; the attempts made to extinguish the bombs which fell in the houses with water, gave occasion to many a bold adventure; miracles were related of heroic women who had saved themselves and others in this way. But they had to lament the death of many brave and worthy men. An apothecary and his son were killed in an operation of this kind.

Whilst lamenting the calamities that had been endured, and congratulating ourselves that these were now at an end, we could not help wondering that the fortress had not made a longer resistance. In the vaults under the nave of the cathedral, which were uninjured, a great number of untouched sacks of flour were found; other provisions were heard of, and an exhaustless supply of wine. It was therefore supposed that the last revolution in Paris, which had placed in power the party to which the commissioners at Mainz belonged, had been the real cause of the early surrender of the fortress. Merlin of Thionville, Rewbell, and others, wished to be in Paris, where, after the defeat of their opponents, they had no longer anything to fear, and an immensity to gain. They wanted, it was thought, first of all to establish themselves firmly in power, to take possession of important places in the government, and acquire large fortunes; then to take advantage of the foreign wars, and, with a continued success of their armies, again excite the popular sentiment, and endeavour thus to regain possession of Mainz, and many other places besides.

No one could wish to remain long amid such devastation and ruin. The King with the guards took their departure first; the regiments followed. Further participation in the horrors of war was not required of me; I obtained permission to return home; but first proceeded to pay another visit to Mannheim.

My first act was to wait upon his Royal Highness Prince Louis Ferdinand, whom I found in good spirits, lying on a sofa, but not quite at his ease, for his wound hindered him from lying comfortably; he could not conceal his desire to return to the theatre of operations as soon as possible.

Thereupon I had a pleasant little adventure in the inn. I was sitting at one end of the long crowded table-d'hôte, and at the other end the King's Chamberlain, Von Rietz, a large, well-made, strong, broad-shouldered man; just such a figure as one might expect to find in an attendant of Frederick William. He and the people about him had been talking and laughing very loud, and in high spirits were now about to leave the table. Rietz came up to me, bowed, and expressed the pleasure he felt in being able at length to make my acquaintance, a thing he had long wished, added some other flattering remark, and then said, he hoped I would pardon him, but he had a personal interest as well in thus meeting me. He then said that he had been told that men of talent and genius were always small, lanky, sickly-looking and ill-natured; of which examples enough had been advanced. This had always vexed him, for he did not think himself altogether a blockhead, and yet he was healthy and strong, and substantial; he was therefore delighted to find in me a man of goodly presence, without being considered the less a genius for it. He was glad of this, and wished us both a long enjoyment of our health and strength.

I replied in equally courteous terms; he shook me by the hand, and it was some consolation to me to find that, whereas the worthy Lieutenant-colonel at Mainz had avoided me probably because he expected to find me the ill-natured person, I had now been honoured for an exactly opposite reason.

At Heidelberg, in the house of my old faithful friend,

Fräulein Delf,* I met my brother-in-law and schoolfellow Schlosser. We discussed many things, and he too had to put up with a discourse on my theory of colours. He listened attentively and good-naturedly to what I said, although he could not give up what he had himself determined upon the subject, and wished, above all things, for me to tell him how far my theory agreed with that of Euler, which he was inclined to follow. I had unfortunately to confess that I had never taken him into account; and that the only thing which concerned me was, to collect innumerable facts, to arrange them, to discover their relationship and position towards each other, and to make them intelligible to myself and others. My method however, as I could show him but few experiments, he could not quite follow.

As the difficulty of such an undertaking became apparent, I showed him a paper I had written during the siege, in which I pointed out how an association of different men might work together, and each contribute his assistance, according to his opportunities and capacity, and thus lend assistance to the undertaking. I laid claim to the help of philosophers, naturalists, mathematicians, painters, mechanists, dyers, and heaven knows how many others, to all of which he listened with patience, as a general description of my plan; but when I proposed to read him the essay, he begged to be excused, and, laughing at me, said, that I was still a child and novice, to imagine that anybody would join me in an undertaking in which I took an interest, that anybody would approve or adopt the plans of another, or that co-operation of any kind whatever could take place in Germany.

He expressed himself upon other subjects in the same way as he has done upon this. He had, no doubt, experienced and suffered much, both as a man of business and an author; and, owing to his earnest character, he had shut himself off from the world, and renounced those happy delusions, to which others abandon themselves often with the best effect. It produced a most unpleasant impression on me when about to turn from the horrors of war

* Goethe speaks of her more fully in the seventeenth Book of his *Wahrheit und Dichtung.*

to the peaceful occupations of private life, to find that I could not so much as hope that anybody would take an interest in an undertaking which occupied me so much, one which I believed useful and interesting to the whole world.*

This again excited the old Adam within me; inconsiderate assertions, paradoxical propositions, and ironical retorts, soon occasioned apprehension and uneasiness to my friends; Schlosser defended himself with great vehemence against such attacks; our hostess did not know what to make of either of us; and at her suggestion my departure took place sooner than was intended; but she managed to prevent it appearing precipitate.

Of my stay in Frankfort there is but little to say, and as little of the remainder of my journey home. During the last months of the year, and beginning of the following one, nothing was spoken or thought of but the atrocities of a half-savage nation intoxicated with victory. However a new kind of life was about to open for me too. The Duke of Weimar, at the close of the campaign, left the Prussian service; the lamentations of the regiment were great amongst all ranks; for they were about to lose a commander, a prince, an adviser, a benefactor and a father, all at the same time. I too was suddenly called to separate from many excellent men, between whom and myself a strong attachment had sprung up; and we parted, not without tears from the best. Veneration for our matchless Prince had brought us together, and bound us to each other; and we seemed to be lost to ourselves in thus being withdrawn from his guidance, and our agreeable and rational intercourse with one another. The country around Aschersleben, the Harz, so conveniently visited from thence, seemed lost to me; and in fact, I have never since wandered very far into it again.

We will now conclude, in order not to touch further upon the great events of the time, or the wild sea of troubles, which, after threatening us for twelve years, at length burst upon, and almost engulfed us.

* Goethe's dissatisfaction with Schlosser cannot have been as great as would appear from what he has here written from memory. For on the 11th of August he writes to Jacobi, "I spent several happy days with Schlosser in Heidelberg; I am very glad of this, and it is a great advantage to me that we have again seen a little more of each other."

NOTES FROM

A TOUR ON THE RHINE, MAINE, AND NECKAR,

IN THE YEARS 1814 AND 1815.

TRANSLATED BY

L. DORA SCHMITZ.

To the Rhine's far-reaching mountains,
　Richly favoured tracts of land,
Meadows mirrored in the river,
　Uplands gaily clad with vine,
Come, and wing'd with thought be always
　Present with your faithful friend.

SAINT ROCH'S FESTIVAL AT BINGEN.

A FEW intimate and sociable friends,* who had spent several weeks in Wiesbaden enjoying its salubrious waters, one day determined to carry out a plan which they had cherished for some time past, to get rid of a feeling of restlessness that had come over them. Mid-day was already past, but a carriage was, nevertheless, ordered, without delay, for a drive into the pleasant country of the Rheingau.† Upon reaching the heights above Biberich, a view was obtained over the extensive and splendid valley of the river, with all the settlements scattered over this most fertile of districts. Still, the view was not altogether as fine as it had often appeared in the early morning, when the rising sun shed his rays upon the numberless large and small buildings—with fronts and sides painted white—that lay along by the river and on the hills. At that time of day we have seen the Johannisberg Monastery in the far distance, standing out more prominently than any other object, while single streaks of light lay scattered about both banks of the river.

It was not long before we found that we were driving through a pious country, for, in Mosbach, we met an Italian, with a well-filled tray of figures, which he was carrying on his head in rather a bold fashion. The images were not exactly like those met with farther north—colourless figures of gods and celebrities—but gaily-coloured images of saints, which seemed more in keeping with the cheerful, joyous region. The Virgin Mary towered above all,

* Goethe's companions on this trip were Zelter of Berlin, and Cramer, the mineralogist, who resided in Wiesbaden.
† The name given to the district along the shores of the Rhine, between Rüdesheim and Nieder-Walluf, which produces some of the finest wines in the world.

and of the fourteen Helpers-in-Need * the chief were here represented; Saint Roch, too, in the black garb of a pilgrim, with his little dog carrying a piece of bread.†

We then drove on to Schierstein, through large cornfields every now and again adorned with walnut-trees. Fertile land extends to the Rhine on our left, on our right to the hills, which, however, are gradually drawing closer to the road. Beautiful, yet dangerous, appeared to us the situation of Walluf, a town built on a tongue of land in the Rhine, at the lower end of a bay. In passing by well-laden and carefully-tended fruit-trees, we saw ships sailing merrily down the river.

The opposite shore now attracts the eye; towns in the midst of large, well-cultivated fertile districts come to view. Soon, however, we have to turn our attention again to our own side of the river; not far off stand the ruins of a chapel on a green meadow, pleasantly situated; its walls are clothed with ivy, wonderfully neat and clean-looking. To our right, the vineyards now come close to the road.

In the little town of Walluf perfect peace seemed to reign, but the chalk-marks, showing where the soldiers had to be quartered, were still visible. Farther on there are vineyards on both sides of the road; even where the ground is flat, or only gently sloping, vineyards and cornfields are met with alternately, but the hills in the distance on our right are completely clothed with vines.

Ellfeld ‡ lies in an open plain, surrounded by hills, which to the north rise to mountains; this town is also situated close to the Rhine, and opposite to it lies a large piece of well-kept meadow-land. § The towers of an old castle and its church at once prove Ellfeld to be a somewhat important provincial town, and, on entering it, we found some houses with architectural decorations of rather an old style.

* These *Helpers* were appealed to in times of trouble. The Catholic Church, however, does not sanction fourteen; and Saint Roch is not one of them, as might be supposed from Goethe's words.
† For an account of the legend of St. Roch, see p. 310.
‡ Usually known by the name of Eltville.
§ The meadow-land spoken of here, and shortly afterwards, is an island in the Rhine, called *Rheinaue* (Rhine meadow).

It would be an interesting study to inquire into the reasons why the first inhabitants of places like this selected such a locality. It would be found, at one time, that the reason was a brook that flowed down from the hills to the Rhine; at another, that the site was a favourable one for embarking and disembarking, or some such local convenience.

We passed pretty children and grown-up persons of good figure; they were all quiet in demeanour and in no way did their appearance betray any kind of hurry. We continually met persons driving, or wandering on foot for pleasure's sake, in the latter case generally with sunshades. The heat during the day was very great, the drought general, and the dust extremely troublesome.

A little below Ellfeld, is a new and handsome-looking country-house, surrounded by gardens prettily laid out. We still pass orchards in the plain to our left, but vineyards are becoming more general. Towns follow closer upon one another, country-houses midway between, so that, on looking back at them, they seem to touch one another.

The vegetation on the plains and hills flourishes upon a gravel soil more or less mixed with clay, and is particularly favourable to the growth of vines, whose roots extend to a good depth. . The ditches at the side for protecting the roads show no other soil.

Erbach, like the other towns, has a clean causeway, the streets are dry, the ground-floors of the houses inhabited and tidily arranged, as can be seen through the open windows. Again we come upon a palatial country-house, the gardens reaching right to the Rhine; the splendid terraces and shady avenues of lime-trees are a pleasure to behold.

The Rhine, at this point, assumes a different character; it is only a portion of the actual river, the fore-lying meadow confines it, and thus turns it into a channel of moderate size, but with a vigorous and rapid stream. To our right, the vineyards now come quite close to the road, supported by strongly-built walls, a small recess in which now attracts our attention. Our carriage is ordered to stop, and we refresh ourselves at a plentiful spring of water that flows from a pipe; this spring is called the Marktbrunnen, and gives its name to the vine grown on the hills of that district.

Soon the vineyard-walls come to an end, the hills are less high, and their gently-sloping sides and ridges are crowded with vines. On our left are fruit-trees. Close to the river are willows, which hide it from view.

In passing through Hattenheim, the road ascends; at the top of the hill, behind the town, the clay soil becomes less mingled with gravel. On both sides are vineyards; the ones on the left supported by walls, those on the right grow on a slope. Reichardtshausen, formerly a monastery, is now the property of the Duchess of Nassau. After passing the last bit of wall we saw a pretty seat under acacia-trees.

Thereupon, on the height, follows a rich, gently sloping plain; but the road soon again runs by the river, which before had lain far below, and at a distance from us. The level country is here laid out in fields and gardens, but where there is the least incline, it is planted with vines. Oestrich lies at some distance from the river, on rising ground, and has a pretty situation; for behind the town the vine-clad hills run down to the river, all the way along to Mittelheim, where the Rhine again shows a splendid breadth. We, then, almost immediately, came upon Langewinkel (Long-corner); the place, certainly, deserves the epithet of *long*, for its excessive length would try the patience of any one driving through the town; but of a *corner* there was nothing whatever to be seen.

In front of Geisenheim, a flat low-lying piece of land extends right to the river, and is, no doubt, flooded whenever the river is high; it is laid out in gardens and clover fields. The meadow in the river (the island), and the little town on its shores, show off prettily against each other. The view on the opposite bank becomes freer. A broad, sloping valley stretches away, between two sloping heights, towards the Hundsrück hills.

As we approach Rüdesheim the low-lying, flat land on our left becomes more and more remarkable, and the idea strikes one that, in remote ages, when the chain of hills around Bingen was still closed in, the water, thus driven and kept back at this point, must have levelled this low piece of ground, and that, by gradually running off, and streaming away with the main current, it at last formed the present bed of the Rhine by its side.

After a drive of three hours and a half, we reached Rüdesheim, where we were immediately induced to alight at the inn *Zur Krone*, which is pleasantly situated not far from the town gate-way.

The inn is built by the side of an old tower, and the view, from the front windows, looks down the Rhine, from the back windows, up the river; we were, however, soon out of doors again. A projecting structure of stone is the place where the surrounding country can best be overlooked. Looking river-upwards from here, the fertile meadow-land is seen in all its perspective beauty. Down the river, on the opposite bank, lies Bingen; further down, in the river, stands the Mäusethurm (Mice Tower). *

Just above Bingen, and close to the river, a hill rises away towards the flat country beyond. It might be imagined to have been a promontory in the remote ages, when the water stood higher. On its eastern slope is seen the chapel dedicated to St. Roch; at present it is undergoing repairs, as it was damaged during the war. On the one side, the scaffolding is still standing, but, nevertheless, a festival is to be held there to-morrow! The people here think that we have come on purpose to attend it, and promise us that there will be plenty of amusement to be had.

We further heard that, during the war, this chapel had been desecrated and laid waste, much to the sorrow of the neighbourhood. This had not, indeed, been done out of caprice and wantonness, but because the site was a favourable position for overlooking the surrounding country, and even commanded a portion of it. The building was, therefore, robbed of all the requisites for Divine service, nay, of all its

* This tower is built on a rock in the Rhine, and its well-known legend relates the fate of Hatto, the cruel and tyrannical bishop of Mayence. After greatly oppressing the people of his district, he found himself visited by a plague of mice wherever he went. In order to escape from his tormentors he at last retired to the tower in the Rhine, which he had built in order to levy a tax from every one who crossed the river at this convenient spot. The mice, however, followed him by the thousand, and devoured him there.

decorations, and besmoked and soiled by being used as a place of bivouac; polluted even by being used as a stable for horses.

All this, however, did not affect the people's belief in their Saint; the Saint who kept the plague and infectious diseases away from those who believed in him.* But to make pilgrimages to the place had been out of the question, for the enemy, who were both suspicious and cautious, had forbidden all religious processions and fêtes, proclaiming them to be dangerous gatherings, which encouraged public spirit and fostered conspiracies. Hence, for a period of four-and-twenty years no festival had been celebrated at the chapel. Yet the faithful who lived in the district around, and who felt convinced of the advantages of a pilgrimage to the place, had, by their great need, been driven to make every effort in their power to visit the shrine. The following curious story is related by the Rüdesheim people about an attempt of this kind. One dark night, in mid-winter, a procession of torches was seen suddenly to leave Bingen, to proceed up the hill, and to assemble round the chapel, to perform their devotions, it was supposed. In how far the French authorities had permitted the approach of the crowd of worshippers was never known. Yet, without their permission, such an undertaking could scarcely have been ventured upon. The true state of the case, it was said, always remained a dead secret. Still, all the Rüdesheim people who flocked to the riverside to witness the scene, declared that they had never in their lives seen anything so strange or so terrible.

After this we walked quietly down the river, and every person we met was rejoicing that the holy shrine in the neighbourhood had been restored. For, although Bingen was no doubt specially interested in its restoration and the busy times that would attend it, still it was a pious and joyful event for the whole country; hence the universal feeling of joy for the morrow.

The intercourse between the inhabitants of the two shores, which had been interrupted, nay, at times completely cut off, for so long, and had been sustained merely by their faith in this Saint, is about to be recommenced by a

* The story of St. Roch is narrated on p. 310.

splendid fête. All the surrounding country is in a state of commotion, for both old and new vows will be offered up in grateful remembrance. Sins will be confessed there, and forgiveness received; in addition to this, among the numerous visitors expected to attend the festival, many persons will meet with friends whom they have, perhaps, not seen for years.

Amid pious and cheerful stories of this kind, and always within sight of the river and the opposite shore, we walked along the whole length of Rüdesheim to the old Roman fort, which is situated at the one end of the town, and in a good state of preservation, owing to its excellent masonry. Count Ingelheim, to whom it belongs, was struck by a happy thought, to make it a place from which visitors might obtain a view both instructive and enjoyable.

One enters into a kind of courtyard, somewhat like a well; it is narrow, with high, black walls, well built but rough in appearance, for the stones are unhewn on the outside—an unpretending rustica. The steep walls can be ascended by means of steps, that have recently been built. Inside of the building we found, in strange contrast, well-arranged rooms and large, desolate vaults blackened by watch-fires and smoke. We wound our way up steps, through dark gaps in the walls, and at last reached the top of the tower, with the most glorious of views. Here we roamed about in the air, admiring the gardens that have been planted and are flourishing upon the old débris. The towers, top of the walls, and flat surfaces are connected by bridges, gay patches of flowers and shrubs in between; these appear to be in need of rain, like the rest of the country.

Rüdesheim lay before and below us in the clear evening light. A castle, belonging to medieval times, is standing not far from this ancient one. There is also a charming view of the vineyards, precious beyond description; gentle inclines and steep gravel hills, nay, even rocks and walls are made use of for the cultivation of vines. The Johannisberg * stands out more prominently than anything else that meets the eye in the way of ecclesiastical or secular buildings.

* A castle not far from Winkel, more fully described on p. 326.

While naming so many of the principal vineyards, we ought, perhaps, not to forget to make due mention of the Eilfer. This wine, like the name of a great and benevolent prince, is always referred to when anything excellent in the country is being spoken of; a wine-year is likewise a subject in every one's mouth. The Eilfer has another quality pertaining to all that is excellent: it is both delightful and plentiful.

As the evening twilight approached, the country around gradually vanished out of sight. The disappearance of the many important individual objects, first led us to think of the full worth of the whole, in which we should have liked to have been lost ourselves; but we had to take leave of the spot.

Our walk back was enlivened by the continual firing of guns from the chapel on the other side of the water. These warlike sounds recalled to our minds the hostelry, on the top of the hill, as a military station. From there the whole valley of the Rhine could be overlooked, and most of the towns, passed on our way hither, were likewise within sight of it.

We were told that, when passing along the heights above Biberich, the St. Roch Chapel must have often been distinctly visible as a white object in the morning sunlight; and we now remembered having noticed it.

Considering all that we had heard, it was not surprising that St. Roch should be regarded as a worthy object of veneration, for, owing to the people's steadfast faith in him, he was at this moment converting the place that had been a military station, and the scene of strife and confusion, into one of peace and reconciliation.

Meanwhile, a stranger had arrived at the inn, and taken his seat at our table. He was thought to be a pilgrim, and so the conversation turned very freely in praise of the Saint. However, to the great astonishment of the well-meaning company, it appeared that the stranger, although a Catholic, was, to a certain extent, opposed to the Saint. For, as he informed us, on one 16th of August, while many persons had been celebrating the feast of St. Roch, his house had been burnt down; on another occasion, on the same fête day, a son of his had been wounded; there was even a third case of misfortune, the particulars of which, however, he did not communicate.

A knowing member of our party thereupon replied that, in individual cases, the main thing depended upon assistance being asked of the Saint to whom the matter specially belonged. That, for instance, for protection against fire, St. Florian had to be appealed to. That, to guard against wounds, prayers should be addressed to St. Sebastian; and, it was possible, that, in the third case he had mentioned, St. Hubert * might have rendered assistance. Moreover, that believers had surely sufficient scope for their appeals, as no less than fourteen saintly Helpers-in-Need had been created. The virtues possessed by these helpers were enumerated; and it was found that there never could be enough.

To rid ourselves of these gloomy reflections, which are not pleasant even to cheerful minds, we again went out into the open air, and enjoyed the bright starry heavens, and remained out so long that the deep sleep we enjoyed afterwards seemed little better than nothing, for we were up again before sunrise. We went out at once to look down the grey valley of the Rhine. A fresh wind came blowing across into our face, a wind favourable both to those coming over to this side of river, as well as to those crossing over to the other.

The boatmen are all busy at work, setting sails to rights; there is firing from the hill; the day has begun as announced the evening before. Already single figures and groups of persons are to be seen in dim outline against the clear sky, round about the chapel, and on the ridge of the hill; but there is as yet little life on the river and its banks.

A fondness for the study of Nature tempted us to go and examine a collection of minerals from the Westerwald,† said to be arranged according to its length and breadth; also

---

* St. Hubert, Apostle of the Ardennes and Bishop of Liège, in the eighth century, was said to have had the power of curing those afflicted in mind. If Goethe remembered this, the jest is rather a doubtful one.

† A hilly district extending from the Seven Mountains to the river Lahn; it is rich in minerals.

some excellent mineral specimens from Rheinbreitbach. This scientific expedition, however, nearly proved destructive to our plan of joining the festival, for, by the time we returned to the Rhine, we found numbers of people starting for the opposite shore, all in the utmost state of bustle. Crowds were pushing their way on board the different boats, and one over-crowded boat after another started on its way.

On the opposite bank, quantities of people and vehicles are to be seen on the move, and boats that have come down the river are landing their passengers. On the hill crowds are wending their way towards the top, by more or less steep paths. The incessant firing shows that a succession of townships are taking part in the pilgrimage.

But now we, too, are to be off; and soon find ourselves midway on the river, our sails and oars vying with hundreds of others. Upon landing we noticed at once, owing to a fondness for geology, that there are some curious rocks at the foot of the hill. The naturalist is thus induced to turn aside from the holy pathway. Fortunately a hammer is at hand. A conglomerate, deserving the greatest attention, is found; a quantity of quartz rock that had been destroyed at the moment of its formation; the pieces are pointed, and have been again united by a quartzose substance. Its excessive hardness prevented our obtaining more than small fragments. I much wish that some naturalist, when passing here, would examine these rocks carefully, determine their relation to the older mountain mass beneath, and be good enough to send me his report together with a few instructive specimens. Gratefully would I acknowledge the receipt!

We now ascended the hill, in company of hundreds of other people, by the steepest of the pathways, that runs zigzag up the rocks; we climbed slowly, often resting and exchanging jokes. It was the Pinax of Cebes * in the truest sense, lively and animated, except that in our case there were not as many misleading byways.

At the top, round about the chapel, we found a great

* A small Greek work which gives an allegorical picture of human life, the aim of which is to prove that the highest happiness consists in the practice of virtue.

crush and commotion, but pushed our way in with the rest. The chapel inside is almost square, each side about thirty feet in length, the choir at the end perhaps about twenty. Here stands the principal altar, not a modern structure, but one in the rich style of the Roman Catholic Church. It is a very high altar, and, in fact, the chapel itself has altogether rather a lofty appearance. There are two other altars of a similar kind in the corners next the main square, and these, too, have not been injured, but are exactly as they were in bygone days. The thought strikes one how this is to be explained in the case of a church so recently ransacked.

The crowd moved from the main entrance towards the chief altar, then turned to the left, where great reverence was paid to some relic lying in a glass coffin. People laid their hands upon it, stroked it, blessed it, and lingered about it as long as they could. However, one person after another was pushed by, and thus I, too, had my turn, with the stream, and was then pushed out of the chapel by a side-door.

Some of the older men from Bingen came up to us in order respectfully to salute our worthy guide, a gentleman in the Duke of Nassau's service;* they praised him as a helpful neighbour; in fact, as the man who had enabled them to celebrate to-day's festival in a suitable manner. We now learned that, when the convent at Eibingen† was abolished, all the fittings of the chapel—altars, chancel, organ, pews, and prie-dieux—were handed over to the community at Bingen for a trifling sum, to assist the restoration of the St. Roch Chapel. As the Protestant party had proved themselves so helpful in the matter, the citizens of Bingen made a vow that they would themselves fetch all the fittings. An expedition was made to Eibingen; all the things were carefully taken from their places, single persons took the smaller articles, others clubbed together and carried the larger pieces, and in this manner they wandered down to the water-side, like a string of ants, carrying pillars and mouldings, pictures and decorations. The boatmen, likewise in accordance

* Cramer, the geologist and inspector of mines.
† A fuller account of this convent is given on p. 321.

with the vow, took the things on board, shipped them across and landed them on the left bank, where pious shoulders again carried them up to the hill-top by various paths. As this was done all at the same time, the procession, as seen from the chapel overlooking the district and the river, must have been one of the strangest imaginable; for decorations in carving and painting, in gilt and lacquer work, were to be seen moving along in motley succession. It was, moreover, a pleasant feeling to think that every one bore their burden with the hope that, in return for their self-imposed labour, they would receive blessings, and be themselves morally the better for it throughout life. The organ, which had likewise been brought over, is, however, not yet in position, but is shortly to be set up in the gallery opposite the chief altar. This account solved the question that had naturally suggested itself upon our remarking that all the decorations, in the one part of the chapel which had but lately been restored, showed signs of age, but were nevertheless in good condition, without any marks of injury, in spite of not being new.

The present state of the chapel must appear all the more edifying, inasmuch as in its happy restoration we have visible proofs of what may be effected by good-will, mutual assistance, and well-ordered arrangements. For that the work has been carried out with fore-thought, is no less evident from the following facts. The chief altar, from a much larger edifice, was to find a place here; hence it was decided to increase the height of the walls by a few feet. In this way the space was considerably increased, and moreover richly decorated. The older members of the community will thus be able now to kneel at the very same altar on the left bank of the Rhine, at which, in their young days, they had knelt on the right bank.

The sacred relics have, likewise, been reverenced for many bygone days. The remains of St. Ruprecht, which it had been customary piously to touch and to praise as helpful in Eibingen, are henceforth to be preserved in the St. Roch Chapel.

A great many persons are animated by a joyful feeling, in again finding themselves near a protector whose power they believe to have long since been proved. It ought to be mentioned here, that it had not been considered becoming to include the sacred relics among the other objects purchased, or in any way to ask a price for them; hence they came as a gift, a pious addition to the other property. It would be well if people had always acted with the same feeling of forbearance in similar cases!

But now the tumult has laid hold of us. Thousands upon thousands of different figures claim our attention. These country-folks do not differ strikingly in their manner of dress, but present an endless variety in the way of physiognomy. The commotion, however, prevents any attempt at making comparisons; any general characteristics would be looked for in vain in the present bustle and confusion. The thread of observation is lost, and one allows oneself to be drawn into the life going on around.

A row of booths—the indispensable accompaniment to a festival—are to be seen at a little distance from the chapel. First of all, there are candles of every description, yellow, white, and painted, to suit the different purses of those attending the fête. Then come prayer-books and *officia* in honour of the Saint about to be celebrated. In vain do we ask for a pleasantly-written pamphlet to enlighten us about the life, works, and the sufferings of the Saint; wreaths of roses, however, are plentiful enough. There are also to be had buns, biscuits, gingerbread-nuts, and other kinds of pastry, as well as all sorts of toys and trinkets to tempt children of different ages.

Processions continue to arrive. The different villages can be distinguished one from the other, and the sight might suggest a variety of reflections to a calm observer. In general, it might be said the children are pretty, not so the young people; and the faces of the older people very worn-looking; there are some very aged persons among them. All are proceeding on their way, singing chants and responses; flags are fluttering, banners waving, as procession after procession comes up, with candles of all sizes. Every community has its own image of the Virgin Mary, carried by children and young girls in new dresses, with large rose-coloured ribbon bows fluttering in the breeze. Specially graceful and pretty to us appeared a Jesus-child carrying a large crucifix, and looking up joyously at the instrument of torture. "Ah," exclaimed a sympathetic on-looker, "all children are just like this one, while they can still look happily out into the world before them!" The child was attired in a dress of golden stuff, and looked most pleasing, and as happy as the little prince.

A great commotion now announced that the chief procession was coming up from Bingen. All who could, hastened to the ridge of the hill to meet it, and we were surprised at the lovely view that was to be obtained over the country around; a splendid change had taken place, and an entirely new scene presented itself to our eyes. The town below is both well-built and well-kept, surrounded by gardens and groups of trees, and lies at the end of an extensive valley, along which flows the river Nahe. And then the Rhine, the Mäusethurm, and the Ehrenburg! In the background, the solemn grey walls of rocks through which the mighty stream has forced its way, and is there lost to view.

The procession is advancing up the hill in the same order as the others. In front the smallest boys, followed by youths and men; holy St. Roch is carried on high, clad in the black velvet garb of a pilgrim, and also with a long royal mantle of the same material edged with gold, from beneath which is seen peeping a small dog holding a piece of bread between its teeth. Immediately after this come boys of a medium age, wearing the short, black habits of pilgrims, shells on their hats and collars, and carrying staffs. Then follow earnest-looking men who do not seem to be either peasants or ordinary citizens. From their weather-beaten faces I fancy they must be boatmen, whose business is both dangerous and anxious, as each moment demands their thoughtful attention, and their whole life is thus one of careful watching.

A red silk canopy now appears; beneath it is carried the consecrated wafer by the bishop, surrounded by the dignitaries of the Church, accompanied by Austrian soldiers,* and followed by the State officials. In this order they

* The fortress of Mainz was at that time garrisoned by Austrian soldiers.

advanced to celebrate the politico-ecclesiastical festival, which was to be the symbol both of the re-acquisition of the left bank of the Rhine, and of the privilege to believe in miracles and signs.

If, however, I am briefly to state what most generally struck me with regard to the different processions, I should say, that the children seemed invariably happy, contented, and pleased, as if by some new, wonderful, and joyful event; the young folks, however, seemed to pursue their way as if indifferent to what was taking place around them; they had been born in evil times, and hence the festival had no memories for them, and those who have no memory of what is good, have no expectation of anything good. The old people, on the other hand, were all affected, as by the remembrance of happy days that had returned, but which were no longer of use to them. From this we perceive that man values his life only in so far as some result can be looked for.

The observer's attention was now, in a somewhat unbecoming manner, withdrawn from the worthy, and in many ways dignified procession, by a great noise behind him, by strange and very violent screams. And I here again made the experience that serious, sorrowful, and even terrible occurrences are often interrupted by an unexpected and absurd incident, as if, in fact, by some farcical interlude.

On the hill behind, a strange cry was heard; the sound was not one of quarrelling, of terror, or of anger, but still wild enough. An excited throng of persons were running to and fro among the rocks and bushes, calling out: stop! here! there! yonder! now! this way! come on! The words were shouted in all possible sorts of tones; hundreds of persons tore about in haste, as if chasing something. The mystery was solved at the very moment that the bishop reached the top of the hill, with the venerable procession.

An active, sturdy youth came running forward, with a delighted expression of countenance, holding on high a bleeding badger that had been captured. The poor, harmless animal had been frightened by the movements of the pious crowds, and driven away from its home; and

x

had now been killed, by the ever merciless hand of man, on the very fête day that ought to have been the most merciful of days, and killed, moreover, at the most joyous moment of the day.

Equanimity and seriousness were, however, soon restored, and our attention attracted by a new and stately procession that was advancing towards the chapel; this was the community from Bidenheim, and was as large as it was orderly. But in this case we likewise failed to find any characteristic feature of the individual town. Confused by so much that was confusing around us, we allowed it quietly to advance towards the scene of the ever-increasing confusion.

All now began to push their way to the chapel, and did their best to obtain admission. We, who had been driven somewhat to the side along one of the paths, preferred remaining in the open air to enjoy the extensive view from the back of the hill up the valley, along which the Nahe flows, unperceived. Here, any one with good eyesight, can survey a district of the utmost variety and fertility as far as the foot of the Donnersberg, the grand ridge of which forms a majestic back-ground to the scene.

We soon perceived that we were approaching the more actual enjoyments of life. Tents, booths, benches, and awnings of various kinds came into view. The welcome smell of fried fat was wafted towards us, and we soon came to a place where a young and active woman—a butcher's daughter—was busy at work over a large, glowing ash-fire, cooking fresh sausages. By preparing them herself, and with the incessant help of a number of nimble servants, she contrived to satisfy the demands of a large concourse of people.

We, too, well provided with steaming fatty food, together with excellent fresh bread, took our seats at a long shaded table, which was already pretty well crowded. Some kindly persons moved closer together, and we found pleasant neighbours, nay, even agreeable society in some people who had come to the festival from the banks of the Nahe. The merry children drank wine like the older people. Brown jugs, with the name of the Saint in white letters on them, passed round the family circles. We, too, had procured jugs of this sort, and set them down before us, filled to the brim.

Thereupon we remarked what great advantage such meetings must be to the people, where a number of single rays are drawn to one centre, by some higher kind of interest, from a large, wide-spread area.

For, at such meetings, people obtain information about several different districts at once. The mineralogist will quickly discover persons who are acquainted with the rocky regions about Oberstein,* with the agates obtained there, and how they are cut and polished, and who can thus give those interested in natural objects some instructive information. The quicksilver mines at Muschellandsberg were also the subject of conversation. New points of interest were opened up, and the hope expressed that good, crystallised amalgamate would be procured there.

The enjoyment of the wine was not disturbed by discussions of this kind. We sent our emptied jugs to be refilled, and were asked to be patient till the fourth hogshead had been tapped. The third had just been finished even at that early hour of the morning.

No one seemed ashamed of their liking for wine, and, to some extent, boasted of the amount they could drink. Pretty women told us that their babes took wine while still fed from the breast. We asked whether it were true that certain clerical gentlemen, and even Electors, ever had succeeded in consuming eight measures of Rhine wine, about sixteen ordinary bottles, within four and twenty hours.

An apparently serious member of our party, in reply to this question, said, that one need only recall what had been said in the Lent sermon, preached by the assistant-bishop of the diocese; after having described to his congregation, in the strongest colours, the terrible evils of drunkenness, he had concluded with these words:

"From what I have said, my devout hearers, you, who have already been graced by repentance and penance, must be convinced that he who thus abuses the glorious gifts of God, commits the greatest of sins. Yet this abuse

* A town on the Nahe above Kreuznach, very picturesquely situated.

of the gift does not exclude it from being our duty to make a good use of it. Is it not written: Wine gladdens the heart of man! Hence it is clear that, in order to make ourselves and others happy, we may, nay, we even ought, to partake of wine. Now, among my hearers of the male sex there is, perhaps, not one but can take to himself two measures of wine, without suffering from any confusion of the senses; but he who, after drinking a third or a fourth measure so far becomes forgetful of himself as not to recognise wife and children, who ill-treats them with quarrelsome words, blows, and kicks, and behaves towards those dearest to him as if they were his bitterest enemies, let him reflect, and keep from such an excess that renders him displeasing to the sight of God and man, and contemptible to those around him. Yet, he who, after enjoying a fourth measure, nay, even a fifth and a sixth, remains so completely himself that he can kindly assist his fellow-Christians, look after his house, and carry out the commands of his superiors in Church and State, let him continue to enjoy his modest portion, and to take it gratefully! Yet let him even beware of going farther without taking good heed, for here, generally, is fixed the limit, beyond which weak men cannot go. For it is, indeed, a rare instance for the All-loving God to grant to man the special mercy of being able to drink eight measures, such as has been conferred upon me, His humble servant. Yet as it cannot be said of me, by any one of you, that I have ever attacked any one in a fit of unwarrantable anger, that I have failed to recognise those in my house, or related to me, or that I have neglected any of my religious duties, or the work required of me, but that, on the contrary, as you can all bear witness, I have ever been ready to prove myself active in the praise and glory of God, as well as in assisting and working for the good of my neighbours, I may assuredly, with a good conscience, and with gratitude, continue in future to enjoy the gift vouchsafed to me.

"And you likewise, my devout hearers, every one of you, take your modest portion in order that, according to the will of the Giver, you refresh your body and cheer your mind! And in order that this may be done, and that, on the other hand, all excess be avoided, be mindful

to act in accordance with the advice of the holy apostle, who says, 'Prove everything and abide by what is best!'"
. The main subject of the conversation continued, of course, to be about wine, as it had previously been. And there now began a dispute about the merits of the different growths; it was pleasant to find that there was no dispute among the magnates themselves as to priority of rank. Hochheimer, Johannisberger, Rüdesheimer, each acknowledged the value of the other; it was only among the gods of minor degree that jealousy and envy prevailed. Thus the favourite red Assmanshäuser was specially subjected to various attacks. A proprietor of vineyards at Oberingelheim, I heard maintain that his were but little inferior to it. The Eilfer was said to have been delicious, but of this there was no proof, as it had already all been drunk. This was admitted by those seated around, for they said that red wines ought to be drunk when young.

Thereupon the people from the Nahe began to praise a wine that grew in their district, called Monzinger. It was said to be light and pleasant to drink of, but that it went to one's head before one was aware of it. We were invited to go and try it. And, in fact, it had been too agreeably recommended for us not to wish to taste it in such good company, even though it might prove somewhat dangerous.

Our brown jugs were now brought to us refilled, and upon seeing the gay white letters of the Saint's name so benevolently active all around, it was felt to be almost a disgrace not to know his story properly, although, of course, all knew this much, that while renouncing all his worldly goods he did not hesitate to risk his own life in order to attend those sick of the plague.

In accordance with a wish that had been expressed, the company now related the graceful legend, and moreover did so as if in competition, children and parents helping one another, as the case might be.

From this we could perceive the real nature of a legend, when flitting from mouth to mouth, from ear to ear. Of contradictions there were none, but an endless variety of forms, which resulted from different persons taking a different interest in the several incidents; thus at one time one circumstance was set aside, and at another brought prominently forward. There was also not a little confusion about the various places to which the Saint had wandered, and where he had resided.

An attempt I made to jot down the story word for word as I heard it there, I found impossible to carry out, so I shall here give it in the form in which it is usually narrated.

Saint Roch, a believer in the Faith, was born in Montpellier, his father being called John and his mother Libera. And, moreover, this same John not only held possession of Montpellier, but of many other places also, and was a godfearing man. He had lived long without having been blessed with children, until, in answer to his prayers to the Virgin Mary, Roch was born to him, and the child came into the world with a red cross on its breast. When the parents fasted, the child was made to fast likewise, and on such days the mother put it to her breast but once to drink. In the fifth year of his age he began to eat and drink very little; in his twelfth year he laid aside all luxury and vanity, and gave his pocket-money to the poor, towards whom he did many good actions in other ways also. He likewise showed himself very industrious in his studies, and was soon distinguished for his ability; and his father, when on his deathbed, addressed some affecting words to him, admonishing him to all that was good. He had not reached the age of twenty when his parents died, and he thereupon divided all the property he had inherited among the poor, renounced his claim as Governor of the provinces, set out for Italy and came to a hospital wherein were many persons suffering from infectious diseases, and these he wished to tend and nurse. But although he was not at once allowed to enter, and was made to consider the danger he would incur, he renewed his entreaty, and when admitted to the sick they were all made well by his touching them with his right hand, and by making the sign of the holy cross over them. Thereupon he went on to Rome, and there also cured many persons suffering from the plague, among others a cardinal, with whom he afterwards resided during the three years he remained there.

When, however, he was himself attacked by the terrible disease, and was taken to the plague-house where all the other sufferers were laid, and where he was, at times, forced to cry aloud with the cruel pain, he arose, went outside of the hospital and seated himself in the porch, in order that the other patients might not be further troubled by his screams. Now, when the passers-by saw him there, they thought that the fault of this lay with those entrusted with the care of the sick, and when they heard that this was not the case, every one looked upon him as foolish and out of his senses, and therefore drove him out of the city. Under the guidance of God, and with the help of his staff, however, he managed, by degrees, to creep to the nearest wood. And when, owing to his great sufferings, he could go no further, he lay down under a hawthorn-tree and rested; and there ran a spring of water close by, from which he refreshed himself.

Not far from this spot stood a country-house, whither a number of great personages had fled from the town, and one of these was called Gotthard, who had a great many servants and hounds with him. A very strange circumstance now occurred, for one of these well-bred hounds one day snatched a piece of bread from the table and ran off with it. Although punished for doing so, the dog, on the second day, watched for a favourable moment and again ran off with the food thus stolen. The Count, thereupon, suspected some mystery, and, accompanied by his servants, followed the dog.

They found beneath the tree a pious pilgrim in a dying state, who entreated them to keep away from him and to leave him, in order that they might not be seized by the same disease. Gotthard, however, determined not to leave the sick man till he was well again, and attended to him to the best of his power. When Roch had regained a little strength, he betook himself to Florence, cured many persons of the plague there, and was himself completely restored to health by a voice from Heaven. He persuaded Gotthard to share his hut in the forest, and to serve God without intermission, which Gotthard promised to do on condition that Roch would never leave him. Thereupon, for a long time, they dwelt together in an old hut. But, at last, after Roch had sufficiently accustomed Gotthard to a hermit's life, he again set out upon his wanderings, and, after a wearisome journey, at length reached his own country, and moreover his native town, which had formerly belonged to him, and which he had presented to his cousin. However, as it happened to be a time of warfare, Roch was taken to be a spy, and was brought before the Governor who no longer recognised him, owing to the great change in his appearance and his wretched clothing, and therefore ordered him to be cast into prison. Roch, however, only thanked God for being allowed to suffer all these misfortunes, and spent five whole years in prison; and moreover would not accept any cooked food that was brought to him, but increased his bodily sufferings with watchings and fastings. When, at last, he saw his end approaching, he begged the gaoler's servant to fetch him a priest. Now the cell in which Roch lay was very dark; yet when the priest entered he found it light, which greatly surprised him; moreover as soon as he beheld Roch he perceived something godlike about him, and fell to the ground half dead in amazement. Thereupon he went straight to the Governor and told him what had happened, and that God had been grievously offended by so pious a man having been shut up in prison so long. As soon as this became known in the town, every one flocked to the tower, but Roch was seized with great weakness and his spirit fled. Yet every one saw a bright light shining through the gaps in the door, and upon opening it the Saint was found lying dead, stretched on the ground, lamps burning at his head and feet. Thereupon, at the command of the Governor, he was buried in the church, with much splendour. He was, moreover, recognised by the red cross on his breast, with which he had come into the world, and great were the cries and loud the lamentations about him.

This happened on the 16th of August in the year 1327, and after some time a church was erected in his honour at Venice, where his body is now preserved. In the year

1414, when a council was being held in Constance, and the plague appeared there, and nothing could be done against it, it suddenly disappeared one day when St. Roch was appealed to, and processions were held in his honour.

This peaceful story could not be listened to quietly amid our surroundings that day. For, at the table where we were sitting, several persons were already disputing about the number of pilgrims and visitors attending the festival. Some said there were 10,000 present, others again maintained that there were more, and that even more were swarming about the ridge of the hill where we were. An Austrian officer, trusting to his military eye, decided in favour of the highest figure.

Other conversations, too, crossed one another. I jotted down in my note-book all kinds of rural remarks and proverbial phrases about the weather that were said to have proved true this year; and when it was found that I was interested in the matter, others were thought of, which I shall give here, as indicating the manners of the people, and some of their more important interests.

"A dry April is not the peasant's will.—If a cricket chirps before the vines begin to shoot, there will be a good year.—A good deal of sunshine in August gives good wine. —The closer that Christmas follows upon a new moon, the harder will be the year that follows; but if it falls towards full moon, or when the moon is on the wane, the milder will be the season.—Fishermen observe the following about the liver of a pike, as having proved true: If the liver is broad towards the little gall-bladder, and the front part pointed and narrow, there will be a long and severe winter.—If the Milky Way shines bright and white in December, there will be a good year.—If the season between Christmas and Twelfth Night is foggy and dark, there will be much sickness during the year that follows. —If during Christmas-night the wine rises in the barrel to such a degree that it runs over, a good wine-year may be expected.—If the bittern is heard early, a good harvest may be looked for.—If the beans grow immoderately high, and the oaks bear much fruit, there will be little corn.—If owls and other birds leave the woods unusually early, and fly towards towns and villages, there will be an unfruitful year.—A cool May gives good wine and hay.—Not too cold and not too wet, fills both barn and barrel.—Ripe strawberries at Whitsuntide foretell a good wine season. —If it rains on Walpurgis-night,* a good year may be looked for.—If the breast-bone of a roasted St. Martin's goose be brown, the weather will be cold; if the bone be white, there will be snow."

A countryman from the hills who had listened, if not with envy, at least with a serious countenance to these numerous proverbs referring to rich fertility, was then asked if any such expressions were customary in his part of the country. He replied that he could not contribute as great a variety, that such mystical phrases were very simple with them, such as—

> "Round of a morning,
> Trampled at noon;
> In pieces at evening,
> Thus it shall ever be,
> And thus it is good."

The company were amused at this happy contentedness, and assured him that there were times when they would themselves be glad to be as fortunate.

Meanwhile several parties, apparently indifferent to those around them, had risen from their seats and left the table, which was so long that one could scarcely see how far it extended; others left exchanging friendly greetings with one another. The company thus gradually dispersed. Only those seated close by us, a few agreeable acquaintances, seemed to hesitate about leaving; we were all loath to part, and turned back again and again to enjoy the pleasant pain of such leave-takings, and finally, by way of comfort, promised impossibilities in the way of re-meetings.

Outside of the tents and booths, as the sun was still high, we at once felt the want of shade, which, however, is promised to our great grand-children by a large plantation of young nut-trees on the ridge of the hill. It is to be hoped that every pilgrim coming hither will be careful of the tender trees, and that some worthy company

* The night that precedes the 1st of May. Saint Walpurgis or Welpurga, was a niece of Saint Boniface, the great Apostle of Germany, whom she assisted in his work.

will be started in Bingen, to protect the plantation, and, by industriously replanting and carefully tending the trees, gradually promote their growth for the use and delight of thousands of their fellow-men.

A new commotion told of some new event. People were seen hurrying to hear the sermon, and all were crowding towards the east side of the chapel. The building here is not quite finished, the scaffolding still standing; thus even while the building is in construction Divine service is being held there. So it was in the days when pious hermits built chapels and monasteries with their own hands. Every bit of hewing, every laying down of a stone was a service rendered to God. Lovers of art will remember the important pictures of Lesueur * representing the deeds of holy St. Bruno. Everything repeats itself in the grand course of the world's history; a careful observer will notice this everywhere.

A stone pulpit built on the outside of the church-wall, supported by corbels, is accessible only from the inside of the church. It is now being entered by the preacher, a clergyman in the flower of manhood; the sun is still high in the heavens, so he is attended by a boy who holds a sunshade over him. The man spoke in a clear intelligible voice, and delivered a very sensible discourse. We believe that we grasped his meaning, and have, at times, repeated his remarks to friends; still it is quite possible that we may not have caught his exact words, and that something of our own has crept into our report of his address. In the following extract, will be found a tolerant mind encouraging zealousness, even though we may not always have given his views in the same powerful and graphic words which we heard that day.

"Devout and beloved hearers! In great numbers you have to-day mounted this hill, in order to celebrate a festival, that for some years past has been interrupted by the ordinance of God. You have come to find a chapel which only a short time ago was desecrated and laid waste, restored, decorated, and consecrated; you have come to enter it with devout steps, and gratefully to fulfil

* Eustache Lesueur who flourished between 1617-1655. The pictures here mentioned are now in the Louvre.

vows made to the Saint specially held in honour here. Now as it is my duty to address a few solemn words to you on this occasion, I think nothing could be more appropriate than our all taking to heart how a man, born, indeed, of pious but yet sinful parents, succeeded in obtaining such a degree of Divine grace, that it enables him to stand in the presence of God, and to intercede for those who faithfully turn to him in prayer, that they may be released from the terrible ills that destroy whole nations, released even from the very jaws of death itself.

"He, like all those whom we honour as saints, has obtained this Divine grace—we may confidently reply—because he possessed the chief of all virtues, including as it does all else that is good: unconditional submission to the will of God.

"For although no mortal man dare presume to imagine that he can become equal to God, or even in any way be like unto Him, still boundless submission to His holy will leads to the first and surest approach to the Supreme Being.

"Have we not an example of this in fathers and mothers who are blessed with a number of children, and who have a loving care for one and all? Yet, if one or other among these children be distinguished for docility and obedience, and follows the parent's commands without questionings and hesitation, straightway doing what they order, and acting as if it lived only in and for its parents, will not this child enjoy great privileges? To his request, or to his intercession the parents will lend an ear, and often cast aside their vexation and displeasure when pacified by his kind caresses. Somewhat thus, in a human way, we must imagine the relation existing between the Saint and God, and which he has achieved by unconditional submission."

We, who were listening to these words, were meanwhile looking up at the pure expanse of the heavens; the bluest of skies was enlivened by light clouds that flitted across. Our position was an elevated one; the view up the Rhine was bright, clear, and open; the preacher was to our left, a little above us, his audience in front of him and of us, a little lower.

The ground upon which the large concourse of people

had assembled, is a large unfinished terrace, not a level piece of ground, but sloping down abruptly at the back. If, at some future day, it were built up and properly laid out according to some architectural plan, it would be one of the finest positions in the world. No preacher, addressing several thousands of persons, ever had a richer landscape lying beyond the place where his congregation stood. And if the architect were to place the multitude upon a neat level flat, perhaps sloping a little upwards at the back, all the congregation would be able to see the preacher, and to hear him comfortably. On the present occasion, as the ground is still in an unfinished state, the people stood one beside the other, on a downward slope, accommodating themselves to circumstances as best they could. A curious, silently-swaying crowd, it seemed, looked down upon from above.

The place from which the bishop was listening to the sermon, could be distinguished only by the conspicuous canopy; he himself was hidden and encompassed by the crowd. This worthy chief of the ecclesiastical dignitaries the ingenious architect might contrive to give a more appropriate and conspicuous position, and thus add to the splendour of the spectacle. Looking thus around, and making these observations, which a practised eye could scarcely help making, did not prevent proper attention being paid to the words of the preacher, who now advanced to the second part of his discourse, and continued somewhat in the following manner.

"Such submission to the will of God, highly as it is to be commended, would, however, have remained without avail had not the pious youth loved his neighbour as himself, nay, even more than himself. For although, trusting to the dispensation of God, he divided his wealth among the poor, in order to go to the Holy Land as a pious pilgrim; he, nevertheless, when on the road, turned aside from his praiseworthy determination. The great misery in which he found his fellow-Christians made him consider it his inevitable duty to assist those who were suffering from one of the most infectious of diseases, without thinking of himself. And he continued this work in various towns, till, finally, he was himself seized by the terrible scourge, and rendered unable further to assist those around him. By being thus active amid danger, he approached nearer to the Divine Presence; 'for as God so loved the world as to sacrifice His only Son for its redemption,' in like manner St. Roch sacrificed himself for his fellow-creatures."

Great was the attention paid to every word that fell from the preacher's lips, and the concourse of listeners extended farther than the eye could reach. All the pilgrims who had wandered hither singly, and all the bands of processionists, had assembled here after having placed their banners and flags against the walls of the chapel, to the left of the preacher, and this added not a little to the picturesqueness of the scene. It was amusing, on the other hand, to notice, in a little courtyard close by, all the various images that had been carried up the hill, standing on their stages as if asserting their privilege to be regarded as the most distinguished members of the audience.

Three Virgin Marys, of different sizes, stood there, new and fresh, in the sunlight; their long, rose-coloured ribbons fluttering merrily in the liveliest of breezes. The Jesus-child in His gold dress still had the same kindly expression of face. Holy Saint Roch, too, more than once looked calmly down upon his own festival—the one image in the black dress, of course, came first in order.

The preacher now turned to the third part of his discourse, and spoke somewhat as follows.

"Yet even this important and difficult task would not have had any blessed result, if St. Roch had expected an earthly reward for his great sacrifices. Such godlike actions can be rewarded only by God, and, moreover, in eternity. The span of time is too short for boundless recompense. And so the Eternal God has bestowed His grace upon this holy man for all ages, and conferred upon him the extreme of blessedness, that of being able, for ever and ever, to be helpful to others from above, as he had been while yet on earth.

"We may, therefore, in every sense, look upon him as an example whereby to measure the degree of our own spiritual growth. If in days of sorrow you have turned to him and have, by the Divine grace, received a happy answer to your prayers, at once lay aside all arrogance and presumptuous pride, and ask yourselves humbly and cheerfully, have we kept his virtues before our eyes? Have we striven to do as he did? Have we, when times were hard, and our burdens well-nigh insupportable, submitted patiently to God's will? Have we checked murmurs that arose in our hearts? Have we lived in the confident hope of having deserved that the troubles were as unexpectedly as graciously put upon us? Have we not only prayed, but implored for release when pestilential and raging disease was among us? Have we in those times of misery stood by our own people, our near or distant relatives, and risked our lives for the sake of our God and His Saint?

"If you can answer these questions in your inmost heart with a yea, as most of you will be able to do, you will carry back home with you a feeling of honest satisfaction. And, if further, as I do not doubt, you can also add: We have, in all these things, not thought of obtaining any earthly reward, but were content with doing the godlike deed, you may rejoice all the more not to have made any vain request, and to have become more like unto the Intercessor.

"Continue to acquire more of these godlike virtues when the times are good, in order that when evil days are at hand, and these often come unexpectedly, you may turn to God through the prayers and vows of His holy Saint.

"In future, therefore, look upon the continued pilgrimages as renewed remembrances that you cannot offer the Supreme Being any greater thanksgiving than a heart made better and enriched with spiritual gifts."

The sermon certainly ended with a good effect upon all present, for one and all had heard the plain words, and all could take to heart the sensible, practical lessons.

The bishop now returned to the chapel, but what took place within was hidden from us. The sounds of a Te Deum could, however, be heard outside. The people streaming in and out presented an animated scene; but the festival was seemingly coming to an end. Processions were beginning to be formed in order to withdraw. The community from Bidenheim, who had been the last to arrive, were the first to leave. We also began to long to be out of the hubbub, and, therefore, took our departure with the peaceful and solemn procession from Bingen. On our way down the hill we noticed traces of the grievous days of the wars. The shrines, representing the different stages in the Passion of our Lord, had evidently been destroyed. When these are rebuilt, it might be managed, by consulting both a religious spirit and an honest appreciation of art,* that every passer-by—whosoever it might be—would regard them with a feeling of sympathetic interest.

Upon reaching Bingen, which is splendidly situated, we did not find much quiet. And after the many remarkable doings of the day, both divine and human, we longed for a plunge into Nature's splendid bath. A boat carried us down the river with the stream. We glided over the remains of the old weir of rocks which time and art have got the better of; the mysterious tower stood upon its imperishable quartz rock, on our left; the Ehrenburg on our right. Soon, however, we turned back, our mind full of those grey precipitous ravines through which, for immense ages past, the Rhine has forced its way.

On our return journey, as had been the case throughout the morning, we were accompanied by bright sunshine, although rising clouds above gave hopes of coming rain that was greatly needed. And at last it came pouring down refreshingly upon everything, and lasted long enough for us, on our homeward drive, to see the whole landscape revived. Thus holy St. Roch had clearly exercised his influence upon other Helpers-in-Need, and thereby proved himself a great blessing even to circumstances that were beyond the actual sphere of his activity.

* Goethe subsequently presented a painting, representing St. Roch, to this chapel, the work of a Louise Seidler.

AUTUMN DAYS IN THE RHEINGAU.*

SUPPLEMENTARY REMARKS TO THE SAINT ROCH
FESTIVAL, 1814.

THE opportunity I had of viewing the places and objects now to be described, I owe to the kindness of the beloved and honoured family Bretano, who arranged many a pleasant hour for me on the banks of the Rhine, in their country-house at Winkel.

The delightful situation of this residence affords an open view on all sides, and the inhabitants—of whom I might reckon myself one for several weeks—could wander merrily about at will, by land or water. We made excursions along both banks of the river by carriage, on foot, and by water, to the most magnificent points, the existence of which were sometimes expected before reached, but, at times, discovered unexpectedly. The country here presents a much greater variety than one would imagine. The eye seems almost unequal to take in all that is to be seen at a time. How, therefore, can mere written words call up any proper recollection of it from the past? Let these pages, however, be dedicated in faithful remembrance of my appreciation of the days spent there, and of my gratitude for having been enabled to have the inestimable enjoyment of those scenes.

1st *September*, 1814.

The sight of the convent of Eibingen raises in one's mind that most melancholy of thoughts, a worthy existence

* Goethe's visit on this occasion lasted from the 31st of August till the 8th of September, 1814. On the 30th he was still in Wiesbaden, as we know from a letter of his to Sulpiz Boisserée.

Y

in a state of decay. The chapel is robbed of all its belongings, the rooms and halls do not show the smallest trace of furniture, the walls of the cells have been knocked in, the doors towards the passages fitted with locks, the gaps left unfilled, and débris lying scattered about. Why all this destruction without aim or object? The reason, we are told, is this: a hospital was to have been established there if the warfare had continued in the neighbourhood. We have, therefore, to be content with the ruins and the forsaken work. It seems, however, as if the empty rooms were made use of at present as a place for keeping soldiers' accoutrements, and for stowing away old, or but little used, implements of war. In the choir are to be seen rows of saddles, and the halls and rooms filled with knapsacks; there is also no dearth of cast-off clothing; so that if one of the nuns, of years gone by, had had the gift of fore-sight she would have been horrified at the devastation and desecration that future days would bring with them. The armorial bearings of the ladies, who, in past times, sought shelter and sustenance here, still adorn the walls of one of the empty halls.

Thereupon we paid a visit to the Brömser buildings,* in Rüdesheim, which contain some curious, but not very pleasing relics from the sixteenth century. There is, however, one family picture of the lords of Kronenburg, from the year 1549, which is particularly good in its way, and worthy the attention of all interested in antiquity and in art.

The town church in the market-place, contains the miraculous image which, in former days, attracted so many devout believers to the monastery of *Noth-Gottes* (Agonia Domini).† The image represents Christ kneeling with upraised hands, is about eight inches high, and probably, is the chief and sole remaining figure of a very old group, depicting the scene on Mount Olivet. The head and body are cut out of wood. The raiment, of fine linen stuff, is gummed on, lying close to the figure, and the folds

---

* The ancient residence of an old aristocratic family which became extinct in the seventeenth century. The present proprietor, Count von Ingelheim, has had the residence partially restored.

† For a more detailed account of this convent, see p. 327.

evenly cut out of the wood; at the arms the linen hangs loose and forms the sleeves, which are stuffed out; the whole image is chalked over and painted. The hands, which are fixed on, are somewhat too long, but the joints and nails are well represented. It belongs to a not incompetent, but unskilful age.

2nd September, 1814.

Towards the middle of Winkel, one has to turn off towards the hills, if a visit to Vollraths * is contemplated. The road at first passes through vineyards; then comes a flat tract of meadow-land, which is unexpectedly found to be damp, and is surrounded by willows. The castle stands on an elevation; at the foot of the hill, to the right and left, are fertile fields and vineyards; a wood of beeches and oaks on the hill at the back.

The courtyard of the castle, which is encircled by dwelling houses and other outhouses of considerable size, bears witness to a state of prosperity in days gone by; the smaller buildings at the back are made use of for farming requirements.

To the right, one enters a garden which, like all around, testifies of a former state of prosperity, and of having been carefully attended to by its proprietor in times past, and now has a peculiar attraction as an often-visited ruin. The fruit-trees, that in former days had been trained to the shape of pyramids and fans, have been allowed to grow wild, their mighty trunks and branches shading the flower-beds, nay, even obstructing the paths, and being laden with excellent fruit, present the strangest appearance. A small country residence, built by the Prince-Elector of the Greiffenklau family, shows the most evident signs of decay when entered. The lower rooms are in a state of utter neglect; the hall, on the first floor, awakens the remembrance of bygone days by its collection of family portraits, which, although not well painted, nevertheless

* The ancient seat of the family Greiffenklau, in whose possession it still remains. It is said to have been built in 1362 by Count Fr. Greiffenklau of Folraz.

recalls the existence of the different personages. In life-size, we see a comfortable-looking Greiffenklau, who may, indeed, feel somewhat proud of himself and his surroundings; two consorts and several sons, prebendaries, soldiers, and courtiers standing round him, and other children and relatives, for whom there was no room below, are represented above as pictures in the painting. There are life-size portraits of Electors, prebendaries, and knights, both in half and full figure, hanging round this desolate, though not devastated hall, where old, rich-looking chairs are still standing in their places amid neglected plants and other rubbish. In the side rooms, gilded leathern hangings are dangling from the walls, and look as if the nails which had supported them had been taken out to be used for some other purpose.

If we turn our eyes from this disorder to the window, a most glorious view is obtained; the wild-looking, but fruitful garden lies directly below and, through a gently widening valley, the town of Winkel is seen in its whole length, while beyond, on the other side of the Rhine, are Lower and Upper Ingelheim in a fertile district. We walked through the neglected garden to the garden-nurseries, and found them in the same forlorn state; the gardener, we were told, was fond of fishing!

Farther off, on a meadow, at the end of the garden, a large well-grown poplar attracted our attention; we were told that it had been planted on the marriage-day of the last Greiffenklau but one, and that his widow delighted in the glories of this place up to the last. After the early death of a son, however, the possession of the beautiful estate passed away to another branch of the family, who, as they reside at some distance, do not seem to be much interested in its preservation. We passed a curious-looking tower, built in a small pond, and then proceeded on to the somewhat imposing residence.

Yesterday, in the convent of Eibingen, we had beheld the devastation that had been caused, wittingly or unwittingly, by change in political relations, in religious ideas, by warfare and other troubles, there we saw a convent that had been destroyed, here, on the other hand, we found the remains of a family mansion that had been allowed to fall to decay of itself. The venerable-looking pedigrees were still hanging on the walls of the corridors; the Greiffenklaus and Sickingens might be seen sending out shoots one against the other, spreading out an endless variety of branches; the most eminent and famous names were linked, on the female side, with those of the Greiffenklaus.

Upon another of this sort of picture were depicted bishops, abbots, priests, and women kneeling under the tree from which they had sprung, praying for salvation. A third picture, of the same kind, had been wantonly or intentionally disfigured by some one who had cut out the head of the founder of the family; probably this had been done by some collector of curiosities, a set of people who cannot be trusted anywhere. Twigs and branches now hovered in mid-air, proclaiming the destruction.

How interesting these galleries were in the good days of old to members of the family, is evident from the fact that plans of many of the estates, with their boundaries, their rightful and doubtful limits, and whatever else there might be worthy of note, were also hung up here and presented to view.

Many things seemed to be missing that had been seen by visitors who had previously been here, but, at last, we discovered a small room, where all the family pictures were lying piled up one on top of the other, and given over to decay. Some were worth being preserved, and probably all once had their own place on the walls. In a few of the rooms there are chairs and bedsteads, presses, and such things, which, in the course of time and from want of care, have gradually become spoilt and useless.

Divine service is still performed in the small chapel, but even this building is not kept very neat. There are in it a few small Greek pictures, which scarcely deserve to have been saved from the general wreck.

From these melancholy surroundings we hastened out into the rich, joyous Nature, and by keeping on the top of the hill, with vineyards to our left, and newly-ploughed fields to our right, we wandered towards the Johannisberg. The limits of the vine plantations also mark the limits of the alluvial soil; where the fields begin we have the natural mountain earth. This is a species of quartz akin to clay-slate, which splits into plates and prisms.

We cannot refrain from looking back to our left towards the river, and at the districts and towns lying along its banks; for now that we know these all severally, we look at with all the greater interest in the landscape as a whole.

One is, however, completely taken by surprise upon reaching the terrace in front of the Johannisberg Castle.* For although all the different places and objects mentioned in our account of the Bingen festival might again be named here, still what our mind would recall at a future day, would be merely what we had beheld at the one point where, on looking to the left and right, the whole scene between Biberich and Bingen presented itself to the eye; everything perfectly distinct to a good eyesight, or one armed with a glass—the Rhine, with all the towns along its shores, its meadowy islands, the opposite banks and their gently-sloping plains. To our left, above, the blue summits of the Altkin and the Feldberg;† directly in front of us the ridge of the Donnersberg, indicating the course taken by the river Nahe. To our right, below, Bingen, and close by, the ominous mountain ravine where the Rhine is lost to sight.

The evening sun, which lingered at our back, illuminated all the various objects that were turned towards us. Light clouds, in curious streaks, stretched from the horizon towards the zenith, and broke the otherwise general clearness of the view; changing bits of sunlight drew our attention first to one point and then to another, and the eye was here and there charmed with single new points of beauty. The condition of the castle itself did not disturb these pleasant impressions. It was uninhabited, it is true, and without furniture, but had not been laid waste.

* An extensive castle, erected in 1722, on the site of an old Benedictine monastery founded in 1162. The castle was presented by Napoleon to Marshal Kellermann in 1807, but was subsequently conferred by the Emperor of Austria on Prince Metternich, and is still the property of this family.

† Peaks in the Taunus range of mountains; the Donnersberg is separated from St. Roch's hill by the river Nahe.

At sunset, the sky became covered from all sides with arrow-shaped, streaky clouds, which kept moving more and more towards the horizon; they indicate a change of weather, which will be determined over night.

3rd September, 1814.

The sky in the morning, which was at first completely clouded, cleared up gradually, with a continuous wind from the north. After having examined an old painting at a picture dealer's in Geisenheim, we went uphill through a copse of oak which, it seems, is cut down every fourteen years to supply tan-yards. Here we again came upon quartz-rock, and farther up found a kind of diluvium. On our left was a deep mountain valley full of old and young oak trees; here the towers and roofs of an old monastery became visible; a wild and lonely situation, completely shut in by the richest green. The place corresponded well with the name of the sanctuary itself, for it is still called *Noth-Gottes* (Agonia Domini), although the mystic picture, which here wailed its distress to the knight, has been removed to the church in Rüdesheim. The place would seem utterly inhospitable, even now, were it not that a small portion of the neighbouring hill had been dug up and tilled.

The path then proceeds upwards to a high-lying and cultivated flat tract of country, until, finally, the Niederwald is reached. Here a long, level and broad road announces the vicinity of important country-houses; and at one end of the road we came upon a hunting-château, with outhouses. In front of the courtyard, or rather from the top of a small tower, a view is obtained of the tremendous ravine through which the Rhine flows. Lorch, Dreieckshausen, Bacharach, were to be seen on either side of the river, and this point seemed to us to form the beginning of an entirely new region, and to be the utmost limit of the Rheingau.

In walking through the wood we obtained a variety of different views, and finally reached a rocky eminence overhanging the lower hill, and from there is seen one of the loveliest views imaginable. Far below us the rapids of the Bingen Loch, just above the Mäusethurm; the Nahe flowing past the bridge at Bingen, farther off the brow of the hill with St. Roch's Chapel, and all pertaining to it—in fact, a grand and, in every way, most varied prospect. In turning round, and looking down, the ruined castle of Ehrenfels was at our feet.

Proceeding through an extensive tract of well-kept forest, we came to a round pavilion, facing the north. Here again, we obtained a view up the Rhine, and found an opportunity of summarising all that we had seen again and again during the last few days. We had become acquainted with the different individual objects, and could now, with the aid of a telescope, nay, even with the naked eye, see and note the more remarkable ones.

In giving a fuller description of the Niederwald, it would have to be remembered that the outlying hills in the Wiesbaden direction draw closer and closer to the Rhine here, driving the stream westwards, and that the rocks of the Niederwald form the point, where it again starts on its northward course.

The steep pathway down towards Rüdesheim led through the most splendid vineyards, clothing the hills, that crowd one upon another here, in the freshest of green, and moreover in such regular stripes that they look as if covered by a curiously-wrought carpet.

4th September, 1814.

Early to church, where the divine service was performed with more than usual solemnity, on account of some endowment of the Greiffenklau family. Children in gay dresses and wreaths knelt at the side steps of the altar, and scattered flowers from their little baskets at certain points of the service; but having been somewhat lavish with their flowers, and yet not wishing to be without any at the solemn moments, they gathered up the flowers that they had already strewn, into their baskets, and offered the gift a second time.

After this we visited the ruined chapel of St. Rhabanus, now converted into the house of a vine-dresser. It is said to have been the first edifice erected in Winkel, and ancient enough it appears to be. The earth, or rather the rubbish piled up where the altar once stood, is said to keep away rats and mice.

After dinner, we left Mittelheim for Weinheim in a boat crowded with people, the wind blowing somewhat briskly from the north-east. The current of the river here runs strong upon the left shore, and has torn away a projecting meadow. The roots of the old willows are bare, and the bark has been ripped from their trunks by the ice. A dam has been thrown up to protect the fields lying beyond from being flooded.

At the end of this dam, towards Lower Ingelheim, we came across some very curious-looking hillocks that have been deposited by the water in remote ages, and this light sand is now driven hither and thither by the wind. Innumerable small shells are mixed with the sand, some of which resemble the turbinidæ found in the tufa limestone by Weinheim. That these snails are still multiplying in the sandy district, may be inferred from the fact that some attentive children showed me a shell with a living animal in it.

At the back of the mill begins a fertile tract of land, which extends as far as Lower Ingelheim. This latter place, which is situated pretty high up on a gentle slope, belongs to the district which was formerly called the Valley of the Holy Roman Empire. Part of Charlemagne's palace * we found utterly demolished, the rest in ruins, and divided into small possessions; its circumference can still be recognised by the high walls, which, however, may belong to a later date. A piece of a white marble pillar is to be seen built into a wall at the gate-

* This palace is described by ancient writers as one of great magnificence. It was destroyed several times and again restored. It suffered most at the hands of the French in 1689. When the last of the halls, that had long stood in tolerable preservation, fell in, in 1831, all that remained of the palace was a heap of ruins. Four columns of syenite, which adorned this palace, were taken to Heidelberg, and used in decorating a covered fountain in that town.

way, with the following inscription from the Thirty-years,' War:—

" 800 years ago this hall, which belonged to the great Emperor Charles, and after him to Louis, son of the benevolent Emperor Charles, but in the year 1044 to the Emperor Henry, was, in the year 1360, the palace of the Emperor Charles, King of Bohemia; the Emperor Charles the Great caused this pillar, together with other pillars of cast metal, to be brought from Ravenna in Italy to this palace, and they were erected in the reign of the Emperor Ferdinand II., and of the King of Spain, Henry IV., and of their prescribed and worshipful government in the Lower Palatinate, on the 6th of April, 1628, when the Catholic Faith was again introduced."

See Münster's History of Ingelheim, in the Valley of the Holy Roman Empire, fol. DCLXXXIX.

The place where the kitchen stood of yore is said to have been discovered by a great many bones of animals, more especially the teeth of boars, having been found in a ditch close by. During the time the district was under French dominion, a number of investigations were made here, and several pillars carried off to Paris.

Lately, while the great high-road was being made, Ingelheim was well paved, and the post-house put into good order. Mrs. Glöckle is the landlady's name, and her house is at present pretty frequently visited by travellers, more particularly by English people of both sexes.

It was night and dark when we reached the ferry, but although some uncomfortable presentiments crossed our minds, we got safely home again.

The 4th of September, 1814, saw us start in a carriage to Rüdesheim, whence we crossed over to Bingen in a rowing-boat, the carriage following in the ferry. We walked along the banks. Gypsum, mixed with a greyish clay, was being unloaded in quantities. Whence can it have been brought? Walked through the town; turned in at *The White Horse*. A melancholy landlady, strangely conscious of her own condition. After being well served at a moderate charge, we drove up St. Roch's hill, past the ruined shrines. St. Roch's Chapel we found open. The man who had superintended its restoration was there, very well satisfied with his work, which may truly be considered a success. The church walls have been heightened so as to obtain the necessary space for the principal altar from Eibingen. The transport of the altar did not cost anything, for the people of Bingen themselves brought everything down from the convent on the other side and up the hill here, the boatmen likewise doing their part without asking for payment. This accounts for all the different things being in such good repair, and that only a few required to be restored.

Some men were busy setting up the organ. Upon asking one of them, whom we took to be the foreman, whether the organ was a good one, he replied, with an air of importance, "It is a soft organ, a nun's organ." They played a few chords to let us hear it, and these seemed quite powerful enough for the size of the chapel.

We then turned towards the view that can never be sufficiently enjoyed, and afterwards examined the rocks. At the top they consist of a kind of clay-slate akin to quartz; at the foot, towards Kempten, of a kind of diluvium, consisting of sharp-edged bits of quartz almost without any connecting substance. It is extremely hard, and on the outside, where exposed to the atmosphere, has acquired the well-known coating of chalcedony. It is justly accounted as belonging to the primeval breccia.

We drove down through the vineyards, leaving Kempten on our right, and soon reached the new and admirable high-road, on both sides of which is good arable land. As it was our intention to go to Upper Ingelheim, we left the high-road and drove to the right over sandy ground, through a wood of young fir. Gently-rising hills soon showed a better soil; finally we came to vineyards, and thereupon reached Upper Ingelheim. This little place lies on a height, at the foot of which runs a brook called the Sulze.

There were but few people to be seen in the neat, well-paved town. At the upper end of it stands an old and completely ruined castle, within the boundaries of which is a chapel which is still used, but is in very bad repair. At the time of the Revolution the armorial bearings on the tombs of the knights were knocked off. The very ancient panes of glass are falling away of themselves. The chapel is a Protestant one.

We noticed a curious custom here. Upon the heads of the colossal stone figures of the knights were hung gaily-coloured, light-looking crowns, made of wire, paper, and ribbands, all plaited together in the form of a tower. The same sort of things, with large paper hearts and writing on them, was also hanging upon cornices. We were told that they were hung up in memory of persons who had died unmarried. These mementos of death were the only decoration of the building.

We then repaired to a wine-house, and the old hostler, in spite of his short breath, did his best to entertain us with stories of both good and evil times. The two Ingelheims used to belong to a district called the *eight townships*, and which, for many ages, enjoyed great privileges. The taxes were small considering the great fruitfulness of the country. Under the French dominion great burdens had to be borne.

In former times only white wine was grown here, but later red wine was also cultivated in imitation of, and even to compete with, the Assmannshäuser; its merits were praised, but as there was no more red Eilfer wine to be procured, we made the best of the white grown that same year.

When we got back to the water-side at Weinheim and asked for a boat, two boys offered their services to row us across. Upon our showing a want of confidence in them on account of their youthfulness, they assured us that they were better up to the work than the older men. And certainly they did take us safely and cleverly across to the right shore.

6th September, 1814.

While out for a walk, and watching the building of a wall, I learned that the limestone, which consists almost wholly of small shells, is procured from the opposite hills in various districts. Now as these shells are the products of fresh water, it becomes more and more evident that, in former ages, there was a restagnation of the river, which became a large lake.

At the water-side, between a bed of willows and the Rhine, I was shown the place where Fräulein von Günderode * committed suicide. To hear the story of this melancholy event at the very spot where it happened, and from persons who lived in the neighbourhood, and had been interested in it, produced an uncomfortable feeling, which is always excited by the scene of any tragedy. In the same way as one cannot enter Eger without fancying oneself surrounded by the spirits of Wallenstein and his followers.

* * * * *

We were relieved from these painful thoughts by inquiring into the daily occupations of people.

Tanning.—A plantation of oaks requires to grow from thirteen to fourteen years before the bark is ready for use. The young oaks are then peeled or cut down altogether; this must be done when they are in sap. The barks are fetched from places at a distance, from the Neckar by way of Heidelberg, from Trèves, etc. As they can be brought by water, the work is greatly facilitated. There are mills for crushing the tan. Skins, American ones, have latterly been brought here across France.

Wine Culture.—The trouble connected with it. Advantages, gain, and loss. In the year 1811, eight hundred casks of wine were produced in Winkel. Great amount of tithes. The goodness of the wine depends upon situation, but also upon a late vintage. In this respect the poor and the wealthy are always at variance, the poor preferring an abundant harvest, the wealthy a good one. It is said that there are better positions round about the Johannisberg; but owing to its being an enclosed district, the vintage there can be delayed unhindered, and hence the greater excellence of the products. The ordinary vineyards are closed some time before the grapes are gathered

---

* Caroline von Günderode had stabbed herself here, in consequence of an unfortunate attachment to the well-known philologist Creuzer, in 1805. Her friend Bettina von Arnim wove her tragic story into a romance, entitled *Die Günderode*, which appeared in 1840.

in, and even the proprietor is not allowed to enter them. If he requires grapes, he has to obtain an order from an official whose duty it is to look after the vines.

* * * * *

And thus we may again close with the happy refrain

*" By the Rhine! By the Rhine!
"'Tis there we grow our wine!"

" *Am Rhein! Am Rhein!*
Da wachsen uns're Reben! "

---

* Opening lines of a popular Rhenish song by Matthäus Claudius, first published in his weekly journal *Der Wandsbecker Bote*, to which paper Goethe had also contributed articles.

ART COLLECTIONS ON THE RHINE, MAINE, AND NECKAR.

1814 AND 1815.

COLOGNE.*

AFTER a pleasant trip down the Rhine, we were greeted by friends and acquaintances, nay, even by strangers, with the unexpected news that Ruben's picture † of the Crucifixion of St. Peter, painted for this his native city, and dedicated to the church of the patron of the town, had been brought back from Paris, and was shortly again triumphantly to be replaced in its former sacred position. We rejoiced that a numerous body of citizens were by this simple, but grand act, enjoying the glorious feeling of now belonging to a ruler who was powerful enough to see that justice was obtained for them in this high sense, and to recover for them a possession of which they had ignominiously been deprived. All the more lively was our interest in visiting the patrons of the fine arts in this city, who felt comforted and cheered by the re-appearance of their Saint,

---

* Goethe's Diary gives the following data: Tuesday, July 25th, Von Stein, the Minister of State, drove me in a carriage as far as Ehrenbreitstein; thence we went in a boat to Cologne. Wednesday, 26th: Examined the cathedral inside and outside, top and bottom, with all its belongings. Private collections, curiosities. Thursday, 27th: Drove round the town; visits; pictures. Wallraf's well-stocked residence; buildings; the rector of the school; also Bonn. Fuchs accompanied me.

† Admitted to be one of Ruben's finest paintings; it had been carried off to Paris by Napoleon in 1802, but after the Peace of Paris (May 30th, 1814) was to be returned to Cologne. The picture had previously been the altar-piece in the cathedral.

and looked upon this public acquisition as a pledge that security and encouragement was promised them for their own private interests.

In the eighteenth century, when the fine arts first began to show signs of life in the districts of the Lower Rhine, it manifested itself mainly in the decoration of the walls and ceilings of churches, monasteries and public buildings, frequently also of large panels with representations of sacred subjects. The more modern style of art provided, in addition, smaller pictures for individual citizens, appropriate for the interior of dwelling houses, and in accordance with domestic tastes. Naturally, favourite subjects were treated with brilliant realism, and people were thus enabled quietly to enjoy splendid works in their own residences.

Such artistic surroundings came to be regarded as necessary objects to the wealthy, and as a sign of superiority among the well-to-do classes. Native artists were employed. A brisk trade with Brabant and Holland brought an immense number of such works into circulation. The fancy for such pictures led to the thought of gain being obtained, and the gain stimulated the fancy; dealers appeared with connections in distant countries, encouraging both art and artists. Among these the name of Jabach * is spoken of with reverence. This excellent man has been painted by Lebrun in life-size, surrounded by his intelligent and well-to-do family. It is still to be seen in Cologne, is in a perfect state of preservation, and deserves to be one of the principal ornaments of a public institution in this city, and one which, it is hoped, may soon be established.

We must, however, now consider the important direction which the love of art has taken in our day. An enthusiastic admiration for the remains of ancient art and its gradual re-appearance out of the dark days of the Middle Ages—which began to show itself towards the end of the last century, and is becoming more and more developed —received abundant encouragement, when churches and

* It is said that Ruben's Crucifixion of St. Peter was painted by order of the Jabach family in memory of Eberhard von Jabach, who died in 1636.

monasteries were abolished, and sacred paintings and other articles were offered for sale. Very precious things that had previously belonged to the community at large, now fell into the hands of private individuals. In Cologne, therefore, several persons felt it to be their duty to rescue and to collect what they could of such treasures. The brothers Boisserée * and Bertram gathered a number of pictures of this kind, with great zealousness as well as knowledge of the subject, and with perseverance and success, at great expense to themselves; this collection forms an instructive and valuable artistic treasure ; it is at present in Heidelberg, and unwillingly missed in Cologne. However, Messrs. Wallraf, Lyversberg, Fochem, and others, possess extremely valuable collections of this kind.

Now as almost all of these paintings had to be carefully cleaned from smoke and dust, the injured parts deftly restored, and the gilt background neatly repaired, there was soon a demand for persons able to restore pictures— a set of persons who are indispensable where a brisk trade in works of art is carried on. A splendid memorial of this kind, where dilettanti and artists have worked together with a spirit of patriotic and artistic appreciation, is presented by the large altar-piece† that has been removed from the Chapel of the Council (*die Rathskapelle*) to the Cathedral.

Still pictures and decorations which had been intended for religious purposes, and which had been removed from

* Sulpiz and Melchior Boisserée had both been brought up to become merchants, but soon gave up the idea of entering mercantile life, owing to their strong preference for study. As will be seen in Goethe's further account, they attended classes at the *Central Schule*, where they had the advantage of hearing lectures by some of the most eminent German scholars, but were especially influenced by Friederich von Schlegel. The brothers, while in Paris in 1803, and still preparing for mercantile life, had received private instruction from Schlegel in philosophy and literature. On their return to Cologne, in 1804, Schlegel received a temporary appointment at the Higher School there, and delivered his famous course of lectures on the History of Literature and on various other subjects, and the brothers Boisserée were amongst his most ardent admirers. Further particulars about their collection of paintings on p. 396.

† On the one panel is Saint Ursula, with the 11,000 virgins; on the other, Saint Gereon, with his followers. The painter was probably Stephan Lochner, who lived in the first half of the fifteenth century.

their places in the churches, owing to the restless and distracted state of the times, did not seem altogether in their proper place in private residences. It thus occurred to the lively and inventive minds of proprietors and artists, to place them amid more appropriate surroundings, and by this means to offer to the sense of taste, what had been ruthlessly snatched from the feelings of piety. Imitation chapels were devised, where the sacred paintings and other articles could be preserved in their old connection and dignity. Coloured glass windows were cunningly imitated upon linen, and painted imitations of articles from monasteries were depicted on the walls, partly in perspective, partly also in bas-relief, so as to look like reality.

This pleasing style of decoration was, however, not allowed to remain in the dark, the cheerful spirit of the inhabitants soon led to its appearing in broad daylight. And artists soon contrived to satisfy demands of this kind, by making the background of narrow courtyards, that were decorated with shrubs and flowers, appear of endless extent by means of well-devised perspective landscapes. All this, and many other things of the kind which most pleasantly strike the visitor as new and significant, bear testimony to a cheerful and pious sensuousness, which seeks both enjoyment and edification, and which, if it proves active in times of oppression and trouble, will in times of security and peace, and an accompanying increase of wealth, very soon show signs of renewed vitality.

In Cologne, therefore, when we attentively consider the many things that have been rescued, preserved and re-animated, we perceive how easy it would be for a government to lend a helping hand in such cases where the appointed superintendents have already cheerfully acknowledged what private individuals have accomplished from a pure interest and love in the subject, and where such happy intentions have been encouraged in every possible way. Delegates, as connoisseurs and lovers of art, would then not remain in ignorance of what works are to be found in the town itself, what comes and goes, or what owners themselves may exchange. While encouraging the activity of individual persons, they would take note of such cases where the life-long efforts of a private person suddenly become the property of the community. For it not rarely happens that a collection becomes a trouble to its owner, who may in various ways come to feel himself hampered by it. Want of space, change of residence, alteration of taste, or a weakened interest in the subject, often lessens the value of artistic works in the eyes of their proprietor, and it is in such cases that a government officer might act for the good of both parties. When respectful attention is paid to a wealthy man he may feel so much flattered, that, if his patriotism is aroused, he may be willing, for some trifling consideration, to hand over his collection, and incorporate it with some public institution, even though he may not be willing to present it as a gift. If he meets with a spirit of indifference in his native town, he will try and obtain gratitude in some distant place. Had this been done, the immense collections of Baron von Hüpsch, which, amid a good deal of rubbish contained the most valuable objects from antiquity, would not have wandered from Cologne to Darmstadt. Nor would Nose's extremely important geological specimens from the Lower Rhine have left Godesberg for Berlin, had he lived in days such as those we are now looking forward to.

Upon inquiring about the collections at present to be found in Cologne, we were first of all referred to that of Wallraf,* the Canon and Professor, who, owing to his enthusiastic attachment to his native city, has devoted his whole life, and all his means—often depriving himself of the first necessaries of life—to collecting everything in any way of interest to his birth-place. Although his attention is chiefly directed to Roman antiquities, sculptures, coins, carved stones and inscriptions, he has at the same time acquired possession of modern works of art of various kinds, paintings, drawings, engravings, books, manuscripts, and even some very important geological speci-

* Ferdinand Franz Wallraf had been a professor at the University of Cologne; when it ceased to exist he received an appointment at the *Central Schule*. His rich collections were bequeathed to the town soon after the publication of this article (1816); they formed the foundation of the subsequent Wallraf-Richarz Museum.

mens. This collection, which it is difficult to inspect, owing to its variety and comprehensiveness, could never be arranged in a private house to afford any enjoyment to the owner himself or instruction to others, for even in the free residence that has been offered to the collector, there is not space enough to hold his numerous possessions, much less, therefore, to exhibit them separately. It is much to be desired that this treasure might soon become the property of the community, in order that the remaining years which may yet be granted to the worthy proprietor, might be devoted to carefully examining and arranging these precious objects, and thus rendering them both enjoyable and useful.

This pre-supposes the existence of a sufficiently large locality, which surely might be found in this extensive city. If such a building were selected, the rooms would, of course, have to be duly considered, in order that the different departments of the collection might be properly arranged. And continual regard would likewise have to be paid to the future; the different rooms would have to be arranged with space enough for any additions that might be expected. A suggestion in this direction would be given by the collection itself, which, as it embraces objects of every description, and points to all quarters, would call for a variety of different rubrics, and in days to come would increase and extend internally. The collection is specially valuable, because it would oblige future conservators to estimate everything according to its kind, and to consider even the most trifling thing as an integral part of the whole. How surprisingly pleasant it would be, if the different rooms were to be tastefully decorated in keeping with the various articles; of this, indeed, we have some examples to admire in several towns, but still we do not know of any general museum in this sense. It is certainly a very pleasant way of receiving instruction when we find sarcophaguses, urns, and all the various articles connected with burials and tombs. arranged side by side in imitation columbaria; when a Roman monument, an altar, or cippus, are surrounded by a decoration reminding us of the Via Appia; when the relics of the early days of the Middle Ages are placed amid decorations belonging to their day, yet harmonising with the later style ; when even objects from the kingdoms of Nature are adorned with pictures of what happens not to be actually represented in the collection. If we were to pursue these thoughts, and imagine the project carried out, many a thing would be accomplished which, even to hint at beforehand, might seem presumptuous. In a district where knowledge can be valued only in so far as it directly affects life, such an arrangement is, in fact, necessary. Here any one who is indifferent, yet inquisitive, would be entertained and stimulated, nay, do what he would he could not fail to be instructed; the connoisseur, on the other hand, would as little allow himself to be led astray by this kind of deception introduced amid the general order, as he would be by the confusion that prevails in the shop of a dealer in curiosities. In Cologne we should have to seek the assistance of the eminent artist, Mr. Fuchs,* in this matter ; he has already, in similar cases, given proof of his inventive talent, taste, and skill Regret would, at the same time, be felt for the loss of Joseph Hoffmann,† who at an early age already accomplished a great deal, and deserved to have lived to see better times.

Every one who takes to heart what has been said above, will feel convinced that, with judicious and active encouragement from high quarters, the establishment of a museum in Cologne, based upon a sound foundation and liberal principles, would at once lead art, ingenuity and industry to work together in order to adorn it. There would, moreover, be no lack of patriotic activity to assist in extending and adding to it. Thus, even at the present moment, while there is as yet but a mere hope of some general point of union, we have a laudable example in the enterprise of General von Rauch, who is collecting all the objects found in the ground turned up where the new fortifications are being made, with the intention of

* Max H. Fuchs, the painter, especially noted in connection with Boisserée's splendid work on the Cologne Cathedral, the architectural drawings for which were made by Fuchs.

† Joseph Hoffmann had died in 1812, but was known to Goethe by having several times competed for the prize offered by the patrons of art in Weimar and, on two occasions, having carried off the prize.

one day handing them over to the public keeping. The many important things already discovered excite the pleasantest hopes, and will secure to the excellent soldier the everlasting gratitude of a town which is showing signs of re-awakening life.

Yet it might not be either necessary or advisable to think of establishing a regular academy of arts in Cologne. Republican forms, that have for ages past been impressed upon men's minds here, are best suited to this part of the country, at least as regards the free arts. An intelligent love of art and art-patronage, everywhere takes the place of actual management; every artist trains pupils of his own in his special department, and every pupil again can freely choose his own master. Here every one can, by his own work as a restorer and dealer in works of art, raise himself to a position that would of necessity become a very pleasant one, were the government to make use of his talents for their purposes, and relieve him from the first cares of life by granting him an adequate pension, or some suitable reward for his unusual labours.

If, in accordance with the general wishes and hopes, a regular intercourse in the fine arts were established on the Rhine and Maine, the interest of travellers could not fail likewise to be aroused. The lover of the fine arts does not always require originals; if he meets with, and takes a fancy to any remarkable picture, of which he cannot hope to obtain the possession, he is satisfied with a copy. This is, at present, to be seen in the pleasure found in the early German style of art, and in the demand there is for copies of paintings of this kind which are highly prized. The central group of the large panel in the Cathedral, spoken of above, has been most successfully copied in miniature by Lieutenant Raabe. A Mr. Beckenkamp also is continually engaged in making copies of it, which at once find purchasers. How many circumstances seem to combine in promising that an active and unfettered artist-life will become cheerfully developed in these districts out of a past age that has never quite died out!

However, before the visitor can enjoy such a diversity

of remarkable objects, he is irresistibly drawn to the Cathedral. Yet when he has looked at this world's wonder—a wonder, however, as yet only in contemplation —when he has looked at it, within and without, in its incompleteness, he is oppressed by a painful feeling which cannot become in any way pleasurable, unless we cherish the wish, nay, the hope, of seeing the building entirely finished. For it is in a state of completion only, that a grandly conceived master-piece can produce that effect which the extraordinary mind of the master had in view: where the immensity is rendered intelligible. When such a work is seen in an unfinished state, neither has the imagination the power, nor has the understanding the readiness to create the complete image or the idea.

This natural feeling, which must affect every one who beholds the unfinished edifice, has suggested an idea to the minds of some young Cologne men, by which its incompleteness may in some measure be made good, and they have formed the happy and bold resolution to complete the Cathedral, at all events in the form of drawings and sketches. Now, although such an undertaking may appear trifling compared with the actual finishing of the building, still even this effort will require as much knowledge as inventive genius, as much actual work as perseverance, as much independence of spirit as influence upon others—if the Brothers Boisserée are to succeed in so far carrying out this splendid artistic work, that it will continue regularly to appear in parts. The original plan had fortunately been found, and the full sketch discovered subsequently, and happily came to the assistance of the measurements and conjectures previously made. Hence, plans, sketches, sections, and perspective drawings will appear from time to time, forming a work which, considering its subject as well as the artists who are engaged with it, deserves to be received with the warmest appreciation. For, to enable the drawings of the excellent Germans Moller,* Fuchs, and

---

* George Moller who so actively assisted the Boisserées with their work on the Cathedral, resided in Darmstadt, and was the architect of the theatre there, which was burned down in 1871, also of that in Mainz, as well as of the Royal residence in Wiesbaden, and of the

Quaglio,* to be engraved in Germany, will require of those who undertake the work, that indestructible love of country which contrives to preserve and to encourage even in evil times, what is indispensable in good days; and accordingly the eminent engravers, Duttenhofer of Stuttgart, and Darnstedt of Dresden have been requested to give their assistance in this important work.

The efforts of private persons have thus brought matters so far, that we are able to form a definite idea of this inestimably precious building, and to imagine the wondrous work as based upon the highest ecclesiastico-Christian requirements, conceived with genius and intelligence, and executed in a perfect style of art and workmanship; and now that we are enabled to enjoy the already existing parts with full appreciation, we cannot refrain from putting the bold question as to whether the present is not the favourable moment for thinking of carrying on the actual building.

But upon inquiring into the circumstances more closely, we make the melancholy discovery that the Cathedral, for twenty years past, has been deprived of every means of support, even for keeping the edifice in a state of repair. Owing to its being an imperial foundation, and because the estates for the preservation of the building were cast in one lot with the estates for the benefices, this church, which required most, had the peculiar and singular fate of becoming the poorest of all; for the other churches have retained or received back their property.

The very first thing, therefore, would be to propose establishing an endowment fund for the complete preservation of the building. Yet even its preservation could not be effected if the idea of continuing the building itself is to be wholly abandoned. Ready money alone would not suffice for such an object; art and skilful workmanship would also need to be aroused, and stimulated anew by the perfect knowledge we now possess of the master's intention. Whatever may be done, the subject

viaduct in the Oelz Valley. Goethe mentions him again later when speaking of Darmstadt.

* The Quaglio here referred to is Angelo, the eldest son of Joseph Quaglio. There were a number of artists of the same name.

must be treated grandly, and this can be done only by the difficulties in connection with the work being neither concealed nor ignored.

In any case, however, the Cathedral, even as it stands, is a fixed centre; it and the many other buildings of the town and the country around, form, within a narrow sphere, a complete history of art. And, in fact, a preparation for a history of this kind both literary and artistic, has been made, inasmuch as the above-mentioned lovers of art, are, with as much enthusiasm as care, devoting their time and energy to the Cathedral, and, at the same time, directing their attention to all the different styles of art which preceded and followed its foundation. Hence old sketches and designs have been collected, tracings made, engravings and drawings of the finest so-called Gothic buildings procured from different countries, more particularly of the important old edifices belonging to the district of the whole Lower Rhine, from the Moselle downwards. This will constitute a work which, in a moderate size and in an instructive form, will illustrate the different epochs of the earlier style of architecture in Germany, from the first days of Christianity up to the appearance of the so-called Gothic style, in the thirteenth century.

The time at the traveller's disposal is too short for him to obtain full information respecting all the various objects of interest in the town; still he did not fail to pay a visit to Mr. Hardy, a prebendary of the Cathedral, a remarkable and cheerful old man of eighty years. He had from early youth shown a talent and taste for art, and is a self-educated man; he was celebrated for his skill in making scientific instruments, had occupied himself with glass grinding, and, incited by his love for the fine arts, had also taken to painting in enamel, with which work he had been most successful. His chief interest, however, had been in making embossments in wax, and even in his earliest youth made some of those extremely fine little works in perspective landscapes and histories—architectural subjects—such as have been attempted by various artists, and may, at the present day, be seen and admired in rings. Later he occupied himself with a species of artistic work that is most pleasing; he embossed half-figures in wax, almost round, his subjects being taken from the seasons and other characteristic and favourite themes, from the merry market-girl, with her basket of fruits and vegetables, to the old farmer saying his prayers before a frugal meal, nay, even devote persons on the point of death. These objects, which are placed, under glass, in boxes about a foot high, are made of coloured wax, the colours harmonising with the subjects represented. They deserve to be carefully preserved in a museum in Cologne; for they forcibly remind the visitor that he is in the birthplace of Rubens, the Lower Rhine, where colour has prevailed and added its glory to works of art. The quiet influence of such a man in his sphere, deserves to be very distinctly portrayed, a task which Canon Wallraf would willingly undertake, for, being the younger man, he, no doubt, owes a good deal to this worthy octogenarian.

A pupil of this worthy man's, a Mr. Hagbold, is engaged with similar works, but hitherto has only produced portraits in profile which, it must be admitted, are good likenesses. The neatness and fineness of the work about the dress and ornaments of these portraits deserve high praise, and if, in future, he were to make them quite round, both as seen from the front in full face, as well as from the side, he could not fail to succeed and become known.

There is another miniature painter who must be mentioned here, a Mr. Lützenkirchen, who, together with eminent talent, shows himself a thoughtful artist, and has already on important occasions won the confidence of persons of note.

In speaking thus of the past and the present in respect to what renders Cologne remarkable, venerable and pleasant, we turn naturally to the question as to what might further be desirable to induce intellectual persons to take up their residence here; it will then be found that philosophy, and the culture which springs from the study of the ancient languages, together with what may be called historical culture, would require to be re-awakened and encouraged here anew—I say anew, for even these advantages did exist, and have not altogether vanished yet. One need only examine the successfully arranged inscriptions in a lapidary style, collected principally by Canon Wallraf, also his pleasant and pithy Latin poems, written for special occasions; one need only look somewhat closely at the historical work which the same gentleman and other persons have done in connection with the ecclesiastical events of their native city. It will be found that there is tooth-work enough, which seems only to be waiting for the wheels to be newly set agoing.

And one is forthwith reminded of the important University which had its seat here. Its position was an advantageous one in the centre of the districts lying between the Moselle, the Meuse and the Lippe, and also as a point of communication with neighbouring countries. Up to the time of the French Revolution, such numbers of students—generally of the Catholic persuasion—flocked from the provinces to the University that they formed, as they called it, a *nation* among themselves. The faculty of medicine, owing to the excellence of its teachers, attracted Dutch students to Cologne up to the very end of the last century, and the town still enjoys its old reputation with the countries round about. During the first years of the French dominion, a hope was even entertained that the old University would be awakened to new life, and the idea has not been entirely abandoned of late years, in fact, was encouraged by the attention paid to the Central School, which was subsequently changed into a higher Secondary school. Considerable property had been left to it, collections too, which increased, rendering it necessary to procure a well-appointed museum for physical objects, and a botanical garden was laid out on an entirely new plan. Now if the art-collections could likewise find a home in these buildings, that formerly belonged to the Jesuits, all that was worth preserving would then be gathered together. It is upon this, as well as upon other things, that the Cologne people found their hope of seeing the old University re-established in the town.

Everything we have been called upon to praise about the city seems to favour this hope, as there can no longer be any question that universities thrive in large towns. The Cologne people maintain that in their city, where the richest treasures of the grand days of the past are to be found, where religious and secular buildings, walls and towers, and a number of different collections furnish illustrations of the history of the past, where shipping and commerce represent the life of the present—everything, in fact, must needs be useful and stimulating both to teachers and students, as there is no longer any question of school or party knowledge, but simply of general views of life, and of genuine knowledge.

That universities, established in small towns, could boast of certain advantages they did not wish to deny, but still it would have to be admitted that these universities were founded in times when young men, who had to be drilled out of a system of dull scholastic restraint into one of conscientious business restraint, were allowed an intermediate time, during which, while studying, they could, so to say, have their fling, and acquire a happy remembrance of accomplished follies. Further, that nowadays this was inadmissible, injurious, and even dangerous; for German youths had generally gained experience on the battlefield, had taken part in great deeds, and the rising generation was already inclined to more serious thoughts; that they no longer wished merely for an adventurous hollow kind of freedom, but for a progressive, extensive limitation. Where, it was said, could this be found better than in a town which contained a world within itself, where every species of activity would present itself to the young men in excellent form, and where they would find their recreation, not in the egotism of comradeships, but in higher views of life, and in the numberless forms of activity pursued by industry and art, where, moreover, the students would need only to cross the river in order to spend their holidays profitably amid the richest districts in the way of mines, foundries, and manufactories.

The Cologne people further maintain that the student would nowhere learn to esteem himself better, or be more esteemed, than in their city, inasmuch as he would necessarily be regarded as a fellow-worker in re-animating a great and ancient existence, restored through the course of time and destiny.

BONN.*

After having carefully examined several churches here, and the ancient monument † that has been erected in public, the travellers were entertained in Bonn by a visit to the collection of curiosities belonging to Canon Pick.‡ This genial and highly intellectual man has conscientiously collected anything and everything in the way of antiquities that came in his way, which of itself is a very praiseworthy proceeding. But he is deserving of greater praise still for having arranged this perfect chaos of odds and ends, with seriousness as well as humour, with appreciation and intelligence, and has thus given the things new life, and rendered them useful as well as enjoyable. But unless one has wandered through his house, and seen how these treasures have become part and parcel of it, no idea whatever can be formed as to what the arrangement is like.

On the walls of the staircase we found a number of portraits, very different in value as works of art, yet taken together they illustrate the costumes of a number of different countries and epochs. The walls of the rooms generally in use, are decorated with engravings and paintings, peculiarly significant, and referring to both sad and joyous incidents in the history of our country—as well as to the fortunes and misfortunes of an arrogant adversary. Above the doors is many an inscribed plate that calls up a thoughtful smile. Thereupon the visitor comes to the actual collection, which presents ever-changing interests, and the visitor's attention is continually forced to take an historical turn. Engravings and coins are found arranged according to the different dates and countries,

---

* Goethe remained only a few hours here. He arrived on the evening of the 27th of July and left the following day for Andernach, and reached Coblenz in the evening, having stopped at Neuwied on his way.

† The statute, in the Cathedral, of the Empress Helena who is said to have founded the church.

‡ The sale of this collection is spoken of in Goethe's *Tag- und Jahresheften.*

utensils of every description, all neatly placed side by side.

We remember, for instance, that one whole wall was decorated with what appeared to be painted pictures, and was remarkable, owing to the different materials of which it was composed: mosaics and inlaying, a patch-work of straw and moss, with cut-up wool in between, a kind of woven stuff like velvet, embroidery and bits of cloth sewed together. By placing such things side by side in this manner a hundred different articles are rendered interesting to the eye, to preserve which would have put even an experienced keeper of curiosities into a state of perplexity; as arranged here they provide food for the mind, and also offer occasion for a discussion on matters of taste. We must here observe that a young cousin of Pick's, well up in science, has arranged a beautiful collection of minerals systematically, and that it is always open both to connoisseurs and amateurs.

After a very enjoyable inspection of an endless number of old articles in the way of ornaments and knick-knacks, a more serious interest was then aroused by a sort of imitation chapel, very appropriately arranged. Windows of old coloured glass had been tastefully put in, by which means a subdued light was shed over the small apartment; when a proper amount of light was allowed to fall in, we found objects of every description, rescued from ruined churches, all set up in appropriate positions: carved priedieux and desks, a completely restored altar, upon the latter a reliquary surmounted by a small figure in wrought silver and ornamented with enamel; also crucifixes and candelebra, all of an ancient date, and reminding one, both in form and subject, of the splendid reliquary in the Cologne Cathedral, in which are preserved the bones of the Magi. The walls are not without their decorations of old paintings, and are here amid surroundings such as they have been accustomed to, and, indeed, look as if they had never known any other home.

Upon proceeding to the next chamber, where old prints and manuscripts are preserved, and other important objects are temporarily arranged, one can only regret that the unsettled state of the times has kept this worthy man from making use of his whole house to exhibit all his possessions in a similar manner.

It was with the greatest delight that we then stepped out on to the garden-terrace, where the talent of an ingenious conservator reveals itself in full glory. Here we found, under the free expanse of the heavens, a number of architectural specimens, pillars and pieces of moulding, as well as fragments of decoration, all grouped into ruins, inscriptions neatly let into walls, works in mezzo-relief tastefully distributed about, large terra-cotta vessels set up as monuments—in short, really stirring, patriotic sentiments were found significantly expressed.

A detailed account of this very successful undertaking would furnish pleasant occupation both for the mind and the imagination. One thing only, by way of example, I will mention here: a small and well-preserved bas-relief, representing the evil consequences of drunkenness, was seen under the branch of a vine, which happened at the time to be laden with bunches of grapes.

If Bonn were a royal residence, and this treasure, its museum of art, the court would possess a collection as generally instructive and attractive as could in any way be desired. And if the collection were increased in the same spirit, the owner and conservator would both derive great enjoyment from it himself, and provide it for others.

While spending our time thus with enlightened and liberal-minded persons in every respect, circumstances turned the conversation upon the University that had formerly existed here. As it seemed a very doubtful matter whether the antiquated High School in Cologne would ever be re-established, an attempt had been made to found a new one in Bonn. It was said that the attempt had failed, because the proceedings—more especially in ecclesiastical concerns—had been carried on in too polemical and not at all in a conciliatory spirit. But that the fear and the party spirit that had existed between the different confessions of Faith had meanwhile abated, and that now the only possible and rational union between Catholics and Protestants, was to be accomplished not by dogmatical and philosophical discussions, but historically, by a system of general culture and sound learning. That, further, an important university on the Lower Rhine was much to be desired, as the Catholic clergy, and hence also the greater portion of the community, were wanting in that breadth of culture which embraces a variety of subjects. That the disinclination, nay, the fear of learning, had originated from the fact that the schism in the Christian Church had been occasioned by philosophy and criticism; that the old church had thus become terrified, and that a separation and a stand-still had been the result. It was further said, however, that with changed circumstances and ideas, what had once separated them might now reunite them, and that the problem which appeared very difficult might, perhaps, be most safely solved in the sense intimated above, and by making use of the opportunity that was now presented.

When we hear the inhabitants of Bonn recommending their town as the seat for a university, we cannot well find any objection to the proposition. They praise the limited size of the place, its peacefulness; they assure us of the esteem in which the student would be held here as a necessary and useful fellow-citizen; they describe the freedom which the young man would enjoy in this splendid part of the country, both inland from the Rhine up and down it, as well as on the other side of the river. It was also said that the reasons why the first attempt to establish a university here had failed, were now well known, and if only these errors were avoided, there was an absolute certainty that their object would be successfully accomplished.

These and other conversations on similar topics were held on the terrace of the palace* garden, and it must be admitted that the view from there is truly charming: the Rhine and the Seven Mountains to the left, on our right a district studded with a number of cheerful-looking houses. This view was so greatly enjoyed that we can scarcely refrain from describing it in words.

* Originally the Electoral Palace, erected in 1717-1730, now the extensive buildings of the Bonn University. The terrace spoken of is better known by the name of the *Alte Zoll*, and is an old bastion standing high above, and overlooking the river.

NEUWIED.

Our chief object, however, bids us move stream-upwards, and to remember Neuwied. This pleasant town, which is built on a tract of land encircled by hills, is noteworthy to us here, on account of the antiquities that have been and are still to be found in the neighbourhood. The opportunity which the enemies of Germany lately seized of crossing the Rhine at this point,* had been made use of by the Romans, who took possession of the secure and pleasant situation, and built forts and dwelling-houses there. Vestiges of a simple old fort were found behind Bieber, a village about half-an-hour's distance from Neuwied, and the remains of a bath were also discovered. Tumbled remains of town-houses are to be found at Heddesdorf, many of which have already been brought to light. It is to be wished that the peaceful times we at present have in prospect will lead to further excavations being made.† The carefully-kept museum in the palace of Neuwied would acquire many additions, and we should obtain further knowledge of the manners and customs of Germany's earliest enemies. Several works have been written on the old roads and walls along the Rhine and Maine, and if the subject is pursued further, we shall eventually have a full account of the whole series.

COBLENZ.

Unwillingly we leave these districts, but mindful of the object in view, we hurry on to Coblenz. This place also might become a centre for collections of anti-

---

* This allusion can refer only to Jourdan's crossing the Rhine, which took place on the 2nd of July, 1796, hence some time before. The one previous to this, under the same general, was made in 1795, in connection with a battle against the Austrians. It was somewhere between Coblenz and Andernach that Julius Cæsar in 55 B.C. erected his famous bridge across the Rhine.

† The first discoveries of old remains here, were made in 1791.

quities, and for encouraging the study of art. The splendid situation of the town, its beautiful streets and buildings, and its well-built houses must be a pleasure to the inhabitants, and attractive to strangers. As this town is destined to be the permanent seat of a government, there will never be any dearth of eminent men, through whose interest in the subject many objects will be discovered and collected; thus, to begin with, it might be well that the few but important relics belonging to the Abbey of Laach,* were judiciously and carefully brought here for preservation.

The School of Law † in Coblenz is a new institution, which, one would think, can scarcely prove a success, isolated as it is; on the other hand the estates of the Secondary School would probably be sufficient to establish a higher kind of Gymnasium, as a preparatory school for the University which it is proposed to establish on the Lower Rhine; and certainly all those connected with such institutions would willingly and actively join a society the aim of which would be to encourage the study of art and antiquity.

When looking from the Karthaus at the exquisite situation of the town and its rich surroundings, one is grieved to think of the unrestorable ruins of the fortress of Ehrenbreitstein, which are now about to be repaired in accordance with the ideas of modern military science. On the other hand, we are glad to find that the beautiful and extensive palace, which lies close to the town, has escaped uninjured, at least, outwardly. The question as to how far it can again become a royal residence, does not belong to our subject; here still we cannot but remember the sad fate which has befallen the Lower Rhine, that by some strange chance all the princely residences there have been laid waste, whereas most of those on the Upper

* A Benedictine abbey on a lake of the same name, in the mountainous and volcanic region of the Eifel, founded in 1093 by Count Palatine Henry II., and secularised in 1802, once one of the wealthiest and most famous in Germany.

† The *École de droit* was founded by the French, who, since the year 1794 had almost continually held possession of Coblenz. When the town again came into the hands of Prussia this essentially French institution was abolished.

Rhine have escaped unharmed. What lovely summer residences the highest and the high of the land would find if the palaces of Poppelsdorf, Brühl, Bensberg, Benrath, and others—which are still in tolerably good preservation—were to be put into order; they would, moreover, bring fresh life to the country around.

In fact, the most advantageous results would arise from this, and especially for the objects we have mainly in view here.*

MAINZ.

The inhabitant of Mainz ought never to lose sight of the fact that he lives in a town which for ages past has always been a military post; ancient as well as modern ruins will remind him of this. An industrious investigator makes use of these to extend his knowledge, and as a means of mental culture; and we are much indebted, therefore, to an active, painstaking man, Professor Lehne, for having more accurately indicated the date and nature of some antiquities that were already known, as well as for having collected and arranged others which he has himself discovered. His map, which shows the position of Roman Mainz and its forts—by way of comparing them with Mainz and its fortifications as they now are—gives a complete survey of the past, which, by being almost swallowed up by the present, is wholly withdrawn from sight. The walls of the very ancient military station, the temple and buildings within it, are all set down on the map; outside of the walls we have the positions of the monument to Drusus, the aqueduct, the artificial pond, and the tombs. In this way the traveller quickly comprehends the relation of the various buildings to one another, whereas, otherwise, they would remain a mystery to him.

The lower rooms of the library-buildings contain a

---

* The wish expressed here by Goethe, has in so far been fulfilled as the palace of Brühl near Cologne and Benrath near Düsseldorf have become royal residences; the palace at Poppelsdorf, close to Bonn, which was presented to the University by King Frederick William III., now contains the Natural History collections. Bensberg, nine miles to the west of Cologne, has become a military school.

well-arranged collection of antiquities. Set up in most conspicuous order we have the tombstones of the Roman soldiers who died in the garrison here, men of all possible nationalities. Their name, birthplace, and the number of the legion to which they belonged, is given upon every stone. The stones were found in rows raised against mounds of earth, behind each of them was an urn containing the bones, proving how greatly valued was the individual man in those times.

In the same hall there are monuments of other kinds, which, like some of the peculiar ancient vases and utensils discovered, are being engraved in copper, and furnished with an explanatory text, a work which, it is to be hoped, will soon appear to satisfy the wishes of lovers of art, and form a new point of interest among them.

In addition to the collection of books the building also contains many things of use to science. What had belonged to the university, that formerly existed here,* in the way of scientific apparatus, of minerals and other objects, has been collected and may serve as the foundation of some future educational establishment.

A number of valuable pictures, that were brought here from Paris, have also found a good position for being enjoyed, and will always help in keeping alive the love of art in the town itself and in the surrounding country.

Count Kesselstüdt, a collector of pictures and antiquities, does not lose any opportunity of adding to his important collection. The paintings of Caspar Schneider, a landscape-painter, justly delight all interested in art. An artist and dealer in works of art, called Arbeiter, possesses a number of beautiful things, which may be had of him at a moderate price. In fact there is so much collected in this town, that there is no doubt that Mainz will prove itself both active and useful in its place in the Art-Union of the Rhine.

In conclusion let us be permitted to express a wish which is quite in keeping with the present and future position of Mainz: that the military genius which presides over this place may arrange and establish a military

* The University of Mainz which was founded as early as 1477 was abolished in 1798.

school here, where even in the midst of peace every one with his eyes open is reminded of war! Activity alone will drive away fear and anxiety; and what displays of the science of fortification and besieging have not over and over again been witnessed here! Every trench, every hill would speak instructively to the young soldier, and daily and hourly impress upon him that this is, perhaps, the most important point where German patriotism will have to steel itself to firmest resolves.*

BIBERICH.

After the many ruins, both of ancient and modern times, which the traveller meets with on the Lower Rhine, and which produce a feeling of thoughtfulness, nay, even of sadness, it is most pleasant to come upon a well-preserved palace; and in spite of standing in the most dangerous of neighbourhoods it is in perfect condition, is inhabited by the Duke, and enlivened by a Court, where the visitor may be received in the most liberal manner. The libraries and collections of minerals, which have fallen into disorder during the long years of war, are now to be re-arranged for the use and enjoyment of the inhabitants themselves, and of the strangers who visit the town. Von Nauendorf, one of the Duke's chamberlains, very willingly allows all those interested in the subject to visit his large and well-arranged collection of minerals.

WIESBADEN.

A great deal has been done here in respect to art, and a number of books procured from monasteries, have likewise been arranged in good order. Noteworthy among these is an old manuscript containing the *Visions of Saint Hildegard*.†

---

* This suggestion of Goethe's has also come to pass, for Mainz not only possesses a military academy, but has, in fact, become a most important military centre.

† "The manuscript here mentioned," says Hempel, "seems to be the work printed in Cologne in 1698: Scivias [sciens vias] seu visionum et revelationum libri ties."

All the objects lately added to the institution have been procured mainly with the view of making the government officers acquainted with what is going on in the world of literature and politics. Hence all the different newspapers and periodicals are kept complete, and in capital order. This is done under the superintendence of the librarian, Mr. Hundeshagen, who is already well-known to the public by his efforts in connection with the palace of Frederick I., at Gelnhausen. Unfortunately the whole of the finished edition of this work of his was destroyed by fire during the bombardment of Hanau; still the copper-plates were luckily saved, so we may hope that the present more promising times may lead to this work being completed. The plan of the fortress of Mainz, published by this talented man, is a further testimony of his industry and ability. A number of young persons are continually at work under his supervision, assisting him in his undertakings.

The cabinet of Mr. Cramer,* the inspector of mines, is one of the chief attractions of this place. It contains a complete and systematic arrangement of the minerals of the Westerwald, and also instructive and splendid specimens from the more important mines there. The genial owner of the collection, who possesses both a theoretical and practical knowledge of his subject, and is also esteemed an able writer in his department, devotes every spare hour he has to entertaining and instructing those who are staying in the town for the sake of its waters, or who are merely paying the place a short visit.

Those interested in architecture will find pleasure and a good style in the great Cursaal, as well as in the newly laid-out streets. These undertakings, which have been clearly encouraged in high quarters, and been granted both privileges and contributions, bear testimony to the talent and energy of Mr. Zais, the architect. The large rooms which are being built in the new houses, awaken the hope that many a project, silently cherished, may be carried out here, and that a town which is so much visited, and is daily increasing in size, may be rendered more im-

* This is the same Mr. Cramer who accompanied Goethe on his trip through the Rheingau with Zelter. See pp. 291, 301.

portant still by art collections and scientific institutions. Several persons interested in art, in natural objects, and antiquities, have already started a society which is to interest itself in everything in any way noteworthy, but especially with regard to the country around Wiesbaden. Von Gerning,* who has mainly devoted his attention to the Taunus hills, might possibly be induced to send his valuable collection here to form a foundation; the goodwill of the Duke, and the readiness of many grateful visitors, would be sure to assist in seeing the collection still further increased.

FRANKFORT.

Amid many years of oppression, of war, and of suffering, this city has continued adding to its buildings in the most splendid and cheerful manner. Any one who has not visited the place for some time would be surprised at the change, and the inhabitants themselves daily admire what they have now been acquainted with for long. The plan, which is designed with great freedom and intelligence, offers the finest spaces for further buildings. Let honour, therefore, be done to the memory of Senator Guillett, and moreover in some public and pleasant locality, for it was he who obtained princely support for his plan for these extensive improvements,† and superintended the work up to the time of his death! The love of the fine arts, in its widest sense, has always been kept active here by private individuals, but the time has now come when the free community feels the desire to take its share in the common endeavour to unite separated collections, and to arrange them for the public benefit; this is the result of a happy coincidence of circumstances.

To begin with, we are met by the welcome news

* Gerning's collection of butterflies, the finest in Europe, was subsequently, according to Goethe's wish, transferred from Frankfort to Wiesbaden. See also p. 363.

† Between the years 1806-1812 the old walls and ramparts were pulled down and the site converted into spacious ornamental grounds; the glacis, too, was subsequently covered with gardens, and bounded by a broad, shaded walk.

that the citizens are seriously considering the project of erecting new library-buildings. The somewhat extensive collection of books belonging to the town had to be removed from its old quarters, to make room for the restorations in connection with the Barfüsser Church; and the books have hitherto been kept in different unsuitable localities. It is, however, now decided to make use of one of the remaining large open spaces where there is sufficient room for other public institutions being attached to it in a worthy manner. Mr. Hess, an architect who has been inspired by the teaching and example of his father, and gained experience by travels abroad and by the contemplation of the grand and tasteful buildings that have already been erected here, has been commissioned to draw up a plan for these proposed buildings. Professor Schlosser, the present able and active librarian, would prove himself greatly to deserve of the thanks of his native city, were he to be entrusted with the arrangement and classification of the books, as well as with any systematic addition that would have to be made; for it may surely be said that the building will form the foundation of many other scientific efforts. This important enterprise can already boast of considerable patriotic donations, for, at the festival in celebration of the restoration of the freedom of the city, very large subscriptions were raised.

Thus this building will, perhaps, draw within its precincts an institution which is already flourishing under the name of *The Museum*. A society of men interested in art, collected sufficient funds to rent some beautiful spacious rooms where they met, from time to time, to enjoy artistic works. This centre soon drew many other things of interest around it; a number of paintings and engravings, together with a considerable sum of money, was bequeathed to it by a Mr. Brönner, and again, all the pictures obtained from abolished monasteries were presented to it.

Chiefly for the sake of these pictures it is to be wished that some arrangements could be made to secure sufficiently large rooms for them to be exhibited in an appropriate manner. For, at present, they are standing piled one on the top of the other, and cannot be examined by lovers of art, without putting kind Mr. Schütz to great inconvenience. This collection is more especially noteworthy inasmuch as the majority of the pictures are by artists from South Germany, the Upper Rhine, with which part of the country Frankfort has had more intercourse than with the Lower Rhine and Brabant. Holbein the Elder,* for some years enjoyed the hospitality of the Carmelites, and we have here an opportunity of examining and estimating his talent as an artist. It is to be hoped that this collection may, in a few years, be exhibited in some public edifice for the enjoyment of all interested in art. How rapidly it might be increased by purchases, presentations and bequests! Hence, those who superintend the construction of the new building need not fear being found fault with for erecting large galleries, even though these may appear disproportionately large for the present requirements; for they might, meanwhile, be made use of in some other very profitable manner.

If Germans look around them and consider what has been done in various towns, even in the worst days, in the way of praiseworthy actions deserving of being imitated, they cannot fail to remember the admirable institution which Prague owes to the Bohemian Estates. Count Sternberg,† a noble-minded patron of the fine arts as well as a patriot, offered his important private collection of paintings for public exhibition in that city, and his example was so fully appreciated by others that they joined him, and presented their collections of art for the same purpose. This was done in such a manner that the various objects continued to belong to their owners, the proprietor's name being affixed to each thing, and they retained full liberty to do with them as they pleased. This society further promised to contribute an annual

* The elder Holbein was born in 1460; his most famous picture representing the Virgin and Child is now in the St. Moritz Chapel in Nürnberg.

† Count Caspar von Sternberg, born in 1761, died in 1838, was a distinguished naturalist especially in the domains of geology and botany. His correspondence with Goethe was published in 1866 in Vienna, and begins with the year 1820. They did not, however, become personally acquainted till the summer of 1822 when they met in Marienbad.

donation in support of a school of art; and some excellent pupils, including members of the aristocracy, have been trained there under the inspiring influence of the talented director, Mr. Bergler.* Why may we not hope to have a similar institution in Frankfort, nay, one exactly like it?

There is already some talk of placing an important and independent institution upon a firm foundation. The chief of all true patrons of art residing here, Mr. Städel,† is even in his old age still enjoying, with appreciation and interest, the treasures of art which he has been collecting all his life; they are exhibited in one of the best houses of the town. Several of the rooms are adorned with choice paintings of the different schools; in a number of cabinets are drawings and engravings, the immense quantity of which, as well as their inestimable value, perfectly astonishes those interested in such things, and very frequently does the visitor return to admire them. It is said that this excellent man who, in his quiet way, has his native city ever at heart, has bequeathed the whole of his collections, together with the spacious building and considerable sums of money, to the town, for the benefit of the public; we may therefore naturally hope that both connoisseurs and amateurs in art, will in all coming ages here find certain encouragement and the surest form of culture.

Dr. Grambs, also possesses a collection of paintings, engravings and drawings that surpass all expectation. The proprietor's remarkable knowledge of art greatly facilitates the visitor becoming quickly enlightened, and obtain-

* Joseph Bergler had been director of the Academy of Arts in Prague since 1800. His drawing of *Wallenstein* Goethe speaks of in his *Tag-und Jahresheften* of 1820. He painted a number of altarpieces.

† Johann Friedrich Städel, who died in 1816, bequeathed his collection of pictures, engravings, his house-property and some £100,000 in money to his native city, in order to found a school of art, which is now attended by between 200 and 300 students. It is to the Städel Art Institute that Frankfort owes its high rank in the artistic world. The collections were formerly exhibited in the somewhat confined locality, 35 Neue Mainzer Strasse, but two years ago a new and handsome building, designed by Sommer, was opened for the reception of these treasures on the south side of the river; here they are now exhibited to the best possible advantage.

ing a thorough insight into the subject. This unwearied patron of the fine arts, who interests himself in all the various living artists, employs and encourages several of the rising artists; a Mr. Wendelstädt is assisting him in this, and thus qualifying himself as a teacher, while the historical knowledge he is acquiring will prove useful to him as a conservator.

Mr. Franz Brentano* possesses a well-arranged collection of excellent paintings which adorn a spacious and well-lighted hall as well as several large rooms. This collection was made by his late father-in-law, Von Birkenstock, who resided in Vienna all his life, but was a Rheinlander by birth, and very well known in the world of learning and art. The same gentleman also possesses a valuable collection of engravings and drawings among which may be found copies of the works of Marc Anton, and other early Italians, such as one rarely has an opportunity of seeing.

Whoever has the good fortune to examine the above collections will assuredly find his ideas on the subject both enriched and stimulated, at whatever stage of knowledge he may happen to be.

Von Gerning is the proprietor of a museum filled with various kinds of treasures which, if arranged in more spacious rooms, would rouse the interest and admiration of lovers of art more than they do at present; for in a private residence justice cannot be done to every single object. His collection of ancient vases, bronzes and other antiquities alone, for instance, would attract attention from all quarters, as an integral part of a large collection.

Mr. Becker, a most admirable maker of medallions, possesses an important series of coins from different periods, carefully arranged to illustrate the history of his subject. He is also the owner of some remarkable paintings, well-preserved bronzes, and ancient works of art of various descriptions.

Single, but important paintings are to be found in

---

* Franz Brentano, a merchant and senator in Frankfort, was an elder step-brother of the poet Clemens Brentano and of Bettina's.

this city in the possession of private persons. At Von Holzhausen's,* on the Oede, is a valuable picture by Lukas Cranach: Christ in the midst of a number of mothers and children; it is remarkable, owing to the happily conceived variation in the motives of maternal love and reverence for the prophet. Some carefully preserved portraits from early times, give us an idea of the importance of this family, and of the love of the fine arts which their ancestors clearly possessed.

Some excellent paintings also adorn the residences of Mr. Leerse and Mrs. de Neufville. One of van der Neer's finest pictures is the property of Mr. Ettling. Lausberg's collection has unfortunately been scattered far and wide.

We should here like to suggest a means by which a patron of the fine arts in this city, might render the greatest service to his fellow citizens, as well as to strangers who visit the place, and moreover with a view to the present as well as the future, when things in Frankfort will have formed and arranged themselves better. The people of Venice, for instance, possess a catalogue of all the paintings in their city, arranged according to the various epochs in the history of art, and according to the years in which the artists flourished; they are given in historical order, and in every case it is stated where the picture is to be found. If some young Frankforter, interested in the subject, were to take this work as his model, and quietly to make the necessary preparations, he might in good time come forward with a catalogue, and thus enable people to obtain instructive information as to what the city possesses. Every methodical classification of scattered elements creates a kind of intellectual intercourse, which is, after all, one of the highest aims in life.

We must further not omit to refer to the various ways in which the interests of collectors are attended to here.

* "Holzhausen's collection is mentioned as still existing, in some of the more recent guides (for instance in Richard's *Passagier auf der Reise*, 1846), as also is Leerse's. Ettling's is again mentioned by Goethe in his *Wahrheit und Dichtung*. Of Mrs. de Neufville's and Lausberg's collections, we have not been able to ascertain anything further," says Hempel in his carefully collected notes.

Mr. Morgenstern, even in his old age, continues to restore paintings with remarkable diligence and accuracy. How well he manages to grasp the spirit and style of the different artists, may be seen from several small copies he has made of some of the finest master-pieces which have passed through his hands, and which he has arranged in a little cabinet in the form of a domestic altar. It is to be hoped that the superintendents of public institutions will keep their eye upon this treasure, in order that it may not leave Frankfort.

Mr. Silberberg has in his possession most excellent engravings, of both old and modern works, and is willing to let collectors have them at a fair bargain. At Mr. Boye's all sorts of artistic and natural objects are to be found. The names of many others—like that of him who will one day undertake to write a guide to enable strangers to find their way about Frankfort—must meanwhile remain unmentioned.

In fact, collectors of works of art could not well find a more favourable place than this city; we need only think of the sales of possessions within the district itself, as well as of the many collections that are sent here by way of speculation. The lover of art can here become acquainted with a number of different masters and their special excellencies, nay, if so inclined, can, at times, for a moderate price, make splendid additions to his stock of treasures. Exhibitions of this kind are often held two or three times during the annual fair, and will, in future, certainly be held more frequently, for owing to the tremendous stir in the world, many a work of art has changed hands, and many a collector has found himself obliged to part with precious treasures for ready money. Frankfort may thus be regarded as an intermediate stage between the Upper and Lower Rhine, between north-eastern and south-western Germany, nay, even between Germany as a whole and foreign countries.

If we now inquire about what instruction is given here in art subjects, we find that something is already being done. There has been established one of those schools for drawing, such as have long been justly popular in Germany, where the object in view is more to cultivate the eye of the private gentleman or artisan, and to diffuse a taste for art, than actually to train a number of artists. The head-master is a Mr. Reges, under the directorship of Dr. Grambs. These schools, in addition to the object just mentioned, have this special advantage, that they are means for discovering talent, as the headmaster can very soon find out where natural ability is allied with carefulness and perseverance, by which qualities alone the true artist of the future can be recognised.

But I would as little advise the establishment of a regular school of art here, as in the other places spoken of, for a continued course of the studies. There would need to be a great many trained artists, a number of aspiring talents, before one could decide to give them a regular form, or even a head. We are quite aware of the esteem due to the different academies of art in the various capitals, directed by eminent men, and surrounded by an abundance of art-treasures; yet even there, a republican form creeps in, before one is aware of it. Thus in Dresden one can detect the pupils of Seidelmann, of Grassi, of Matthäi, Kügelgen, and of Hartmann, as well as those who have studied under Zingg, Klengel, or Friedrich. A general course of instruction is extremely valuable; each separate youth, on the other hand, likes to be taught by some special master, and if he follows merely the one, he will be powerfully influenced by his confidence in his teacher, and a certain quiet conviction of his own.

But if eminent men are not exactly to be invited to Frankfort, it should be made convenient for them to reside here; they might be placed in a position that enabled them to rent suitable apartments, and other advantages also might be granted to them. The directors of the art institutions in the town might entrust them with the education of the most promising pupils, and pay them a fair reward in return. Nay, the young man might choose his own teacher, according to the style of art he meant to study, or according to the liking and confidence he felt towards any special artist. Wealthy parents would pay for the instruction given to their children, and benevolent patrons of art for such of their protégés whom they thought promising. If an artist of this sort were a married man, or otherwise not disinclined to make an addition to his income, he might take young men into his house, and have a regular establishment of his own, and those trained to the profession might lend him their assistance as subordinate teachers. As there would be scope for several men acting thus in this free city, it might lead to splendid results.

That young men should be trained in a practical manner is demanded by modern times. With a master, such as we have spoken of, they would learn to draw, to paint, to copy, and to restore pictures; and those with inferior talent would not, as frequently happens where too much is expected in a regular course of instruction, fall into a state of vexation and despair. If very eminent talent were discovered in some special case, there would be time enough to send the student to some higher school elsewhere.

That those whose duty it is to superintend such matters, would likewise see that these masters were adequately provided with everything that they might not themselves be able to procure in the ways of models and lay figures, need scarcely be mentioned. There is already a collection of casts of ancient statuary in the garden of Von Bethmann,* and what may not be expected of a man whose love and interest in such things is kept in lively activity by great wealth!

Proposals of this kind we may all the more readily suggest, as they are in accordance with the spirit of the age, and in all educational establishments, experience teaches us that it is much more advantageous to carry these on in a liberal, humanising manner, than to keep them within narrow limits, in a constrained, monastic fashion. Let the Frankfort citizen look back upon the history of those times, when a number of artists flourished one besides the other, and shortly one after the other, without their having been subjected to any academical restraint, where the family circle took the place of school

* Bethmann's Museum now contains Dannecker's famous piece of sculpture, Ariadne on the Panther; it was nearly finished at the time Goethe is speaking of, but was not exhibited there till some time afterwards.

and academy. Let him but recall the times of Feyerabend, Merian, Roos and Schütz,* and he will find the path indicated by which the artist of this free city can best attain his full development and intention.

We are now called upon to mention some other excellent artists. Mr. Schütz, known by the cognomen of *Der Vetter* (the cousin), works at that style of landscape-painting which, since the days of Sachtleben, has uninterruptedly taken the Rhine as its subject. His drawings in sepia are remarkable for their purity and careful work; the clearness of the water and of the sky are inimitable. The way he has depicted both banks of the river, the meadows, the rocks, and the stream itself, is as faithful as it is pleasing; the feeling one experiences when travelling on the Rhine seems to be communicated or re-awakened when looking at his pictures. In his oil-paintings this artist has very successfully made use of the opportunity of depicting the changes of tone in the colouring that are produced by the time of day and year, no less than by atmospheric influences.

In Grambs's house there are some most valuable watercolours by Mr. Radl, describing scenes around Frankfort, and some of the delightful valleys of the Taunus hills; these, while being true to Nature, leave nothing to be desired either in the way of choice of subject, artistic distribution of light and shade, or of colouring.

It would be also the pleasant duty of the head of the art department to make the public at home, as well as abroad, acquainted with such artists as these. Allow us here to make a suggestion, which even though it may appear somewhat strange, undoubtedly deserves a trial. We have made no secret of the fact that anything in the way of endowment we do not at all approve of in connection with the art schools. On the contrary, our proposal would be this: a clever artist, who has no actual orders for pictures, or who cannot afford to work on chance, should

---

* All these were distinguished citizens of Frankfort. The first mentioned family were famous in connection with the book trade and the art of wood engraving in the sixteenth century. The Schützs here mentioned were a family all distinguished as painters; with one member of the family Goethe became intimately acquainted in Rome in 1788.

receive orders from the head of the art department for carefully executed pictures, be offered a fair remuneration for them, and these pictures might then be sold to collectors for a smaller sum. The loss which this would entail would be a greater act of benevolence towards the artist than by merely granting him a pension without conditions. If he possesses real merit, and in this way becomes more generally known, orders for pictures will accumulate, and he could then, with a little forethought, fix his own price for them. A sufficiently large fund might fix a certain sum for this purpose, and those who had the management of it might quite well avoid any reproaches of favouritism by getting up public exhibitions and lotteries for works of this kind, or even by holding auctions. In this way men of acknowledged honesty and intelligence would bring renewed animation and life into the period to which we are at present looking forward.

But as we are favouring republican forms by such new arrangements, let us here add that it would, on the other hand, very well become a free citizen, not readily inclined to be controlled by any one, to develope social virtues in himself; for experience, from the earliest times up to our own day, teaches us that the native of a free city does not readily unite with his equals. Nothing is more natural than that independence should strengthen our confidence in our own nature, and as certainly, in the course of years, must a man's character become more and more abrupt; now when each individual allows himself to act thus independently, the consequence will be that persons who might have been united by the most admirable of bonds, are often found living entirely apart. Even mutual interests are no longer able to bring such minds together, even for a moment; lovers of flowers will quarrel over flowers, collectors of coins over coins—if their minds have been accustomed unconditionally to give way to their personal feelings and passions.

How pleasant it is, therefore, to learn that here in Frankfort there exists a society of men interested in matters of art, who meet in turn at each other's houses, where they hold instructive discussions about the engravings each has in his possession. By this means a very extensive and difficult branch of art, where everything depends upon the value of the individual print, will by degrees have been attentively examined. A far greater advantage, however, is derived from the fact that what is possessed by others become thus, as it were, our own mental property. To become acquainted with and to love excellent things which we do not ourselves possess, and can never hope to possess, is in reality the chief virtue of civilised man, for the object of the ruder and more selfish man is often merely to seek the possession of an article, to acquire a surrogate for the appreciation and love in which he himself is wanting. If meetings of this kind are held in the various branches of art, the rising generation will become united by a common and cheerful bond of peace, in the same way as in times of trouble the one half of the community nobly unite for defence and attack, while the other half meets to give counsel and assistance for the benefit of their native land.

Having now spoken of the highest motives which urge us to encourage art and science, and of the purely moral and intellectual means which deserve to be made use of for the purpose, we must also refer to a prejudice which is at times met with. The collector of works of art often keeps too strictly aloof from the dealer in works of art. This way of acting dates from those early times, when the wealthy man very highly prized what he himself possessed, simply because he possessed it, and, in fact, very often greatly over-estimated its value. In the present and more active intercourse in the world, a collector cannot avoid exchanging or parting with many a thing to a third person who happens to be interested in it—it may be a thing which the collector no longer values, or in which his interest has become lessened. In Frankfort, especially, where there is such a constant in-and-out-pouring of works of art, one can hardly imagine the existence of a stationary collection, and in future days certainly no lover of art will be found fault with for having—as far as his means would admit—endeavoured to keep alive his interest in art by changing his possessions.

We do not require to look far to find instances that

industrial pursuits can in our day, as of old, very well be united with a love for science and art; in the book-trade, pleasant prospects for art are already evident. Mr. Brönner has arranged a number of finely-bound books in a convenient, well-kept and prettily decorated room, and besides these, he has, of course, the latest engravings, and even paintings, for the inspection of visitors, some also for sale. Mr. Wenner, when in Rome, took an active interest in the German artists residing there, gave some commissions to Messrs. Riepenhausen, Overbeck, and Cornelius, and undertook the publication of the latter's etchings of scenes from *Faust*. They have been most faithfully and carefully engraved by Ferdinand Ruscheweyh, as lovers of art may see for themselves by examining the specimen-prints. Mr. Wenner has also introduced to his native city excellent engravings after Canova and Thorwaldsen, inasmuch as he has facilitated the means for exhibiting and procuring them. Mr. Wilmans also, a man interested in art, possesses some valuable paintings; his efforts in the domain of literature and art are universally known. It is to be wished that a more detailed account, than can be given by a traveller, might be made of all the art-collections and the various endeavours to encourage art—which shed a glory over this free and re-awakening city—and that this account might soon be published by one or other of the existing firms; and the sooner this is done the better!

Having expressed this wish, both with regard to Frankfort as well as to the other towns previously spoken of, we must request those who may undertake the work, not to do this in too heavy a style, but rather to present their information in the form of a brightly-written pamphlet, which a visitor to the town would be glad to purchase for some small sum; further, to make merely a small edition of the work so that the following one may be enlarged, and rendered more vivid still. For everything that is to exercise its influence upon the day must have a fresh appearance, and what is asked for here is not a work for preserving, but one for perusing.

That an active spirit is at work among the other arts also, is evident from an academy for singing which has been started by Mr. Düring of his own accord, and from a pure love of the art. This institution has already so far proved successful that young persons of both sexes, who have studied under Mr. Düring, have upon various festive occasions given performances of music in the churches of both persuasions, to the enjoyment and edification of the congregations. This they have done also at public concerts. Every Sunday morning a rehearsal is held to which, upon notice being given, visitors are admitted. A larger building might be granted to this institution, which would at once derive great advantages from the additional space. The idea commends itself to all lovers of music, and there is no fear of its lacking support, or of its failing to cultivate the individual voices, for Frankfort possesses in Mr. Schmidt an able musical conductor, and the opera can boast of several talented persons who not only charm people by their vocal skill, but who regard it as their duty to make their art more generally appreciated, and to extend its influence by giving instruction in the theory of music.

Having now expressed many a sincere wish, and spoken of a number of important projects and far-reaching plans, we have finally to mention an institution which is established upon the securest foundation, and, at the present moment, is showing signs of renewed activity by doing away with hindrances that formerly existed, and by setting aside obstacles that had arisen accidentally. We refer to the endowment which Dr. Senckenberg,[*] of revered memory, a physician and man of extensive knowledge, has bequeathed to his native city. The institution is divided into two parts, the one being devoted to practical, the other to theoretical work. The first, the town hospital, is established in a palatial building built for the purpose by the founder, and possesses considerable capital. From the very outset large donations and bequests have been presented to it, and it has thus gradually acquired great wealth which increases year by year, owing to its surplus funds.

[*] The Senckenberg Society, founded in 1763 by the distinguished physician of this name, is still one of the chief interests in Frankfort. In 1868 a new building was erected for the library belonging to the several learned departments in common; a botanic garden, an anatomical museum, and a hospital.

All the more interest and good-will therefore we feel towards the other part of the institution, which, from being devoted to theoretico-scientific purposes, does not enjoy the same patronage. It embraces the house, courtyard and garden of the former residence of the proprietor. The house, in which one of the attendants resides, contains, it is true, rooms of but moderate size which would not afford sufficient space for what they are expected to contain, unless the things were arranged in the best possible order. There is also an excellent library, which extends up to the time of the immediate successors of Haller; it contains the most important ancient anatomical and physiological works, and would, if well-arranged, enlarged, and thrown open to the public, enable the town-library to dispense with an important department in science.

A cabinet of minerals, which had up till now been merely an appendix to the library, is being arranged and classified; it contains a great number of excellent specimens, but only groups of things, without any internal connection. The fossils, collected during fortunate times, surpass all expectation.

The botanic garden is spacious enough for containing the specific plants required by the institution, and together with these there might, with careful management, be added plants important to the physiological branch of the science, and crowns our whole knowledge of vegetable life.

The old chemical laboratory is no longer of any use, owing to the advance which science has made. A new laboratory, however, built for some other school, stands directly by the side of Senckenberg's garden-wall; and is at present isolated and unused.

The anatomical museum is both convenient and spacious; the preparations exhibited there do not all belong to the institution.

After thus briefly mentioning the different parts of the institution, it is now our duty to examine its present condition, and at the same to express our wishes and hopes in connection with it. In the first instance we must, above all things, keep in view the intention of the founder who, as a scientific and enlightened man, imagined that he could not better provide for the wants of his hospital, than by placing by its side an institution for study and instruction. His object was to present the medical men of his native city with a centre where they could meet for scientific discussions. He invited some members of the profession, together with others of his fellow-citizens, to become its guardians, called upon them to meet once a month at his house, and encouraged the plan of lectures being delivered in various branches of science.

His early and unfortunate death interrupted a beginning of this kind, which he was himself about to make. Still the institution could boast of an active and truly flourishing period of existence during the time when Reichard, the author of the *Frankfurter Flora*, was head-physician. However, there was no increase in the funds destined for the support of this department, and for this reason, that in a mercantile city people are more inclined to be interested in practical work than in scientific pursuits, and, in fact, feel themselves more called upon to get rid of present evils than to prepare for coming ones. Accordingly the hospital alone received donations and bequests, and the scientific department was neglected.

It fell more and more into oblivion, and suffered from troubles both internal and external. A medical school, which was intended to throw new life into the subject, was started and then failed. The burdens of war were and are still being borne with the other evils that follow in its wake; in short, the institution is, at present, so poor that it cannot undertake the smallest thing at its own expense. It has even had to depend upon the generosity of outsiders, for the purchase of cabinets to contain the collection of minerals.

But even in this case we find cause for re-awakening hope. Dr. Lehr, the head-physician, who died recently, and to whom Frankfort owes the inoculation of cow-pox, has incorporated his library with that of Senckenberg's, and bequeathed to it a collection of portraits of celebrated medical men, together with 9,000 gulden, the interest of which is to be added to the salary of the head-physician, on condition that he delivers lectures on botany during the summer months, without expecting fees.

Dr. Neuburg, the principal medical officer attached to this institution, who is well-known for his knowledge, activity and generosity, and who is at present busily at work arranging the Natural History collections, proposes, as soon as he has examined the objects and the gaps that require filling up, to hand over the duplicates of his conchyliae and birds to the institution. And the library and museum also, when once they have been exhibited in good order to the patriotic citizens of Frankfort, cannot fail to draw many single possessions to it, and arouse many benevolent actions.

As regards the study of botany, it is evident, from what has been already said, that it is receiving sufficient attention meanwhile. Dr. Neeff, with the assistance of the horticulturists Bäumert and Isermann, may be trusted to complete the laying-out of the garden in an appropriate manner, and having it in readiness by next spring.

Still, a great deal would be accomplished for botany in Frankfort, if those interested in the subject were to associate, to visit and to communicate with one another, and moreover associate in such a manner that every one undertook to direct his attention to some special branch of the subject. The Dutch and English have set us the best possible example in this respect; the former, by the formation of a society, the members of which have undertaken the task of bringing ornamental flowers to the highest state of perfection; the latter, by a number of horticulturists having determined to devote their attention to special plants—to gooseberries for instance—in doing which each cultivates only one species with the greatest possible care. If this should appear trivial or even ludicrous to many, from their scientific heights, it must be remembered that a wealthy man, interested in such things, likes to possess plants both rare and striking to the eye, and that the fruit-gardener has, in like manner, to apply his knowledge to the requirements of the table of the rich. With such a society Frankfort would, at once, occupy an important position in the field of botany.

If the Senckenberg garden is to be devoted entirely to medical and physiological requirements, the lecturer at the institution would be greatly assisted, were he to be allowed the privilege of taking his students to the gardens of such gentlemen as Messrs. Salzwedel, Jassoy and Löhr, in and around Frankfort, or to the grounds belonging to Mr. Metzler, beyond Oberrad. This would give pleasure and encouragement both to proprietors and visitors. In an enterprising city, all those in any way interested in the same objects ought to endeavour to make each other's acquaintance; and hence botanists, florists, cultivators of fruit, and market gardeners, ought not to keep aloof from one another, for they might mutually instruct and be of service to one another.

As regards chemistry much might be done here in the simplest manner, for there is no want either of an appropriate building, or of persons willing and able to promote its interests. The laboratory that has been built close to the Senckenberg Institution is a new one, and adapted to every requirement; it has been standing untenanted and unused ever since the medical school ceased to exist, and the general wish must necessarily be that it should be incorporated with the Senckenberg Institution. A decree from the high quarters cannot now be long deferred, as times have become peaceful again. Dr. Kestner is anxiously awaiting this decision, and we may venture to hope that every support will be given him in return for his exertions in the matter. It is certain that with a regular course of lectures in chemistry many of the more enlightened citizens will find one of their chief wishes fulfilled. An opportunity for becoming acquainted with the whole domain of modern chemistry, which embraces the greater part of physical science, ought to be granted to every large town, and to Frankfort in particular. Here the physician in practice would conveniently hear of the latest discoveries and opinions. The pharmaceutist would have an opportunity of learning more about the nature of the various preparations and mixtures, which he has for long made merely according to prescription.

Again, others who have made their wealth in important manufactures, would be greatly interested in hearing of the latest discoveries; others, also, who are striving after higher culture, would be benefited by a knowledge of chemistry; even those unwilling to give up their faith in chemico-mystic ideas, would here find satisfaction in perceiving that many things which our forefathers in olden days knew of only piece-meal, or vaguely suspected as a whole, now, from day to day, prove themselves connected with and in one another, even explaining one another. Perhaps in no other branch can scientific inquiry show more clearly the ideal in reality, than in the domain of chemistry.

If it were possible to invite some able physicist to work hand in hand with the lecturer on chemistry, and to bring forward what is contained and suggested in many of the branches of physics, to which the chemist lays no claim—and if further he were enabled to procure the instruments necessary for illustrating the phenomena without going in for any very extensive apparatus, both costly and requiring a great deal of space, Frankfort would be attending to important and secretly-felt wants; this would at the same time save a lamentable loss of time and energy which might be directed to nobler objects. A fitting locality for such scientific work might be found in the anatomical museum. In place now of dwelling upon the fact that Dr. Behrends—a worthy disciple of Sömmering's, and head of this department— has sent in his resignation, and that Dr. Lucia, an active and able comparative anatomist, is about to leave for Marburg, let us make some general remarks about the relation in which anatomy stands to the Senckenberg Institution as it is at present. The founder, when conceiving a picture of a complete medical institution, perhaps made somewhat of a mistake by not having paid attention to the special conditions in which his undertaking was placed. Those acquainted with the science of anatomy—professors at our different universities—will be the first to acknowledge that anatomy is one of the most difficult sciences to teach. A library, diagrams, preparations, and a hundred appliances that take up a great deal of time, are required as the foundation; but in addition to this a human corpse is required as the subject of examination and instruction. And yet where is this body to be obtained? Everywhere the existing legal restrictions are being less strictly observed, or entirely disregarded, and the professor of anatomy, in a humane age, is invariably regarded as acting inhumanly towards sufferers and mourners.

Let all that has been said above be regarded merely as the reflections of a traveller hurrying on his way. The man of business who remains on the spot may see the circumstances in a different light.

And yet all that we have said would be altogether fruitless did we not venture to maintain that such a well-planned institution, one that does honour both to its founder and to the city itself, cannot succeed or prove in the smallest degree useful, notwithstanding the efforts of those in connection with it, unless the state of its funds be improved. The possibility of doing this does not lie very far off, and we have no hesitation in asking both the professional and non-professional members of the committee to consider in how far it might be practicable to employ a portion of the surplus funds of the hospital to the scientific institution; and, further, we must urgently request these excellent gentlemen—when they are agreed upon this point—to obtain consent from head-quarters as soon as possible. We are aware of the difficulties that may arise from such conditions, but they might be settled with one word: a free city ought to show a free spirit; and with a renewed existence * and in order to efface the terrible evils of the past, it has, above all things, to free itself from old prejudices. It is incumbent upon Frankfort to shine on every side, and to be active on every side. It is true, that theoretical work and scientific instruction belong to universities, but they do not belong to these exclusively. Intellect is welcome everywhere.

* On the dissolution of the German Empire, Frankfort, together with Aschaffenburg, Hanau, Fulda and Wetzlar, was made over as a grand-duchy to Carl von Dalberg, but in 1814 again became one of the four free cities of the German confederation, which privilege it continued to enjoy till the year 1866.

Consider what has been the influence of the universities in Berlin, Breslau and Leipzig, upon the practical life of the citizens, and it will further be found that the chemist and physicist is in his very element in London and Paris, the busiest and most enterprising of cities. And Frankfort has undoubtedly the right, from its circumstances, its position and its power, to compete with other cities in carrying out such praiseworthy objects.

Supplementary Remarks on Frankfort upon Maine.

The Senckenberg endowment is a very important institution; its scientific department is under the superintendence of Dr. Neuburg, a man of unwearied energy, and as ready to sacrifice himself to its interests as to fight in its cause. As several desirable objects have been effected during the course of the year by his exertions, and the active support of the other gentlemen connected with it, the governing body of the hospital will, in the end, be unable to refuse its assistance to the scientific department. The spirit to perceive the necessity of this, to recognise the great usefulness of the institution, and also to see that the original purpose of the founder is finally accomplished, must already be active in the minds of the Frankfort public, or shortly show signs of activity.

Senckenberg left a collection of minerals and fossil shell-fish; the minerals were the less important part, and were arranged in the disordered confusion of the earlier system of mineralogy. For more than forty years this collection lay covered with dust, without any attention being paid to it, and it was not till this year that a few mineralogists—among whom Dr. Buch deserves to be specially mentioned—undertook to arrange it according to the systems of Werner and Leonhard, with the full intention, moreover, of enriching it with a number of specimens it did not possess, and of thus making it complete.

It is to be regretted that the active zeal of these gentlemen has found but little encouragement, and that, in spite of their having devoted a good deal of time to it, and even been at some personal expense in connection with the work—they are only very gradually accomplishing their object. The undertaking, moreover, only a short time ago, very nearly fell through altogether, owing to a proposal made by some of the governing body which fortunately, however, was rejected. The proposal was that in order somewhat to assist this part of the institution, the building itself had better be let out on lease! The existing trouble would have benefited as much by this as an incurable disease may be said to be benefited by death.

The anatomical museum has obtained considerable advantages through the unwearied exertions of Dr. Cretzschmar, who is lecturing there. He is also endeavouring, by his own industry as well as that of his students, to replace some of the preparations which the institution has lost of late years. Several successful preparations of injected blood-vessels and skeletons of birds and other objects in comparative anatomy—among which are some very abnormal parts of the *Testudo mydas*—serve as convincing proofs of this.

The botanic garden also has received various additions. A not inconsiderable number of plants were obtained for the hot-houses, not purchased out of the endowment fund; a number of wild flowers from the country around Frankfort, which had been declined by the Wetteraner Flora, were given in the garden. Owing to the limited extent of the botanic garden, a rule has been made to cultivate mainly medicinal or economical plants, or such as are rarely to be found in the neighbourhood, for there is not space enough to introduce any great variety of plants. Mr. Stein, the chemist, and a very well-informed man in other respects, has made several excursions in the neighbourhood, and presented the garden with several rare plants found on these occasions. The green-house was presented with various rare exotic plants, such as the *Laurus Camphora, Epidendron Vanilla,* etc. There has not been sufficient time yet, during the past rainy summer, to put the hitherto neglected garden into complete order, still a part of it has been systematically arranged under the superintendence of the very able botanist Mr. Becker of Offenbach, who joined in the work from a pure love for science.

The whole garden will, no doubt, be in perfect order by next summer.

The library has acquired a considerable number of the best old medical works, but could not procure any of the newer ones on account of the limited funds at its disposal. It is pretty complete up to the period in which Senckenberg died, as he possessed the books and left them to the institution. Other works were obtained subsequently, it is true, and Dr. Lehr increased the collection by bequeathing his stock of books to it; but of late years many gaps in medical literature have remained unfilled.

The chemical laboratory, which was built under the Prince Primate in behalf of the special medical school, but again became the property of the town, and also the adjoining bit of garden on the site of the old wall, have been handed over to the scientific department as a gift by the Senate, at the request of the governing body. It is much to be wished that Senckenberg's will might be fulfilled in this point also, for he knew how to estimate the importance of chemistry, and wished to know the study pursued in some appointed branch of his institution; this is all the more to be desired as this science in our day has overtaken and outstripped almost every other one.

The signs of dilapidation in the greenhouse, and the great age of the other buildings, the want of many indispensable objects, both of a scientific and other kind, may well be said to offer a melancholy prognosis, from the luke-warm manner in which everything that concerns the institution is treated, and which stands in glaring contrast to the earnest wishes of the lamented founder. It is greatly to be wished that contributions from some of our wealthier citizens, even though it were in small sums, might avert the impending ruin of so useful an institution.

A great deal has hitherto been done for the hospital, the funds of which are kept distinct from those of the scientific department. During last year again a considerable sum was laid by as a balance after all expenses had been paid. Praiseworthy as may be the generosity of the Frankforters towards their hospital, still it is melancholy to perceive how little appreciation there is among them for the science and art of medicine, which the founder so much wished to encourage, and the study of which is so beneficial in its results. They would unquestionably be acting more in accordance with the spirit of the founder if but a small portion of the annually increasing funds of the hospital were devoted to the sister-institution, at all events, if this institution were not so hardly dealt with in doubtful cases, as not unfrequently occur. It should be remembered that the greatest loss to both institutions would be the omission of doing good, and that no accumulated capital, however important it may seem to him who has been in the habit of amassing it from youth upwards, is in the smallest degree able to take the place of the actual achievement of good. The sacrifices which the one part of the endowment rendered to the other at the time of its first establishment, should alone be sufficient to induce the administrators to support this part of the endowment; the loss of the institution would deprive the Frankfort physicians—who like ordinary workmen are paid merely for every case they attend, and who have neither distinction nor encouragement of any kind to expect in return for the danger and difficulties in connection with their professional life—of every assistance of progressing with the age.

Mr. Städel, a patron of art, like few others, has just died in his eighty-ninth year. In his will he bequeaths his house, his collections, and his personal property, which is valued under 13,000 gulden, to founding an institution for the fine arts. Dr. Grambs, a collector of ability and likewise a patron of art, is appointed executor of this last will.

OFFENBACH.

In this well-built and cheerful-looking town, which is steadily increasing in size, the collection of stuffed birds belonging to Privy-Councillor Meyer is deserving of every attention. This praiseworthy man, as the inhabitant of a favourable district, is both a good sportsman and a naturalist, and has arranged a complete series of inland birds. He employs several artists for making drawings of these creatures, and has in this manner encouraged the study of a very necessary branch of art connected with Natural History—that of making accurate copies of organic objects; among these the many different forms of birds and the varying formation of the several parts of their body, and their light, delicate, and variously-coloured plumage, demands great nicety of discernment in the artist, and his utmost care. A work of Mr. Meyer's has long since given his country a proof of the services he has rendered to science, and he has this year again earned the thanks of naturalists by the publication of his *Account of the Birds of Livonia and Esthonia*. The artists he employs in his own house and elsewhere, are chiefly Messrs. Gabler and Hergenröder. The latter's sister is celebrated as a painter of flowers. Miss Stricker of Frankfort, who likewise shows great talent in this direction, has not as much time to devote to the work as could be wished.

HANAU.

Of late years this town has acquired a favourable and well-tested reputation in connection with Natural History. By a strange but lucky coincidence several zealous investigators in the different branches of this splendid science found themselves residents of the town. Dr. Gärtner, the worthy veteran among botanists in Germany, has long since won his reputation by his participation in the *Wetterauische Flora*. Leisler's able studies embraced the whole domain of zoology, but he devoted himself chiefly to birds and mammals. Dr. Kopp promoted the interests of chemistry and physics with the best success, although his attention was mainly directed to mineralogy. Schaumberg, who enjoys a high reputation, more especially as an artistic naturalist, and whose collection is undoubtedly the most important private cabinet in Germany, offers an abundance of excellent specimens. Privy-Councillor Leonhard, and Mertz the clergyman, now dead, have also proved themselves active workers in the field of mineralogy. The public are already acquainted with the large tabular work published by the two latter in conjunction with Dr. Kopp. Leonhard, who is continually engaged with his periodical, has also published a topographical mineralogy, and we may shortly expect from him, in conjunction with Dr. Kopp and Gärtner junior—a very intelligent chemist and physicist —an introduction to mineralogy, accompanied by a number of engravings both in colour and black. These propædeutics for the Natural History of the inorganic kingdom, which are the fruit of many years' laborious study, and fill a very important gap in our literature, may be looked forward to with a feeling of perfect confidence.

These men considered it a good thing to direct the endeavours of individual persons to *one* object, in order, by their mutual efforts, to bring matters more further forward. Hence, even amidst the stormy days of ruthless dissension among the nations in 1808, it was proposed to establish a society to promote the interests of natural science. The small number of the members gave both character and an appearance of reality to the enterprise. Very soon other eminent men joined them from neighbouring as well as from distant parts, and this literary society gradually extended beyond the boundaries of the province, to every part of scientific Europe. Suitable premises, granted by the government, afforded an opportunity for starting a museum. This useful institution was presented with gifts from all quarters. Still its funds remained very limited, till Karl von Dalberg,* who was interested in its success, granted it, in 1811, a considerable annuity out of his own purse, and this the society continued to enjoy for several years. The epidemic which followed the retreat of the French, robbed the society of many of its most valued members. There is a pleasant hope that the present government, like that of past days, will consider the institution worthy of its attention, and continue to grant the use of the building, and by this means give a founda-

* Primate of the Rhenish Confederation, previously Archbishop of Mainz.

tion and continued support to a very deserving institution, which would otherwise inevitably cease to exist.

It may readily be imagined that, as there are so many industrious naturalists in Hanau, there must likewise be various important collections to be found in the town.

The museum of the Wetterau Society embraces all the different branches of science, and has hitherto been continually receiving additions; for most of its members had, in accordance with the wise directions of the regulations, endeavoured to justify the election which enabled them to enjoy the honourable distinction of being members of the society. However, the examination of this museum excites less interest as a whole, than the private collections possessed by several of the scientific men of the town. In the latter we find the character of the individual man more vividly expressed, and perceive the industry and care with which such things are created, which indeed is not often accomplished, except at the cost of a whole life-time.

Among the zoological cabinets, the most important is that of the late Dr. Leisler, and the Schaumberg collection. The latter, however, since its owner removed to Kassel, can no longer be said to belong here; Leisler's collection also will not much longer remain in Hanau as his heirs have determined to sell it.

In order, in some way to celebrate the memory of this excellent man, the following remarks may be added. He occupied himself in his earlier years with entomology, but subsequently devoted himself heart and soul to the study of mammals, birds and fishes; yet ornithology remained longest the subject of his inquiries. Merely to show, in passing, what services he has rendered to the study of the birds of his country, we must mention that his endeavour was to become acquainted with, and to give an accurate account of, the different colours of birds. Now most water birds moult twice in the year, thus the same bird is clothed in different colours in spring and in autumn, in youth and in old age. He has collected, with untiring zeal, every single species of the most different colours and stages of transition. And as he was a sportsman, and intimately acquainted with the art of stuffing animals, his collection possesses great advantages in several

2 c

respects, and, with the exception of Meyer's, no other collection in Germany at all events, can be compared with it.

Of late year he had been engaged with the study of bats, but as he possessed an excellent memory he never wrote down anything, and thus his studies would all have been lost to us, had not one of the last of his pupils made some of these so entirely his own, that he is now writing a monograph on these strange creatures, which is shortly to be published.

The fishes are all admirably stuffed and of unusual size. The series of the fresh-water fish of Germany is almost complete, and there are a number of specimens from the sea, of great beauty. The collection of insects is of considerable extent. Out of 1,600 specimens, butterflies form the larger half.

In conclusion be it remarked that Leisler, before he devoted himself to medicine, had studied law with much success, and that he was well spoken of as a philosophical writer after the publication of a system of natural laws.

Dr. Gärtner, the industrious and eminent botanist, to whom many in the profession owe their training, has rendered no small service to science by his gift of a number of carefully-dried specimens of plants. After the publication of the *Wetterauische Flora* mentioned above, he devoted himself without interruption, and with unwearied industry, to the study of the vegetation of his native country. He discovered a number of phanerogamous plants and more than 200 *cryptogamiæ*, an account of which from his masterly hand, is certainly much to be wished. His herbarium, which is most extensive as regards the *cryptogamiæ*, is arranged in the neatest possible manner. Of late Gärtner has also turned his attention with the utmost diligence to the zoology of his country. His collections of mammals, birds and shells, are a proof of this. But although he has numerous specimens of shells from other countries, some of which are very rare, he, nevertheless, considers his collection of those from the province of Hanau much more valuable, for this branch of natural science was first cultivated by him in the *Wetterau*. He distributed the objects he obtained from the surrounding country, among his friends, and in this way aroused an interest in a study which appeared to be almost wholly neglected in Germany. In earlier years, Gärtner also occupied himself with chemistry, physics and mineralogy, and thus deserves the name of naturalist in its very widest sense. He has also rendered most active service in collecting and arranging the Wetterau collection, and also in editing the reports published by this scientific society. It is to be regretted that age, and also his health which has suffered from his unwearied exertions, will at present not permit him to engage in any very active work.

The mineral cabinet belonging to Privy-Councillor Leonhard, with its over 7,000 specimens, is divided into two parts, a oryctognostic and a geognostic section. The oryctognostic section is arranged in accordance with the method of classification adopted in the systematico-tabular survey and characteristics of mineral bodies; still the changes that have become necessary from the advance of the science, have not been disregarded. Very pleasant is the methodical way in which all the objects are arranged and exhibited. In the case of each one of these specimens care has been taken to show its characteristic points, and attention has, moreover, been paid to the freshness of the specimens; regularity of form also has been attended to with a very pleasant result. But in addition to this the collection is remarkable on account of its high degree of completeness. Scarcely any of the latest discoveries are wanting, and the series it possesses of a variety of different species, renders it both important and instructive for the study of the relative occurrence of fossils—a consideration hitherto much neglected, and only now again demanding attention.

Privy-Councillor Leonhard has deserved the thanks of the public for having founded a mineralogico-mercantile institute. It is an establishment that advances the cause of science, inasmuch as it offers the means for obtaining fossils from various districts and countries, either in exchange for others or at a moderate price, and either singly or in a systematic series. Full confidence ought to be placed in this undertaking as it is not done with any view to making money, but wholly from a love of science.

Among the educational establishments for the encouragement of art, the School for Drawing deserves to be honourably mentioned. *Hofrath* Westermayr, who is at the head of this establishment—which receives only a trifling support from the State—has rendered the school very important services. Since his return from Weimar, the taste for art has been considerably awakened, and we observe, with pleasure, that many of the wealthier inhabitants are beginning to form small collections of pictures. The number of pupils attending the school is at present between 200 and 300. The institution possesses funds—the fruits of the labours of the teachers—which might be very usefully employed for procuring paintings and other objects of art.

The wife of *Hofrath* Westermayr also works actively for the good of the school. In addition to this lady-artist, the names of Tischbein, Carteret, Berneaud, Franz Nickel and Deiker, deserve to be mentioned among the artists of the town. We must, however, not omit Krafft, a man of genial disposition, and also the profound student Bury, both of whom are an honour to their native city, and even when thought of at a distance.

Painting in enamel is executed chiefly by Carteret and Berneaud, and both may justly claim the title of artists. Besides these two, Franz Nickel, a native of Hanau, has greatly distinguished himself in this branch of painting; he resided in Madrid for many years, and there occupied the position of assistant teacher at the Academy.

Among the collections of paintings here, that belonging to Mr. W. Leisler, a merchant and younger brother of the naturalist, deserves to be specially mentioned.

The jewellery manufactories of the town are peculiarly remarkable. They have existed since the year 1670, and may be said to have been the nursery of similar establishments in many of the capitals of Germany and of Europe generally, all of which, however, have failed to equal their original. Hanau workmen enjoy a very favourable reputation, and are in request everywhere. The present most famous firms—the Brothers Toussaint, Souchai, as well as Collin, Bury, Müller and Junger—not only uphold the reputation of their works, but strive continually to bring their productions to a greater degree of perfection. It may truly be said that Hanau produces work that cannot be manufactured either in Paris or London, and not unfrequently even surpasses that produced by industrious Geneva. We must further mention the extensive size of the ateliers of the above workers-in-gold, where the raw material is exhibited through all the different stages up to the finished articles, and of these there is the greatest possible variety.

The carpet manufactories of Messrs. J. D. Leisler and Co. deserve special attention, from the fact that the material known by the name of *drawn Wilton-carpeting* is manufactured here in the greatest perfection. And there is not only an extensive selection of tasteful designs in the most beautiful and brightest colours, but any special pattern that may be wanted can be produced. This manufactory also produces unclipped and pile carpets of a velvet species, Venetian and Scotch carpets, etc. The treaty which formerly existed between Holland and France was very unfavourable for the sale of these goods, and during that time it was almost solely the German Courts that sent in orders for the manufactured articles.

The manufacture of silk tapestries in Hanau also deserves mention, for in early times this town provided most of the German Courts with the most tasteful *ameublements*. During the stormy period of the last ten years, the Brothers Blachierre have, however, thought it advisable to produce only such fabrics as are used by all classes of society. Hence, the woollen and silk goods of Hanau are now produced less with a view to artistic taste, than for general usefulness, and these have been a great benefit to the public, and are largely exported. The hope is now entertained that, with the re-opened free traffic by sea, this manufacturing town will recover some of its former prosperity.

ASCHAFFENBURG.

In this town also are to be found early German paintings from abolished monasteries, by Grünewald and others, perhaps even some of Dürer's; also some few but valuable objects of art. Were but some of the almost too numerous treasures in the capital brought here, and exhibited for the enjoyment and instruction of the public, this finely-situated town would then at all events receive some compensation for what it lost by the removal of the Court!* Many persons visiting the place would moreover be induced to remain here for a time.

Now that the treasures which Paris had accumulated, are again finding their way out into the world, and are being distributed over Europe, arousing an interest and proving their usefulness, it would be a grand undertaking for the principal governments in Germany—from a pure feeling of conviction and earnest will—to do that which as a vanquished nation it had unwillingly to agree to; in other words, to see that things of which the royal residencies possess a superfluity should be distributed among the provincial towns. It is well for small States to keep their moderately large collections together, but large States cannot do better than to distribute their wealth of art-treasures over the whole country. This will not only help in producing artists, but encourage collectors of artistic objects, and the more frequently the latter are met with, the greater will be the attention paid to artists themselves.

Unwillingly we break our journey here, but we must not allow ourselves to be tempted too far eastwards by the wealth there. We must now return to where the Maine draws closer to the Rhine.

DARMSTADT.

The Grand Duke's museum here will probably always be considered the principal institution of the kind in the province, and its admirable arrangements may very justly serve as a guide to all similar undertakings. Spacious

* Up to the year 1806 Aschaffenburg had been the capital of a principality of the same name; it then became a part of the grand duchy of Frankfort, but in 1814 was handed over to Bavaria in exchange for districts on the river Inn, in Salzburg, and in Tyrol, which the latter had delivered up to Austria.

halls contain the utmost variety of objects arranged without ostentation but with order, dignity and neatness, so that, while being instructed we are conscious of a feeling of admiration together with our enjoyment.

The excellent casts of splendid statuary, no doubt, deserve to be mentioned first; then there are numerous busts, parts of the body, and bas-reliefs, all placed in good positions, favourable both as regards effect as well as for examining the works. Facsimiles in cork of all the more important Roman monuments, nay, of all the Italian and some of the earlier German monuments as well, afford the architect an opportunity of making very important comparisons.

Several rooms are occupied by a large collection of paintings, where every lover of art, according to his interest in the subject, can either quietly enjoy the pictures themselves, or obtain historical information concerning the earlier and more modern masters.

When now about to make the vain endeavour to furnish some account of the other treasures, we cannot refrain from expressing the wish that a catalogue—even though it were one of a most general kind—might soon be forthcoming for the benefit of travellers. For how otherwise can the visitor expect to find his way about among the endless treasures, in spite of their admirable arrangement. It is not saying too much to maintain that the visitor will here find masterpieces of art and curiosities, from every century and every country, handed down to us as worthy our attention and interest. Vases and urns of every description, goblets and trinkets, bronzes from every century, among which are costly candelabra and brass lamps for a number of wicks; reliquaries from the earliest Byzantine times, of bronze and enamel, and ivory ones from a later date; ecclesiastical appurtenances of every description; inestimably precious drawings by the first masters; Chinese and Japanese articles both from earlier and more modern times; articles in glass, valuable either on account of their material, form, or fine cutting. We should have to continue in this brief manner, to give the reader merely some general idea of this model collection, and yet should not be able to enumerate all the various things.

There are, for instance, a great number of early German church paintings which, if restored and renovated, would serve admirably for decorating an imitation chapel.

But what strikes the visitor almost more than the treasures themselves, is the activity and energy observable in connection with the institution as one that is continually being further developed. Every department shows this same activity; everywhere one finds something new being added; everywhere some arrangement is being improved upon, so that every year the visitor is struck by the creative and industrious spirit at work. Even though, when speaking of the Cologne collection, we could not but regret the removal of Von Hüpsch's* treasures to the Darmstadt Museum; still, when seen here we cannot but rejoice over the happy fate that awaited its chaotic condition; for it has here become more fully developed, carefully arranged and incorporated with an already thriving and well-ordered world.

A Natural History collection, as rich as it is complete, exists by the side of this Art collection. In a number of well-lighted galleries are exhibited the products of the three kingdoms of Nature, and these are under the superintendence of energetic men, who see that they are kept in order for the benefit of visitors; at the same time the arrangement of the objects is continually undergoing some improvement for the sake of those already acquainted or anxious to examine the objects. Even though we can speak here merely in a general way, we must not omit to mention a collection which is devoted to comparative anatomy, and where are arranged and exhibited, those remarkable fossils—remains of gigantic animals from primeval times—frequently found in the broad valleys of the Rhine. Very affecting it was, to the writer, to find here a number of specimens that had been collected with enthusiastic interest by Merck,* the friend of his youth, since dead; these specimens were rescued from oblivion and given

* Herr von Hüpsch's collection spoken of in the article on Cologne formed the nucleus of this museum.
† Johann Heinrich Merck was born in Darmstadt in 1741, and committed suicide in 1791. He is very frequently mentioned by Goethe in his *Wahrheit und Dichtung*, Books 12–19.

a home here, owing to the Duke's affection for Merck, and great care was bestowed upon them by the naturalists who succeeded him.

We here found fulfilled a wish previously expressed, that drawings of very rare natural objects, such as one may never have an opportunity of seeing, should be exhibited in the form of illustrations by the side of the other objects actually possessed. Thus the enormous antlers dug up in Ireland, we here found represented on paper (by way of trial), and exhibited to the amazement of all beholders. We trust that the project now entertained, of depicting these and other similar objects on the spaces above the cabinets, may very soon be carried out.

A most extensive library, appropriately and neatly arranged, next attracts the traveller's admiration, and excites the wish that he had more time to devote to its treasures. And, moreover, if he had come here an utter stranger, and perfectly unacquainted with the existing circumstances, his attention would at once turn to the spirit which gave life to and kept in life, such a large institution. He could not for a moment remain in ignorance of the fact that the Prince must have a great and decided love for such things, and that he has bestowed his full confidence in some able man whom he allowed to work and to act without hindrance and according to plans of his own; from this it again follows that the Director must have under him only such men who work with him in the same spirit, at the same pace, without pausing yet without hurry, and towards one end. Then only can such admirable arrangements, as we find here, not appear marvellous; but still, where separation, disorder, and caprice are so often met with here on earth, it is likely, nevertheless, to appear marvellous. Delightful, therefore, it must be to every one to find that his Royal Highness the Grand Duke has, throughout so many years and amid the most unfavourable circumstances, remained true to his interest in these things, further that Privy-Councillor Schleiermacher continues to enjoy the Prince's confidence in so high a degree, that his two sons, under his direction, superintend the Art collection and the Library, and have even turned the physical apparatus to use by giving courses of lectures; and again that Fehr has the management of the mineralogical and geological departments, including the collection of *conchifera*, while Bekker devotes his attention to the rest of the animal kingdom. When we find, upon looking over the many galleries, that they all seem living parts of one great whole, and when further we observe that, during the course of the year, every department has systematically been increased, we cannot but entertain the wish that every conservator would examine this collection from an artistic, antiquarian, and scientific point of view, but also, and more particularly from its ethical side—and take it as his model.

That there is no dearth of industrious artists in the town, is what may be expected from such favourable conditions. Moller has every opportunity for exercising his talent as an architect in a city which is daily increasing in size; where private residences are continually being erected, and projects for public buildings are always being entertained. He has likewise, for several years past, been engaged in copying ancient German buildings, and the Boisserées' work on Cologne Cathedral will furnish unequivocal testimony with regard to his industry, accuracy, as well as artistic taste. The newly-discovered original sketch of Cologne Cathedral is in his hands, and a facsimile of it is to be published by him in the Boisserées' work. The study of German architecture will be indebted to Moller for some of its finest contributions, for he is at present engaged on the ancient buildings of his own district—in Mainz, Oppenheim, Worms, Spires, Frankfort, etc.—and is having these engraved on copper.

Mr. Primavesi, who is celebrated for his etchings of landscapes, is also busily at work. He has undertaken the arduous task of sketching all the districts along the shores of the Rhine, from its two sources downwards. The work is to be published in two parts, accompanied with a short account of the different places. In this way all the remarkable points on the borders of Germany's chief river will also be brought into artistic connection.

HEIDELBERG.

This town, which is remarkable in very many respects, engages the visitor's attention at once in more than one way. The object which we are at present pursuing, however, leads us first of all to that collection of old paintings which was brought here from the Lower Rhine, and has for some years past been regarded as a special attraction of the place, nay, of the whole surrounding country.

I have just paid a second visit to the Boisserées' collection, which I have not seen for a year, and have more fully been considering both its significance and the object it has in view; but although I am not in any way disinclined to offer a few words to the public about it, I find myself face to face with all the difficulties I anticipated. For as the chief advantage of plastic art consists in its representations not being expressible in words, although some intimation of them may no doubt be given, a man of any penetration knows that in such a case he would be undertaking an impossibility unless he set some limit and goal to his task. He will at once perceive that the best and most profitable course to pursue will be to follow an historical method, and he will determine to pay due regard to the well-arranged and well-stocked collection by endeavouring not merely to give an account of the pictures themselves, but of their relation to one another; he will guard against making comparisons to things that exist elsewhere, although of course he will have to show the connection between the different epochs in art, that come under discussion here, with remote attempts in art separated from it both by time and place. And hence he will see that full justice is done to the precious works now engaging our attention, and have them treated in such a manner that an able historian will gladly assign them their position in the large sphere of the world of art in general.

By way of an introduction to this, and in order that the peculiar character of the collection may be more distinctly understood, it is above all things necessary to speak of how it originated. The brothers Boisserée, who in conjunction with Bertram, are its proprietors at present, and allow all lovers of art to share their enjoyment of it, were in the first instance brought up with the idea of becoming merchants, and their studies had been directed to this object, both at home and abroad, in the chief mercantile cities. Meanwhile, however, on every occasion that presented itself, they endeavoured to satisfy their inclination for higher culture as well; and some good opportunities presented themselves, for a number of eminent German scholars had been called to hold appointments in the new School established in Cologne. By this means they acquired a degree of culture that was rarely met with in that part of the country. They had from youth upwards, it is true, been surrounded by old and modern works of art, and must have been born with and trained to find pleasure and interest in them; still it was in reality an accident that aroused in them the wish to possess such things, and gave rise to one of the most praiseworthy of enterprises.

The reader may remember the story of the youth who found a thole-pin on the sea-shore, and who was so pleased with the thing that he procured an oar for it, then a boat, and finally masts and sails; whereupon he took short trips along the coast, and finally struck boldly out to sea, continued to invest in ships of larger size, and eventually became a rich and prosperous man. Like him, the two brothers of whom we are speaking, one day purchased, for a very trifling sum, a church painting which they happened to find exposed for sale at a fair, and this purchase was soon followed by others. By possessing the pictures, and having them restored, they gradually acquired a knowledge of the paintings, and thus what had originally been a mere fancy, became a passion which only increased with their knowledge of the subject and the actual possession of good and excellent works. It was no sacrifice to them to lay out a large part of their wealth, and to devote the whole of their time, to accomplish the object they had in view, whether this had to be done by expensive journeys, new purchases, or any other undertaking.

It became their wish at the same time to rescue the

early German architectural works from oblivion, to give illustrations of the better ones in all their purity, and thus to form some opinion regarding the deterioration of this style of architecture. One endeavour succeeded another, and the brothers are now in a position to publish a work unusually magnificent for Germany, containing some 200 illustrations, which, as regards rarity, fidelity, successful preservation and restoration, but more especially as regards their purely historical sequence, could hardly be equalled.

But now, in order to make ourselves as intelligible as possible, it will be necessary to turn back to early times—in the same way as any one about to work out a genealogical tree has to force his way back as far as possible from the branches towards the root. But in so doing, we shall always assume that the reader has this collection either actually present before him or in mind, also that he is acquainted with the works of art about to be discussed, and that with an unbiassed mind he has the sincere wish to join us in obtaining instruction.

* * * * *

Military and political troubles had brought the Roman empire into such a state of anarchy and degradation, that good institutions of every kind, and artistic ingenuity in particular, disappeared from the face of the earth. Art, which a few centuries previously, had occupied so high a position, was completely lost sight of amid the fierce military proceedings. The most obvious proof of this is furnished by the coins belonging to these degenerate times, when the many good and bad emperors considered it no dishonour to be represented upon the worst copper pence as perfect caricatures, and gave their soldiers some beggarly pittance in place of honourable pay.

It is to the Christian Church that we are indebted for the preservation of art, even though it be like a spark among a heap of ashes. For although the new doctrine, with its more inward, meek moral tendencies, had to reject that form of art which expressed mere outward strongly sensuous ideas, and to set aside, if not to destroy, works of that class, still in the historical element of this religion there lay more varied, more infinite seeds than in any other, and it was but natural that it sprung up of itself, without either the intention, or the interference of the new religionists.

The new religion acknowledged a supreme God, not as majestically conceived as Jupiter, but more human; for He is the Father of a mysterious Son, who was to represent the moral qualities of the Deity on earth. These two are accompanied by a fluttering, innocent dove, as a shaped and subdued flame, forming a wonderful triplet, around which again are assembled a host of blessed spirits in numberless gradations. The mother of this Son could be honoured as the purest of women, for even in heathen antiquity the state of virginity and maternity had been conceived unitable. By her side is an old man, and a misalliance is sanctioned in heaven in order that the new-born God may not want an earthly father both for the sake of appearances and to attend to his needs.

What power of attraction this Divine-human Being exercised during His growth to manhood, and at last, in His full activity, is evident from the number and variety of His disciples and adherents of both sexes who, although differing in age and character, have gathered around Him; also from the Apostles who sprung up from among the multitude, the Evangelists, the many believers from every rank and profession, and the many martyrs who have suffered in His cause, from Stephen upwards.

Now when it is found that this new covenant is founded upon an earlier one, the traditions of which extend back to the creation of the world, and which are more historical than dogmatic; and further, when it is considered that the first parents, the patriarchs and judges, the prophets, kings and restorers—every one of whom are in some way distinguished or distinguishable—it is both intelligible and natural that art and religion should unite, and that the one should appear unable to exist without the other.

Hence, while Hellenic art began with generalities, and long afterwards lost itself in specialities, Christian art had the advantage of being able to start with an immense number of individualities, and of gradually rising to generalities. In looking back at the mass of historical and mythical personages mentioned above, and bearing in mind that every one of them is famous for some important and characteristic action, and that, further, the new covenant, in order to justify its existence, was endeavouring to find itself symbolically in the earlier one, and referred in a thousand different ways to historical and earthly as well as heavenly and spiritual relations—it would indeed seem as if we ought to possess some memorials in plastic art of the first centuries of the Christian Church.

However, the world as a whole was in too distracted and oppressed a condition for this; the ever-increasing state of disorder drove culture from the West, and Byzantium alone remained a stronghold for the Church, and for that form of art connected with it.

But, unfortunately, even the Orient in those times presented a melancholy appearance, and, from an artistic point of view, the above-mentioned personages cannot be said to have flourished immediately, although they did prevent the old mummified style of art losing all its significance. Some distinction was always made between the figures; but to render this distinction more obvious, the different names were inscribed on or below the pictures, in order that, in the ever-increasing number of saints and martyrs, one was not honoured in place of another, but that each—as was but fair—should receive his due. Thus it became an ecclesiastical affair to get pictures manufactured; and this was done according to prescribed rules under the superintendence of the clergy, and the pictures were then, amid consecrations and miracles, dedicated to the established form of divine service. It is in this manner, even in our own day, that the sacred pictures, which members of the Greek Church worship at home or on their travels, are manufactured in Susdal and its neighbourhood, under the superintendence of the clergy; consequently there has arisen, and must be, a great uniformity among them.

But to return to Byzantium and to the period mentioned above; it will be found that religion itself assumed an absolutely diplomatico-pedantic character, while its festivals took the form of Court and State pageants.

It is to this limitation and obstinacy of their system that we have to ascribe the circumstance, that even the iconoclasts did no injury to the condition of art, for after the victory of the leading party, the restored pictures had to be precisely like the old ones, if they were again to receive due honour.

How the most melancholy of all phenomena crept in · that of painting the Virgin brown (the consequence probably of Egyptian, Ethiopian, or Abyssinian influences), and that the face of the Saviour on the cloth held by St. Veronica, should likewise be made the colour of a Moor—will perhaps be more definitely pointed out when a careful examination is made of the history of art in those countries. All this, however, indicates a state of continual deterioration, the complete cessation of which took place even later than might have been expected.

We must now endeavour to make clear what the Byzantine School—of which we have but little to say in the way of praise — *did* possess of great intrinsic merit, artistically transmitted to it as a grand inheritance from its earlier Greek and Roman ancestors, but which had been preserved by it as if transmitted by guilds.

When above we not unjustly termed its style mummified, it must be remembered that when the inside of a body has been removed, the shape of the frame asserts its right by means of the dried and hardened muscles. And so it is here, as a further examination will show.

The highest aim of plastic art is to adorn some definite place, or to contribute an ornament to some indefinite place; it is this requirement that gives rise to everything which we term artistic composition. In this the Greeks, and after them the Romans, were master-spirits.

Everything, therefore, that is to please as a decoration, must be articulated, and moreover in that higher sense where the different parts will stand in correlation to one another. To effect this it becomes necessary for the work to have a centre, a top and bottom, and two sides, these being the first elements of symmetry; and if these be perfectly intelligible to the understanding, the work may be called a decoration of the lowest form. The more numerous its parts become and the more that the original symmetry becomes interwoven with these parts, concealed or alternating in contrasts, or presented to the eye as manifest secrets—the more pleasing the decoration will be; and it becomes perfect when it no longer occurs to us to think of the first elements, but strikes us as something spontaneous and accidental.

Now the Byzantine School has always adhered to strict, dry symmetry, and although its pictures have thereby become stiff and unpleasant, there are cases where a certain gracefulness has been produced by a change in the position of the figures standing beside one another. This excellence, together with the great variety of subjects offered by the traditions of the Old and New Testaments, was spread over the whole of the converted world, by artists and workmen from the East.

What took place in Italy thereupon is well known. Practical talent had entirely disappeared, and everything that required culture was dependent upon the Greeks. The gates of the temple of St. Paul beyond the walls, were cast in Constantinople in the eleventh century, and the different fields decorated in a hideous fashion with engraved figures. It was at this time that Greek schools for painting were established in Italy; Constantinople sent architects and workers in mosaics, and they decorated the devastated West with a melancholy style of art. When, however, in the thirteenth century the feeling for the truth and the loveliness of Nature awoke again, the Italians turned immediately to what had been esteemed an excellence in the Byzantines: symmetrical composition and definiteness of character. They succeeded in this the more readily, as their appreciation of form quickly showed itself. It was not likely to have been lost to them altogether. Magnificent buildings from antiquity had been before their eyes for centuries. The remaining portions of those that had fallen to ruins or been destroyed, were now at once turned to some ecclesiastical or other public use. The most splendid statues escaped destruction, and the two collossi likewise were never destroyed. And every ruin even had its shape. A Roman, in particular, could not set his foot on the ground without touching something in the way of form, could not dig in his garden or in his

2 D

field without bringing to light the most exquisite pieces of workmanship. What happened in Siena, Florence, and elsewhere, must not detain us here, the less so as every lover of art can obtain the most detailed information about this, as well as about all the other subjects discussed here, in D'Agincourt's extremely valuable work.

The fact that the Venetians, as inhabitants of coasts and low-lying countries, soon became conscious of an appreciation for colour, is an important fact for us here; for we shall make use of this as a means of passing over to the Netherland School where we meet with the same characteristic.

Thus we are now approaching the object we specially have in view, the Lower Rhine; and for its sake we have not hesitated to make the long digression.

In a few words let us recall the circumstance, that the districts along this glorious river were invaded by the Romans, that the invaders erected fortresses there, settled on its banks, and powerfully influenced the culture of the country around. And when we find that even their principal colony there bears the name of the wife of Germanicus,* there can be no doubt that some great enterprises in art had been made there in those days. For artists of various kinds—architects, sculptors, potters and coiners—were, of course, a necessary part of such undertakings as is proved by the numerous remains that have and are still being dug up.

How far the mother of Constantine the Great, the wife of Otto, may have influenced it subsequently, remains for historians to decide. Our object here renders it more necessary to turn to the legend, to discover some universally applicable idea in or behind it.

Ursula, a British princess, and Gereon, an African prince, it is said, came to Cologne from Rome; the former

* The first settlement, where Cologne now stands, was made by the Ubii at the suggestion of the Roman general Marcus Vipsanius Agrippa in 37 B.C., and received the name of Urbs Ubiorum. Its subsequent name Colonia Agrippina, it obtained, not as Goethe here supposes from Agrippina, the wife of Germanicus, but from his daughter of the same name, afterwards wife of the Emperor Claudius, who was born in the town of the Ubii and in the year 50 A.D. sent a Roman colony to the place.

with a host of noble maidens, the latter surrounded with a body of heroes. Quick-witted men, who have seen through the haze of the tradition, have commented on the legend somewhat as follows:—When two parties spring up in a kingdom and keep irrevocably apart from one another, the weaker party will move away from the centre and endeavour to get nearer the borders. There, there will be more room for factions, tyranny will not immediately reach so far. There, a prefect or governor may, at all events, make a strong position for himself with the aid of the discontented party, either by tolerating their sentiments and opinions, or by joining in these himself.—This idea has a great charm for me, for we have experienced similar, nay, exactly the same state of things, in our own day, and has even occurred more than once.—A host of the noblest and bravest Christian emigrants set out one after the other for the famous and beautifully situated colony of Agrippina, where, after being warmly welcomed and protected, they enjoyed a happy and pious time in the loveliest of districts; but finally had miserably to submit to the violence of a contending party. If we examine the kind of martyrdom they had to endure, and how Ursula and her companions submitted to it, we do not find a mere repetition of those absurd stories of how delicate, innocent and highly cultured persons were butchered and murdered in brutal Rome, by hangmen and savage animals for the amusement of a mad crowd from the lower and higher ranks; no, in Cologne we see a bloody massacre of the one party by the other, who wishes speedily to be rid of it. The murder of the noble maidens resembles the massacre of St. Bartholomew's Eve, a September day. Gereon seems to have fallen with his followers in a similar way.

If the Theban legion,* too, was cut to pieces on the

* A mythical legend, so called from the legion having been raised in Upper Egypt, and leads us back to the days of Diocletian (313). The legion was intended to make war against the Bagaudae, a people on the Rhone; the soldiers, however, being Christians, refused to join in the heathen rites expected from the army. Maximilian thereupon, at the command of Diocletian, caused the whole legion of 10,000 men to be cut to pieces. According to the legend the whole legion with

Upper Rhine at the same time, we shall find it an epoch where the ruling party is not exactly endeavouring to oppress a growing party, but endeavouring to destroy one that has reached its own height.

All that has hitherto been said—although given with the utmost brevity and in a very general way—is most necessary in order to obtain some idea of the Netherland School of art. The Byzantine School of painting, in all its ramifications, had for many years prevailed over the whole of Western Europe and likewise on the Rhine, and employed trained journeymen and youths belonging to the district to execute works for churches; hence there are many specimens of that dry style of art, exactly like the melancholy productions of the Byzantine School itself, to be found in Cologne and its neighbourhood. Yet nowhere, perhaps, in the history of art does the national character, the climatic influence, play so beautiful a part as in the Rhine countries; for which reason we shall devote special care to the development of this point, and beg the reader's kind attention to our further remarks.

We shall pass over the important epoch when Charles the Great established a series of royal residences along the left bank of the Rhine, from Mainz to Aix-la-Chapelle, because the culture which resulted from this, had no effect whatever upon the art of painting, which is mainly the subject of discussion here. The gloomy rigidness of the Oriental School did not show any signs of brightening up, even in the Rhine countries, till the thirteenth century. Then, however, all at once, we find a joyous appreciation of Nature forcing its way through, and moreover not exactly in the form of merely copying individual existing things, but as a pleasant feasting of the eye, as it looked around the sensuous world. Faces of boys and girls as round as apples, oval heads of men and women, prosperous-looking old men with flowing or curly beards; the whole generation good, pious and cheerful, and all depicted with a delicate, nay, a soft brush, although

---

their leader suffered death without making any resistance. Their relics are preserved at St. Maurice, south of the lake of Geneva, and partly at Turin.

characteristic enough still. It is the same with regard to the colours; these also are cheerful, clear, nay, even powerful, not actually harmonious but still not gaudy, and always pleasing and agreeable to the eye.

The material and technical characteristics of the pictures here discussed, are the gold background, the nimbus round the head bearing the name of the saint. The brilliant metallic back-ground also frequently shows the stereotyped kind of flower, in tapestry fashion, or is made to look like gold carving by means of brown outlines and shadings. That these pictures may be ascribed to the thirteenth century is proved by the age of the churches and chapels, where they were found hung up in accordance with the purpose for which they were originally painted. The strongest proof, however, is that the cloisters and other spaces in various churches and monasteries—where the same characteristics are to be met with—were painted at the time when those buildings were erected.

Among the pictures in the Boisserées' collection, the one of Saint Veronica* may justly be mentioned first, inasmuch as in several respects it serves as evidence of what we have just said. At some future time, perhaps, it may be discovered that this picture, as regards composition and drawing, is a sacred one in the usual Byzantine style. The blackish-brown face—darkened subsequently very likely —with the crown of thorns, has a wonderful expression, both noble and sorrowful. The corners of the cloth are held by the saint, who is scarcely a third of life-size. She is standing behind it, and is covered by it up to her breast; most graceful are both attitude and gesture. The bottom of the cloth touches the floor of which there is some indication, and in the corners of the picture, on either side, are seated three little angels singing; if standing, they would at most be a foot in height; they are so beautifully and artistically arranged in two groups that the highest demands of composition are perfectly satisfied. The whole conception of the picture points to a traditional style of art, well thought out and carefully executed; what abstraction it must have required to place the figures

* The well-known picture by *Meister* Wilhelm, now in the Pinakothek in Munich.

there introduced in three different dimensions, and everywhere to symbolise the whole! The little figures of the angels, more especially the action of the head and hands, is so beautiful, that no further remark need be made about this. Now, although we claim the right to give this picture a Byzantine origin, still the grace and softness with which the figure of the saint and the children are delineated, oblige us to assume that it belongs to the Lower Rhenish period described above. The painting exercises an incredible charm upon the spectator, because of its combining the double element of severity of conception and gracefulness of execution; and this is in no small measure increased by the contrast between the fearful Medusa-like head, the graceful virgin, and the pretty children.

Similar reflections are suggested by other large panels, upon which are depicted, in half life-size, apostles and patriarchs with the same soft, pleasant brush, and in the same cheerful, agreeable colouring between gold battlements and other architectural ornamentations resembling coloured carving. But these, at the same time, point to new considerations. For, towards the end of the so-called Middle Ages, plastic art in Germany had far outstripped painting; it was more indispensable to architecture, more in keeping with mere sensuousness, and more within the reach of artistic talent. The painter, when wishing to avoid what is more or less mannerism, and about to contemplate existing objects for himself, has two paths to choose between: the imitation of Nature itself, or the imitation of already existing works of art. Therefore, we shall in no way be detracting from the merits of the Netherland artists of this epoch, by raising the question whether the holy men who are depicted with such exquisite delicacy and softness, rich and yet freely draped, are not copies of carved figures, either coloured nor uncoloured, which stood between real architectural gold carvings of a similar description. We consider ourselves specially justified in forming this supposition, from the skulls lying at the feet of these saints and painted in the decorated squares; from these we draw the conclusion that the pictures are copies from some reliquary, with its ornamentations and figures. Such a picture becomes all the more pleasant, inasmuch as it will possess a certain earnestness—which plastic art always has in advance of painting—and will shine through it in a kindly style of treatment. Everything that we have here maintained may, at some future day, be more fully confirmed when the remains of the early Christian Church, now so widely scattered, come to be examined with unbiased attention.

It will be found that even at the commencement of the thirteenth century Wolfram von Eschenbach, in his *Parcival*, speaks of the painters of Cologne and Maestricht almost proverbially as being the best in Germany, therefore no one can be surprised at our having said so much in praise of the old paintings of these districts. We shall now, however, have to turn our whole attention to a new epoch that began with the fifteenth century, in order to note its main characteristics. But before proceeding to the discussion of the new style of treatment which was then adopted, we must once more mention the subjects which were specially offered to the painters of the Lower Rhine.

We have already observed that the chief saints of this district were noble maidens and youths, and that the manner of their deaths presented nothing of those objectionable incidents that were so inconvenient to art when the deaths of other martyrs had to be described. But the highest piece of good fortune, which the artists of the Lower Rhine enjoyed, was that they possessed the bones of the three Magi, which had been brought to Cologne from Milan. It would be in vain to search through history, traditions, or legends, for a subject more favourable, suggestive, pleasing. or graceful, than was offered by this. Beneath crumbling walls, and beneath a miserable roof, a new-born infant, yet with a look of consciousness about him, is being nursed on his mother's lap, and watched by an old man. Before him are kneeling the noble and great of the earth, offering reverence to childhood, treasures to poverty, crowns to humility. A numerous suite stand amazed at the strange end to a long and perilous journey. It is to this exquisite subject that the artists of the Lower Rhine owe their good fortune, and it is not to be wondered at that, for centuries, they were never weary of repeating the same subject. We now, however, come to the important step which Rhenish art made between the end of the fourteenth and the beginning of the fifteenth century. Artists had long since found themselves obliged to examine the variety which Nature presented, owing to the number of different characters they were called upon to depict; but hitherto they had been satisfied with obtaining a mere general impression, even though every now and again something in the manner of portraits is met with in them. At the time of which we are now speaking, we find express mention made of *Meister* Wilhelm, who was said to be unsurpassed in copying the human face. Of his peculiar style we have the most remarkable evidence in the *Dombild* in the Cologne Cathedral,* and it may, moreover, be regarded as the turning-point in the history of art on the Lower Rhine. It is to be wished that its real value may continue to be appreciated by historical criticism. For it is at present by being so enveloped by the incense of adoration, that it is to be feared it will soon become as clouded to the eyes of the mind, as it was in former days to the eyes of the body by the dirt of lamps and candles. It consists of a central picture and two side-panels. In all these we find the background of gold in the style of the paintings described above. The carpet, also, behind the figure of the Virgin, is of the stamped kind, and gaily coloured. In the other parts of the picture this style of proceeding, otherwise so frequently met with, has been entirely avoided; the artist had come to perceive that he could produce brocade and damask, and other things that change in colour, whether bright or glittering, with his own brush, and hence had no further need for such mechanical contrivances.

The figures in the principal picture, as well as those in the side-panels, are symmetrical with the centre, but with a great variety of important contrasts in the way of form and gesture. The traditional Byzantine prin-

* The celebrated picture in the chapel of St. Agnes in the cathedral. It appears doubtful whether the painting is by *Meister* Wilhelm; for it has been supposed to be the picture alluded to by Dürer in his diary of his travels in the Low Countries, where he mentions having paid two " white pennies" to see the picture which "*Meister* Stetfau" had painted in Cologne.

ciple still predominates, but is treated with grace and freedom.

A kindred species of this style of national peculiarity, is to be found in the throng surrounding the principal group: the maidens around Saint Ursula, and the knights accompanying Gereon, all appear, as it were, in oriental masks. But the two kings kneeling are perfect portraits, and we are disposed to maintain the same of the Virgin. We will not add more about this rich piece of composition and its various points of excellence, for the *Annual, for Lovers of Early German Times and Art,** gives a very welcome copy of this admirable work, together with a full account of it; we should offer the treatise our undivided thanks, were it not that the account is pervaded by a kind of enthusiastic mysticism, the effect of which is not beneficial either to art or to the cause of knowledge.

As this picture bears evidence of the master's great practical experience, others of the same description may be found when a careful investigation is made, even though a number may in the course of time, have become wholly destroyed and others left altogether uncared for, owing to a subsequent and different style of art. To us they would be an important document, showing a decided step made by art to rid itself of a stereotyped reality, and to work itself free from a general national type of face to the perfect reality of a portrait. From this deduction we feel convinced that the painter of this picture, be his name what it may, was truly German in mind and origin, and hence that there is no need to appeal to any Italian influence in explanation of the merits of his style.

As the picture was painted in 1410, it belongs to the time when Johann van Eyck† was already a distinguished

---

* *Taschenbuch für Freunde altdeutscher Zeit und Kunst,* published in Cologne. Wallraf's account of the same picture appeared in the volume for the year 1816.

† Johann van Eyck, also known by the name of John of Bruges, is said to have been born in 1370, and began studying painting under his elder brother Hubert. He is specially famous as the improver and supposed inventor of oil-painting, by having discovered a means of giving consistency to colours without drying them in the sun, and by adding a waterproof varnish that added to the clearness and brilliancy of the colours.

artist, and thus serves in some way to account for the incomprehensible excellence of Eyck's style, for it shows us what sort of artists lived contemporaneously with this admirable painter. We called the *Dombild* (Cathedral picture) the point at which the early Netherland School took a new turn, and we here add that we consider Eyck's works as belonging to the period when the revolution of that style was completed. Even in the early Byzantine, Lower Rhenish pictures, we find the stereotyped carpets sometimes treated in perspective, even though somewhat awkwardly. In the Cathedral Picture there is no perspective, the simple gold background precludes this. Now Eyck cast aside everything of the stamped style as well as the gold back-ground; a free space was thus gained, upon which not merely the principal figures, but all the subordinate figures were represented as perfectly life-like in face, figure, and dress, and every detail also was accurately described.

Difficult as it always is to give an account of such a man as Eyck, we shall, nevertheless, venture upon an attempt, in the hope that the reader may one day have an opportunity of examining his works. And, to begin with, we shall not hesitate for a moment to rank Eyck among the chief of those whom Nature has endowed with artistic talents. He, moreover, had the good fortune to live in an age when art had reached a high degree of technical excellence universally practised, and which had reached a certain limit. In addition to this he had become aware of a higher, nay, the very highest technical advantage in painting; for, be it as it may with regard to the discovery of oil-painting, we do not hesitate to maintain that Eyck was the first who mixed the oily substances—previously merely been smeared over the pictures when finished—among the colours themselves, and that he used the oils that dried the quickest, colours that were clearest and covered least thickly; this he did in order that, when laying on the paints, the light of the white ground, and that colour upon colour, might shine through according as he wished. Now, as the whole force of colour—which is in itself dark—is not excited by light being reflected from it, but by being made to shine through, the highest physical and artistic requirements were satisfied by this discovery and style of treatment. The appreciation for colour, too, was innate in Eyck, as the Netherlander. The power of colour was known to him as well as to his contemporaries, and thus he brought matters so far—to speak merely of drapery and tapestry—that the appearance of the canvas far surpassed that of the reality. This, of course, could be done only by the genuine artist, for actual sight is dependent upon an endless number of coincidences both as regards the eye itself as well as the objects to be seen; while, on the other hand, the artist paints according to rules, as to how the objects are to be distinguished from one another by light, shade, and colour, and to be viewed, in their utmost visibleness, by good, sound eyesight. Eyck, further, made himself master of perspective, and was intimately acquainted with the variety presented by landscapes, more particularly with an endless number of different buildings, and these now took the place of the scanty background of gold or tapestry.

It will seem strange when we add that, while Eyck cast aside the material and mechanical imperfections of the old style of art, he omitted to retain a technical excellence which had, up to that time, been silently preserved—the principle of symmetrical composition. Still, this was the natural result of an extraordinary mind like his, for when breaking through the material shell he was not likely to stop and consider that there might be another ideal mental limit beyond, one which he would fight against in vain, and to which he would have to submit, or else create another according to his own idea. Eyck's compositions, therefore, are of the greatest truth and beauty, although they do not satisfy the actual demands of art, and it seems, in fact, as if he had intentionally not made use of anything that his predecessors possessed or practised. In those of his pictures we have become acquainted with, there is no group to be compared with those of the little angels by the side of Saint Veronica, spoken of above. Now as nothing that is meant to please the eye, can exercise any charm unless it possesses symmetry, Eyck—as a man of taste and fine feeling—of course produced this after his own fashion, and moreover, has done so in such a manner that the effect is more agreeable and forcible than what is merely symmetrical in art and wanting in *naïveté*, for then the work will appeal only to the understanding, and only awaken our power of calculation.

If our readers have followed us thus far patiently, and those who are acquainted with the subject agree with us that every advance from a stiffened, antiquated, artificial condition to a free, life-like truth to Nature, is immediately followed by a loss which can be rectified only very gradually, and often not for many years—we may now pass on and examine Eyck's peculiar style, for we shall be inclined unconditionally to honour his individual characteristics. Even the earlier artists of the Netherland School had been inclined to depict the affecting subjects offered by the New Testament in a kind of sequence; and we find that Eyck's great work, which adorns this collection, also consists of a central picture and two side-panels; we have the thoughtful artist, with a fine feeling and appreciation for his subject, depicting a connected trilogy. On our left we have the most youthful-looking maiden receiving from a heavenly youth the announcement of some strange event. In the central picture we see her as a happy, astonished mother, honoured in her son. On the right hand picture again, we find her leading her child into the temple to be presented to the Lord; she herself appears almost the matron with the earnestness of her presentiment of what is before the boy whom the High Priest is welcoming with delight. The expression of the face of the Virgin in all three pictures, and her figure and attitude in each case —at first kneeling, then sitting, and at last standing—are all alike charming and dignified. The position of the different persons towards one another, on all of the three paintings, bears evidence of very refined feeling. In the scene in the temple there is, moreover, a species of parallelism which is accomplished, apart from the central piece, by a contrast of characters—a kind of mental symmetry so deeply felt and so significant that the spectator is attracted and interested, although it is an excellence that cannot be measured by the standard of perfect art.

Thus Johann van Eyck, as an artist of admirable thought

and feeling, managed to produce an increased variety among his principal figures; and is equally successful in his representation of the different localities. The Annunciation takes place in a closed room, narrow but lofty, the light coming in through the wing of an upper window. Everything in the room is neat and orderly as befitting innocence, whose thoughts are confined to itself and its immediate surroundings. The seats against the walls, the prie-dieux, the bedstead, all are neat and smooth. The bed is covered with red and curtained, everything described in the most admirable manner, even the brocaded back of the bed. The central picture, on the other hand, presents the freest of views, for the noble but ruined chapel of the centre serves more as a frame for the various objects than to conceal them. To the left of the spectator is a town somewhat in the distance, with a number of streets and houses full of bustle and activity; the town comes into the picture, as it were, from the background, leaving a broad open field. This latter, which is adorned with various kinds of rural objects, extends away to a well-watered district. To the right of the spectator a view is obtained of a portion of a round temple several stories in height; the interior of this rotunda, is depicted on the adjoining panel, and contrasts most admirably in height, width, and brightness, with the other panel representing the Virgin's little room.

When we repeat that every object in the three pictures is described in the most perfect manner, and with the utmost accuracy, a general idea may be formed of the excellence of these well-preserved paintings. And all the various parts are treated with the same care, from the dilapidated, tumble-down walls and the grass growing on the decaying thatched roof to the bejewelled goblets of gold, from the drapery of the figures to the countenances, from the nearest point to the most distant part in the picture; and there is not a spot upon these panels which would not gain by being examined with a magnifying glass.—The same may be said of a single panel upon which Lucas * has depicted the Madonna suckling her child.

* Lucas of Leyden, 1494-1533. The picture mentioned above is now in the Pinakothek in Munich.

This leads us to speak of the important circumstance that Eyck's ideas of synimetry—a matter so urgently demanded by us—are shown more in his surroundings, and thus offer an artistic and pleasant expedient in place of the uninteresting background of gold. And although his figures may not move or stand towards one another altogether in accordance with the rules of art, still we have a definite locality which prescribes a distinct limit, and makes it appear as if their natural and, so to say, accidental gestures had been regulated in the most pleasant manner.

But all that has been said, in spite of our endeavour to be accurate and definite, must remain mere words, unless the reader has himself seen the pictures. It is exceedingly to be wished, therefore, that the proprietors would publish accurate copies—of moderate size in the first instance—of these pictures, in order that those who have not had the good fortune to see the paintings, might examine and judge for themselves about what has been stated of them.

In expressing this wish, we remember with all the more regret the loss we have sustained by the early death of Epps, a young man of promising talent, whose taste had been educated by the works of this collection. His name, is still held in honour by all who knew him, especially by those amateurs who possess copies of ancient works from his hand, and which he made with the utmost fidelity and diligence. Still there is no need to despair utterly, for a very skilful artist has associated himself with the proprietors, and is now devoting himself to the care of the important collection. He would give the best evidence of his admirable talent and conscientious spirit were he to undertake to make copies of the pictures, and to publish them in the manner suggested above. Were such a work in the possession of all those interested in art, many other remarks might be added here, which, as things are at present, would only confuse the imagination; this generally happens when any attempt is made to describe a picture in words.

Very unwillingly do I make a break here, for the very things which would now, in their turn, have to be discussed, offer a great deal both of what is pleasing and enjoyable. Of Johann van Eyck himself we must not add more at present, for we shall have to return to him when speaking of subsequent artists. In the artists who directly follow him we need as little assume any foreign influence. In fact, when endeavouring to estimate the value of any unusual degree of talent, it is but a poor expedient rashly to speculate where the man may have derived all his advantages. A child growing up to manhood does not find Nature presented to him in all its simplicity and nakedness; for the divine power of his ancestors has created for him a second world in the already existing world. Enforced habits, usages, popular customs, venerable traditions, precious monuments, useful laws, and the many glorious productions of art, enthral and influence him to such a degree, that he is never quite able to distinguish between what is original in him and what hereditary. He makes use of the world as he finds it, and is perfectly right in so doing.

An artist may, therefore, be called original when he treats the objects around him in an individual, national, and, above all, in a traditional manner, and succeeds in forming them into one well-arranged whole. Hence, when speaking of a man of this kind, it is our duty first of all to consider what ability he possesses, in how far it has been developed, and then to inquire into his immediate circumstances and in how far they offered him subjects, contrivances, and ideas; only at the last may we look around and examine not only what he knew of foreign things, but more especially in what way he made use of them. For the spirit of much that is good, pleasant, and useful, flits about the earth often for centuries before its influence is directly felt. We often wonder, when reading history, at the slow progress made by mere mechanical contrivances. The Byzantines had the precious works of Hellenic art before their eyes without being able to rise out of the wretchedness of their mummified style of painting. Can we detect in Albrecht Dürer's works any special evidence of his having been in Venice? This excellent artist can in all cases be comprehended only from his own works.

This is the kind of patriotism I should wish to see, for it is a kind to which every kingdom, every country and province, nay, to which every town is entitled; for by exalting the character of the individual man—which consists in his not allowing himself to be mastered by circumstances, but by mastering and directing them himself—we are conferring upon every nation, and part of a nation, the right and honour of likewise possessing a character of its own, which will reveal itself in the artist, or a man eminent in some other way. It is in this manner that we shall proceed when discussing such estimable artists as Hemmelinck,* Israel van Mecheln, Lucas van Leyden, Quintin Messis,† and others. All of them keep within their native sphere, and our duty will be, as far as possible, to refuse to admit any foreign influence upon their merits. Thereupon, we have Schoreel, and later, Hemskerck, and several others, whose talents were cultivated in Italy, but who, nevertheless, could not cast aside their Netherland origin. In these cases there may be found some evidence of the example set by Leonardo da Vinci, Correggio, Titian, and Michel Angelo, but the Netherlander remains the Netherlander, nay, their national characteristics predominate to such a degree that they, in the end, shut themselves up within their own magic circle, and refuse every kind of foreign culture. In this way Rembrandt gives proof of the most eminent artistic talent, and he found material and stimulus enough in his own immediate surroundings, without having the slightest knowledge that such people as the Greeks or Romans ever existed.

If we have succeeded in giving the account we proposed, it will now be time to turn to the Upper Rhine, and endea-

* *Hans Hemmelinck* (also called Memlinc) was born in 1440, and was alive 1509. His most celebrated picture is a large altarpiece now in the Marien Kirche in Dantzig, which represents, on three panels, *The Last Judgment, Hell, and the Abode of the Blessed*. The work was formerly ascribed to other artists, but is now generally acknowledged to be Hemmelinck's; it bears the date 1487.

† *Quintin Messis*, 1460–1530, is said to have originally been a smith, and is hence often called the Smith of Antwerp; he is further said to have taken up painting from having fallen in love with the daughter of an artist.

vour to find out the main excellencies and characteristic features of the Upper German school, and, moreover, in the different localities—in Swabia, Franconia, and Bavaria. In this case, too, our first duty will be to make clear to ourselves the difference, nay, the contrast between the two schools, in order that the one school may appreciate the good points of the other; that the eminent men of both may receive their due, and that the one party may acknowledge the progress made by the other; in short, that everything good and excellent arising from the principles of both schools may be brought prominently forward. In this manner we shall gladly give German art of the fifteenth and sixteenth centuries its due honour, and the froth of over-estimation, which is even now so objectionable to connoisseurs and lovers of art, will gradually disappear. With a feeling of assurance we may then look further to the east and south, and with good-will join our associates and neighbours there.

In offering the public these pages, which are addressed to the present day, we may be allowed to hope that they may exercise both a kindly influence upon the age itself, and also be supported and encouraged by it. This can be accomplished only by a fulfilment of the reasonable wishes we have expressed, and by an inquiry being made into the problematical suggestions proposed, but more particularly by the continued activity of those interested in the subjects. The Boisserées' collection of plates has meanwhile been making considerable progress. Moller, too, has finished the first engraving of the original plan of the Cologne Cathedral, and has also published two parts of his valuable drawings of early German buildings and monuments; they are executed in the most careful and neatest manner. We must also add that, following the example of the forerunner of the art-treasures which required to be rescued from their state of bondage, and which greeted us on our arrival in Cologne—others likewise which were distributed over all parts of the world, are now returning to their original homes. In this way an appreciation for art will again be awakened in every country and province, and a new direction given both to the study and the actual practice of art.

SUPPLEMENTARY REMARKS ON HEIDELBERG.

With regard to the Boisserées' collection, we have still to add that, within the past year, it has been considerably increased, more especially with admirable paintings belonging to the Upper German School. Of such masters who had not been previously represented, paintings have been acquired of Wohlgemuth,* Altdorfer, and Bouckelaer, and also of an excellent Cologne artist hitherto quite unknown—Johann von Melem, after the style of Schoreel; all are important pictures, some of them even masterpieces. Of such masters as were already represented, additional works have been obtained of Martin Schön, J. J. Walch, a portrait-painter contemporary with Dürer, one by Dürer himself and one by Johann Mabuse. Mabuse is one of the most eminent early painters of the Netherland School, and is also remarkable for the variety he exhibits in his treatment of his subjects; all the greater, therefore, is the good fortune of this collection to have gained possession of several of his master-pieces, perfect treasures in the way of execution and preservation, and these pictures, moreover, are from different periods of the artist's life. But, perhaps, the most precious of all, is the late addition of Dürer's *Descent from the Cross*.

We must further not omit to mention that the proprietors of this collection, owing to their extensive and favourable connections, have the immediate prospect of increasing it systematically, and of making it more and more complete. They entertain a well-founded hope of soon recovering several extremely precious works for the elucidation of the history of German art, which have for centuries been scattered about in foreign lands, and of including these among the other works they possess of the kindred sphere of art.

* * * * * *

On the Lower Rhine adequate institutions for the study

* Michael Wohlgemuth, who lived from 1434 to 1519, was a painter and engraver in wood in Nürnberg. Albrecht Altdorfer (1488-1538), who lived principally in Regensburg, is regarded as one of the most eminent successors of Albrecht Dürer.

of science and art are being established, and as far as I know, everything that could be desired is being done and industriously carried forward. If it should be our good fortune to visit the Upper Rhine again, Mannheim, Schwetzingen, and the Duke's collection of German antiquities at Erbach would offer the finest material; Carlsruhe also, with its gardens and botanical institutions, its beautiful collections of objects in Natural History and Art, and its new and important buildings, would offer an opportunity for the most suggestive considerations.

We must now offer the Upper Rhine our congratulations upon its enjoying the rare advantage of possessing, in Mr. Hebel,[*] a national poet thoroughly imbued with the spirit of his native country, one who looks from the highest stage of culture down upon his immediate surroundings, throwing out the network of his talents, as it were, to fish up the peculiarities of his countrymen and contemporaries, in order afterwards to depict these to them for their own amusement and edification. In doing this we are led to think of the manuscripts about to be returned to Heidelberg,[*] and thus of the literary collections of the early German period, and are reminded of the early stages of poetic art in the same way as we have hitherto recalled the early forms of painting, and find that the remarks just made apply to this case likewise; for here, too, the order of the day is over-estimation, misrepresentation, and an unfortunate kind of accommodation. However, in this respect also, we have the assuring hope that when the extravagant delight in things newly discovered or newly observed, has somewhat abated, it will

---

[*] Johann Peter Hebel (1760–1814) had since 1791 been a teacher at the Gymnasium in Carlsruhe, and afterwards held the position of Director of the school. Goethe's attention had been drawn to him upon the publication of the first edition of his *Allemannische Gedichte*, and the second edition he himself reviewed in the *Jena Allegmeine Literatur Zeitung*.

† Boisserée writes to Goethe from Heidelberg on December 2, 1815: "You will be glad to hear that the Pope has consented to allow the thirty-nine manuscripts belonging here to be returned from Paris; Prince Hardenberg announced the fact to the University the day before yesterday. There is as yet no reply to the other request respecting the larger portion which is meanwhile still in Rome." See also p. 423.

soon give place to a true knowledge of the subject and well-directed activity.

The primary object of these pages which, it is true, originated quite accidentally, was merely to discuss art and antiquity; but how can these two subjects be conceived apart from science, and these three again apart from Nature? Hence, bit by bit, everything that fell in the way of the eye and hand fitted in with the rest. A kindly acceptance of what is herewith presented, and what, in reality, can be looked upon merely as a continual offering of thanks on the part of the traveller for the many acts of kindness he has met with, may encourage him to make a continuation.

In conclusion I cannot refrain from mentioning, that fortune seems to be favouring the wishes and projects of all lovers of art. For a second original plan of the Cologne Cathedral has been found in Paris, of which I can give some account, having seen it myself, and can confirm the reports I had heard previously.

Of this plan, and of the other sketches that accompany it, the following remarks may be added. The largest is, in respect to size and style of drawing, the exact counterpart of the one now in Darmstadt.* The latter represents the northern tower, whereas the new one describes the southern one, with only this difference that it likewise includes the whole of the adjoining central gable, together with the principal entrance and the windows. Hence, the injury done to the one in Darmstadt, by a piece having been torn off, can be repaired. The newly-discovered plan is altogether some three feet and two inches (Rhenish) in breadth, and thirteen feet two inches in length.

On the second sheet we have the plan of the southern tower to the right of the main entrance given on the same scale, and drawn by the same hand in the most careful manner possible. On a third is a sketch of the second storey of the tower from the east, giving the diameter of the end which joins the nave of the church; this is drawn on a different scale and by a different hand, less finely and carefully, but is also original, inasmuch as, like the

* The plan was at that time being engraved by Moller of Darmstadt, for Boisserée's work on the Cologne Cathedral, see p. 417.

principal sketch, it not only differs in one essential point from the actual building, but also to some extent differs from the principal sketch itself. To judge from the subject alone, it is clear that the last-mentioned drawing was made merely to be of assistance during the actual work of building, and for this very reason is specially remarkable and instructive. It is thought to be the work of the superintendent of the *Bauhütte*.* Both drawings are of the same size, over three feet long and two and a half feet broad, are made on parchment and are in a good state of preservation.

As regards the preservation of the large sketch, it has not suffered any great injury except in a few small points. But, on the other hand, it shows many signs of wear, and has here and there been touched up by a subsequent hand, unnecessarily however. Both for this reason, and because the sketch and the accompanying sheets treat of the one tower furthest advanced in construction, and also because nothing whatever was known in Cologne itself about this second sketch, but only of the one at present in Darmstadt, formerly preserved in the archives of the Cathedral, it may be assumed that the sketch was used in the *Bauhütte*, and that it had been taken from Cologne long ago. This might have happened the more readily as the architects of Cologne were often called to foreign parts.

* * *

We at present, it is true, find patriotic Germans devoting themselves zealously, in thought, to the enjoyment of their sacred architectural monuments, in maintaining those that are completed or but half completed; and we also find that in some places the necessary funds exist, while in other cases endeavours are being made to re-acquire money that has drifted into other channels. Still we cannot but experience a feeling of uneasiness when we observe that not only the pecuniary resources are in a miserable state, but that the resources of art itself and of workmanship have almost entirely disappeared. In vain do we look around for a number of persons capable and willing to

* The name of a society of artists founded for the preservation of architectural works.

undertake such work. On the other hand history teaches us that in former days masons' work was done by members of a large and extensive closed guild, and executed under the strictest forms and regulations.

Stone-masons had, in fact, risen to a very favourable position in the civilised world, from having obtained a place midway between the fine arts and the trades. They called themselves a *fraternity*, and their statutes were ratified by the Emperor. The society originated from the immense power and perseverance of mankind, but at the same time from the demand for these gigantic buildings which had to be erected almost simultaneously. An enormous number of boys, youths, and men, trained for the purpose, were at work all over Germany, in every one of the principal towns. The chiefs of this large army of workers had their head-quarters in Cologne, Strassburg, Vienna and Zürich; and each stood at the head of his district according to its geographical position.

When we examine the internal organisation of this society, we come upon the word (*Hütte*) hut or lodge, at first in its simple meaning, of a space covered by boards or planks where the stone-mason executed his work, but then also in its figurative sense as the seat of the judge, of the archives and of the upholder of all rights. When a building was to be begun, a plan was drawn up by the master, which, when approved of by the architect, was placed in the hand of the artist as a document and agreement. All arrangements about apprentices, workmen and servants, their learning or receiving stated work, their artistic, technical and moral obligations, are specified in full detail, and all their actions based upon the most delicate code of honour. On the other hand, they enjoyed great advantages by belonging to the fraternity, a most effectual one being to make themselves understood to others of their craft by secret signs and sayings, throughout the whole building-world; that is to say, throughout the whole civilised, semi-civilised, and uncivilised world.

When we think of the numberless multitudes of men of every degree of skilfulness, organised in this manner, working hand in hand with their master, certain of daily occupation for their livelihood, provided for in case of old age or illness, inspired by religion, animated by art, and controlled by custom, we begin to comprehend how such immense structures were planned, undertaken, and, if not actually completed, still carried out further than would otherwise have been conceivable. When further we bear in mind that it was one of the rules and conditions of the fraternity, that the enormous edifices were constructed for a *daily wage*, in oder that the smallest detail might receive the utmost care, we may well give heed and with hesitation ask ourselves what we, in our day, could accomplish of a similar description.

If at some future day we may be enabled to give some fuller account of the Stone-mason Fraternity, our thanks will be due to worthy Dr. Ehrmann, of Frankfort, a man of eminent intelligence, who has kindly communicated to me from his wealth of antiquarian possessions, a collection of records and reports, together with some notes and a pamphlet of his own.

*   *   *   *   *

Our efforts in regard to art in the south-west have been supplemented by a very desirable undertaking of Dr. Büsching's in the north-east, communicated to the *Weekly Reports for Patrons of the History of Art and Learning in the Middle Ages*; and these ought not to remain unknown to any one interested in that period. His casts in iron of old Silesian coins, also commend themselves as worthy of imitation, even though made of a different material; the amateur would thus have in his hand miniature mementos of art, the originals of which he could hardly hope ever to possess.

Extremely pleasant as well as significant it is to us to be able, in conclusion, to add the news that, at the most gracious intercession of their Majesties the Emperor of Austria and the King of Prussia, His Holiness the Pope has handed over to the University of Heidelberg not only the works that belonged to the former library of the Palatinate, found in Paris, but has likewise ordered the return of other eight hundred and forty-seven volumes which had originally belonged to the collection, and are at present in the library of the Vatican. Every German knows the value of this gift too well, for there to be any need of further comment in regard to it. We may be permitted to add here that many of the wishes entertained by Germany have been fulfilled since the traveller was met in Cologne by the joyful tidings of the return of its patron saint!

COMPLETE CATALOGUE

OF

BOHN'S LIBRARIES,

CONTAINING

STANDARD WORKS OF EUROPEAN LITERATURE IN THE ENGLISH LANGUAGE, ON HISTORY, BIOGRAPHY, TOPOGRAPHY, ARCHÆOLOGY, THEOLOGY, ANTIQUITIES, SCIENCE, PHILOSOPHY, NATURAL HISTORY, POETRY, ART, FICTION, WITH DICTIONARIES, AND OTHER BOOKS OF REFERENCE. THE SERIES COMPRISES TRANSLATIONS FROM THE FRENCH, GERMAN, ITALIAN, SPANISH, SCANDINAVIAN, ANGLO-SAXON, LATIN, AND GREEK. PRICE 3s. 6d. OR 5s. PER VOLUME (WITH EXCEPTIONS). A COMPLETE SET IN 651 VOLUMES, PRICE £144 17s. 6d.

Catalogues sent Post-free on Application.

LONDON:
GEORGE BELL AND SONS, YORK STREET,
COVENT GARDEN.
1883.

August, 1853.

COMPLETE CATALOGUE
OF
BOHN'S LIBRARIES.

STANDARD LIBRARY.
A SERIES OF THE BEST ENGLISH AND FOREIGN AUTHORS, PRINTED IN POST 8VO.

281 *Vols. at* 3s. 6d. *each, excepting those marked otherwise.*

Addison's Works. With the Notes of Bishop HURD, much additional matter, and upwards of 100 Unpublished Letters. Edited by H. G. BOHN. *Portrait and 8 Engravings on Steel.* In 6 vols.

Alfieri's Tragedies, including those published posthumously. Translated into English Verse, and edited with Notes and Introduction, by EDGAR A. BOWRING, C.B. 2 vols.

Ascham's Scholemaster. By Prof. I. E. B. Mayor. *In the press.*

Bacon's Essays, Apophthegms, Wisdom of the Ancients, New Atlantis, and Henry VII., with Introduction and Notes. *Portrait.*

Ballads and Songs of the Peasantry of England. Edited by ROBERT BELL.

Beaumont and Fletcher, a popular Selection from. By LEIGH HUNT.

Beckmann's History of Inventions, Discoveries, and Origins. Revised and enlarged. *Portraits.* In 2 vols.

Bremer's (Miss) Works. Translated by MARY HOWITT. *Portrait.* In 4 vols.
Vol. 1. The Neighbours and other Tales.
Vol. 2. The President's Daughter.
Vol. 3. The Home, and Strife and Peace.
Vol. 4. A Diary, the H—— Family, &c.

Brink's Early English Literature to Wiclif.

British Poets, from Milton to Kirke WHITE. Cabinet Edition. In 4 vols.

Browne's (Sir Thomas) Works. Edited by SIMON WILKIN. In 3 vols.

Burke's Works. In 6 Volumes.
Vol. 1. Vindication of Natural Society, On the Sublime and Beautiful, and Political Miscellanies.
Vol. 2. French Revolution, &c.
Vol. 3. Appeal from the New to the Old Whigs; the Catholic Claims, &c.
Vol. 4. On the Affairs of India, and Charge against Warren Hastings.
Vol. 5. Conclusion of Charge against Hastings; on a Regicide Peace, &c.
Vol. 6. Miscellaneous Speeches, &c. With a General Index.

Burke's Speeches on Warren Hastings; and Letters. With Index. In 2 vols. (forming vols. 7 and 8 of the works).

—— **Life.** By PRIOR. New and revised Edition. *Portrait.*

Burns, Lockhart's Life of. By W. S. Douglas.

Butler's (Bp.) Analogy of Religion, and Sermons, with Notes. *Portrait.*

Camoëns' Lusiad, Mickle's Translation. Edited by E. R. HODGES.

Cary's Translation of Dante's Heaven, Hell, and Purgatory. Copyright edition, being the only one containing Cary's last corrections and additions.

Carafas (The) of Maddaloni: and Naples under Spanish Dominion. Translated from the German of Alfred de Reumont.

Carrel's Counter Revolution in England. Fox's History and Lonsdale's Memoir of James II. *Portrait.*

Cellini (Benvenuto), Memoirs of Translated by ROSCOE. *Portrait.*

Cervantes' Galatea. Translated by GORDON GYLL.

—— **Exemplary Novels.** Translated from the Spanish by W. K. KELLY.

—— **Don Quixote de la Mancha.** 2 vols.

Chaucer's Works. Edited by ROBERT BELL. New Edition, improved. With Introduction by W. W. SKEAT. 4 vols.

Classic Tales, containing Rasselas, Vicar of Wakefield, Gulliver's Travels, and Sentimental Journey.

Coleridge's (S. T.) Friend. A Series of Essays on Morals, Politics, and Religion.

—— **(S. T.) Biographia Literaria, and two Lay Sermons.**

—— **Aids to Reflection.** *In the press.*

—— **Lectures on Shakespeare.** *In the press.*

Commines. (*See Philip de Commines.*)

18

Condé's Dominion of the Arabs in Spain. Translated by Mrs. Foster. In 3 vols.

Cowper's Complete Works. Edited, with Memoir of the Author, by Southey. Illustrated with 50 Engravings. In 8 vols.
Vols. 1 to 4. Memoir and Correspondence.
Vols. 5 and 6. Poetical Works. Plates.
Vol. 7. Homer's Iliad. Plates.
Vol. 8. Homer's Odyssey. Plates.

Coxe's Memoirs of the Duke of Marlborough. Portraits. In 3 vols.
⁎ An Atlas of the plans of Marlborough's campaigns, 4to. 10s. 6d.

——— **History of the House of** Austria. Portraits. In 4 vols.

Cunningham's Lives of Eminent British Painters. New Edition by Mrs. Heaton. 3 vols.

Defoe's Works. Edited by Sir Walter Scott. In 7 vols.

De Lolme on the Constitution of England. Edited, with Notes, by John Macgregor.

Emerson's Works. 3 vols.

Foster's (John) Life and Correspondence. Edited by J. E. Ryland. In 2 vols.

——— **Lectures at Broadmead** Chapel. Edited by J. E. Ryland. In 2 vols.

——— **Critical Essays.** Edited by J. E. Ryland. In 2 vols.

——— **Essays—On Decision of Character,** &c. &c.

——— **Essays—On the Evils of Popular Ignorance,** &c.

——— **Fosteriana: Thoughts, Reflections,** and Criticisms of the late John Foster, selected from periodical papers, and Edited by Henry G. Bohn (nearly 600 pages). 5s.

Fuller's (Andrew) Principal Works. With Memoir. Portrait.

Gibbon's Roman Empire. Complete and Unabridged, with Notes; including, in addition to the Author's own, those of Guizot, Wenck, Niebuhr, Hugo, Neander, and other foreign scholars; and an elaborate Index. Edited by an English Churchman. In 7 vols.

Goethe's Works, Translated into English. In 8 vols.
Vols. 1. and 2. Autobiography, 20 Books; and Annals. Portrait.
Vol. 3. Faust.. Two Parts. By Miss Swanwick.
Vol. 4. Novels and Tales.
Vol. 5. Wilhelm Meister's Apprenticeship.

Goethe's Works—continued.
Vol. 6. Conversations with Eckermann and Soret. Translated by John Oxenford.
Vol. 7. Poems and Ballads, including Hermann and Dorothea. Translated by E. A. Bowring, C.B
Vol. 8. Götz von Berlichingen, Torquato Tasso, Egmont, Iphigenia, Clavigo, Wayward Lover, and Fellow Culprits. By Sir Walter Scott, Miss Swanwick, and E. A. Bowring, C.B. With Engraving.
Vol. 9. Wilhelm Meister's Travels.
Vol. 10. Tour in Italy, 2 Parts, and Residence in Rome.
Vol. 11. Miscellaneous Travels. Switzerland, France, Mainz & Rhine Tour.

——— **Correspondence with Schiller.** See Schiller.

Greene, Marlowe, and Ben Jonson, Poems of. Edited by Robert Bell With Biographies. In 1 vol.

Gregory's (Dr.) Evidences, Doctrines, and Duties of the Christian Religion.

Guizot's Representative Government Translated by A. R. Scoble.

——— **History of the English Revolution of 1640.** Translated by William Hazlitt. Portrait.

——— **History of Civilisation,** Translated by William Hazlitt. In 3 vols Portrait.

Hazlitt's Table Talk. A New Edition in one volume.

——— **Lectures on the Comic** Writers, and on the English Poets.

——— **Lectures on the Literature** of the Age of Elizabeth, and on Characters of Shakespear's Plays.

——— **Plain Speaker.**

——— **Round Table; the Conversations** of James Northcote, R.A.; Characteristics, &c.

——— **Sketches and Essays, and** Winterslow (Essays Written there). New Edition.

Hall's (Rev. Robert) Miscellaneous Works and Remains, with Memoir by Dr. Gregory, and an Essay on his Character by John Foster. Portrait.

Hawthorne's Tales. In 2 vols.
Vol. 1. Twice Told Tales, and the Snow Image.
Vol. 2. Scarlet Letter, and the House with the seven Gables.

Heine's Poems, complete, from the German, by E. A. Bowring, C.B. 5s.

Hungary: its History and Revolutions; with a Memoir of Kossuth from new and authentic sources. Portrait.

A CATALOGUE OF

Hutchinson (Colonel), Memoirs of with the Siege of Latham House.

Irving's (Washington) Life and Letters. By his Nephew, PIERRE E. IRVING. In 2 vols.

────── Complete Works. In 15 vols.
Vol. 1. Salmagundi and Knickerbocker Portrait of the Author.
Vol. 2. Sketch Book and Life of Goldsmith.
Vol. 3. Bracebridge Hall and Abbotsford and Newstead.
Vol. 4. Tales of a Traveller and the Alhambra.
Vol. 5. Conquest of Granada and Conquest of Spain.
Vols. 6 and 7. Life of Columbus and Companions of Columbus, with a new Index. Fine Portrait.
Vol. 8. Astoria and Tour in the Prairies.
Vol. 9. Mahomet and his Successors.
Vol. 10. Wolfert's Roost and Adventures of Captain Bonneville.
Vol. 11. Biographies and Miscellanies.
Vols. 12-15. Life of Washington. Portrait.

For separate Works, see Cheap Series.

James's (G. P. R.) Richard Cœur-de-Lion, King of England. Portraits. 2 vols.

────── Louis XIV. Portraits. 2 vols.

Jameson's Shakespeare's Heroines: Characteristics of Women. Moral, Poetical, and Historical.

Junius's Letters, with Notes, Additions, and an Index. In 2 vols.

La Fontaine's Fables. Translated from the French by E. WRIGHT, jun.

Lamartine's History of the Girondists. Portraits. In 3 vols.

────── Restoration of the Monarchy, with Index. Portraits. In 4 vols.

────── French Revolution of 1848, with a fine Frontispiece.

Lamb's (Charles) Elia and Eliana. Complete Edition.

────── Dramatic Poets of the Time of Elizabeth; including his Selections from the Garrick Plays.

Lanzi's History of Painting. Translated by ROSCOE. Portraits. In 3 vols.

Lappenberg's Anglo-Saxon Kings. 2 vols.

Lessing's Dramatic Works. Complete, with Memoir by HELEN ZIMMERN. Portrait. 2 vols.

────── Laokoon. (By BEASLEY) Hamburg Dramatic Notes, Representation of Death (by Miss ZIMMERN), Frontispiece.

Locke's Philosophical Works, containing an Essay on the Human Understanding, &c., with Notes and Index by J. A. ST. JOHN. Portrait. In 2 vols.

Locke's Life and Letters, with Extracts from his Common-Place Books, by Lord KING.

Luther's Table Talk. Translated by WILLIAM HAZLITT. Portrait.

Machiavelli's History of Florence, The Prince, and other Works. Portrait.

Martineau's, Harriet, History of England, from 1800-15.

────── History of the Peace, from 1815-1846. 4 vols.

Menzel's History of Germany. Portraits. In 3 vols.

Michelet's Life of Luther. Translated by WILLIAM HAZLITT.

────── French Revolution, with Index. Frontispiece.

Mignet's French Revolution from 1789 to 1814. Portrait.

Milton's Prose Works, with Index. Portraits. In 5 vols

Mitford's (Mary R.) Our Village. Improved Ed., complete. Illustrated. 2 vols.

Molière's Dramatic Works. Translated by C. H WALL. In 3 vols. Portrait.

Montesquieu's Spirit of the Laws. A new Edition revised and corrected. 2 vols. Portrait.

Neander's Church History. Translated: with General Index. In 10 vols.

────── Life of Christ. Translated.

────── First Planting of Christianity, and Antignostikus. Translated. In 2 vols.

────── History of Christian Dogmas. Translated. In 2 vols.

────── Christian Life in the Early and Middle Ages, including his 'Light in Dark Places.' Translated.

Ockley's History of the Saracens Revised and completed. Portrait.

Percy's Reliques of Ancient English Poetry. Reprinted from the Original Edition, and Edited by J. V. PRICHARD. In 2 vols.

Philip de Commines, Memoirs of, containing the Histories of Louis XI. and Charles VIII, and of Charles the Bold, Duke of Burgundy. To which is added, The Scandalous Chronicle, or Secret History of Louis XI. Portraits. In 2 vols.

Plutarch's Lives. By G. LONG and A. STEWART. 4 Vols.

Poetry of America. Selections from 100 American Poets, from 1776—1876. Edited by W. J. LINTON. Portrait.

Ranke's History of the Popes. Translated by E. Foster. In 3 vols.

—— Servia and the Servian Revolution.

Reynolds' (Sir Joshua) Literary Works. *Portrait.* In 2 vols.

Richter (Jean Paul Fr.) Levana and Autobiography. With Memoir.

—— Flower, Fruit, and Thorn Pieces. A Novel.

Roscoe's Life and Pontificate of Leo X., with the Copyright Notes, and an Index. *Portraits.* In 2 vols.

—— Life of Lorenzo de Medici, with the Copyright Notes, &c. *Portrait.*

Russia, History of, by WALTER K. KELLY. *Portraits.* In 2 vols.

Schiller's Works. Translated into English. In 6 vols.
Vol. 1. Thirty Years' War, and Revolt of the Netherlands.
Vol. 2. *Continuation of* the Revolt of the Netherlands; Wallenstein's Camp; the Piccolomini; the Death of Wallenstein; and William Tell.
Vol. 3. Don Carlos, Mary Stuart, Maid of Orleans, and Bride of Messina.
Vol. 4. The Robbers, Fiesco, Love and Intrigue, and the Ghost-Seer.
Vol. 5. Poems. Translated by EDGAR BOWRING, C.B.
Vol. 6. Philosophical Letters and Æsthetical Essays.

—— Correspondence with Goethe, translated by L. DORA SCHMITZ. 2 vols.

Schlegel's Philosophy of Life and of Language, translated by A. J. W. MORRISON.

—— History of Literature, Ancient and Modern. Now first completely translated, with General Index.

Schlegel's Philosophy of History. Translated by J. B. ROBERTSON. *Portrait.*

—— Dramatic Literature. Translated. *Portrait.*

—— Modern History.

—— Æsthetic and Miscellaneous Works.

Sheridan's Dramatic Works and Life. *Portrait.*

Sismondi's Literature of the South of Europe. Translated by Roscoe. *Portraits.* In 2 vols.

Smith's (Adam) Theory of the Moral Sentiments; with his Essay on the First Formation of Languages.

Smyth's (Professor) Lectures on Modern History. In 2 vols.

—— Lectures on the French Revolution. In 2 vols.

Spinoza's Works. 2 vols. *In the press.*

Sturm's Morning Communings with God, or Devotional Meditations for Every Day in the Year.

Sully, Memoirs of the Duke of, Prime Minister to Henry the Great. *Portraits.* In 4 vols.

Taylor's (Bishop Jeremy) Holy Living and Dying. *Portrait.*

Thierry's Conquest of England by the Normans. Translated by WILLIAM HAZLITT. *Portrait.* In 2 vols.

Ulrici (Dr.) Shakespeare's Dramatic Art. Translated by L. D. Schmitz. 2 vols.

Vasari's Lives of the Painters, Sculptors, and Architects. Translated by Mrs. FOSTER. 5 vols.

Wesley's (John) Life. By ROBERT SOUTHEY. New and Complete Edition. Double volume. *With Portrait.* 5s.

Wheatley on the Book of Common Prayer. *Frontispiece.*

HISTORICAL LIBRARY.
21 *Vols. at* 5s. *each.*

Evelyn's Diary and Correspondence. *Illustrated with numerous Portraits, &c.* In 4 vols.

Pepys' Diary and Correspondence. Edited by Lord BRAYBROOKE. With Notes, Important Additions, including numerous Letters. *Illustrated with many Portraits.* In 4 vols.

Jesse's Memoirs of the Reign of the Stuarts, including the Protectorate. With General Index. *Upwards of 40 Portraits.* In 3 vols.

Jesse's Memoirs of the Pretenders and their Adherents. 6 *Portraits.*

Nugent's (Lord) Memorials of Hampden, his Party, and Times. 12 *Portraits.*

Strickland's (Agnes) Lives of the Queens of England, from the Norman Conquest. From official records and authentic documents, private and public. Revised Edition. In 6 vols.

—— Life of Mary Queen of Scots. 2 vols.

A CATALOGUE OF

COLLEGIATE SERIES.
10 Vols. at 5s. each.

Carlyle's Dante. The Inferno. Translation. Text and Notes. Second Edition. *Portrait.*

Dante. The Purgatorio. By S. Dugdale.

Dobree's Adversaria. By Prof. Wagner. 2 vols.

Donaldson's Theatre of the Greeks. Illustrated with Lithographs and numerous Woodcuts.

Keightley's Classical Mythology. New Edition. Revised by. Dr. L. Schmitz. With 12 plates.

Herodotus, Turner's (Dawson W. Notes to. With Map, &c.

Herodotus, Wheeler's Analysis and Summary of.

Thucydides, Wheeler's Analysis of.

New Testament (The) in Greek. Griesbach's Text, with the readings of Mill and Scholz, Parallel References, a Critical Introduction and Chronological Tables. *Two fac-similes of Greek MSS.* 3s. 6d.; or with Lexicon, 5s. Lexicon Separately, 2s.

PHILOSOPHICAL LIBRARY.
12 Vols. at 5s. each, excepting those marked otherwise.

Comte's Philosophy of the Sciences. By G. H. Lewes.

Draper (J. W.) A History of the Intellectual Development of Europe. By John William Draper, M.D., LL.D. A New Edition, thoroughly Revised by the Author. In 2 vols.

Hegel's Lectures on the Philosophy of History. Translated by J. Sibree, M.A.

Kant's Critique of Pure Reason. Translated by J. M. D. Meiklejohn.

—— Prolegomena and Metaphysical Foundations. E. B. Bax. 5s.

Logic; or, the Science of Inference. A Popular Manual. By J. Devey.

Miller's (Professor) History Philosophically considered. In 4 vols. 3s. 6d each.

Tennemann's Manual of the History of Philosophy. Continued by J. R. Morell

ECCLESIASTICAL AND THEOLOGICAL LIBRARY.
15 Vols. at 5s. each, excepting those marked otherwise.

Bleek (F.) An Introduction to the Old Testament, by Friedrich Bleek. Edited by Johann Bleek and Adolf Kamphausen. Translated from the German by G. H. Venables, under the supervision of the Rev. E. Venables, Canon of Lincoln. New Edition. In 2 vols.

Chillingworth's Religion of Protestants. 3s. 6d.

Eusebius' Ecclesiastical History. With Notes.

Hardwick's History of the Articles of Religion. To which is added a Series of Documents from A.D. 1536 to A.D. 1615. Together with Illustrations from Contemporary Sources. New Edition, revised by Rev. F. Procter.

Henry's (Matthew) Commentary on the Psalms. *Numerous Illustrations.*

Pearson on the Creed. New Edition. With Analysis and Notes.

Philo Judæus, Works of; the contemporary of Josephus. Translated by C. D. Yonge. In 4 vols.

Socrates' Ecclesiastical History, in continuation of Eusebius. With the Notes of Valesius.

Sozomen's Ecclesiastical History, from A.D. 324-440; and the Ecclesiastical History of Philostorgius.

Theodoret and Evagrius. Ecclesiastical Histories, from A.D. 332 to A.D. 427 and from A.D. 431 to A.D. 544.

Wieseler's Chronological Synopsis of the Four Gospels. Translated by Canon Venables. New Edition, revised.

22

BOHN'S VARIOUS LIBRARIES.

ANTIQUARIAN LIBRARY.

35 Vols. at 5s. each.

Bede's Ecclesiastical History, and the Anglo-Saxon Chronicle.

Boethius's Consolation of Philosophy. In Anglo-Saxon, with the A. S. Metres, and an English Translation, by the Rev. S. Fox.

Brand's Popular Antiquities of England, Scotland, and Ireland. By Sir HENRY ELLIS. In 3 vols.

Chronicles of the Crusaders. Richard of Devizes, Geoffrey de Vinsauf, Lord de Joinville.

Dyer's British Popular Customs, Present and Past. An Account of the various Games and Customs associated with different days of the year. By the Rev. T. F. THISELTON DYER, M.A. With Index.

Early Travels in Palestine. Willibald, Sæwulf, Benjamin of Tudela, Mandeville, La Brocquière, and Maundrell; all unabridged. Edited by THOMAS WRIGHT.

Ellis's Early English Metrical Romances. Revised by J. O. HALLIWELL.

Florence of Worcester's Chronicle, with the Two Continuations: comprising Annals of English History to the Reign of Edward I.

Gesta Romanorum. Edited by WYNNARD HOOPER, B.A.

Giraldus Cambrensis' Historical Works: Topography of Ireland; History of the Conquest of Ireland; Itinerary through Wales; and Description of Wales. With Index. Edited by THOS. WRIGHT.

Henry of Huntingdon's History of the English, from the Roman Invasion to Henry II.; with the Acts of King Stephen, &c.

Ingulph's Chronicle of the Abbey of Croyland, with the Continuations by Peter of Blois and other Writers. By H. T. RILEY.

Keightley's Fairy Mythology. Frontispiece by Cruikshank.

Lepsius's Letters from Egypt, Ethiopia, and the Peninsula of Sinai.

Mallet's Northern Antiquities. By Bishop PERCY. With an Abstract of the Eyrbiggia Saga, by Sir WALTER SCOTT. Edited by J. A. BLACKWELL.

Marco Polo's Travels. The Translation of Marsden. Edited by THOMAS WRIGHT.

Matthew Paris's Chronicle. In 5 vols.
FIRST SECTION: Roger of Wendover's Flowers of English History, from the Descent of the Saxons to A.D. 1235. Translated by Dr. GILES. In 2 vols.
SECOND SECTION: From 1235 to 1273. With Index to the entire Work. In 3 vols.

Matthew of Westminster's Flowers of History, especially such as relate to the affairs of Britain; to A.D. 1307. Translated by C. D. YONGE. In 2 vols.

Ordericus Vitalis' Ecclesiastical History of England and Normandy. Translated with Notes, by T. FORESTER, M.A. In 4 vols.

Pauli's (Dr. R.) Life of Alfred the Great. Translated from the German. To which is appended Alfred's Anglo-Saxon version of Orosius, with a literal Translation, and an Anglo-Saxon Grammar and Glossary.

Roger De Hoveden's Annals of English History; from A.D. 732 to A.D. 1201. Edited by H. T. RILEY. In 2 vols.

Six Old English Chronicles, viz.:—Asser's Life of Alfred, and the Chronicles of Ethelwerd, Gildas, Nennius, Geoffrey of Monmouth, and Richard of Cirencester.

William of Malmesbury's Chronicle of the Kings of England. Translated by SHARPE.

Yule-Tide Stories. A Collection of Scandinavian Tales and Traditions. Edited by B. THORPE.

ILLUSTRATED LIBRARY.

84 Vols. at 5s. each, excepting those marked otherwise.

Allen's Battles of the British Navy. Revised and enlarged. Numerous fine Portraits. In 2 vols.

Andersen's Danish Legends and Fairy Tales. With many Tales not in any other edition. Translated by CAROLINE PEACHEY. 120 Wood Engravings.

Ariosto's Orlando Furioso. In English Verse. By W. S. ROSE. Twelve fine Engravings. In 2 vols.

Bechstein's Cage and Chamber Birds. Including Sweet's Warblers. Enlarged edition. Numerous plates.
*** All other editions are abridged.
With the plates coloured. 7s. 6d.

23

A CATALOGUE OF

Bonomi's Nineveh and its Palaces.
New Edition, revised and considerably enlarged, both in matter and Plates. *Upwards of 300 Engravings*

Butler's Hudibras. With Variorum Notes, a Biography, and a General Index. Edited by HENRY G. BOHN. *Thirty beautiful Illustrations.*

———; *or, further illustrated with 62 Outline Portraits.* In 2 vols. 10s.

Cattermole's Evenings at Haddon Hall. 24 *exquisite Engravings on Steel, from designs by himself* the Letterpress by the BARONESS DE CARABELLA.

China, Pictorial, Descriptive, and Historical, with some Account of Ava and the Burmese, Siam, and Anam. *Nearly 100 Illustrations.*

Craik's (G. L.) Pursuit of Knowledge under Difficulties, illustrated by Anecdotes and Memoirs. Revised Edition. *With numerous Portraits.*

Cruikshank's Three Courses and a Dessert. A Series of Tales, *with 50 humorous Illustrations by Cruikshank.*

——— **Punch and Judy.** With 24 Illustrations. 5s. With Coloured Plates. 7s. 6d.

Dante. Translated by I. C. WRIGHT, M.A. New Edition, carefully revised. *Portrait and 34 Illustrations on Steel, after Flaxman.*

Didron's History of Christian Art in the Middle Ages. From the French. *Upwards of 150 outline Engravings.*

Dyer (T. H.) The History of Pompeii; its Buildings and Antiquities. An account of the City, with a full description of the Remains, and an Itinerary for Visitors. Edited by T. H. DYER, LL.D. *Illustrated with nearly 300 Wood Engravings, a large Map, and a Plan of the Forum.* A New Edition, revised and brought down to 1874. 7s. 6d.

Gil Blas, The Adventures of. 24 *Engravings on Steel, after Smirke, and 10 Etchings by George Cruikshank.* 6s.

Grimm's Gammer Grethel; or, German Fairy Tales and Popular Stories. Translated by EDGAR TAYLOR. *Numerous Woodcuts by Cruikshank.* 3s. 6d.

Holbein's Dance of Death, and Bible Cuts. *Upwards of 150 subjects, beautifully engraved in fac-simile,* with Introduction and Descriptions by the late FRANCIS DOUCE and Dr. T. F. DIBDIN. 2 vols. in 1. 7s. 6d.

Howitt's (Mary) Pictorial Calendar of the Seasons. Embodying the whole of Aiken's Calendar of Nature. *Upwards of 100 Engravings.*

——— **(Mary and William) Stories of English and Foreign Life.** *Twenty beautiful Engravings.*

India, Pictorial, Descriptive, and Historical, from the Earliest Times. *Upwards of 100 fine Engravings on Wood, and a Map.*

Jesse's Anecdotes of Dogs. New Edition, with large additions. *Numerous fine Woodcuts after Harvey, Bewick, and others.*

———; *or, with the addition of 34 highly-finished Steel Engravings.* 7s. 6d.

King's Natural History of Precious Stones, and of the Precious Metals. *With numerous Illustrations.* Price 6s.

——— **Natural History of Gems** or Decorative Stones. *Finely Illustrated.* 6s.

——— **Handbook of Engraved Gems.** *Finely Illustrated.* 6s.

Kitto's Scripture Lands and Biblical Atlas. 24 *Maps, beautifully engraved on Steel,* with a Consulting Index.

———; *with the maps coloured,* 7s. 6d.

Krummacher's Parables. Translated from the German. *Forty Illustrations by Clayton, engraved by Dalziel.*

Lindsay's (Lord) Letters on Egypt, Edom, and the Holy Land. New Edition, enlarged. *Thirty-six beautiful Engravings, and 2 Maps.*

Lodge's Portraits of Illustrious Personages of Great Britain, with Memoirs. *Two Hundred and Forty Portraits, engraved on Steel.* 8 vols.

Longfellow's Poetical Works. *Twenty-four page Engravings, by Birket Foster and others, and a Portrait.*

———; *or, without illustrations,* 3s. 6d.

——— **Prose Works.** 16 *page Engravings by Birket Foster, &c.*

Loudon's (Mrs.) Entertaining Naturalist. Revised by W. S. DALLAS, F.L.S. *With nearly 500 Woodcuts.*

Marryat's Masterman Ready; or, The Wreck of the Pacific. 93 *Woodcuts.* 3s. 6d.

——— **Poor Jack.** *With 16 Illustrations, after Designs by C. Stanfield, R.A.* 3s. 6d.

——— **Mission; or, Scenes in Africa.** (Written for Young People.) *Illustrated by Gilbert and Dalziel.* 3s. 6d.

——— **Pirate; and Three Cutters.** New Edition, with a Memoir of the Author. *With 8 Steel Engravings, from Drawings by C. Stanfield, R.A.* 3s. 6d.

——— **Privateers - Man One Hundred Years Ago.** *Eight Engravings on Steel, after Stothard.* 3s. 6d.

——— **Settlers in Canada.** New Edition. *Ten fine Engravings by Gilbert and Dalziel.* 3s. 6d.

Maxwell's Victories of Wellington and the British Armies. *Steel Engravings.*

Michael Angelo and Raphael, their Lives and Works. By DUPPA and QUATREMÈRE DE QUINCY. *With 13 Engravings on Steel.*

Miller's History of the Anglo-Saxons. Written in a popular style, on the basis of Sharon Turner. *Portrait of Alfred, Map of Saxon Britain, and 12 elaborate Engravings on Steel.*

Milton's Poetical Works. With a Memoir by JAMES MONTGOMERY, TODD's Verbal Index to all the Poems, and Explanatory Notes. *With 120 Engravings by Thompson and others, from Drawings by W. Harvey.* 2 vols.

Vol. 1. Paradise Lost, complete, with Memoir, Notes, and Index.

Vol. 2. Paradise Regained, and other Poems, with Verbal Index to all the Poems.

Mudie's British Birds. Revised by W. C. L. MARTIN. *Fifty-two Figures and 7 Plates of Eggs.* In 2 vols.

————; or, *with the plates coloured,* 7s. 6d. per vol.

Naval and Military Heroes of Great Britain; or, Calendar of Victory. Being a Record of British Valour and Conquest by Sea and Land, on every day in the year, from the time of William the Conqueror to the Battle of Inkermann. By Major JOHNS, R.M., and Lieutenant P. H. NICOLAS, R.M. *Twenty-four Portraits.* 6s.

Nicolini's History of the Jesuits: their Origin, Progress, Doctrines, and Designs. *Fine Portraits of Loyola, Lainès, Xavier, Borgia, Acquaviva, Père la Chaise, and Pope Ganganelli.*

Petrarch's Sonnets, and other Poems. Translated into English Verse. By various hands. With a Life of the Poet, by THOMAS CAMPBELL. *With 16 Engravings.*

Pickering's History of the Races of Man, with an Analytical Synopsis of the Natural History of Man. By Dr. HALL. *Illustrated by numerous Portraits.*

————; or, *with the plates coloured,* 7s. 6d.

*** An excellent Edition of a work originally published at 3l. 3s. by the American Government.

Pictorial Handbook of Modern Geography, on a Popular Plan. 5s. 6d. *Illustrated by 150 Engravings and 51 Maps.* 6s.

————; or, *with the maps coloured,* 7s. 6d.

Pope's Poetical Works. Edited by ROBERT CARRUTHERS. *Numerous Engravings.* 2 vols.

Pope's Homer's Iliad. With Introduction and Notes by J. S. WATSON, M.A. *Illustrated by the entire Series of Flaxman's Designs, beautifully engraved by Moses (in the full 8vo. size).*

———— **Homer's Odyssey, Hymns,** &c., by other translators, including Chapman, and Introduction and Notes by J. S. WATSON, M.A. *Flaxman's Designs beautifully engraved by Moses.*

———— **Life.** Including many of his Letters. By ROBERT CARRUTHERS. New Edition, revised and enlarged. *Illustrations. The preceding 5 vols. make a complete and elegant edition of Pope's Poetical Works and Translations for 25s.*

Pottery and Porcelain, and other Objects of Vertu (a Guide to the Knowledge of). To which is added an Engraved List of Marks and Monograms. By HENRY G. BOHN. *Numerous Engravings.*

————; or, *coloured.* 10s. 6d.

Prout's (Father) Reliques. Revised Edition. *Twenty-one spirited Etchings by Maclise.* 5s.

Recreations in Shooting. By "CRAVEN." New Edition, revised and enlarged. *62 Engravings on Wood, after Harvey, and 9 Engravings on Steel, chiefly after A. Cooper, R.A.*

Redding's History and Descriptions of Wines, Ancient and Modern. *Twenty beautiful Woodcuts.*

Rennie's Insect Architecture. New Edition. Revised by the Rev. J. G. WOOD, M.A.

Robinson Crusoe. With Illustrations by STOTHARD and HARVEY. *Twelve beautiful Engravings on Steel, and 74 on Wood.*

————; or, *without the Steel illustrations,* 3s. 6d.

Rome in the Nineteenth Century. New Edition. Revised by the Author. *Illustrated by 34 Steel Engravings,* 2 vols.

Sharpe's History of Egypt, from the Earliest Times till the Conquest by the Arabs, A.D. 640. By SAMUEL SHARPE. With 2 Maps and upwards of 400 Illustrative Woodcuts. Sixth and Cheaper Edition. 2 vols.

Southey's Life of Nelson. With Additional Notes. *Illustrated with 64 Engravings.*

Starling's (Miss) Noble Deeds of Women; or, Examples of Female Courage, Fortitude, and Virtue. *Fourteen Illustrations.*

Stuart and Revett's Antiquities of Athens, and other Monuments of Greece. *Illustrated in 71 Steel Plates, and numerous Woodcuts.*

A CATALOGUE OF

Tales of the Genii; or, the Delightful Lessons of Horam. *Numerous Woodcuts, and 8 Steel Engravings, after Stothard.*

Tasso's Jerusalem Delivered. Translated into English Spenserian Verse, with a Life of the Author. By J. H. WIFFEN. *Eight Engravings on Steel, and 24 on Wood, by Thurston.*

Walker's Manly Exercises. Containing Skating, Riding, Driving, Hunting, Shooting, Sailing, Rowing, Swimming, &c. New Edition, revised by "CRAVEN." *Forty-four Steel Plates, and numerous Woodcuts.*

Walton's Complete Angler. Edited by EDWARD JESSE, Esq. *Upwards of 203 Engravings.*

———; or, *with 26 additional page Illustrations on Steel,* 7s. 6d.

Wellington, Life of. From the materials of Maxwell. *Eighteen Engravings.*

Westropp's Handbook of Archæology New Edition, revised. *Numerous Illustrations.* 7s. 6d.

White's Natural History of Selborne. With Notes by Sir WILLIAM JARDINE and EDWARD JESSE, Esq. *Illustrated by 40 Engravings.*

———; or, *with the plates coloured,* 7s. 6d.

Young, The, Lady's Book. A Manual of Elegant Recreations, Arts, Sciences, and Accomplishments. *Twelve Hundred Woodcut Illustrations, and several Engravings on Steel.* 7s. 6d.

———; or, *cloth gilt, gilt edges,* 9s.

CLASSICAL LIBRARY.

95 Vols. at 5s. each, excepting those marked otherwise.

Æschylus translated into English Verse by A. SWANWICK.

———, Literally Translated into English Prose by an Oxonian. 3s. 6d.

———, Appendix to. Containing the Readings given in Hermann's posthumous Edition of Æschylus. By GEORGE BURGES, M.A. 3s. 6d.

Ammianus Marcellinus. History of Rome from Constantius to Valens. Translated by C. D. YONGE, B.A. Dble. vol., 7s. 6d.

Antoninus. The Thoughts of the Emperor Marcus Aurelius. Translated by GEO. LONG, M.A. 3s. 6d.

Apuleius, the Golden Ass; Death of Socrates; Florida; and Discourse on Magic. To which is added a Metrical Version of Cupid and Psyche; and Mrs. Tighe's Psyche. *Frontispiece.*

Aristophanes' Comedies. Literally Translated, with Notes and Extracts from Frere's and other Metrical Versions, by W. J. HICKIE. 2 vols.
Vol. 1. Acharnians, Knights, Clouds, Wasps, Peace, and Birds.
Vol. 2. Lysistrata, Thesmophoriazusæ, Frogs, Ecclesiazusæ, and Plutus.

Aristotle's Ethics. Literally Translated by Archdeacon BROWNE, late Classical Professor of King's College.

——— Politics and Economics. Translated by E. WALFORD, M.A.

——— Metaphysics. Literally Translated, with Notes, Analysis, Examination Questions, and Index, by the Rev. JOHN H. M'MAHON, M.A., and Gold Medallist in Metaphysics, T.C.D.

Aristotle's History of Animals. In Ten Books. Translated, with Notes and Index, by RICHARD CRESSWELL, M.A.

——— Organon; or, Logical Treatises. With Notes, &c. By O. F. OWEN, M.A. 2 vols., 3s. 6d. each.

——— Rhetoric and Poetics. Literally Translated, with Examination Questions and Notes, by an Oxonian.

Athenæus. The Deipnosophists; or, the Banquet of the Learned. Translated by C. D. YONGE, B.A. 3 vols.

Cæsar. Complete, with the Alexandrian, African, and Spanish Wars. Literally Translated, with Notes.

Catullus, Tibullus, and the Vigil of Venus. A Literal Prose Translation. To which are added Metrical Versions by LAMB, GRAINGER, and others. *Frontispiece.*

Cicero's Orations. Literally Translated by C. D. YONGE, B.A. In 4 vols.
Vol. 1. Contains the Orations against Verres, &c. *Portrait.*
Vol. 2. Catiline, Archias, Agrarian Law, Rabirius, Murena, Sylla, &c.
Vol. 3. Orations for his House, Plancius, Sextius, Cœlius, Milo, Ligarius, &c.
Vol. 4. Miscellaneous Orations, and Rhetorical Works; with General Index to the four volumes.

——— on the Nature of the Gods, Divination, Fate, Laws, a Republic, &c. Translated by C. D. YONGE, B.A., and F. BARHAM.

Cicero's Academics, De Finibus, and Tusculan Questions. By C. D. YONGE, B.A. With Sketch of the Greek Philosopher.

———— Offices, Old Age, Friendship, Scipio's Dream, Paradoxes, &c. Literally Translated, by R. EDMONDS. 3s. 6d.

———— on Oratory and Orators. By J. S. WATSON, M.A.

Demosthenes' Orations. Translated, with Notes, by C. RANN KENNEDY. In 5 volumes.
    Vol. 1. The Olynthiac, Philippic, and other Public Orations. 3s. 6d.
    Vol. 2. On the Crown and on the Embassy.
    Vol. 3. Against Leptines, Midias, Androtrion, and Aristocrates.
    Vol. 4. Private and other Orations.
    Vol. 5. Miscellaneous Orations.

Dictionary of Latin Quotations. Including Proverbs, Maxims, Mottoes, Law Terms, and Phrases; and a Collection of above 500 Greek Quotations. With all the quantities marked, & English Translations.

————, with Index Verborum. 6s. Index Verborum only. 1s.

Diogenes Laertius. Lives and Opinions of the Ancient Philosophers. Translated, with Notes, by C. D. YONGE.

Epictetus. Discourses, with Encheiridion and Fragments. Translated with Notes, by GEORGE LONG, M.A.

Euripides. Literally Translated. 2 vols.
    Vol. 1. Hecuba, Orestes, Medea, Hippolytus, Alcestis, Bacchæ, Heraclidæ, Iphigenia in Aulide, and Iphigenia in Tauris.
    Vol. 2. Hercules Furens, Troades, Ion, Andromache, Suppliants, Helen, Electra, Cyclops, Rhesus.

Greek Anthology. Literally Translated. With Metrical Versions by various Authors.

———— Romances of Heliodorus, Longus, and Achilles Tatius.

Herodotus. A New and Literal Translation, by HENRY CARY, M.A., of Worcester College, Oxford.

Hesiod, Callimachus, and Theognis. Literally Translated, with Notes, by J. BANKS, M.A.

Homer's Iliad. Literally Translated.

———— Odyssey, Hymns, &c. Literally Translated.

Horace. Literally Translated, by SMART. Carefully revised by an OXONIAN. 3s. 6d.

Justin, Cornelius Nepos, and Eutropius. Literally Translated, with Notes and Index, by J. S. WATSON, M.A.

Juvenal, Persius, Sulpicia, and Lucilius. By L. EVANS, M.A. With the Metrical Version by Gifford. *Frontispiece*

Livy. A new and Literal Translation. By Dr. SPILLAN and others. In 4 vols.
    Vol. 1. Contains Books 1—8.
    Vol. 2 Books 9—26.
    Vol. 3. Books 27—36.
    Vol. 4 Books 37 to the end; and Index.

Lucan's Pharsalia. Translated, with Notes, by H. T. RILEY.

Lucretius. Literally Translated, with Notes, by the Rev. J. S. WATSON, M.A. And the Metrical Version by J. M. GOOD.

Martial's Epigrams, complete. Literally Translated. Each accompanied by one or more Verse Translations selected from the Works of English Poets, and other sources. With a copious Index. Double volume (660 pages). 7s. 6d.

Ovid's Works, complete. Literally Translated. 3 vols.
    Vol. 1. Fasti, Tristia, Epistles. &c.
    Vol. 2. Metamorphoses.
    Vol 3. Heroides, Art of Love, &c.

Phalaris, Bentley's Dissertation on. 5s.

Pindar. Literally Translated, by DAWSON W. TURNER, and the Metrical Version by ABRAHAM MOORE.

Plato's Works. Translated by the Rev. H. CARY and others. In 6 vols.
    Vol. 1. The Apology of Socrates, Crito, Phædo, Gorgias, Protagoras, Phædrus, Theætetus, Euthyphron, Lysis.
    Vol. 2. The Republic, Timæus, & Critias.
    Vol. 3. Meno, Euthydemus, The Sophist, Statesman, Cratylus, Parmenides, and the Banquet.
    Vol. 4. Philebus, Charmides, Laches, The Two Alcibiades, and Ten other Dialogues.
    Vol. 5. The Laws.
    Vol. 6. The Doubtful Works. With General Index.

———— Dialogues, Analysis and Index to. With References to the Translation in Bohn's Classical Library. By Dr. DAY.

Plautus's Comedies. Literally Translated, with Notes, by H. T. RILEY, B.A. In 2 vols.

Pliny's Natural History. Translated, with Copious Notes, by the late JOHN BOSTOCK, M.D., F.R.S., and H. T. RILEY, B.A. In 6 vols.

Pliny the Younger, The Letters of. MELMOTH's Translation revised. By the Rev. F C T. BOSANQUET, M.A.

Plutarch's Morals. By C. W. KING, M.A.

Propertius, Petronius, and Johannes Secundus, and Aristænetus. Literally Translated, and accompanied by Poetical Versions, from various sources.

Quintilian's Institutes of Oratory. Literally Translated, with Notes, &c., by J. S. WATSON, M.A. In 2 vols.

Sallust, Florus, and Velleius Paterculus. With Copious Notes, Biographical Notices, and Index, by J. S. WATSON.

Sophocles. The Oxford Translation revised.

Standard Library Atlas of Classical Geography. *Twenty-two large coloured Maps according to the latest authorities.* With a complete Index (accentuated), giving the latitude and longitude of every place named in the Maps. Imp. 8vo. 7s. 6d.

Strabo's Geography. Translated, with Copious Notes, by W. FALCONER, M.A., and H. C. HAMILTON, Esq. With Index, giving the Ancient and Modern Names. In 3 vols.

Suetonius' Lives of the Twelve Cæsars, and other Works. Thomson's Translation, revised, with Notes, by T. FORESTER.

Tacitus. Literally Translated, with Notes. In 2 vols.
Vol. 1. The Annals.
Vol. 2. The History, Germania, Agricola, &c. With Index.

Terence and Phædrus. By H. T. RILEY, B.A.

Theocritus, Bion, Moschus, and Tyrtæus. By J. BANKS, M.A. With the Metrical Versions of Chapman.

Thucydides. Literally Translated by Rev. H. DALE. In 2 vols. 3s. 6d. each.

Virgil. Literally Translated by DAVIDSON. New Edition, carefully revised. 3s. 6d.

Xenophon's Works. In 3 Vols.
Vol. 1. The Anabasis and Memorabilia. Translated, with Notes, by J. S. WATSON, M.A. And a Geographical Commentary, by W. F. AINSWORTH, F.S.A., F.R.G.S., &c.
Vol. 2. Cyropædia and Hellenics. By J. S. WATSON, M.A., and the Rev. H. DALE.
Vol. 3. The Minor Works. By J. S. WATSON, M.A.

SCIENTIFIC LIBRARY.

56 Vols. at 5s. each, excepting those marked otherwise.

Agassiz and Gould's Comparative Physiology. Enlarged by Dr. WRIGHT. *Upwards of 400 Engravings.*

Bacon's Novum Organum and Advancement of Learning. Complete, with Notes, by J. DEVEY, M.A.

Bolley's Manual of Technical Analysis. A Guide for the Testing of Natural and Artificial Substances. By B. H. PAUL. 100 *Wood Engravings.*

BRIDGEWATER TREATISES.—

——— **Bell on the Hand.** Its Mechanism and Vital Endowments as evincing Design. *Seventh Edition Revised.*

——— **Kirby on the History, Habits,** and Instincts of Animals. Edited, with Notes, by T. RYMER JONES. *Numerous Engravings, many of which are additional.* In 2 vols.

——— **Kidd on the Adaptation of** External Nature to the Physical Condition of Man. 3s. 6d.

——— **Whewell's Astronomy and** General Physics, considered with reference to Natural Theology. 3s. 6d.

——— **Chalmers on the Adaptation** of External Nature to the Moral and Intellectual Constitution of Man.

BRIDGEWATER TREATISES—*cont.*

——— **Prout's Treatise on Chemistry,** Meteorology, and Digestion. Edited by Dr. J. W. GRIFFITH.

——— **Buckland's Geology and** Mineralogy. 2 vols. 15s.

——— **Roget's Animal and Vegetable Physiology.** *Illustrated.* In 2 vols. 6s. each.

Carpenter's (Dr. W. B.) Zoology. A Systematic View of the Structure, Habits, Instincts, and Uses, of the principal Families of the Animal Kingdom, and of the chief forms of Fossil Remains. Revised by W. S. DALLAS, F.L.S. *Illustrated with many hundred Wood Engravings.* In 2 vols. 6s. each.

——— **Mechanical Philosophy, As-** tronomy, and Horology. A Popular Exposition. 183 *Illustrations.*

——— **Vegetable Physiology and** Systematic Botany. A complete Introduction to the Knowledge of Plants. Revised, under arrangement with the Author, by E. LANKESTER, M.D., &c. *Several hundred Illustrations on Wood.* 6s.

——— **Animal Physiology.** In part re-written by the Author. *Upwards of 300 capital Illustrations.* 6s.

BOHN'S VARIOUS LIBRARIES.

Chevreul on Colour. Containing the Principles of Harmony and Contrast of Colours, and their application to the Arts. Translated from the French by CHARLES MARTEL. Only complete Edition. *Several Plates.* Or, with an additional series of 16 Plates in Colours. *7s. 6d.*

Ennemoser's History of Magic. Translated by WILLIAM HOWITT. With an Appendix of the most remarkable and best authenticated Stories of Apparitions, Dreams, Table-Turning, and Spirit-Rapping, &c. In 2 vols.

Hogg's (Jabez) Elements of Experimental and Natural Philosophy. Containing Mechanics, Pneumatics, Hydrostatics, Hydraulics, Acoustics, Optics, Caloric, Electricity, Voltaism, and Magnetism. New Edition, enlarged. *Upwards of 400 Woodcuts.*

Hind's Introduction to Astronomy. With a Vocabulary, containing an Explanation of all the Terms in present use. New Edition, enlarged. *Numerous Engravings. 3s. 6d.*

Humboldt's Cosmos; or, Sketch of a Physical Description of the Universe. Translated by E. C. OTTÉ and W. S. DALLAS, F.L.S. *Fine Portrait.* In five vols. *3s. 6d.* each; excepting Vol. V., *5s.*

*** In this edition the notes are placed beneath the text, Humboldt's analytical Summaries and the passages hitherto suppressed are included, and new and comprehensive Indices are added.

—— **Travels in America.** In 3 vols.

—— **Views of Nature; or, Contemplations of the Sublime Phenomena of Creation.** Translated by E. C. OTTÉ and H. G. BOHN. With a complete Index.

Hunt's (Robert) Poetry of Science; or, Studies of the Physical Phenomena of Nature. By Professor HUNT. New Edition, enlarged.

Joyce's Scientific Dialogues. By Dr. GRIFFITH. *Numerous Woodcuts.*

—— **Introduction to the Arts and Sciences.** With Examination Questions. *3s. 6d.*

Knight's (Chas.) Knowledge is Power. A Popular Manual of Political Economy.

Lectures on Painting. By the Royal Academicians. With Introductory Essay, and Notes by R. WORNUM, Esq, *Portraits.*

Lilly's Introduction to Astrology. With numerous Emendations, by ZADKIEL.

Mantell's (Dr.) Geological Excursions through the Isle of Wight and Dorsetshire. New Edition, by T. RUPERT JONES, Esq. *Numerous beautifully executed Woodcuts, and a Geological Map.*

—— **Medals of Creation;** or, First Lessons in Geology and the Study of Organic Remains; including Geological Excursions. New Edition, revised. *Coloured Plates, and several hundred beautiful Woodcuts.* In 2 vols., *7s. 6d.* each.

—— **Petrifactions and their Teachings.** An Illustrated Handbook to the Organic Remains in the British Museum. *Numerous Engravings. 6s.*

—— **Wonders of Geology; or, a Familiar Exposition of Geological Phenomena.** New Edition, augmented by T. RUPERT JONES, F.G.S. *Coloured Geological Map of England, Plates, and nearly 200 beautiful Woodcuts.* In 2 vols., *7s. 6d.* each.

Morphy's Games of Chess. Being the Matches and best Games played by the American Champion, with Explanatory and Analytical Notes, by J. LÖWENTHAL. *Portrait and Memoir.*

It contains by far the largest collection of games played by Mr. Morphy extant in any form, and has received his endorsement and co-operation.

Schouw's Earth, Plants, and Man; and Kobell's Sketches from the Mineral Kingdom. Translated by A. HENFREY, F.R.S. *Coloured Map of the Geography of Plants.*

Smith's (Pye) Geology and Scripture; or, The Relation between the Holy Scriptures and Geological Science.

Stanley's Classified Synopsis of the Principal Painters of the Dutch and Flemish Schools.

Staunton's Chess-player's Handbook. *Numerous Diagrams.*

—— **Chess Praxis.** A Supplement to the Chess-player's Handbook. Containing all the most important modern improvements in the Openings, illustrated by actual Games; a revised Code of Chess Laws; and a Selection of Mr. Morphy's Games in England and France. *6s.*

—— **Chess-player's Companion.** Comprising a new Treatise on Odds, Collection of Match Games, and a Selection of Original Problems.

29